Sustainability and Social Change in Fashion

Sustainability and Social Change in Fashion

LESLIE DAVIS BURNS

FAIRCHILD BOOKS

NEW YORK · LONDON · OXFORD · NEW DELHI · SYDNEY

FAIRCHILD BOOKS
Bloomsbury Publishing Inc
1385 Broadway, New York, NY 10018, USA
50 Bedford Square, London, WC1B 3DP, UK

BLOOMSBURY, FAIRCHILD BOOKS and the Fairchild Books logo are trademarks of
Bloomsbury Publishing Plc

This edition first published in the United States of America 2019
Reprinted 2019

Cover design by Eleanor Rose
Cover photograph © Patrick Ryan/Stone/Getty Images

Bloomsbury Publishing Inc does not have any control over, or responsibility for,
any third-party websites referred to or in this book. All internet addresses given
in this book were correct at the time of going to press. The author and publisher
regret any inconvenience caused if addresses have changed or sites have
ceased to exist, but can accept no responsibility for any such changes.

Library of Congress Cataloging-in-Publication Data

Names: Burns, Leslie Davis, author.
Title: Sustainability and social change in fashion / Leslie Davis Burns.
Description: New York : Fairchild Books, [2019] | Includes index. | Identifiers: LCCN 2018021859
    (print) | LCCN 2018033167 (ebook) | ISBN 9781501334078 (epdf) | ISBN 9781501334061
    (pbk.) | ISBN 9781501334085 (ePDF)
Subjects: LCSH: Clothing trade—Environmental aspects. | Clothing trade—Social aspects. |
    Fashion—Environmental aspects. | Fashion—Social aspects.
Classification: LCC HD9940.A2 (ebook) | LCC HD9940.A2 B87 2019 (print) | DDC 746.9/2—
    dc23
LC record available at https://lccn.loc.gov/2018021859

ISBN: PB: 978-1-5013-3406-1
         ePDF: 978-1-5013-3407-8
         eBook: 978-1-5013-3408-5

Typeset by Lachina
Printed and bound in the United States of America

To find out more about our authors and books visit
www.fairchildbooks.com and sign up for our newsletter.

Extended Contents vi
Preface xi

1 Overview of Sustainability and Social Change in Fashion 1

2 Diversity, Equity, Inclusion, and Social Justice 27

3 Product Life Cycle 53

4 Longevity of Use 81

5 Supply Chain Assurance and Transparency 111

6 Sustainable Business Logistics and Retailing 141

7 Sustainable Communities 161

8 Goals, Plans, and Trends in Creating Sustainable Supply Chains 183

Glossary 210
Photo Credits 217
Index 218

Preface xi

Tenets of Sustainability and Social Change in Fashion   xii
   Diversity, Equity, Inclusion, and Social Justice   xii
   Product Life Cycle   xii
   Longevity of Use   xii
   Supply Chain Assurance and Transparency   xii
   Sustainable Business Logistics and Retailing   xii
   Sustainable Communities   xii
Acknowledgments   xiii
Sustainability and Social Change in Fashion **STUDIO**   xiv
Instructor's Resources   xiv

1

Overview of Sustainability and Social Change in Fashion   1

Defining Sustainability and Social Change   3
   Sustainability   3
   Social Change   4
Business Frameworks for Sustainability and Social
   Change   4
   Corporate Social Responsibility Framework   4
   Triple Bottom Line Framework   5
   Conscious Capitalism   5
   Certified B Corporations™   6
The Global Fashion Industry   6
   Historical Context   6
   Today's Fashion Supply Chain Network   8
Sustainability and Social Change in the Global
   Fashion Industry   9
   Sustainability and Fashion   10
   Social Change and Fashion   10
Issues and Challenges around Sustainability in the
   Global Fashion Industry   10
   Textile Production   11
   Apparel Production   16
   Textile–Apparel–Retail Supply Chain   18
   *Over-consumption and Postconsumer
      Textile Waste*   19

Summary   21
Key Terms   21
References and Resources   21
Case Study: Should Everlane Pursue Becoming a B
      Corporation™?   24
Call to Action Activity: What's in Your Closet?   24
Responsible Wool Standard: Conversation with
      Jeanne Carver   25

2

Diversity, Equity, Inclusion, and Social Justice   27

Overview of Diversity, Equity, Inclusion, and Social
      Justice   28
   Diversity   29
   Equity   31
   Inclusion   32
   Social Justice   32
Inclusive and Equitable Fashion Products   33
   Universal Design   33
   Advancing Cultural and Ethnic Sustainability   40
Diverse and Inclusive Imagery and Promotion of
      Fashion Products   40
Company Policies, Procedures, and Advocacy   43
   Internal Diversity Programs   43

Supplier/Vendor Diversity Programs 43
External Policy Advocacy 44
Summary 45
Key Terms 46
References and Resources 46
Case Study: Kowtow: Adding a Unisex/Gender
        Neutral Collection 47
Call to Action Activities: Creating an Infographic
        around Diversity, Equity, and Inclusion 48
Call to Action Activities: Acknowledging Fashion
        Brands That Create Universal Designs 48
Activate. Commentate. Motivate: Conversation with
        Caryn Franklin 49
Company Highlight: Adaptive Apparel That's
        Fashionable? ABL Denim Meets the
        Challenge 52

Industry Standards, Certifications,
        and Labeling Programs 67
Summary 72
Key Terms 73
References and Resources 73
Case Study: Strategies for Lululemon Athletica
        Inc. to Decrease Their Environmental
        Impact 75
Call to Action Activity: "I Pledge _____" Activity 76
Fashion Positive: Conversation with Annie
        Gullingsrud 77
Company Highlight: Pratibha Syntex and
        Responsible Water Management 79

3

Product Life Cycle 53

Product Life Cycle and Product Life Cycle
        Assessment 54
Life Cycle Assessment of Cotton 55
Life Cycle Assessment of a Pair
        of Levi's® 501® Jeans 55
Self-Assessment Tools for Fashion
        Brand Companies 56
Strategies to Decrease the Environmental Impact
        of Fashion Products 58
Use of Environmentally Responsible
        Materials 58
Reduced Water Consumption 60
Decreased Reliance on Fossil Fuels and
        Increased Use of Renewable Energy
        Sources 61
Reduced Textile Waste 63
Laws, Regulations, Industry Standards, and
        Certifications 66
Laws and Regulations 66

Longevity of Use 81

Historical Perspective 83
The Fashion Process and Forms of
        Obsolescence 84
The Fashion Process 84
Forms of Obsolescence 84
Slow Fashion Movement 85
Use of Small-Scale, Traditional Techniques 86
Local Sourcing 86
Co-creation/Co-production 86
Environmental, Social, and
        Cultural Sustainability 87
Economic Sustainability 87
Designing for Durability 88
Strategies for Design and Merchandising
        for Longevity of Use 88
High Quality and Durable Fabrics and
        Construction Techniques 89
Classic Design or Design for Style-
        Adaptability 91
Fewer and Trans-Seasonal Collections/Lines 91
Modular and/or Multi-Functional Design 93
Size, Style, and Technical Alterability 94

Upcycling 97
*Creating an Emotional and/or Experiential
    Connection between the Item and
    the Wearer* 99
Consumer/User Attitudes and Behavior 101
    *Reducing Consumption and Buying Fewer and
      Higher Quality Items* 101
    Caring for Fashion Items 101
    Repairing and/or Altering Fashions 102
    Sharing Fashions 102
Summary 102
Key Terms 103
References and Resources 103
Case Study: Heritage Brand Collaborations:
    Pendleton Woolen Mills 105
Call to Action Activity: Longevity of Use: Cost-Per-
    Wearing Analysis 106
Slow Fashion Zero Waste Design: Conversation with
    Katherine Soucie 107
Company Highlight: Alabama Chanin: Thoughtful
    design. Responsible production. Good
    business. Quality that lasts. 109

Supply Chain Traceability 120
Supply Chain Transparency 121
*International Standards and Legal Mandates for
    Transparency* 121
*Company Reporting for Supply Chain
    Transparency* 122
Social Compliance Programs 124
    Codes of Conduct 124
    Factory Auditing 125
    *Industrywide Initiatives, Organizations, and
      Certifications* 128
    Hierarchy of Social Compliance Programs 131
Summary 132
Key Terms 133
References and Resources 133
Case Study: Picture Organic Clothing: Supply Chain
    Assurance and Transparency 135
Call to Action Activity: Consumer Perceptions of
    Supply Chain Transparency 136
Better Buying: Conversation with Marsha
    Dickson 137
Company Highlight: Everlane: Radical
    Transparency 139

Supply Chain Assurance and Transparency 111

Sourcing and Supply Chain Management
    in the Fashion Industry 113
    Supply Chain and Sourcing 113
    Supply Chain Management 113
Supply Chain Management Issues in the Fashion
    Industry 115
    Risk Management 116
    Risk Management Issues 116
Supply Chain Assurance 119
    Responsible Sourcing 119
    Responsible Production 119
    Responsible Purchasing 120
Supply Chain Traceability and Transparency 120

Sustainable Business Logistics and Retailing 141

Business Logistics 142
    Accurate Sales Forecasting 143
    Minimal Transportation 143
    *Environmentally Sustainable Modes
      of Transportation* 144
Packaging 146
    Labels 147
    Product Protection 147
    Shipping Container Materials 147
    *Shipping Container and Packaging Size and
      Volume* 148
    Packaging Filler 148

Return Plan   148
Sustainable Operations of Fashion Brand
      Companies   149
Sustainable Fashion Retailers   151
   Sustainable Retailers of New
      Fashion Products   151
   Sustainable Retailers of Previously Owned
      Fashion Products   152
   Connecting Consumers with Sustainable Fashion
      Brands   154
Summary   154
Key Terms   155
References and Resources   156
Case Study: Sustainable Packaging for
      Icebreaker   156
Call to Action Activity: Volunteer at a Local Thrift
      Store   157
Retailing Slow Fashion and Independent Designer
      Collections: Conversation with Amy
      Tipton   158
Company Highlight: thredUP Inc.   160

7

Sustainable Communities   161

What Are Sustainable Communities?   163
   Social Enterprise and Social Entrepreneur   163
   Financial Stability of Social Enterprises   164
Types of Social Enterprises in the Fashion
      Industry   166
   Social Objectives and Business Objectives Are
      Directly Aligned   166
   Social Objectives and Business Objectives
      Overlap   169
   Social Objectives and Business Objectives
      Are Unrelated   170
   Corporate Foundations   172
Social Awareness and Policy Advocacy   173
   Heightening Social Awareness   173
   Policy Advocacy   173

   Fashion as a Vehicle to Advance Philanthropic
      and Advocacy Efforts   174
Summary   175
Key Terms   176
References and Resources   176
Case Study: Conscious Step: Marketing Socks to
      Fight Poverty   177
Call to Action Activity: Becoming Part of the
      Solution   178
Making a Difference in Communities: Conversation
      with Treana Peake   179
Company Highlight: Krochet Kids intl.: Together,
      We Empower People to Rise Above
      Poverty   181

8

Goals, Plans, and Trends in Creating Sustainable Supply Chains   183

Sustainability Goals and Plans   185
   Sustainability Plans   186
   Examples of Sustainability Plans   187
Trends in Environmental, Social, Cultural, and
      Economic Sustainability   189
   Environmental Sustainability: Creating a Circular
      Economy   189
   Social and Cultural Sustainability: Beyond
      Auditing   192
   Economic Sustainability: Scalability   194
   Consumer Engagement: Redefining
      Fashion Consumption   195
Leadership throughout the Sustainable Fashion
      Supply Chain   200
Summary   203
Key Terms   203
References and Resources   203
Case Study: Scalability and LooptWorks: Use Only
      What Exists   205

Call to Action Activities: Fashion Transparency
          Index: Brand Analysis and
          Engagement 206
Call to Action Activities: Upcycling Collaboration
          Project 207
Zero Waste Design and University/Industry
          Upcycling Collaboration: A Conversation
          with Elizabeth Shorrock 207
Company Highlight: Loomstate: It's All
          Connected 209

Glossary 210
Photo Credits 217
Index 218

I love fashion! In fact, I do not remember a time when I was not immersed in both the art and craft of creating fashion; knowing at an early age that I would eventually want to be part of the industry that brings fashions to consumers. I also love the processes of research and education. As such, I am fortunate to have a career that has allowed me to combine all three: research, teaching, and fashion. The fashion industry was very different when I started as a professor in the early 1980s, a time when the industry was changing dramatically with global expansion, introduction of technologies that reduced the time needed for design and production, and increased availability of low-cost trendy fashions. What would these changes mean for my teaching and research, and for my love of fashion? I soon found out.

In 1996, the Kathie Lee Gifford sweatshop scandal hit; and, in 1997, the *NY Times* published an article about environmentally unsafe conditions in Nike's footwear factories in Vietnam. More news reports of sweatshop conditions around the world and the environmental impact of textiles surfaced. United Students against Sweatshops chapters popped up on many campuses. I became uncomfortable teaching about business practices I knew were contributing to the depletion of human and natural resources. But, what could I do to create a better tomorrow for the fashion industry? I then realized—who best to make those changes than the corporate decision makers of the future—my students. Fortunately, at the time there were many faculty addressing these difficult issues in our courses and Educators for Socially Responsible Apparel Business (now Educators for Socially Responsible Apparel Practices) was created as a forum for exchanging ideas. I taught my courses using a corporate social responsibility paradigm, striving to instill in my students that every one of them, regardless of their role/position in a company, could make a positive difference through asking questions within the corporate environment,

convening like-minded colleagues, and making the right decisions. As part of my own professional development, I met with industry leaders, visited socially responsible factories, and completed the Lead Auditor Training Course offered by the Worldwide Responsible Accredited Production (WRAP) organization. I attended industry forums such as the Ethical Sourcing Forum held annually in New York City. I read all I could about strategies companies were using to make a positive difference: zero waste design, sourcing sustainable materials, supply chain transparency, creating inclusive fashions, and social enterprises contributing to the sustainability of communities. I felt hopeful that change could happen! That said, I knew much work was still needed.

It is well-documented that the current global fashion industry is not sustainable—overconsumption by consumers and traditional practices of fashion brand companies continue to exhaust both human and natural resources. Creating truly sustainable fashion supply chains requires commitments, plans, and implementation of multiple interrelated strategies leading to social change by all fashion brand companies. This book provides a framework for that work—six tenets of sustainability and social change in fashion that integrate the various strategies fashion brand companies are taking to improve the industry. It provides an overview of concepts, applications, legal and regulatory issues, and tools available to professionals throughout the fashion industry. It provides examples of successful fashion brand companies that are leaders in sustainability and social change, and calls to action for each and every person in the fashion community to contribute to these efforts and become leaders within their own organizations. The overall goal of this work is that by understanding the interrelated complexities of the strategies, you will have the knowledge and tools to make informed decisions to create a positive impact in your current and/or future work environment.

Tenets of Sustainability and Social Change in Fashion

I have organized strategies that enhance economic, environmental, social, and cultural sustainability and create social change around the following six tenets of sustainability and social change in fashion.

Diversity, Equity, Inclusion, and Social Justice

Equity, inclusion, and social justice are a result of fashion companies' intentional decisions to ensure diversity, fairness, and equity in their product development, operations, and promotions of fashions. Universal design strategies are often used in creating inclusive and equitable fashion products resulting in fashion products that are ability inclusive, size inclusive, and gender inclusive. In addition, equity and inclusion are advanced through diverse and inclusive imagery and promotion of fashion products.

Product Life Cycle

Environmental sustainability is advanced when product life cycle—materials, production, use, maintenance, and end-of-life—are taken into account in the design and production of fashions. Fashion brand companies have incorporated a number of strategies to decrease the environmental impact of fashion products: sourcing responsible materials, reducing water consumption, decreasing reliance on fossil fuels, and reducing both pre-consumer and postconsumer textile waste. Industry standards, certifications, and labeling programs provide assurances and transparency around these strategies.

Longevity of Use

Longevity of use focuses on creating fashion products that consumers/users love, have a connection to, and want to keep and wear. The slow fashion movement provides insights for fashion brand companies to implement a number of strategies to extend the life of fashions: creating high quality fashions made with durable fabrics and construction techniques, classic designs, fewer and trans-seasonal collections, modular or multi-functional designs, fashions that can be altered, upcycled fashions, and products that create an emotional and/or experiential connection with the wearer.

Supply Chain Assurance and Transparency

Supply chain assurance (responsible sourcing, production, and purchasing) and supply chain traceability and transparency (knowing and communicating where, how, and by whom products are made) are integral to advancing social and cultural sustainability. Government regulations, media coverage of industry practices associated with human trafficking and other labor issues, and consumer advocacy for human rights are pushing companies to effectively implement social compliance programs. Moving "beyond auditing" will further advance this work.

Sustainable Business Logistics and Retailing

Fashion brand companies use a variety of sustainable business strategies in their operations and in getting the fashion goods to the ultimate consumer (packaging, shipping, and distributing fashion merchandise). These strategies are intentional decisions around reducing the environmental impact of modes of transportation, packaging, and internal business practices. Sustainable fashion retailers take sustainability into consideration in their offerings of new and/or previously owned fashion products.

Sustainable Communities

Is it possible for a successful fashion brand company to have a mission that puts social objectives (e.g., eliminating hunger and poverty) as important as (or even more important than) its business objectives (e.g., profit)? The answer is *yes*. Social enterprises and other fashion brand companies advance sustainable communities through programs that enhance the health and well-being of their employees, contribute to the communities in which they have operations, and contribute to communities where there are social needs.

The strategies covered in these tenets of sustainability and social change in fashion are interrelated and not mutually exclusive. Indeed, socially responsible fashion brand companies utilize multiple strategies that exemplify several of the tenets. A chapter is devoted to each tenet and includes an overview of strategies for social change, examples of industry best practices, rules or regulations associated with implementing the strategies, tools available for professionals in the fashion industry, and calls to action for professionals throughout the fashion industry to make a difference. The book ends with an overview of sustainability plans that set goals and integrate strategies for further advancing economic, environmental, social, and cultural sustainability.

Examples of socially responsible fashion brand companies are highlighted throughout the book. Please know that these are only a few examples of amazing companies around the world that are making a difference through their products, operations, and contributions. I wish I could have included information about every company I discovered during my research and interviews. The good news is that there were far too many to include within the page restrictions of this book.

Acknowledgments

This book would not have been possible without the assistance and support of many people. I greatly appreciate everyone now and previously at Fairchild Books who worked with me on this book, particularly Amanda Breccia, Joe Miranda, and Edie Weinberg—your insights and suggestions were invaluable! Words cannot express my thanks to all of the individuals, companies, and organizations who provided images, reviewed text material, and agreed to be interviewed—kindred spirits around a passion for improving the fashion industry. I'd also like to thank the anonymous reviewers who provided thoughtful commentary and guidance through the book's revisions. And, lastly, I'd like to thank Bill Boggess for his encouragement, patience, and support through this process. What a remarkable journey this book has taken, from initial notes made on a long plane flight through its countless reorganizations—I can still say that I love fashion and I am hopeful for the future of the fashion industry!

The Publisher wishes to thank the following reviewers: Melinda Adams, University of Incarnate Word; Brenda Brandley, Lethbridge College; Milly Brown, Plymouth Art College (UK); Kelly Cobb, University of Delaware; Maritza Cantero Farrell, Lasell College; Lori A. Faulkner, Ferris State University; Kate Fletcher, University of Arts London (UK); Kimberly Guthrie, Virginia Commonwealth University; Tasha Lewis, Cornell University; Mark O'Connell, Seneca College.

The Publisher wishes to gratefully acknowledge and thank the editorial team involved in the publication of this book:

Acquisitions Editor: Wendy Fuller

Development Manager: Joseph Miranda

Editorial Assistant: Bridget MacAvoy

Art Development Editor: Edie Weinberg

Production Manager: Claire Cooper

Project Managers: Chris Black and Morgan McClelland, Lachina

Leslie Davis Burns
Responsible Global Fashion LLC

Sustainability and Social Change in Fashion STUDIO

Fairchild Books has a long history of excellence in textbook publishing for fashion education. Our new online STUDIOS are specially developed to complement this book with rich ancillaries that students can adapt to their learning styles. *Sustainability and Social Change in Fashion Studio* features online self-quizzes with scored results, personalized study tips, and flashcards with terms/definitions.

STUDIO access cards are offered free with new book purchases and also sold separately through www.fairchildbooks.com.

Instructor's Resources

Instructor's Resources offered online for teachers are Instructor's Guide, which provides suggestions for planning the course and using the text in the classroom, supplemental assignments, and lecture notes; Test Bank, which includes sample test questions for each chapter; and PowerPoint-presentations that include images from the book and provide a framework for lecture and discussion

1

Overview of Sustainability and Social Change in Fashion

Objectives

- Describe environmental, economic, social, and cultural sustainability issues in the global fashion industry.
- Compare the business frameworks fashion brand companies have adopted to address these issues and challenges.
- Explain issues and challenges associated with textile production, apparel production, supply chain processes, and over-consumption and textile waste and how the global fashion industry is addressing them.

What do these fashion brands/companies have in common?

- Jeanne Carver of Imperial Stock Ranch produces wool from sheep raised using sustainable agricultural practices, certified by the Responsible Wool Standard.
- Rachel Faller of Tonlé creates innovative fashions using zero waste design techniques.
- Granted Clothing produces heirloom hand-knit woolen sweaters designed to be worn and cherished for years and passed on to the next generation.
- With a commitment to gender inclusive design, GFW Clothing is designed to fit one's body rather than gender.
- Patagonia uses only 100 percent organic cotton, fleece made from postconsumer recycled plastic soda bottles, and offers a line of certified Fair Trade USA apparel.
- Everlane's commitment to "radical transparency" results in full disclosure and visual documentation of factories along with transparent pricing of all merchandise.
- Through their Krochet Program, Krochet Kids intl. creates jobs in Northern Uganda through capacity building training of crocheters (see Figure 1.1).

What do they have in common? They all have a mission and core values of contributing to a more sustainable and socially responsible global fashion industry. They have challenged traditional industry processes, chosen to value human rights and environmental stewardship as equal to financial gain, and built alliances to foster social change. Indeed, business practices such as these are imperative to the future of the global fashion industry.

a

b

Figure 1.1 Through its lines of crocheted hats, Krochet Kids intl. creates sustainable communities of women in Northern Uganda who sign each of the hats they create.

Why are sustainability and social change so important to the future of the global fashion industry? Over-consumption and traditional industry practices within the global fashion industry have contributed to the depletion of human and natural resources. Therefore, companies designing, producing, marketing, and retailing fashion products need to re-think their supply chain to be more sustainable and to foster social change. Fortunately, the business practices of numerous successful fashion brands/companies have resulted in a reduction in the natural resources required for production and distribution, a reduction in textile waste, an increase in the standard of living for workers, and an increase in the transparency of operations for investors and consumers. Whereas fashion brands/companies throughout the world have made tremendous strides in contributing to a more sustainable and socially responsible global fashion industry, there is still much work to do, and this work is the responsibility of everyone who is part of the global fashion community—designers, product developers, sourcing analysists, merchandisers, retailers, and consumers. Each and every individual and company can make a difference!

Defining Sustainability and Social Change

This book provides a framework around fashion design and merchandising for sustainability and social change. The terms **design** and **merchandising** are used broadly to encompass a variety of processes throughout the fashion supply chain. For the purposes of this book, the term design refers to the processes in creating a fashion product that include design, product development, pattern making, and production systems. The term merchandising refers to the various buying and selling processes across the supply chain, including product and consumer research, marketing, and retailing of fashion products. Because there are multiple perspectives and definitions for the concepts of *sustainability* and *social change*, definitions in the context of this book are provided.

Sustainability

Sustainability, or *the ability to be sustained*, has numerous meanings depending on how the term is applied. The definition by the U.S. Environmental Protection Agency (EPA)—"the ability to maintain or improve standards of living without damaging or depleting natural resources for present and future generations"—is used in this book, as it reflects social, economic, and environmental aspects of sustainability (U.S. EPA, 2016b). Therefore, to understand sustainability and its relationship to the global fashion industry, the interrelationships among environmental, economic, social, and cultural dimensions are examined.

Environmental Sustainability

We are well aware that sustaining the earth's finite natural resources is imperative for the health of the planet and its inhabitants. According to the U.S. EPA,

practices to enhance **environmental sustainability** focus on two broad goals: 1) reducing consumption of non-renewable resources and 2) ensuring that consumption of renewable resources does not exceed their long-term rates of natural regeneration (U.S. EPA, 2016a).

Reducing Consumption of Non-Renewable Resources. **Non-renewable resources** are resources of economic value that cannot be replaced by natural means on a level equal to their consumption. Most fossil fuels (e.g., oil, natural gas, and coal) are non-renewable natural resources because once consumed, they cannot be replaced.

Ensuring Long-Term Regeneration of Renewable Resources. **Renewable resources** are resources of economic value that can be replaced or replenished naturally over time or are always available. Renewable energy resources include solar energy and energy from wind. The natural fibers cotton, wool, silk, and flax are renewable resources if they are produced using sustainable agricultural practices that do not deplete the soil or damage the environment.

Economic Sustainability

Economic sustainability is the ability for individuals, companies, communities, and countries to sustain indefinitely a defined level of economic production. To be sustainable, economic production must serve the common good, be self-renewing, and build human capacity. When integrated with social and environmental sustainability, economic sustainability occurs when social and environmentally sustainable practices are financially feasible.

Social Sustainability

Social sustainability is the ability for a social system or social unit, such as a community, to function indefinitely at a defined level of social well-being through shared structures and processes (Social Sustainability, 2016). These processes and structures allow for individuals' health and well-being, including nutritious food, clean water, adequate shelter, education, realization of personal potential, participation in governance, citizenship, service to others, and cultural expression. In his review of definitions of social sustainability, Stephen McKenzie (2004, p. 18) noted "socially sustainable communities are equitable, diverse, connected and democratic, and provide a good quality of life."

Cultural Sustainability

Culture is defined as the beliefs, way of thinking, customs, language, and artifacts (e.g., arts, clothing, and built structures) of a particular society, group, or organization. Physical artifacts are important symbols of a culture and serve as tangible representations of cultural values and norms. **Cultural sustainability** results from strategies for maintaining the aspects of culture that create positive, equitable, and enduring relationships among the current members and future members of the society, group, or organization and that retain the value of the physical artifacts that represent the culture.

Social Change

Social change is reflected in the discernible transformation of culture and social institutions (social processes, social interactions, organizations) over time; that is, apparent changes in how people within a society think and behave. All societies go through social change—as a result of changes in the physical environment (climate change, deforestation), population (migration), isolation and contact with other groups, social structure (degree to which authority or conformity is valued), and technologies (technology changes society by changing our environment to which we, in turn, adapt). However, the frequency and nature of social change varies among societies. When work, play, family, religion, and other activities are less integrated and dependent upon one another within a society, social change tends to be easier and more frequent; when work, play, family, religion, and other activities are highly integrated and have rigidly defined roles, social change tends to be more difficult and less frequent.

Business Frameworks for Sustainability and Social Change

Within a capitalistic economic system whereby industry and trade are controlled by private owners rather than the state, strategies and business practices that promote sustainability and foster social change have focused on the ability to be in business long term to make positive contributions to the community, broader society, and planet. As such, several business frameworks are used to address environmental, economic, social, and cultural sustainability issues. The four frameworks most commonly used by fashion brands/companies are

- Corporate social responsibility framework
- Triple bottom line framework
- Conscious capitalism
- Certified B Corporations™

It should be noted that these business frameworks are not mutually exclusive. For example, certified B Corporations™, such as Eileen Fisher and Patagonia, also have numerous corporate social responsibility initiatives. In fact, on a fundamental level, the overall goal of each is the same—to create opportunities and structures for businesses to enhance environmental, economic, social, and cultural sustainability and to foster positive social change through their business practices.

Corporate Social Responsibility Framework

One of the most common frameworks used by companies today is the corporate social responsibility framework. **Corporate social responsibility (CSR)**, **corporate responsibility (CR)**, or **social responsibility (SR)** refers to business initiatives that are part of a company's overall business plan and that contribute to sustainable development. CSR initiatives typically go beyond what is required by law to enhance environmental, social, economic, and/or cultural sustainability. As noted on the website of fashion brand Patagonia (2016a), "Corporate Responsibility (CR) is a broad-based movement in business that encourages companies to take responsibility for the impact of their activities on customers, employees, communities and the environment." CSR has received much attention by marketing and management scholars (see Aguinis & Glavas, 2012, for a bibliography of journal articles and books).

Companies that use this framework often have CSR professionals and/or divisions/departments within the company structure. For example, Columbia Sportswear Company, headquartered in Portland, Oregon, USA, has a team of CSR professionals who integrate the company's CSR initiatives across the company's divisions (Columbia Sportswear, 2016).

Triple Bottom Line Framework

The phrase **triple bottom line**, first used in 1994 by John Elkington (founder of SustainAbilty, a British consulting agency), describes three bottom lines that companies need to address—economic prosperity (profit), social justice (people), and environmental quality (planet). *Profit* refers to the traditional financial performance of the company (sales, profit, jobs created) or economic sustainability; *people* refers to measurements related to the performance of the company around social responsibility (health and safety, human rights, community impact) or social sustainability; and *planet* refers to measurements related to the performance of the company around environmental responsibility (carbon footprint, recycling and reuse of resources, water and energy use, pollution reduction) or environmental sustainability (Elkington, 1999; Elkington, 2004). Within this framework, companies use measurements for all three performance indicators, consider all three when assessing the cost of doing business, and treat each with equal importance in strategic planning, when making decisions, and when introducing initiatives. This framework provides an easily understood way of reflecting a company's commitment to economic, social, and environmental sustainability. However, critics of this framework question whether performance indicators across the three components can be accurately

measured and compared to ensure equivalent treatment (Triple Bottom Line, 2009).

Conscious Capitalism

Corporate social responsibility and triple bottom line frameworks typically overlay initiatives on traditional profit-oriented business plans/structures. In their book, *Conscious Capitalism: Liberating the Heroic Spirit of Business* (2013), John Mackey (cofounder of Whole Foods) and Raj Sisodia (cofounder of the Conscious Capitalism Institute) challenged business leaders to re-think their business models and outlined four interconnected and mutually reinforcing principles of **conscious capitalism**:

1. Higher purpose—the business aspires to a purpose that "enriches the world by its existence." The business' employees are a team "passionate and committed to their work and relish the opportunity to be part of something larger than themselves." Questions addressed by companies: Why does our business need to exist? What core values represent the enterprise and unite all of our stakeholders?

2. Stakeholder integration—the business "cares profoundly about the well-being of its customers" and "embraces outsiders as insiders inviting suppliers into the family circle" and a business that "genuinely cares about the planet and all the sentient beings that live on it," shared sense of purpose, and core values.

3. Conscious leadership—leaders of the business are motivated by a higher purpose and creating value for all stakeholders. The business is "self-managing, self-motivating, self-organizing, and self-healing" and "chooses and promotes leaders because of their wisdom and capacity for love and care." Interactions within the business rely on trust, accountability, transparency, integrity, loyalty, fairness, personal growth, love, and care.

4. Conscious culture and management—the business "exists in a virtuous cycle of multifaceted value creation, generating social, intellectual, emotional, spiritual, cultural, physical, and ecological wealth

and well-being for everyone it touches, while also delivering superior financial results year after year, decade after decade."

Such companies do what is right because it is right. Fortunately, companies that are built and organized around these four principles do exist. For example, fashion brand company Patagonia prides itself on its business culture and strategies that are aligned with conscious capitalism.

Certified B Corporations™

In an effort to certify and communicate sustainable business practices to investors, clients, and consumers, **B Corporations**™ and *benefit corporations* were introduced. B Corporations™ certification is overseen by B Lab, "a nonprofit organization dedicated to using the power of business to solve social and environmental problems." Corporations who meet the "standards of verified, overall social and environmental performance, public transparency, and legal accountability" may be certified B Corporations™ and market themselves accordingly (B Lab, 2016) (see Figure 1.2). Over fifty apparel, footwear, and accessory companies are currently certified as B Corporations, including twenty-six apparel companies. Examples include Eileen Fisher, Indigenous Designs Corporation,

Certified

Figure 1.2 The certified B Corporations™ logo indicates that the company has met standards associated with social and environmental sustainability.

Oliberte Limited, Patagonia, Inc., Olukai, MUD Jeans, and Threads 4 Thought. These corporations exemplify some of the best industry practices around sustainability and social change.

The Global Fashion Industry

In our current business context, economic, environmental, social, and cultural sustainability are important issues that must be addressed through business practices that affect social change. Unfortunately, the global fashion industry has a history of exploiting both natural and human resources. Therefore, as we evaluate the status of our industry, examine effective business strategies, and plan for a more sustainable and socially responsible future, there is much we can learn from the history of the global fashion industry (Welters, 2015). How did we come to this point in our industry's existence and what can we learn from our past to make our future better?

Historical Context

Pre-Industrial Revolution

Up until the mid-1700s, fabrics and clothing were handmade for one's own use, for one's family, or for local clients. In many countries, all aspects of creating clothing—spinning, weaving, and sewing processes—occurred in homes with all members of the family contributing to the enterprise. In England, spinning typically took place in the home but local professional hand-weavers often were hired to weave the cotton or wool fabrics. In either case, fabric and the clothing made from fabrics were valued possessions reflecting the natural resources available (e.g., cotton, wool, flax, silk, leather) and the time devoted to handwork, such as weaving, knitting, embroidery, and cutting and sewing the garments themselves. As valued materials, fabrics or garments were rarely thrown away. Scraps of leftover fabrics were used to make quilts or rugs. Garments were often reconstructed to fit multiple individuals over time. Clothing no longer suitable for wearing was repurposed to extend the life of the fabric by cutting and/or sewing the fabric into new usable goods.

Industrial Revolution

This all changed with the onset of the **Industrial Revolution**. Starting in the mid-1700s in England and continuing through the late 1880s in Europe and the United States, the societal change known as the Industrial Revolution brought us the introduction of machine-made products, use of steam power, and increased number of factories. As with other industries, the growth and development of the ready-to-wear fashion industry was highly affected by the Industrial Revolution. The spinning of yarns and weaving of fabrics were the first processes to be mechanized. Early inventions included the flying shuttle loom invented by Thomas Kay in 1733, the spinning machine invented by James Hargreaves in 1764, the water-powered spinning machine invented by Sir Richard Arkwright in 1769, a mechanized power loom invented by Reverend Edmund Cartwright in 1785–1787, and a mechanized power loom invented by Francis Cabot Lowell in 1813. Work in the textile mills was labor intensive and factories attracted women and children, particularly from rural areas, or immigrants in the United States, providing cheap labor for the industry. The invention of the cotton gin (engine) by Eli Whitney, patented in 1794, mechanized the process of removing seeds from cotton fibers. This invention also had an impact on the social structure of the United States, as the economic development of the South, which the United States attributed to the growing cotton industry, justified the expansion of slavery in southern states.

Taking mechanization to the next step of the production process—sewing garments—mechanized sewing machines were introduced by Walter Hunt in 1832, Elias Howe in 1845, and Isaac Singer in 1846. As the sewing machine was adapted for factory use, sewing factories sprung up. These factories required relatively little investment—sewing machines, a room to house the sewing machines, and labor trained in sewing. In the United States, the influx of immigrants in the late 1800s and early 1900s provided a steady supply of workers, many

of whom were young women desperate for any job. Companies also solicited workers to cut, sew, and trim garments in their homes; often with entire families, including children, participating in the activities. This practice, known as *homework*, led to the proliferation of contractors and subcontractors, a practice still prevalent in the global fashion industry today. The factories and homework became part of what was referred to as the "sweated" industry, in that work was "sweated off" to contract factories and homework. Factories were characterized by low wages, long hours, and unsanitary and dangerous working conditions—and thus became known as **sweatshops**.

As we will see throughout the history of our industry, it often took a tragic event to bring attention to the industry and to force social change. One of the first of these tragic events was the fire of the Triangle Shirtwaist Factory in 1911 in Manhattan, New York City, which claimed the lives of 146 young immigrants, some as young as fourteen years old. It is still considered one of the worst industrial disasters in U.S. history (Kheel Center, 2011). The tragedy brought widespread media attention to the working conditions in apparel factories as survivors and witnesses shared their stories of trying to escape only to find doors locked and fire escapes ineffective. Many of those who died jumped from the ninth-floor windows rather than burn alive. The tragedy brought a rallying voice to workers and activists that led to increased power of the International Ladies' Garment Workers' Union as well as changes to government regulations around labor and safety. As a result of this event, most large factories became unionized and were regularly inspected. Collective bargaining raised the wages of sewing operators although they were still lower than other industrial/manufacturing jobs.

Search for the Cheap Needle

Throughout the 1900s, ready-to-wear clothing became affordable and available (through diversified distribution and retailing channels) to the growing middle classes, particularly in the United States and Western Europe. As demand for ready-to-wear clothing grew so did companies' exploration for more efficient production and distribution channels. Since the production of textiles and of garments is labor intensive, meaning that a relatively large part of the costs of production is due to labor costs, as wages of operators in textile mills and sewing factories increased in the United States and Western Europe, companies began operations in locations with lower wages. Until the mid-1990s, ready-to-wear apparel was designed and manufactured by companies primarily for distribution in the same country as where the clothing was produced (domestic production). Therefore, the *search for the cheap needle* moved clothing production first to domestic factories in low-wage areas of a particular country; for example, production in the United States moved from the northeast to the south and west. As wages in these areas of a country rose, companies turned to off-shore production in developing countries throughout the world where wages were lower. As the economies of countries increased along with subsequent wage increases, production continued to move to lesser developed countries.

With the increase in off-shore production, trade among countries for textiles and clothing also increased, with developed countries serving as the primary consumers of clothing being manufactured in less-developed countries. The advent of the World Trade Organization in 1995 encouraged international trade and economic development of lesser developed countries through industries such as textile and clothing production. Because the clothing manufacturing industry requires little investment and employs many people, sewing factories are often one of the first manufacturing industries introduced and these industries are often regarded as important for economic development. For example, according to the World Trade Organization (2015), in 2014, over 90 percent of Haiti's total merchandise exports were clothing, over 80 percent of Bangladesh's total merchandise exports were clothing, and over 50 percent of Cambodia's total merchandise exports were clothing. Unfortunately, the potential for increasing the economic development, along with corrupt governments, often justify low wages

and allow for unhealthy and dangerous working conditions in textile and apparel factories. As in the past, it took a horrific event to bring attention to the industry and to force social change. That event was the collapse of the Rana Plaza building, home to several apparel factories, in Savar, Bangladesh (outside of Dhaka), on April 24, 2013. Over 1,100 people were killed and over 2,400 injured in one of the worst industrial disasters of our time. This event and current strategies to address working conditions in Bangladesh and other countries are discussed in greater detail later in this chapter.

Today's Fashion Supply Chain Network

The current global fashion industry is a dynamic collection of interconnected individuals, companies, and systems that make up the supply chain network necessary to design, manufacture, and deliver a fashion product to the ultimate consumer (see Figure 1.3). These networks include those involved with materials (e.g., fibers, fabrics), creating fashion brands (e.g., designers, product developers, merchandisers), manufacturing fashion brands (e.g., contract factories), and retailing the final product through an array of brick-and-mortar and non-store retailing venues (e.g., buyers, managers). From an economic perspective, value is added at each stage of the process with the final price of the fashion product *supposedly* reflecting of the value of the combined resources used and respective profits of companies throughout the supply chain.

However, the price of apparel does not always reflect the true value of the product. Indeed, unlike many consumer goods, the price of clothing over time has actually gone down (Thompson, 2012). According to the U.S. Bureau of Labor Statistics (2014) "apparel costs increased more slowly than overall inflation during the late 1970s, and the trend has continued ever since." In 1900, apparel spending accounted for 14 percent of expenditures; this fell to 12 percent in 1950, and to 4 percent in 2003.

Does this mean that consumers are buying less? No. In fact, global apparel expenditures continue to rise.

Figure 1.3 Tonlé's factory in Cambodia is part of a network of companies that make up today's fashion supply chain.

According to a study conducted by SinoInteractive, an E-commerce and digital marketing agency in China, "sales across the global apparel market continue to grow and are expected to exceed US$1.4 trillion in 2016" (Global Apparel Sales, 2016). Therefore, with extremely low wages for sewing operators in developing countries, the growth of inexpensive fast fashion, and the increased competition among fashion brands and retailers, consumers in developed countries worldwide can now purchase clothing at such low prices and quality that the clothing is viewed as disposable—to be worn once or twice and then thrown away. In fact, a consumer can purchase a V-neck T-shirt at Forever 21 for as little as $3.90, at Walmart for $4.06, at Zara for $5.00, and at H&M for $5.99. Such low prices for clothing are common and now expected by consumers.

Fabrics and clothing, once viewed as valued possessions, no longer carry value and the price of the merchandise does not reflect the natural and human resources required to produce and sell it. With the growth of contract factories, particularly but not exclusively in developing countries, exploitation of factory workers continues. And as the sheer volume of clothing increases, the fashion industry continues to exploit natural resources, including land and water. Fortunately, numerous fashion brands/companies are working to reverse these trends and contribute to a more sustainable and socially responsible global fashion industry.

Sustainability and Social Change in the Global Fashion Industry

Sustainability and social change in the global fashion industry go hand in hand. Companies throughout the fashion supply chain are striving to be more environmentally, socially, economically, and culturally sustainable, which in turn drives social change. Similarly, social change serves as spur and catalyst for fashion brand companies to take action.

Sustainability and Fashion

In the context of this book, sustainability refers to optimizing the interconnected relationships among environmental, economic, social, and cultural systems for long-term prosperity and improved quality of human life. When the term is applied to the global fashion industry, sustainability occurs

- within the supply chain (e.g., business practice that contributes to the economic sustainability of a particular company) and
- within the broader context in which the industry exists (e.g., business practice that contributes to the environmental sustainability of a world region or the social sustainability of a community).

In the global fashion industry, environmental, economic, social, and cultural sustainability are highly integrated around a broader term—**sustainable development**. According to the World Business Council on Sustainable Development (2015), sustainable development "takes into consideration environmental impact, economic efficiency, and the quality of life." Sustainable development in the fashion industry is exemplified by companies that have continued financial success over time and have contributed to the economic development of a community or region with business practices that foster social equity and environmental responsibility. As we will see throughout this book, both large corporations and small fashion/brand companies contribute to sustainable development.

Social Change and Fashion

Fashion is both a reflection of and a catalyst for social change. Fashion, as a cultural artifact reflects the norms and values of a society, community, or organization. Fashion brands can also be used to facilitate social change, particularly around social

Figure 1.4 Work of the Obakki Foundation facilitates social change by providing education and clean water in African communities.

justice issues. For example, The Obakki Foundation is the philanthropic counterpart to the luxury brand, Obakki. The focus of the Obakki Foundation is providing clean water and education in Cameroon and South Sudan, Africa. Through the work of the Obakki Foundation, twelve schools have been built and nine hundred water wells have been drilled. One hundred percent of the proceeds from the Scarves for Water program were used to drill water wells in several African communities (see Figure 1.4). Similarly, the global fashion industry reflects normative business practices of a society or country. The fashion supply chain can also foster changes in ways of thinking and behavior toward a more environmentally, economically, socially, and culturally sustainable world. For example, advances in technologies for using textile waste have reinforced practices by both industry and consumers to reduce the amount of clothing thrown away.

Issues and Challenges around Sustainability in the Global Fashion Industry

Some may view a goal of enhancing sustainability and fostering social change as inherently counter to the concept of fashion. Does not fashion, by its very nature, invoke business practices that utilize (some would say *exploit*) human and natural resources to satisfy consumers' growing appetite for inexpensive and quickly changing clothing? In fact, in the introduction of their book *Sustainable Fashion: What's Next?* (2015), authors Janet Hethorn and Connie Ulasewicz ask the question "How do we design, develop, produce, wear, and reuse fashion in sustainable ways and still participate in fashion?" (p. xxiv). Is that even possible? When we start examining the issues and challenges associated with textile production, apparel design and production, and distribution, trying to address the issues may appear a daunting, if not impossible, task. However, fashion brands/companies are taking on this challenge through innovative technologies, reforms in social systems, and as the slogan for Winter Sun, a fair trade apparel company, states, "be[ing] the change you want to see happen."

Following is a brief overview of the primary issues and challenges around sustainability in the global fashion industry and general ways in which the fashion industry is fostering social change in response to these issues and challenges. Although the strategies being used to address these issues and challenges are examined in greater detail throughout the book, an integrated overview is provided here as a framework for the more specific discussions in the forthcoming chapters. Issues and challenges exist throughout the supply chain, including consumer use and disposal. Therefore, issues and challenges introduced here will focus on

- Textile production
- Apparel production
- Textile–apparel–retail supply chain
- Over-consumption and postconsumer textile waste

Textile Production

Cotton Production

Cotton is one of the most important fibers in the apparel industry and represents almost half of the total fiber used to make clothing. Cotton production is global in nature with more than 250 million people

in some thirty-five countries employed in the cotton industry (Global Organic Cotton, 2016c; WWF, 2016). China, India, United States, Pakistan, Brazil, and Uzbekistan are the largest producers of cotton. The environmental impact of the conventional cotton production is most evident in the use of chemical fertilizers, pesticides, and herbicides used in growing cotton and in the large amounts of water used in the growing and processing of cotton. Although cotton is grown on only 2.5 percent of the world's agricultural land, it accounts for 16 percent of all pesticide and 6.8 percent of all herbicide use worldwide (Global Organic Cotton, 2016b). These pesticides are washed out of soils and pollute groundwater and rivers. In addition, if pesticides are not appropriately handled workers may become ill or die. Cotton fiber and fabric production also use a large amount of water. It is estimated that an average of 10,850 liters of water are required to create one pair of cotton jeans (Chapagain et al., 2005). In addition, "social and environmental impacts of water use are generally not translated into the price of products at all" (Chapagain et al., 2005, p. 32).

One of the issues that has received a great deal of media attention is the use of child and forced labor with cotton production in Uzbekistan (ILRF, 2016). Uzbekistan, located in Central Asia, is one of the largest world exporters of cotton. For many years the government of Uzbekistan has forced adults and children (some as young as ten) to pick cotton. Schools are closed during harvest season and quotas are allocated for amounts to be harvested. The Uzbek government has detained activists seeking to monitor the situation and refuses to address the problem.

The processing stages of cotton, including dyeing, bleaching, and finishing also have environmental, economic, and social risks. These processes use large amounts of chemicals, including heavy metals, formaldehyde, azo dyes, and chlorine bleach, that can cause pollution through the textile mills' wastewater. These chemicals may be hazardous to the workers at the textile mills, and many can be found as residues on the finished product.

How are the environmental, social, and economic impact of cotton production and processing being addressed by the global fashion industry? One of the most evident practices is growing and using certified **organic cotton**. Organic cotton eliminates the use of synthetic fertilizers and pesticides and conserves water, which lessens irrigation and erosion (Global Organic Cotton, 2016a). Certified organic cotton is grown according to internationally recognized organic farming standards and a number of organic cotton certifications exist, including the Global Organic Textile Standard and the USDA National Organic Program. These certifications are discussed in greater detail in Chapter 3. According to Textile Exchange's Organic Market Report (Textile Exchange, 2016a), organic cotton represents a US$15.7 billion market value with both large corporations (e.g., Nike, H&M) and smaller companies (e.g., Indigenous, Outerknown, Picture Organic Clothing) adopting organic cotton as a preferred fiber for their merchandise (see Figure 1.5). In addition, many improvements have been made over the past twenty years in reducing or even eliminating hazardous chemicals and increasing the practice of recycling chemicals. Wastewater is also treated to reduce pollution. In addition, several industry-wide collaborations have also been initiated to improve sustainability in the cotton industry. These include the Better Cotton Initiative, certified Fairtrade Cotton Standard, and the Responsible Sourcing Network's Pledge against the use of Uzbek cotton. These will be discussed in greater detail in later chapters.

Fair trade is a global system that supports farmers and artisans in developing countries to make trade fair through paying a living wage, providing opportunities for advancement, employing environmentally sustainable practices, building long-term trade partnerships, ensuring healthy and safe working conditions, and providing financial and technical assistance. Fairtrade International is an international organization that developed fair trade standards for a number of industries including small-scale cotton producers. Through their independent certification company, FLO-CERT, producers who meet the standards can be certified and allowed to market themselves as certified Fairtrade using the Fairtrade Mark. Fair trade standards ensure

Figure 1.5 Fair trade fashion brand Indigenous Designs uses organic cotton for their merchandise.

that minimum prices are paid for the cotton, that premium prices are also paid to be used for social and economic investments, and that cotton is grown according to environmental sustainability standards (Fairtrade International, 2016; Fairtrade America, 2016).

Fashion brands/companies have also come together to ban the use of cotton from Uzbekistan. Over 270 companies and industry associations have signed the Responsible Sourcing Network's pledge to "commit to not knowingly source Uzbek cotton for the manufacturing of any of our products until the Government of Uzbekistan ends the practice of forced child and adult labor in its cotton sector. Until the elimination of this practice is independently verified by the International Labor Organization, we will maintain this pledge" (Responsible Sourcing Network, 2016). Companies who have signed this pledge include Adidas Group, American Eagle Outfitters, Carrefour, Carter's, Columbia Sportswear, Fast Retailing Co. Ltd (Uniqlo), Fruit of the Loom, Gap Inc., H&M, Inditex (Zara), J. Crew, Levi Strauss & Co., lululemon athletica, Nike, Patagonia, Primark, and PVH Corp.

Wool Production

Second to cotton, wool is the next most popular natural fiber used for clothing. Wool production is worldwide, although Australia is the largest producer of merino wool, the most common type of wool for clothing. Sustainability and ethical issues associated with wool production include possible overgrazing of land; greenhouse emissions caused by methane produced by sheep; water consumption by sheep and in processing wool; use of chemicals in cleaning (scouring) and processing wool, which may lead to wastewater pollution; and the possibility of inhumane treatment of sheep (particularly the practice of mulesing). The possible inhumane treatment of lambs and sheep has received a great deal of media attention by PETA and other animal rights and protection groups. **Mulesing** is the practice whereby flesh is stripped from the buttocks of Merino lambs to create scarred skin with no wrinkles or folds. This practice is intended to prevent blowflies from laying eggs in the folds of the animal's skin. However, not only is mulesing painful to the lambs, but it can also cause inflammation and even death. Mulesing is primarily practiced in Australia

and New Zealand, leading producers of merino wool (Animals Australia, 2016; Jenkin, 2012).

How are these sustainability and ethical issues being addressed by the global fashion industry? Textile Exchange has recently initiated the Responsible Wool Standard to "provide the industry with a tool to recognize the best practices of farmers; ensuring that wool comes from farms with a progressive approach to managing their land, and from sheep that have been treated responsibly." "The Responsible Wool Standard is an independent, voluntary standard, which means that companies can choose to become certified. On farms, the certification ensures that sheep are treated with respect to their five freedoms and also ensures best practices in the management and protection of the land. Through production, certification ensures that wool for certified farms is properly identified and tracked" (Textile Exchange, 2016c). (See Figure 1.6 and Responsible Wool Standard: A Conversation with Jeanne Carver at the

Figure 1.6 Imperial Stock Ranch in central Oregon, USA, produces high quality wool grown and processed with sustainable practices, becoming the first wool supplier to receive the Responsible Wool Standard certification from Textile Exchange.

end of the chapter.) The European Union Eco label "eco wool" certifies that the wool has been sheared from sheep that are allowed to roam; that chemical flea dipping has not been used; and that the fleece has not been treated with chemicals, dyes, or bleaches.

Voluntary bans as well as policies and procedures to eliminate the practice of mulesing were initiated in Australia and New Zealand. The goal was to eliminate the practice by 2010, although there are reports that the practice may still occur. Fashion brands/companies typically ban wool suppliers who are still practicing mulesing. In addition, the International Wool Textile Organization publishes Guidelines for Wool Sheep Welfare available to wool producers. To ensure retail partners and consumers regarding their land management practices and ethical treatment of sheep, Icebreaker (2016), a fashion brand/company headquartered in New Zealand that supports approximately 15,000 sheep, provides extensive transparency of their supply chain. Standards, certifications, photos, and videos of supply chain partners are publicly available.

Manufactured Fibers

Manufactured fibers (aka man-made fibers) are fibers manufactured from cellulosic materials (e.g., rayon, acetate, lyocell), synthetic polymers (e.g., polyester, nylon, acrylic), protein (e.g., milk protein fiber), or inorganic materials (e.g., glass, metal). Manufactured fibers made from cellulosic materials (aka **regenerated cellulosic fibers**, or cellulosic fibers) and synthetic polymers (commonly called **synthetic fibers** or synthetics) are most common for apparel and will be the focus of this discussion. The first regenerated cellulosic fiber, using wood pulp as the base material, was commercialized in the early 1900s as "artificial silk" and later became known as rayon. With the invention of nylon in the 1930s, DuPont was the first company to successfully market synthetic fibers. Since the invention of polyester in the 1940s, demand for synthetic fibers has continued to grow. The growth rate for polyester fibers has been higher than other synthetics, with polyester now accounting for over 70 percent of the total demand for fibers (Carmichael, 2015).

All cellulosic and synthetic fibers rely on chemical solutions that are moved through a spinneret into a chemical (e.g., sulfuric acid) or water-based bath where the fiber is hardened. Depending on the fiber, washing and bleaching processes may be needed to prepare the fiber for finishing. Fibers are treated through mechanical, thermal, and chemical processes to create particular properties and performance of the fiber. Because fiber length and characteristics are controlled, cellulosic and synthetic fibers are used for a wide variety of end use applications, including clothing, interior textiles, and industrial uses.

Regenerated Cellulosic Fibers. The three types of manufacturing techniques or generations of regenerated cellulosic fibers and their environmental impact are (Mass, 2014; O EcoTextiles, 2012)

1. Viscose process (first generation) for rayon—in this process, cellulose (wood pulp) is treated with caustic soda and carbon disulfide. Although chemicals do not remain as a residue on the fiber, disposing of the chemicals used in the processing can create pollution in wastewater.

2. High Wet Modulus (HWM) process (second generation) for rayon—HWM process increases the wet strength of rayon. Similar to the viscose process, disposing of chemicals used in the process can be polluting.

3. Lyocell (third generation)—according to the Federal Trade Commission, lyocell is the generic name for a "cellulose fiber obtained by an organic solvent spinning process" and is considered a subclass of rayon (Federal Trade Commission, 1996). The lyocell process reuses up to 99.8 percent of the solvent and the remaining emissions are broken down.

Rayon (viscose and HWM) and lyocell are produced from renewable cellulosic plants such as beech trees, pine trees, and bamboo. All are biodegradable; although all may not be made from plants harvested in environmentally responsible ways. Lenzing Viscose® and Lenzing Modal® HWM rayon are made from sustainably harvested beech trees certified by PEFC (Programme for the Endorsement of Forest Certification).

The lyocell process is the most environmentally responsible processing method among the processes for regenerated cellulosic fibers. This has sometimes caused confusion for fashion brands/companies and consumers. For example, in 2003, bamboo was introduced as an environmentally responsible fiber because the cellulose base (bamboo) was renewable. However, the viscose processing method was used. The Federal Trade Commission now requires that if the viscose method is used it must be labeled as rayon made from bamboo.

Lenzing's Tencel® lyocell is one of the most common lyocell fibers available. Not only is Tencel® lyocell made from eucalyptus grown on land unsuitable for food crops, the plants require less water than cotton, non-toxic solvents are use, the filament fibers use a water-based bath, and solvents are washed from the fiber and reused. In addition, Tencel® lyocell is more odor-resistant (prevents the growth of bacteria which causes odors) than viscose rayon, HWM rayon, or cotton. Therefore, products made with Tencel® lyocell do not need to be washed as often as those made from these other fibers.

Synthetic Fibers. The environmental impact of synthetic fibers is well-established. Fibers such as nylon and polyester "are produced from polymer solution obtained from the by-product of non-renewable petroleum resources" (Chen & Burns, 2006, p. 251; Lewin, 2006). In addition, synthetics do not decompose and when disposed of in landfills they release heavy metals, including antimony, and other additives into soil and groundwater.

How has the environmental impact of synthetic fibers been addressed by the global fashion industry? Reduction of consumption of non-renewable resources in the fashion industry includes using renewable energy resources and using recycled polyester, nylon, and other synthetic fibers in closed-loop recycling systems (Baugh, 2015). These strategies will be discussed in greater detail in Chapter 3. According to Textile Exchange's 2016 Preferred Fiber and Materials Market Report, recycled polyester, lyocell, biobased synthetics, recycled cotton, recycled wool, and organic cotton

are the preferred fibers among fashion brands/companies for environmental sustainability. Leaders in the industry for use of recycled polyester include Nike, H&M, The North Face, Patagonia; and leaders in the industry for the use of lyocell include Inditex (Zara), H&M, G-Star Raw, Lindex, and Eileen Fisher (Textile Exchange, 2016b).

Leather Production

The process of preserving and softening animal skins to create leather for apparel and accessories dates back to prehistoric times, with techniques independently developed by societies throughout the world. The process of creating leather includes three stages that require large amounts of fresh water and chemicals. The process results in pollutants that include both solid wastes and wastewater characterized by organic and inorganic compounds.

1. *Pre-Tanning Stage*—hides are cured using salt to remove excess water. Hair is removed from the hides using a liming process. Hides are then delimed to lower the pH of the material so that the it can be treated with enzymes to soften it. This process is referred to as baiting. The hides then undergo a pickling process that prepares them for mineral tanning.

2. *Tanning Stage*—hides are treated to produce a durable product using either vegetable or mineral tanning methods. Until the mid-1800s leather was created through vegetable tanning using the tannins from bark, leaves, and other plant materials. In the mid-1800s chrome tanning was invented. It uses chromium sulfate or chromium salts to produce a softer and more supple leather product. Most leather produced today uses the chrome tanning method. Of the three stages, the tanning stage creates the greatest environmental impact. With chrome tanning, all minerals are water soluble but not all are absorbed by the hide. Thus, the discharged wastewater contains chrome and other minerals. Vegetable tanning results in solid waste discharge, which is also a pollutant but less harmful than effluents from mineral/chrome tanning.

3. *Post-Tanning and Finishing Stage*—hides are treated to enhance the desired qualities of the leather; e.g., buffing, embossing, and finishing with protective agents.

The negative impacts of tanning leather on the environment and human health are well-established (Gullingsrud, 2017; Hasnat, Rahman, & Mosabbir, 2013; Mwinyihija, 2010). Over the past twenty-five years, a number of strategies have been implemented to address the negative impact of leather production processes.

- Legislation—many countries have legislation regulating effluent discharge by tanneries. Whereas these legislative efforts have resulted in less pollution for the enforcing countries, many tannery operations moved to countries with less-restrictive environmental laws.

- Certifications and labeling—a number of certifications and associated labeling are available for materials and products that meet specific environmental standards. These are discussed in greater detail in Chapter 3. An example specific to leather is the *Leather from Italy—Full Cycle* certification and label (Italian national standard UNI 11239), which guarantees that the leather is entirely made in Italy, from raw hide through finished leather.

- New technologies—technological advancements are underway including sulfide-free unhairing processes, non-chrome tanning processes, natural dyestuffs, and reduced water consumption.

- State-of-the-art treatment plants—in most countries, tannery wastewater is treated, although to differing levels. However, even with treatment, pollutants are not necessarily destroyed. New technologies for recovering and processing by-products are underway.

Apparel Production

As noted earlier in this chapter, the global ready-to-wear fashion industry has had a history of exploitation of factory workers. Unfortunately, this is still the case today, including human trafficking and **modern slavery**, "an umbrella term that includes forced labor, debt bondage, servitude, and trafficking for the purposes of labor exploitation" (Skrivánková, 2017, p. 3). A type of modern slavery, **forced labor**, describes a situation in which a worker performs work or services involuntarily under threat of penalty or punishment. As noted by Pietra Rivoli in her book, *The Travels of a T-shirt in the Global Economy* (2015):

> Since the rise of the industry in eighteenth century England, ideal workers for low-end textile and apparel work have been those who endure repetitive drudgery not just cheaply but willingly and uncomplainingly (pp. 105–106).

Such laborers tend to be women and/or those in a community who are desperate for work.

> Like their sisters in time, textile and clothing workers in China today have low pay, long hours, and poor working conditions. Living quarters are cramped and rights are limited, the work is boring, the air is dusty, and the noise is brain numbing. The food is bad, the fences are high, and the curfews inviolate. As generations of girls and seamstresses from Europe, America, and Asia are bound together by this common sweatshop experience—controlled, exploited, overworked, and underpaid—they are bound together, too, by one absolute certainty, shared across both oceans and centuries: This beats the hell out of life on the farm (pp. 109–110).

Despite the horrid factory conditions, the financial autonomy of workers and self-determination are viewed as preferable to staying and working on a farm. Therefore, from the time of the Triangle Shirtwaist Factory fire in 1911 the apparel industry has been associated with sweatshops. In general, a sweatshop is a workplace where workers are exploited, including being denied a living wage or benefits; working excessively long hours, often

Figure 1.7 The collapse of the Rana Plaza building in Bangladesh brought widespread attention to the global apparel industry and empowered workers to protest unsafe conditions.

without overtime pay; suffering poor working conditions; undergoing arbitrary discipline, including verbal and/or physical abuse; and/or having no ability to organize to negotiate better terms of work.

As earlier noted, another horrific factory tragedy brought attention to factory conditions, worker strife, and the necessity for social change in the apparel industry. The collapse of the Rana Plaza building, home to several apparel factories, in Savar, Bangladesh (outside of Dhaka), on April 24, 2013, made headline news. Over 1,100 people were killed and over 2,400 injured in one of the worst industrial disasters of our time (see Figure 1.7). Prior to its collapse, building owners had been informed of cracks in a structural pillar and in the ceiling of the building. In fact, the day before the collapse, an engineer deemed the building unsafe. Despite these warnings, the building owner, Sohel Rana, assured factory owners that the building was safe and factory employees were urged to return to work. The tragedy brought the world's attention to the unsafe factory conditions and corruption within the Bangladesh government. Through dramatic media coverage during the days following the collapse, we watched in horror as the extent of the tragedy unfolded. Consumers were shocked to see their favorite brands identified as being made in one of the clothing factories housed in the building; brands including Inditex (Zara), Mango, The Children's Place, Walmart, and JCPenney, just to name a few.

How are the issues around apparel production being addressed by the global fashion industry? Future chapters explore the role of industry alliances (e.g., Bangladesh Safety Accord, Alliance for Bangladesh Worker Safety), creating and implementation of social compliance programs (codes of conduct, factory auditing, organizational commitments), and supply chain transparency as means by which many companies within the fashion industry strive to improve workplace conditions and the lives of workers. Improved supply chain transparency by fashion brands/companies provides investors, retailers, and consumers with information about the location of contract factories, visual evidence of the working conditions within the factory, strategies to ensure compliance with codes of conduct, efforts to improve the community where the factories are located, and other sustainable development efforts of the fashion brand/company.

Textile–Apparel–Retail Supply Chain

Sustainable development is dependent on business practices throughout the fashion supply chain. The issues and challenges that emerge across the supply chain include

- Energy use
- Use of hazardous chemicals
- Use of conflict minerals

Energy Use

Energy use in the fashion supply chain results from

- Mechanization of processes throughout the supply chain from raw materials through retail distribution,
- Globalization and increased specialization among companies and countries along the supply chain with raw materials being shipped to processing facilities then shipped to production facilities and then shipped to distribution centers before they are available to the ultimate consumer, and
- Energy use by consumers in the maintenance of clothing.

How are issues of energy use being addressed by the global fashion industry? Strategies include reduction of overall energy usage, reduction in a company's reliance on energy sources that are non-renewable (e.g., fossil fuels) and an increase use of energy sources that are renewable (e.g., solar, wind). For example, in 2008, Nike launched an energy and carbon program that resulted in an increase use of energy from renewable resources and a reduction of the energy use of their contract factories by half since the program started (Nike, 2016).

Environmentally responsible companies are also examining their supply chains to minimize the degree to which raw materials, component

parts, or finished products are shipped. Whereas it is acknowledged that sourcing materials or production close to the ultimate consumer does not guarantee that a fashion company is committed to sustainability, if the manufacturing processes that are closer to the consumer are environmentally responsible then shortening or reducing the size of supply chains makes sense from an environmental perspective (Kovacs, 2016). Strategies around resource use in getting merchandise to the consumer are discussed in greater detail in Chapter 6.

Use of Hazardous Chemicals

Many types of chemicals are used across the fashion supply chain, primarily in the production and finishing of textiles and fabrics. In textile production and processing, pesticides are used in cotton production; agents are used to clean and bleach fibers; and softeners, dyes, chemicals, and fixing agents are used to process and finish fabrics to add color, water repellency, stain protection, and wrinkle resistance properties. Many of the chemicals used in textile processing are hazardous. Textile mills that process textiles using wet processing techniques use a great deal of water for processes such as scouring, desizing, bleaching, and dyeing. The wastewater created through these processes can be hazardous and if not appropriately treated can pollute rivers, lakes, or other bodies of water in which the wastewater is disposed (TEonline, n.d.).

How are these issues around the use of hazardous chemicals being addressed by the global fashion industry? As discussed earlier in this chapter, many fashion brands/companies are using fibers that are being produced without the use of hazardous chemicals or with recycled chemicals. In addition, companies and associations have implemented **restricted substance lists (RSL)** that reflect compliance with or exceeding legal limits of use of hazardous substances across their supply chains. Lists include substances, test methods, prohibition or limitation values, and country- or state-specific requirements. For example, the American Apparel and Footwear Association (AAFA) regularly publishes a Restricted Substance List (AAFA, 2017). "The RSL is intended to provide apparel and footwear companies with information related to regulations and laws that restrict or ban certain chemicals and substances in finished home textile, apparel, and footwear products around the world" (p. 2). Chemicals included in this RSL include asbestos, azo dyes, dioxins and furans, disperse dyes, flame retardants, fluorinated greenhouse gases [perfluorocarbons (PFCs), hydrofluorocarbons (HFCs)], metals, organotin compounds, pesticides, phthalates, soluble heavy metals, solvents, and other miscellaneous chemicals (e.g., formaldehyde).

Companies themselves have published RSLs as guides for their operations and for their suppliers' operations. For example, the objectives of Levi Strauss & Co. Restricted Substance List (2014) are to

1. Ensure that materials, chemicals, and other goods used or supplied for the fabrication, manufacture, or processing of LS&CO-labeled and/or distributed products comply with the applicable chemical content and chemical exposure laws of every governmental jurisdiction in which those products are fabricated, manufactured, processed, or distributed; and

2. Protect the health and safety of consumers and others handling LS&CO-labeled and/or distributed finished products.

Greenpeace (2016), the global environmental organization, launched their "Detox My Fashion" campaign in 2011 to compel the fashion industry to take responsibility and eliminate the use of hazardous chemicals throughout their supply chains. The initiative secured commitments from seventy-six international fashion brands, retailers, and suppliers as well as secured policy changes in Europe and Asia. Each year Greenpeace publishes the "Detox Catwalk," which reports the steps taken by the fashion brands in reducing the use of hazardous chemicals as well as providing information about their suppliers' use of hazardous chemicals. Future chapters further explore these strategies used by fashion brands/companies in reducing and eliminating the use of hazardous chemicals.

Use of Conflict Minerals

Conflict minerals—tin, tungsten, tantalum, and gold—are mined under conditions that violate human rights or finance armed conflicts in Democratic Republic of the Congo (DRC) or its adjoining countries (e.g., Angola, Republic of Congo, Uganda). According to the Conflict Minerals Rule of the U.S. Security Exchange Commission, any publicly traded corporation must identify sources of these minerals if they originated in DRC or the adjoining countries, report of processes for assessment of compliance with Conflict Minerals Rule, and provide a listing of smelters and refiners that are used in any of the corporation's products. Although we may not always realize it, apparel often includes metal hardware such as zippers, buttons, or functional trim; or as part of accessories such as belts. Therefore, as of 2017 fashion brand corporations such as Nike, VF, or Columbia Sportswear, must file this report. Fashion retailer corporations such as Macy's (2016) must also file a report as to how their suppliers are complying with the Conflict Minerals Rule. It should be noted that this SEC rule is currently under review.

Over-consumption and Postconsumer Textile Waste

How many clothing items do you own? How often do you wear them? How often do you launder them? It is estimated that worldwide 80 billion new pieces of clothing are purchased every year; representing a 400 percent increase than what we consumed twenty years ago (The True Cost, 2015). In addition, per capita spending on clothing is also expected to continue to grow worldwide (Statista, 2016). For example, per capita spending on apparel from 2012 to 2025 is expected to grow only 14 percent in the United States (from $686 to $781), 21 percent in EU-27 (from $663 to $804), 33 percent in Japan (from $814 to $1,080), 47 percent in Canada (from $831 to $1221), and 56 percent in Australia (from $1,050 to $1,643); but 172 percent in Russia (from $272 to $740), 246 percent in China (from $109 to $377), and 283 percent in India (from $36 to $138). Clearly, consumers buy more clothing than they need and consumption is expected to continue to grow.

A result of over-consumption of apparel, particularly inexpensive low-quality clothing is **postconsumer textile waste**. Whereas textile waste occurs throughout the manufacturing process, the largest amount occurs as postconsumer waste. The U.S. Environmental Protection Agency (2015) estimated that in 2013 only 15 percent of all postconsumer textile waste (2.3 million tons) was recovered (i.e., recycled, reused, etc.). This means that approximately 85 percent (12.83 million tons) of all postconsumer textile waste was not recovered. Some have suggested that the amounts are higher; others lower. However, even with differing statistics, it is fair to say that a great deal of postconsumer textile waste is generated each year and most of it ends up in landfills (see Figure 1.8).

How is the issue of over-consumption being addressed by the global fashion industry? Strategies

Figure 1.8 Increases in postconsumer textile waste have resulted in multiple strategies to reduce the amount that goes into landfills.

have focused on two areas: 1) reducing consumption of clothing and 2) reducing postconsumer textile waste that goes into landfills.

Reducing Consumption of Clothing

The first area—reducing the amount of clothing purchased—may seem counterintuitive to something the fashion industry would want to promote. However, a number of fashion brands/companies have promoted purchasing clothing that can be worn for a longer period of time, buying only what one needs, and repairing worn clothing. For example, in her book *Sustainable Fashion and Textiles: Design Journeys* (2014), Kate Fletcher explores the role of **slow fashion**, challenging fashion designers to create a more sustainable fashion industry through systems thinking, quality over quantity, longevity of use, and local sourcing. To varying degrees, strategies associated with the slow fashion movement have been adopted by numerous fashion brands/companies. For example, fashion brand Nau designs and markets high quality apparel with closed-loop fibers (e.g., recycled polyester), designed with as little waste as possible, and that can be worn not only across seasons but for years.

Other fashion brands/companies encourage consumers to repair clothing so that it can be worn for a longer time period. For example, Patagonia's Worn Wear (Patagonia, 2016b) program encourages repairing garments for extended life. Nudie Jeans, a Swedish apparel denim brand, has a "Repair and Take Care of Your Jeans" section on their website. They offer several ways for you to repair your Nudie jeans: 1) selected Nudie jeans stores worldwide will repair them for free, 2) you can order a free Nudie jeans repair kit and do it yourself, or 3) you can find someone who will repair them for you. Details of these and other strategies for design and merchandising for longevity of use are discussed in greater detail in Chapter 4.

Reducing Postconsumer Textile Waste

Postconsumer textile waste is being addressed through a number of strategies around collecting, recycling, upcycling, and re-selling used clothing and other textile products (Hawley, 2015). For example, the association Secondary Materials and Recycled Textiles (SMART) provides resources and services for the multi-billion dollar (U.S.) global industry of recovering and reusing postconsumer waste. Heightened consumer awareness, new technologies, and partnerships with leading fashion brands/companies have resulted in a growth in recycling of clothing donated to charity, repurposing used textiles for new end uses, and reclaiming fibers (e.g., wool, cotton) from textile waste to be used again. Partnerships with fashion brands/companies has fostered the attention to these strategies. For example, Levis Strauss & Co. has recently partnered with Evrnu™ technology company to create jeans made from fabrics with at least 50 percent postconsumer cotton waste (Samaniego, 2016). Details for these and other strategies for tackling textile waste throughout the supply chain are discussed in Chapters 3, 4, and 6.

Summary

The future of the global fashion industry is dependent on strategies around sustainability to foster social change. As applied to the global fashion industry, sustainability includes four interrelated aspects: environmental, economic, social, and cultural sustainability. Social change is reflected in the discernible transformation of culture and social institutions (social processes, social interactions, organizations) over time; that is, apparent changes in how people within a society think and behave.

Strategies and business practices that promote sustainability and foster social change have focused on the ability to be in business long term to make positive contributions to the community, broader society, and planet. As such, several business frameworks have addressed environmental, economic, social, and cultural sustainability issues. These frameworks include corporate social responsibility, triple bottom line, conscious capitalism, and certified B Corporations™.

The global fashion industry has a long history of exploitation of human and natural resources. Today, over-consumption and industry practices contribute to the depletion of human and natural resources. With limited natural resources and the importance of human rights, companies designing, producing, and marketing fashion products need to re-think their supply chain to be more sustainable and to foster social change. Fortunately, the business practices of numerous successful fashion brand/companies have resulted in a reduction in the natural resources required for production and distribution, a reduction in textile waste, an increase in the standard of living for workers, and/or an increase in the transparency of operations for investors and consumers.

Key Terms

B Corporations™	modern slavery
conflict minerals	mulesing
conscious capitalism	non-renewable resources
corporate responsibility (CR)	organic cotton
	postconsumer textile
corporate social responsibility (CSR)	waste
	regenerated cellulosic
cultural sustainability	fibers
design	renewable resources
economic sustainability	restricted substance list
environmental	slow fashion
sustainability	social change
fair trade	social responsibility (SR)
forced labor	social sustainability
High Wet Modulus	sustainable development
(HWM)	sustainability
Industrial Revolution	synthetic fibers
lyocell	sweatshops
manufactured fibers	triple bottom line
merchandising	viscose

References and Resources

Aguinis, Herman. (2011). "Organizational Responsibility: Doing Good and Doing Well," in S. Zedeck (ed) *APA Handbook of Industrial and Organizational Psychology* (Vol. 3): 855–79. Washington, DC: American Psychological Association.

Aguinis, Herman, & Glavas, Ante. (2012). "What We Know and Don't Know About Corporate Social Responsibility: A Review and Research Agenda," *Journal of Management*, 38(4): 932–68.

American Apparel and Footwear Association (2017, March). *Restricted Substance List*. Retrieved on June 7, 2017, from https://www.aafaglobal.org/AAFA/Solutions_Pages/Restricted_Substance_List.

Animals Australia (2016). "Mulesing." Retrieved on July 27, 2016, from http://www.animalsaustralia.org/issues/mulesing.php.

B Lab (2016). "Certified B Corporations." Retrieved on July 6, 2016, from https://www.bcorporation.net/.

Baugh, Gail (2015). "Fibers: Exploring Healthy and Clean Fiber," in J. Hethornand & C. Ulasewicz (eds) *Sustainable Fashion What's Next?* (2nd ed.): 313–45. NY: Fairchild Books.

Better Cotton Initiative (2016). "About BCI." Retrieved on July 7, 2016, from http://bettercotton.org/.

Business Dictionary (2016). Social Sustainability. Retrieved on July 25, 2016, from http://www.businessdictionary.com/definition/social-sustainability.html.

Carmichael, Alasdair (2015, January/February). "Man-Made Fibers Continue to Grow." *Textile World*. Retrieved on July 13, 2016, from http://www.textileworld.com/textile-world/fiber-world/2015/02/man-made-fibers-continue-to-grow/.

Chapagain, A.K., Hoekstra, A.Y., Savenije, H.H.G., & Gautam, R. (2005, September). "The Water Footprint of Cotton Consumption." Value of Water Research Report Series No. 18. UNESCO Institute for Water Education. Retrieved on July 27, 2016, from http://waterfootprint.org/media/downloads/Report18.pdf.

Chen, Hsiou-Lien, & Burns, Leslie Davis (2006). Environmental Analysis of Textile Products, *Clothing and Textiles Research Journal*, 24(3): 248–61.

Columbia Sportswear Co. (2016). "About Us—Corporate Responsibility." Retrieved on July 26, 2016, from https://www.columbia.com/About-Us_Corporate-Responsibility.html.

Elkington, John (1999). *Cannibals with Forks: Triple Bottom Line of 21st Century Business*. Oxford, UK: Capstone Publishing Ltd.

Elkington, John (2004). "Enter the Triple Bottom Line." Retrieved on July 20, 2016, from http://www.johnelkington.com/archive/TBL-elkington-chapter.pdf.

Fairtrade America (2016). "Cotton." Retrieved on July 20, 2016, from http://www.fairtradeamerica.org/en-us/fairtrade-products/cotton.

Fairtrade International (2016). "Cotton." Retrieved on July 20, 2016, from http://www.fairtrade.net/products/cotton.html.

Federal Trade Commission (1996, April 12). "FTC Approves 'Lyocell' for Use in Fabric Content Labeling." Retrieved on July 25, 2016, from https://www.ftc.gov/news-events/press-releases/1996/04/ftc-approves-lyocell-use-fabric-content-labeling.

Fletcher, Kate (2014). *Sustainable Fashion and Textiles: Design Journeys* (2nd ed.). London: Routledge/Taylor & Francis Group.

"Global Apparel Sales to Climb Past $1.4 Trillion in 2016" (2016, July 12). *Apparel*. Retrieved on July 20, 2016, from http://apparel.edgl.com/news/Global-Apparel-Sales-to-Climb-Past-$1-4-Trillion-in-2016106121.

Global Organic Cotton Community (2016a). "Organic Cotton." *HELVETAS, Textile Exchange, and ICCO*. Retrieved on July 27, 2016, from http://www.organiccotton.org/oc/Organic-cotton/Organic-cotton.php.

Global Organic Cotton Community (2016b). "The Risks of Cotton Farming." *HELVETAS, Textile Exchange, and ICCO*. Retrieved on July 27, 2016, from http://www.organiccotton.org/oc/Cotton-general/Impact-of-cotton/Risk-of-cotton-farming.php.

Global Organic Cotton Community (2016c). "World Cotton Production." *HELVETAS, Textile Exchange, and ICCO*. Retrieved on July 27, 2016, from http://www.organiccotton.org/oc/Cotton-general/World-market/World-cotton-production.php.

Greenpeace (2016). "The Detox Catwalk 2016." Retrieved on July 26, 2016, from http://www.greenpeace.org/international/en/campaigns/detox/fashion/detox-catwalk/.

Gullingsrud, Annie (2017). *Fashion Fibers: Designing for Sustainability*. NY: Fairchild Books/Bloomsbury.

Hasnat, Abul, Rahman, Istiakur, & Pasha, Mosabbir (2013). Assessment of Environmental Impact for Tannery Industries in Bangladesh. *International Journal of Environmental Science and Development*, 4(2): 217–20.

Hawley, Jana (2015). "Economic Impact of Textile and Clothing Recycling," in J. Hethorn & C. Ulasewicz (eds). *Sustainable Fashion What's Next?* (2nd ed.) 204–30. NY: Fairchild Books.

Hethorn, Janet, & Ulasewicz, Connie (2015). *Sustainable Fashion: What's Next?* (2nd ed.). NY: Fairchild Books.

Icebreaker (2016). "Ethics." Retrieved on July 27, 2016, from https://www.icebreaker.com/en/icebreaker-ethics/ethics-landing.html.

Imperial Stock Ranch (2016). "Traceable and Responsible." Retrieved on July 27, 2016, from http://imperialstockranch.com/2016/05/traceable-and-responsible/

International Labor Rights Forum (2016). Cotton Campaign. Retrieved July 27, 2016 from http://www.laborrights.org/industries/cotton.

Jenkin, Nicola (2012, December 10). "Should We Be Sheepish about Wool's Sustainability Record?" *Source Intelligence*. Retrieved on July 20, 2016, from http://source.ethicalfashionforum.com/digital/should-we-be-sheepish-about-wools-sustainability-record.

Kheel Center, Cornell University (2011). "The 1911 Triangle Factory Fire." Retrieved on July 20, 2016, from https://trianglefire.ilr.cornell.edu/.

Kovacs, Mandy (2016, July 5). "Sustainable Sourcing: Are Shorter Supply Chains Key to Sustainability?" Retrieved on July 22, 2016, from http://www.just-style.com/management-briefing/sustainable-sourcing-are-shorter-supply-chains-key-to-sustainability_id128282.aspx.

Levi Strauss & Co. (2014, July). "Restricted Substance List." Retrieved on July 26, 2016, from http://levistrauss.com/wp-content/uploads/2014/09/July-2014-RSL-English.pdf.

Lewin, Menachem (Editor) (2006). *Handbook of Fiber Chemistry* (3rd ed.). Boca Raton, FL: CRC Press/Taylor & Francis Group.

Mackey, John & Sisodia, Raj (2013). *Conscious Capitalism: Liberating the Heroic Spirit of Business.* Boston: Harvard Business Review Press.

Macy's (2016, May 31). "Conflict Minerals Report." Retrieved on July 27, 2016, from https://www.macysinc.com/assets/docs /social-responsibility/Conflict_Minerals_Report.pdf.

Mass, Ed (2014). "Rayon, Modal, and Tencel—Environmental Friends or Foes." *Yes It's Organic.* Retrieved on July 21, 2016, from http://www.yesitsorganic.com/rayon-modal-tencel -environmental-friends-or-foes.html#ixzz4Fd5t4cbp.

McKenzie, Stephen (2004). *Social Sustainability: Towards Some Definitions.* Hawke Research Institute Working Paper Series, No. 27. Retrieved on July 26, 2016, from http:// naturalcapital.us/images/Social%20Sustainability%20-%20 Towards%20Some%20Definitions_20100120_024059.pdf.

Mwinyihija, Mwinyikione (2010). *Ecotoxicological Diagnosis in the Tanning Industry.* NY: Springer.

Nike (2016). "Nike Aims to Minimize Our Environmental Footprint." Retrieved on July 25, 2016, from http://about.nike .com/pages/environmental-impact.

O EcoTextiles (2012, February). "Eucalyptus Fiber by Any Other Name." Retrieved on July 19, 2016, from https://oecotextiles .wordpress.com/category/fibers/viscose/.

Patagonia (2016a). "Corporate Responsibility." Retrieved on July 26, 2016, from http://www.patagonia.com/corporate -responsibility.html.

Patagonia (2016b). "Worn Wear." Retrieved on July 26, 2016, from http://www.patagonia.com/worn-wear.html.

Responsible Sourcing Network (2016, May 27). "Cotton Pledges Against Forced Labor in the Uzbek Cotton Sector." Retrieved on July 25, 2016, from http://www.sourcingnetwork.org/the -cotton-pledge.

Rivoli, Pietra (2015). *The Travels of a T-shirt in the Global Economy* (2nd edition). Hoboken, NJ: Wiley.

Samaniego, Danielle (2016, May 11). "Levi Strauss & Co. + Evrnu Create First Pair of Jeans from Post-Consumer Cotton Waste." *Unzipped Blog.* Retrieved on July 27, 2016, from http://www .levistrauss.com/unzipped-blog/2016/05/levi-strauss-co-evrnu -create-first-pair-of-jeans-from-post-consumer-cotton-waste/.

Senge, Peter, Smith, Bryan, Kruschwitz, Nina, Laur, Joe, & Schley, Sara (2008). *The Necessary Revolution: How Individuals and Organizations Are Working Together to Create a Sustainable World.* NY: Doubleday.

Skrivánková, Klára (2017, July). *Base Code Guidance: Modern Slavery.* Anti-Slavery International and Ethical Trade Initiative. London: Ethical Trade Initiative.

Statista (2016). "Per Capita Expenditure on Apparel Worldwide in 2015 and 2025, by Region (in U.S. Dollars)." Retrieved on July 18, 2016, from http://www.statista.com/statistics/279749 /global-per-capita-apparel-expenditure/.

TEonline (n.d.) "Textile Chemicals." Retrieved on July 25, 2016, from http://www.teonline.com/knowledge-centre/textile -chemicals.html.

Textile Exchange (2016a). "Organic Cotton Market Report: Overview." Retrieved on July 22, 2016, from https://textileexchange.org /downloads/2016-organic-cotton-market-report-overview/.

Textile Exchange (2016b). "Preferred Fiber and Materials Market Report: Overview." Retrieved on July 22, 2016, from https:// textileexchange.org/downloads/2016-preferred-fiber-and -materials-market-report/.

Textile Exchange (2016c). "Responsible Wool Standard." Retrieved on July 20, 2016, from http://responsiblewool.org/.

The True Cost (2015). "Environmental Impact." Retrieved on July 21, 2016, from http://truecostmovie.com/learn-more /environmental-impact/.

Thompson, Derek (2012, April 5). "How American Spends Money: 100 Years in the Life of the Family Budget." *The Atlantic.* Retrieved on July 15, 2016, from http://www.theatlantic .com/business/archive/2012/04/how-america-spends-money -100-years-in-the-life-of-the-family-budget/255475/.

Triple Bottom Line (2009, November 17). *The Economist.* on Retrieved on July 20, 2016, from http://www.economist.com /node/14301663.

United States Department of Labor Bureau of Labor Statistics (2014, April). "One Hundred Years of Price Change: The Consumer Price Index and the American Inflation Experience." Retrieved on July 15, 2016, from http://www. bls.gov/opub/mlr/2014/article/one-hundred-years-of-price -change-the-consumer-price-index-and-the-american -inflation-experience.htm.

United States Environmental Protection Agency (2015, June). "Advancing Sustainable Materials Management: 2013 Fact Sheet." Retrieved on July 22, 2016, from https://www.epa.gov /sites/production/files/2015-09/documents/2013_advncng _smm_fs.pdf.

United States Environmental Protection Agency (2016a). "Resource Consumption." Retrieved on July 7, 2016, from https://cfpub.epa.gov/roe/chapter/sustain/resource.cfm.

United States Environmental Protection Agency (2016b). "Sustainability." Retrieved on July 7, 2016, from https://cfpub .epa.gov/roe/chapter/sustain/index.cfm.

Welters, Linda (2015). "The Fashion of Sustainability," in J. Hethorn & C. Ulasewicz (eds). *Sustainable Fashion What's Next?* (2nd ed.): 4–26. NY: Fairchild Books.

World Business Council for Sustainable Development (2015, June). "Evaluation of Smart Community Infrastructures: Towards a Standardized Approach." Retrieved on July 26, 2016, from http://www.wbcsd.org/Pages/eNews/eNewsDetails .aspx?ID=16506&NoSearchContextKey=true.

World Wildlife Fund (2016). "Sustainable Agriculture—Cotton." Retrieved on July 27, 2016, from http://www.worldwildlife.org /industries/cotton.

World Trade Organization (2015). "Merchandise Trade by Product—Clothing." Retrieved on July 15, 2016, from https:// www.wto.org/english/res_e/statis_e/its2015_e/its15_merch _trade_product_e.pdf.

Case Study: Should Everlane Pursue Becoming a B Corporation™?

Everlane, headquartered in San Francisco, California, USA, designs, markets, and retails men's and women's apparel. As a pure play online apparel retailer, they focus on direct marketing to the consumer. The company was started in 2010 by Michael Preysman and now includes a team in San Francisco and a small team in New York City. Everlane is organized around three areas: design and production, creative and marketing, and engineering and operations. From its inception, Everlane has prided itself in "pushing boundaries and challenging conventions" primarily around production, pricing, and transparency. They invite customers to challenge them and ask questions about the integrity of their contract factories and how the prices of products are determined. Their website provides evidence of their socially responsible values and business practices. See https://www.everlane.com.

The leadership team at Everlane is considering whether to lead the company in becoming a certified B Corporation™. Currently, over twenty-five apparel companies have earned this certification, including Eileen Fisher, Patagonia, and Indigenous. Certification is overseen by B Lab, a nonprofit organization "dedicated to using the power of business to solve social and environmental problems" (B Lab, 2016). The leadership team will be reviewing the advantages and disadvantages and will make a decision whether to include this endeavor as a strategic goal for the company. You will take the role of the analyst asked to research the certification criteria and processes, analyze this information in relation to Everlane, and provide a recommendation to the leadership team.

1. What is a B Corporation? What are the criteria and certification processes used for a company to be certified?

2. Research Everlane as a company—their history, mission, values, and organizational structure. Describe the current product categories and pricing. Who is the target customer for Everlane?

3. Describe and explain at least three advantages and three disadvantages for Everlane to pursue certification to become a B Corporation.

4. What is your recommendation as to whether Everlane should pursue certification to become a B Corporation? Provide justification for this recommendation.

5. Include a reference list and be sure to cite your resources.

Note: The background for this case study is based on publicly available information. The business problem is speculative only and is not based on publicly available and/or documented information from Everlane.

Call to Action Activity: What's in Your Closet?

1. Go to your closet and select one of your favorite clothing items. Describe the item, brand, fiber content, and country of origin. Include a photograph or sketch of the item.

2. Describe and explain at least two general issues (in relation to textile production, apparel design, apparel production, and/or supply chain) that may be evident in the design, production, and/or distribution of this item. Be sure to cite resources used in your explanations.

3. Go to and explore the website of the brand. Describe what business practices, if any, they employ that address issues of environmental, economic, social, and cultural sustainability. Be sure to cite the website.

4. Write a professionally worded email to the brand/company that includes the following:

    a. Introduce yourself, describe your interest in sustainability and social responsibility, and explain why you are writing this email.

    b. Outline at least one issue you believe that the fashion brand/company is addressing well and why and at least one issue you believe that the fashion brand/company should be addressing and why. Be sure to include rationales for each.

    c. Thank the company for reading the email and for their consideration in addressing the issues. Include your name and signature.

5. Your paper will include your responses to questions 1 through 4, a reference list, and a photograph or sketch of the item.

Responsible Wool Standard: Conversation with Jeanne Carver

Jeanne Carver
Imperial Stock Ranch
Maupin, Oregon, USA

Imperial Stock Ranch in central Oregon, USA, produces high quality wool grown and processed with sustainable practices. The ranch has become the first wool supplier to receive the Responsible Wool Standard certification from Textile Exchange. Jeanne Carver, co-owner of Imperial Stock Ranch spoke about sustainability and her work in promoting sustainable practices in the wool industry (see Figure 1.9).

Figure 1.9 Jeanne Carver, co-owner of Imperial Stock Ranch, is a leader in sustainable wool certification.

Q: How do you define sustainability? How do you apply this definition to your wool business?
A: I define sustainable agriculture as environmentally sound, economically viable, and socially responsible. That is, leaving the land better than how you found it and ensuring the health of the animals. Let me explain each.

Environmentally sound—agriculturalists and all land managers have a calling to conserve our natural resources. We work to improve, not just maintain, our land. Therefore, we constantly monitor and revise our conservation management plan.

Economically viable—if we cannot make a living then we will not be there to steward the land. Both the value and the volume of the harvest allow us to continue to do good work. I believe that conservation and economic sustainability go hand in hand—if the land wins then we win; and if the animals are well cared for and healthy, it will have a positive impact to the bottom line.

Socially responsible—taking care of the people who are part of our team is essential. Our workers are our family. Social also includes community—our close and extended neighborhoods—those who live next door, in town, in the region, and in the state. When working with textile mills and cut-and-sew facilities, we are committed to working as close to home as possible. We view this as part of social sustainability. In fact, the Oregon Department of Economic Development estimated that in the past ten years we have contributed over $10 million to the economy of the region and state. In addition to environmental, economic, and social aspects of sustainability, I also include a fourth leg—cultural sustainability—that is, preserving the traditions and values of both the agriculture and textile communities and industries, which are vital to this country's strength.

Q: How did you get involved with the Responsible Wool Standard and why do you think it is important?
A: The Responsible Wool Standard (RWS) was developed by Textile Exchange (TE). I first became aware of the work of TE when I attended the 2014 Textile Sustainability Conference held in Portland, Oregon. The conference was an eye-opening experience for me. I was both intrigued and inspired. TE was then just starting to talk about wool. Their original work focused on organic cotton. After cotton, they turned to development of the Responsible Down Standard (RDS). Then they started exploring a wool standard. It just so happened that Nancy Hales (Portland's First Lady at the time) spoke at this conference and mentioned the collaboration of Imperial Stock Ranch and Ralph Lauren in creating the USA sourced wool sweater worn by U.S. athletes during the opening ceremonies of the 2014 winter Olympics. Representatives from TE and other brands connected with me about our operations at Imperial Stock Ranch.

Our involvement with the Responsible Wool Standard came about from our work with brand partners. In 2015, we were approached about the idea of being third party certified under this developing "standard," which had a focus on both land management and animal husbandry practices. Our family ranch is in its 146th year of continuous operation raising sheep, cattle, grains, and hay. In 1999, we shifted from commodity sale of wool to selling "value-added" wool products such as yarn, fabric, clothing, accessories, and home textiles, working with supply chain partners as close to home as possible (all within the United States). Because of this work, and our move into value-added food markets, we understood that customers want more and more to know what's behind the products they purchase. Brands are at risk with their choices in sourcing and manufacturing partners, and the practices of those partners. Just as we've seen in the growth of niche markets in the food sector, working together in textiles for a certified traceable product held to identifiable standards gives people increased confidence in both their purchases and brand loyalty. As a producer, the RWS reflects what we already believe and practice on the ground. And it intentionally ties the entire supply chain together—raw material producers, processors, manufacturers, and brands. This broadens and strengthens our "community," which includes the customer, all part of the same story and making us stronger.

Some brands further differentiate themselves, as Patagonia has done, by adding additional criteria to the RWS to create their own standard. Imperial Stock Ranch is currently certified as an RWS and PAT Plus supplier of wool. The RWS is not without challenges, but it is a growing voluntary standard around the world. Updates as of fall 2017 show certified wool producers in Australia, New Zealand, Uruguay, and Argentina, in addition to the United States. Supply chain partners in eight countries are certified, including the United States where we have four facilities certified to deliver traceable product.

Q: You have partnered with a number of fashion brands, including Ralph Lauren, J Crew, Ethan Allen, and Zady. What advice would you have for a fashion brand wanting to source wool in the United States?
A: Marketing our wool fibers to fashion brands has been challenging. Imperial Stock Ranch is not a textile mill. Brands typically want to source yarns or fabrics and do not want to handle the complicated supply chain from acquiring the raw wool to managing the processing, spinning, dyeing, and weaving. The single best raw wool resource for mills or brands to secure a traceable American wool supply is Chargeurs Wool USA. Brands have gone out looking for U.S. wool at its origin and stumbled across Imperial Stock Ranch. Because we had built strong relationships with mills, I have handled the supply/value chain for the brands. The Responsible Wool Standard will help with marketing a fully traceable certified American wool supply by providing a place where brands can go to find wool that meets the standard.

Diversity, Equity, Inclusion, and Social Justice

Objectives

- Describe relevant issues in the fashion industry related to diversity, equity, inclusion, and social justice.
- Explain strategies in the fashion industry that result in equitable and inclusive fashion products and imagery and promotion of fashion products.
- Explain how principles of universal design are applied to the design and creation of fashion products.
- Explain programs and initiatives that companies in the fashion industry have implemented to create more equitable and inclusive workplaces and communities.

New York City–based apparel brand Universal Standard *gets it* when it comes to women's apparel sizing. With their Universal Fit Liberty program,

> If a piece from our core collection no longer fits due to size fluctuation, we'll replace it with your new size, within a year of purchase, free of charge. All returned clothing will be laundered and donated across a number of charities supporting women in need. We believe your clothes should always fit, feel, and look good. And, women deserve to live their lives without feeling bullied by their size (Universal Standard, 2017).

Founded by Polina Veksler and Alexandra Waldman in 2015, Universal Standard addresses the issue that "size had become the dividing line determining who had the privilege and freedom to dress with quality and style." They do so by offering high quality, trans-seasonal, and stylish "elevated basics" in women's sizes 6–32 through direct-to-consumer retail (see Figure 2.1). As a size-inclusive brand, Universal Standard epitomizes strategies that successfully address diversity and equity issues within the fashion industry (Sherman, 2016).

The focus in this chapter is on diversity, equity, inclusion, and social justice within the fashion industry. Similar to other industries, organizations, and institutions, the fashion industry has faced challenges around these issues. Because of systemic and institutionalized inequities within all sectors of the fashion industry, historically marginalized groups of individuals have not had equitable opportunities to succeed in the fashion industry. In addition, non-inclusive fashion products and imagery of fashions result in customers having limited options and limited exposure to diverse perspectives of what are considered fashion norms and ideals of attractiveness. To address these challenges, fashion brands, companies, and organizations have developed and implemented numerous strategies for creating more diverse, equitable, and inclusive workplaces, product lines, and product imagery. The chapter begins with an overview of diversity, equity, inclusion, and social justice as they apply to the fashion industry, including challenges the fashion industry is facing. The chapter then outlines strategies by which fashion brands and companies are addressing these issues, including inclusive and equitable fashion products, diverse and inclusive imagery and promotion of fashion products, internal policies and procedures, and external policy advocacy.

Overview of Diversity, Equity, Inclusion, and Social Justice

The terms diversity, equity, inclusion, and social justice are applied to fashion because of two parallel aspects of fashion directly related to these terms:

1. *Fashion products and practices including apparel, accessories, and other forms of adornment.*

Figure 2.1 Alexandra Waldman and Polina Veksler founded size-inclusive fashion brand, Universal Standard.

Throughout history, clothing and adornment have reflected and communicated individual and social statuses including age, gender, ethnicity, socioeconomic status/class, culture, and ideals of attractiveness. Thus, individuals have sought out and worn specific clothing items to communicate such statuses. Fashion also reflects normalized ideals of attractiveness, and imagery associated with fashions reinforces these normalized ideals.

2. *The industry that creates, manufactures, distributes, and advertises these fashions.* Historically marginalized groups have been the foundation of the ready-to-wear fashion industry. Lower class and/or immigrants have historically worked in the factories producing fashion products. The ready-to-wear fashion industry also employs a large number of women throughout segments of the industry—design, manufacturing, and retailing.

Thus, to fully understand the dynamics of social change within the industry today, a discussion of diversity, equity, inclusion, and social justice is imperative.

Diversity

The term **diversity** describes the demographic mix of a people that includes both individual differences (e.g., personality, life experiences, perspectives) and group/social differences (e.g., race, ethnicity, socioeconomic status, gender, sexual orientation, gender identity, country of origin, and ability as well as cultural, political, religious, or other affiliations). Why is diversity important? First, by acknowledging and promoting diversity, stereotypic perceptions and associations based on individual and group/social differences can be countered, resulting in reduced prejudice and negative behaviors based on these individual and group/social differences. Second, increased awareness of the value of diversity in decision making in all areas and at all levels of a company results in increased diversity of workforce of the company. Lastly, consumers are increasingly purchasing from companies whose goods and services meet diverse consumer needs and whose

imagery of products reflects diverse characteristics of its customer base. Numerous demographic characteristics have been addressed in diversity initiatives by companies in the fashion industry. The characteristics are described in this section, and the strategies used by fashion brands and companies are discussed later in the chapter.

Age

Stereotyping and discrimination based on differences in age is referred to as **ageism**, usually that of younger persons against older. Ageism in the fashion industry is reflected in limited availability of fashion products that address older consumers' wants and needs, in limited number of older individuals in the imagery associated with fashions, and workplace age discrimination within some companies.

Gender

Gender refers to the physical and/or culturally and socially constructed characteristics of women and men. **Gender identity** is how an individual conceptualizes and experiences their gender, regardless of whether or not it conforms with the gender culturally associated with their assigned sex at birth. **Gender expression** refers to "an individual's presentation—including physical appearance, clothing choice and accessories—and behavior that communicates aspects of gender or gender role. Gender expression may or may not conform to a person's gender identity" (American Psychological Association, 2015).

With regard to fashion products, distinctions between men's and women's apparel and accessories are commonplace, and fashion products reflecting fluidity of gender expression are limited. When shopping for fashion, whether online or at a brick-and-mortar store, one must often define one's gender, as fashion retailers still typically divide options by "men" and "women" or online as "shop men" and "shop women." Similarly, fashion imagery reflecting gender fluidity is also limited. In addition, gender inequality and discrimination within the fashion industry has been manifested in a number of ways. For example, the term *glass runway* refers to workplace discrimination of women in leadership roles within all areas of the fashion industry as evidenced by the relatively smaller number of women as compared to men in leadership roles in this predominantly female-oriented industry (Ghanem, 2017).

Culture, Race, and Ethnicity

The term **culture** has many meanings. For the purposes of this discussion, culture refers to the sum of knowledge, beliefs, attitudes, values, customs, and meanings that defines a group's particular way of life. "Culture is transmitted through assumptions, language, material objects, dress, rituals, institutions, and art from one generation to the next" (Dictionary.com, 2017).

Historically, the term **race** referred to a social construct that separated individuals into groups based on physical appearance (e.g., skin color), cultural and/or ethnic identity, and/or power structures within a society. Scholars now note that "*race* is not a biological category but an idea, a social construction—created to interpret human differences and used to justify socioeconomic arrangements in ways that accrue to the benefit of the dominant social group" (Adams, Bell, & Griffin, 2007, p. 118). **Ethnicity** refers to groups of individuals who identify with a common cultural heritage, including language, social, religious, and/or national experiences.

Cultural identity, **racial identity**, and **ethnic identity** refer to how individuals view themselves as belonging to a particular cultural, racial, or ethnic group.

Cultural, racial, and ethnic identity are often communicated through dress and appearance. For example, **traditional** or **national dress/clothing** reflects the history and identity associated with groups, countries, and/or world regions through symbolic elements (e.g., motifs, styles, accessories, etc.) (see Figure 2.2). Depending on the degree of acceptance of *Western clothing* or *Western style* (clothing styles associated with Western Europe and North America) traditional dress may be worn on a day-to-day basis or may be worn only for

Figure 2.2 Traditional dress of the women in Sacred Valley of the Incas in Peru includes styles, colors, motifs, and accessories.

ceremonial occasions. Religious beliefs and identity are also represented through symbolic elements in clothing and appearance norms, e.g., necklace with a Christian cross, jilbab and hijab worn by Muslim women, and kippah or yarmulke worn by Jewish boys and men.

Cultural mixtures of symbols, folklore, and practices often result from acculturation, assimilation, or cultural exchange. For example, the acceptance of and/or adaptation of Western style clothing by individuals throughout the world reflects the status associated with the dress style. **Cultural appropriation** or **ethnic appropriation** is the unauthorized and inappropriate borrowing or using of symbolic elements representing a particular culture or ethnic group by individuals who are not part of that particular culture or ethnic group. Cultural appropriation is often the case when the symbolic elements are copied from a minority culture by members of a dominant culture or when the elements copied reinforce "historically exploitative relationships" among countries or cultures (Arewa,

2016). Cultural or ethnic appropriation in fashion results when these symbolic elements are borrowed (e.g., adopting elements of clothing from indigenous cultures, wearing jewelry or clothing with religious symbolism without the belief in those religions) where the meanings associated with the symbolic cultural elements are lost or distorted or even viewed as mocking the culture's history and identity.

Socioeconomic Status

"**Socioeconomic status** is the social standing or class of an individual or group. It is often measured as a combination of education, income and occupation. Examinations of socioeconomic status often reveal inequities in access to resources, plus issues related to privilege, power and control" (American Psychological Association, 2017). Fashion and class systems have always been connected. Wealth and socioeconomic status are often communicated by symbols associated with those who have acquired certain privileges within the society and have the ability to afford particular fashions. Historically, **sumptuary laws** were used to regulate consumption. In the case of fashion, such laws restricted the wearing of particular materials (e.g., furs, metals, fabrics), colors, jewels, decorative techniques (e.g., embroidery), or clothing styles to those who were of particular rank or status. Today, status and/or wealth are reflected in the wearing of rare (and therefore expensive) gemstones and precious metals and/or wearing fashions with visible labels of expensive designer/luxury brands. In the current ready-to-wear fashion industry, class issues continue to be associated with specific fashion products and imagery of fashion products, thus limiting those without the class privileges the ability to acquire or obtain certain fashions (Gee, 2017).

Disability

Disability refers to a "condition or function judged to be significantly impaired relative to the usual standard of an individual or group. The term is used to refer to individual functioning, including physical impairment, sensory impairment, cognitive impairment, intellectual impairment

mental illness, and various types of chronic disease" (Disabled World, 2017). The three dimensions of disability include body structure and function (and impairment thereof), activity (and activity restrictions), and participation (and participation restrictions) (Disabled World, 2017). In fact, a person may be disabled in some environments but not in others. From a social perspective, a person experiences disability when impairment substantially limits a major life activity, or when there is a history or perception of such a limitation. Fashion products that address the unique needs of individuals with disabilities are designed to proactively remove restrictions and/or allow for participation in the activity. Such options are limited. In addition, the imagery associated with fashion rarely reflects individuals with disabilities. Although legal strides have been made to reduce discrimination in the workplace and create greater access for individuals with disabilities, additional work is still needed in fashion industry workplaces as well as in fashion products and imagery.

Ideals of Attractiveness

Ideals of attractiveness are aspirational characteristics that represent a society's norms of beauty and aesthetics. Ideals of attractiveness are directly related to media imagery associated with fashion including fashion images in magazines, advertising, television, film, and other outlets. The fashion industry has been charged with promoting limited and often unattainable ideals of attractiveness in the hiring, use, and representation of models who are predominantly young, very thin, able-bodied, and white.

Equity

Within diverse societies there are disparities among people based on these individual and/or group/social differences. **Equity** takes into consideration the fact that these social identifiers (age, gender, race, socioeconomic status, physical ability, etc.) do, in fact, affect equality. Equity is a goal not a process. The goal of equity is to promote justice, impartiality, and fairness within the processes and distribution of resources by systems and/or institutions within the society. In an equitable environment, an individual or a group is given resources it needs for equal advantage to others in order to succeed. Achieving equal advantage does not necessarily mean offering equal services; in fact, more or different services may be necessary to achieve equality of opportunity. For companies, equity is advanced through initiatives for historically underrepresented and/or marginalized populations of employees to have equal access to professional growth opportunities (PCC, 2017).

Inclusion

Inclusion refers to the degree to which diverse individuals are able to participate fully in the decision-making processes within an organization

or group. Whereas a truly "inclusive" group is necessarily diverse, a "diverse" group may or may not be "inclusive" (PCC, 2017). For companies, inclusiveness results in greater democratic decision making and decisions that reflect the diversity of both the workforce and the customers for which the company is serving (see Figure 2.3). For example, a fashion brand company that has a core value of inclusiveness in decision making would hire, support, and value the contributions of employees across ages, genders, ethnic/cultural identities, physical abilities, and socioeconomic statuses.

Social Justice

Social justice is both a goal *and* a process. The goal of social justice is full and equal participation of all groups in a society that is mutually shaped to

Figure 2.3 Diversity of employees of this fashion start-up company reflects a commitment to inclusiveness.

meet their needs. To achieve this goal the process of social justice is to ensure the distribution of resources is equitable so that all members of society are physically and psychologically safe and secure. Social justice involves individuals who have a sense of their own actions as well as a sense of social responsibility toward and with others and the society as a whole (Adams, Bell, & Griffin, 2007). What role does fashion play in social justice? Through **solution-based design**, many fashion designers are approaching fashion design from the perspective of creating fashions that are part of solutions to larger societal, economic, health, and political problems (Friedman, 2016). For example, founded in 2014, New York-based Care + Wear "is a leading provider of innovative healthwear focused on creating positive and effective healing experiences for patients everywhere" (Care + Wear, 2017). **Healthwear** (medically related apparel and accessories created to address challenges created by illness or disability using tools and techniques of fashion) by Care + Wear includes such products as Ultra-Soft Antimicrobial PICC Line Covers for patients suffering from conditions like cancer or Lyme disease, Chest Access Shirts for patients with

chest ports, and gloves for wheelchair users (see Figure 2.4). "By designing functional and fashionable products in collaboration with patients, clinicians and hospitals, we hope that we can help patients live comfortably, safely, and stylishly" (Care + Wear, 2017). In addition, as introduced in Chapter 1 and discussed in later chapters, numerous fashion brands facilitate social change and promote social justice through advocacy, humanitarian, philanthropic, and community development initiatives.

Inclusive and Equitable Fashion Products

The fashion industry has addressed issues and challenges around diversity, equity, inclusion, and social justice in a number of ways, including creating, manufacturing, and distributing inclusive and equitable products. These are fashion items that reflect the diverse wants and needs of consumers regardless of age, ability, gender, religion, and socioeconomic status and fashions that do not exploit cultural or ethnic symbolic representations. Strategies used by fashion brands include universal design and designs that advance cultural/ethnic sustainability.

Universal Design

One of the most common strategies associated with inclusive and equitable products is universal design. The Centre for Excellence in Universal Design (2017a) defines **universal design** as:

> the design and composition of an environment so that it can be accessed, understood and used to the greatest extent possible by all people regardless of their age, size, ability or disability. An environment (or any building, product, or service in that environment) should be designed to meet the needs of all people who wish to use it. This is not a special requirement, for the benefit of only a minority of the population. It is a fundamental condition of good

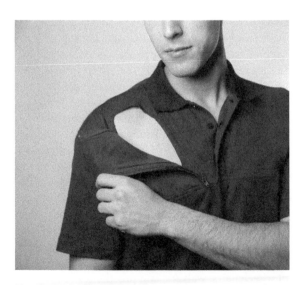

Figure 2.4 Care + Wear creates healthwear such as Chest Access Shirts for patients with chest ports.

design. If an environment is accessible, usable, convenient and a pleasure to use, everyone benefits. By considering the diverse needs and abilities of all throughout the design process, universal design creates products, services and environments that meet peoples' needs. Simply put, universal design is good design.

Other terms used to describe this design approach include **inclusive design** and **barrier-free design** (often when applied to the built environment).

Based on the work of the Center for Universal Design and North Carolina State University (Connell et al., 1997), seven principles of universal design guide designers and product developers in creating products that meet the needs of all people who wish to use it:

1. Equitable use
2. Flexibility in use
3. Simple and intuitive to use
4. Perceptible information
5. Tolerance for error
6. Low physical effort
7. Size and space for approach and use

See Table 2.1 for a complete listing of the Principles of Universal Design (Connell et al., 1997) and design solutions related to apparel (Park et al., 2014).

The principles of universal design are used by designers during the design process for fashion apparel (see Figures 2.5a and 2.5b). The principles of universal design are also used to analyze existing garments and their potential for use resulting in benefits for a broader range of consumers. As noted by Park et al. (2014), a number of clothing items epitomize universal design. For example, the Japanese kimono is worn by both men and women and can be adjusted to fit a range of sizes.

In addition to the obvious benefits of universal design to customers of fashion, fashion brands and companies can also benefit from incorporating

universal design principles (Centre for Excellence in Universal Design, 2017b). These benefits include

- Enhanced customer satisfaction with the apparel products
- Increased market reach—available to a greater number of people
- Potential for market crossover—accessibility and usability can generate widespread demand (If a product is simple, clear, easy to access, and easy to use, a consumer will be more likely to adopt it.)
- Positive brand image—positively contributing to society

Although the principles of universal design have been applied to the design of apparel and accessories for a number of specialized groups to create a wide variety of fashions, the current discussion around inclusive design in fashion will include

- Ability inclusive
- Size inclusive
- Gender inclusive

Ability Inclusive

Fashion brands/companies have incorporated principles of universal design to create fashions that can be worn by anyone, regardless of ability. For example, fashion brand Janska® creates wraps, capes, shawls, and accessories made from soft fleece fabrics that are ability inclusive (Janska®, 2017). In addition, fashion brands/companies have incorporated principles of universal design in the creation of **adaptive clothing** or **adapted clothing**, designed specifically for people with physical disabilities or who have difficulty dressing themselves. The primary challenges to independent dressing are closures such as buttons and zippers, pulling garments over the head, and putting on trousers. Adaptive clothing is specifically designed for ease of dressing and movement by using Velcro® hook and loop fasteners and/or easy to snap open backs to make it easier for a caregiver. The use of wheelchairs, walkers, and prosthetics can also

Table 2.1 Principles of Universal Design and Design Solutions for Apparel

	Design Principle	Guidelines	Design Solutions
1	**Equitable Use** The design is useful and marketable to people with diverse abilities.	1a. Provide the same means of use for all users: identical whenever possible; equivalent when not. 1b. Avoid segregating or stigmatizing any users. 1c. Provisions for privacy, security, and safety should be equally available to all users. 1d. Make the design appealing to all users.	Relaxed silhouette that fits a wide range of consumers of different sizes and shapes.
2	**Flexibility in Use** The design accommodates a wide range of individual preferences and abilities.	2a. Provide choice in methods of use. 2b. Accommodate right- or left-handed access and use. 2c. Facilitate the user's accuracy and precision. 2d. Provide adaptability to the user's pace.	Versatile way of dressing.
3	**Simple and Intuitive Use** Use of the design is easy to understand, regardless of the user's experience, knowledge, language skills, or current concentration level.	3a. Eliminate unnecessary complexity. 3b. Be consistent with user expectations and intuition. 3c. Accommodate a wide range of literacy and language skills. 3d. Arrange information consistent with its importance. 3e. Provide effective prompting and feedback during and after task completion.	Easy donning and doffing.
4	**Perceptible Information** The design communicates necessary information effectively to the user, regardless of ambient conditions or the user's sensory abilities.	4a. Use different modes (pictorial, verbal, tactile) for redundant presentation of essential information. 4b. Provide adequate contrast between essential information and its surroundings. 4c. Maximize "legibility" of essential information. 4d. Differentiate elements in ways that can be described (i.e., make it easy to give instructions or directions). 4e. Provide compatibility with a variety of techniques or devices used by people with sensory limitations.	Easy to understand the dressing procedure. Simple yet thoughtful design. Minimal design details.
5	**Tolerance for Error** The design minimizes hazards and the adverse consequences of accidental or unintended actions.	5a. Arrange elements to minimize hazards and errors: most used elements, most accessible; hazardous elements eliminated, isolated, or shielded. 5b. Provide warnings of hazards and errors. 5c. Provide fail safe features. 5d. Discourage unconscious action in tasks that require vigilance.	Design that does not hinder body movement. Optimized fit for size flexibility.

Table 2.1 Principles of Universal Design and Design Solutions for Apparel (*continued*)

	Design Principle	Guidelines	Design Solutions
6	**Low Physical Effort** The design can be used efficiently and comfortably and with a minimum of fatigue.	6a. Allow user to maintain a neutral body position. 6b. Use reasonable operating forces. 6c. Minimize repetitive actions. 6d. Minimize sustained physical effort.	Easy donning and doffing and easy maintenance.
7	**Size and Space for Approach and Use** Appropriate size and space is provided for approach, reach, manipulation, and use regardless of user's body size, posture, or mobility.	7a. Provide a clear line of sight to important elements for any seated or standing user. 7b. Make reach to all components comfortable for any seated or standing user. 7c. Accommodate variations in hand and grip size. 7d. Provide adequate space for the use of assistive devices or personal assistance.	Flexible size and fit. Easy donning and doffing.

References: Connell et al., 1997; Park et al., 2014.

 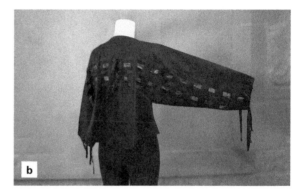

Figure 2.5 Principles of universal design were used in this digitally printed and laser cut cotton sateen jacket and silk vest designed by Jean Parsons and Kristen Morris. The jacket showcases digitally printed silk ribbons passed through laser cut slits. Original photographs provided by the designers.

make both dressing and movement challenging. Adaptive clothing allows for enhanced movement and comfort while sitting in a wheelchair, with prosthetics, or when using a walker. For example, ABL Denim is an inclusive design fashion brand company that offers a variety of denim fashions for individuals with limited mobility or dexterity and sensory processing issues (see company highlight at the end of the chapter) (see Figure 2.6). As a

resource for individuals, Buck & Buck® (2017) offers an *Adaptive Clothing Guide* for a variety of needs including those with dementia, arthritis, physical stiffness, foot problems, and delicate skin.

Size Inclusive

Sizing of women's, men's, and children's ready-to-wear is based on several factors (Burns, Mullet, & Bryant, 2016):

Figure 2.6 ABL Denim is an inclusive design fashion brand company creating fashionable adaptive clothing.

- Standardized sizing categories that vary by country and/or region of the world (e.g., U.S./Canada, U.K., France/European, Italy, Australia, Japan sizing categories);

- Standardized sizing categories by gender and, in some cases, age and relative size (e.g., misses, women's, women's plus size, men's, men's big-and-tall, junior, girls' preteen, boys' husky);

- Companies' **grade rules** used in creating patterns for the size range they produce resulting in variation in sizing among brands and styles produced.

Fashion brands often limit the range of sizes they offer by focusing on historically traditional sizing categories (e.g., women's sizes UK X–16, U.S./Canada 4–14) and/or using less specific sizing options (e.g., XS, S, M, L, XL, XXL). For women, the term **plus-size clothing** (e.g., women's sizes UK 14–32, U.S./Canada Plus 0X–4X, 14–28, 12W–28W) and for men, the term **big-and-tall clothing** (and plus-size clothing) are used to describe apparel sizes that are

larger than the traditional sizing categories. Fashions with **petite sizing** are designed and sized for women who are 5 feet 4 inches tall or less (e.g., women's U.S./Canada 0P–20P). These "specialty size" markets—plus-size, big-and-tall, petite—are considered growth opportunities for fashion brands and companies (Russell, 2017, June 1). As such, many fashion brands offer styles in a variety of size classifications. For example, Eileen Fisher offers styles in regular, petite, and plus sizes. **Size inclusive** fashion brands offer a broader range of sizes and do not make distinctions among regular, plus, and/or petite. For example, Universal Standard, the New York-based fashion brand highlighted in the introduction to this chapter, offers high quality fashions in women's U.S./Canada sizes from 6–32 (see Figure 2.7). Kade & Vos uses 3D design techniques to create women's undergarments that fit all shapes and sizes. Created in 2008, The Curvy Fashionista fashion lifestyle blog (http://thecurvyfashionista.com/) serves as a resource for consumers of plus-size and size inclusive fashions.

Gender Inclusive

The terms **gender inclusive fashion**, **unisex fashion**, and **gender neutral fashion** refer to fashions worn by individuals of all genders and reflect an individual's gender expression. Gender inclusive fashions include men's fashions that incorporate styles and styling details traditionally worn by women (e.g., floral prints, softer fabrics, skirts), women's fashions that incorporate styles and styling details traditionally worn by men (e.g., suit jackets, bomber jackets, tuxedos), and fashions that are traditionally worn by individuals of all genders (e.g., T-shirts, denim jeans) using gender inclusive sizing. It should be noted that referring to fashions, per se, as *gender fluid* fails to acknowledge the complex aspects of gender identity that shift across situations or time.

Of course, women's fashions have integrated men's styling for years, as adopting men's apparel reflected adopting symbols of the power structure within the society. On the other hand, historically, mainstream men's fashions have not adopted styling typically worn by women, thus avoiding symbolism associated with weakness in the society. What is currently

Figure 2.7 Universal Standard fashions are size inclusive, offering merchandise in U.S./Canada sizes 6–32.

evident in both men's and women's fashions is the range of styling available to all genders (Knoepp, 2017; Paget, 2016). No longer does a woman who prefers masculine fashion styles have to shop for traditional men's fashion outlets; instead she can find fashion brands that span the range of masculinity and femininity in sizing that fits her. A number of **tomboy brands** focus on creating fashions with men's styling in traditionally female sizing. New York City-based Kirrin Finch's menswear-inspired apparel is designed to fit a wide range of female sizes for what they refer to as a "dapper style" androgynous look. Wildfang, headquartered in Portland, Oregon, USA, creates and sells "the best men's styles, but for women" (see Figure 2.8). As they note on their website (Wildfang, 2017):

We're Liberating Menswear, One Bowtie at a Time.

We are modern-day female Robin Hoods, raiding men's closets and dispensing the styles we love through a single destination. From wingtips and blazers to exclusive content and inspiration, Wildfang aims to bring out the best in you by serving both your tomboy fashion sense and your

Figure 2.8 Wildfang fashions reflect the growing trend of tomboy brands.

tomboy spirit, 24/7/365. Because, while it's true that fashions change with the seasons, badass incidentally never goes out of style.

Fashion brands often market themselves as offering gender neutral and/or unisex lines. For example, GFW Clothing, designed and made in the United Kingdom, was founded in 2015 (part of Gender Free World Ltd) by individuals who believed access to clothing was restricted by gender. GFW Clothing styles are designed to fit one's body rather than one's gender (see Figure 2.9). For example, three body shapes and seven sizes are offered for each shirt design. In addition, GFW Clothing reflects the following values (Gender Free World, 2017):

1. To be seen as an individual regardless of physical or sexual characteristics.

2. To be free of the dominant societal norms which restrict choice such as assuming that a woman likes pink things!

3. To be free to love who you like regardless of their biology or gender.

4. Celebrating masculinity and femininity across its spectrum in the spirit of free expression.

Other gender neutral fashion brands include Muttonhead, headquartered in Toronto, Canada (https://www.muttonheadstore.com/); sixty-nine, headquartered in Los Angeles, California, USA (sixty-nine.us); and NotEqual, headquartered in New York City. These brands offer styles of tops, jackets, and pants in a range of sizes and body types. In addition, unisex/gender neutral has also made it to haute couture. Canadian designer Rad Hourani became an invited member of the Chambre Syndicale de la Haute Couture in Paris. In presenting his first Paris Haute Couture show in January 2013, he became the first designer in the history of fashion to present a unisex haute couture collection (Rad Hourani, 2017).

Figure 2.9 Gender neutral fashions such as GFW are designed to fit one's body rather than one's gender.

Advancing Cultural and Ethnic Sustainability

As noted earlier in the chapter, traditional/national dress and/or appearance norms are considered physical artifacts of a culture and incorporate symbolic elements that reflect the history and identity associated with cultures, countries, and/or world regions. Fashion designers have long been inspired by traveling to or observing cultures other than their own and incorporating aspects of traditional and/or national dress into couture and ready-to-wear fashions. In fashion, cultural and ethnic sustainability is advanced through the appropriate use of the symbolic elements (design of fabrics/materials, apparel, and/or accessories) found in traditional/national dress and/or appearance norms associated with a particular religious, ethnic, or cultural group. Appropriate use occurs when the value of the aspects of the dress that represent the culture is retained and when aspects of culture that create positive, equitable, and enduring relationships among the current members and future members of the society, group, or organization are maintained.

Because of widespread cultural exchange and incorporation of cultural/ethnic elements in symbols in fashion, designers and merchandisers of fashion are often confused about when the fashions are cultural *appreciation* (advancing cultural and ethnic sustainability) and when the fashions are cultural *appropriation* (unauthorized and inappropriate borrowing and/or using of symbolic elements). Questions asked include: Who owns the cultural/ethnic symbolism, can the symbolism be borrowed without exploitation, and who decides? "Context, particularly as it relates to power relationships, is a key factor in distinguishing borrowing from exploitative cultural appropriation" (Arewa, 2016). Also, when original sources are not acknowledged or compensated, they are also considered cultural appropriation. Court rulings may soon decide, as the United Nations World Intellectual Property Organization is exploring legal ramifications for those who "borrow" aesthetic symbols from indigenous cultures ("traditional cultural expressions") without those cultures benefiting.

Courts withstanding, negative public reactions toward images reflecting cultural insensitivity are growing. For example, the March 2017 "diversity" issue of *Vogue* included an editorial with supermodel Karlie Kloss dressed as a Japanese fashion Geisha along with "one of fashion's favorite set-ups when it comes to shooting in other countries: using, as a prop, a decidedly unglamorous, often stereotypical human cultural symbol wearing traditional garb—in this case, a sumo wrestler—posed next to the beautiful white supermodel wearing designer clothing" (Mau, 2017). Upon the extensive public backlash, Kloss apologized for participating in the shoot.

How can designers avoid cultural appropriation in their design work? Asking the following questions provides designers with a deeper understanding of the cultural or ethnic symbolism and appropriate credit and use of these symbols (Calmese, 2017).

- What is my inspiration and what is the cultural context and meaning of the symbols I am borrowing?

- What is the power structure that underlies my being inspired by and borrowing the symbols? Am I part of the dominant culture and are the symbols part of a minority or marginalized culture?

- Is my design altering and/or mocking the original cultural context and meaning of the symbols?

- How does the ethnic/cultural group benefit from my design? Was permission granted to use the symbols? How will credit be given?

- How can I collaborate with those whose culture I am inspired by?

Diverse and Inclusive Imagery and Promotion of Fashion Products

Fashion products are promoted in a variety of media and platforms on live models and mannequins and through imagery of models wearing fashion products including

- Runway shows (live, print, digital, and video images)
- Fashion editorials (print and digital)
- Advertising (print, digital, and video) in magazines, on billboards, on television, and on social media
- Social media influencers
- Retailer visual displays (online and in brick and mortar stores)

Fashion advertising and promotional imagery communicates and reinforces ideals of physical attractiveness, which can affect the identity and self-esteem of individuals receiving those visual messages. Therefore, diverse and inclusive fashion imagery promotes a broader perspective of ideals of attractiveness and subsequently enhances and reinforces the positive self-esteem of consumers. Diverse and inclusive imagery and promotion of fashions is achieved through the use of models of multiple ages, ethnicities, physical abilities, genders, and ideals of physical attractiveness and through imagery that respects genders and does not perpetuate negative stereotypes. Some progress is being made. For example, Ashley Graham was the first plus-size model to appear on the cover of American *Vogue* and has appeared on runway fashion shows of designers including Michael Kors (see Figure 2.10).

Figure 2.10 Ashley Graham walks the runway for Michael Kors collection during New York Fashion Week, February 2017.

However, the reality is that models used in fashion promotions and imagery are still predominantly young, thin, female, and Caucasian. Caryn Franklin, Debra Bourne, and Erin O'Connor founded the initiative "All Walks Beyond the Catwalk" (All Walks, 2017) to "challenge the fashion industry's dependence on unachievable and limited body and beauty ideals by respecting diversity" (see Conversation with Caryn Franklin at the end of this chapter). Working with fashion designers, industry creatives, and fashion colleges, they have heightened awareness and created meaningful changes in the industry to promote diversity in fashion imagery and promotions. "We call for racial, age, size and body diversity in our imagery; design training that accommodates all bodies and gender enlightened thinking that empowers young women and young men."

Realizing the negative impact of fashion promotions using very thin models both for the models and for consumers viewing the models, several countries have passed legislation restricting such images; thus, recognizing and advocating for greater diversity of ideals of physical attractiveness and for the health of models. For example, French laws require photographs of models in advertisements that have been retouched to be labeled as *photographie retouchée* (retouched photograph). In addition, French, Italian, and Spanish laws restrict underweight models. In Italy and Spain, models are required to reach a minimum body mass index (BMI) that takes into account an individual's height and weight. "Under World Health Organization guidelines an adult with a BMI below 18.5 is considered underweight, 18 malnourished, and 17 severely malnourished. The average model measuring 1.8m (5ft 9in) and weighing 50kg (110 lb) has a BMI of 16" (Gayle, 2017). In France, models are required to provide medical certificates that indicate they are of healthy weight (Weil & Diderich, 2017). As stated by France's Minister of Social Affairs and Health Marisol Touraine, "Exposing young people to normative and unrealistic images of bodies leads to a sense of self-depreciation and poor self-esteem that can impact health-related behavior." Recently, luxury brand groups Kering and LVMH Moët Hennessy Louis Vuitton joined forces to require casting of female models to be above French size 32 for women (U.S. size 0) and male models to be above size 42 for their runway and fashion shoots. In addition, models must present recent health certificates before being cast (Diderich, 2017).

Within companies, decisions around diverse, inclusive, and equitable imagery in fashion promotions are typically the responsibility of individual fashion creatives employed by fashion brands, advertising firms, and media. The result is that fashion creatives who place a priority on diversity create more inclusive promotional strategies for their particular company or clients, but such decisions vary greatly across and even within companies. In general, to create diverse and inclusive imagery, fashion creatives must prioritize diversity in the catwalks, advertising, and promotions including

- Greater diversity in size, age, genders, and skin tones of models
- Broader beauty ideal beyond young, white, thin models
- Advertising messages that promote positive self-esteem
- Less objectification of women in advertising and promotions
- Less hyper-sexualized imagery associated with fashion products

In some cases, however, companies have articulated principles, strategies, and priorities to guide decision makers. For example, a U.K. retailer, Marks and Spencer, has published Principles of Responsible Marketing (2017) in which it outlines ethical marketing practices for the company (see Table 2.2 for the complete list of principles). One such principle

Table 2.2 Marks and Spencer's Principles of Responsible Marketing

Our approach includes, but is not limited to, the following principles:

- As an absolute minimum, all our marketing, advertising and promotions must comply with the relevant laws, regulations and self-regulatory codes;
- We will never mislead our customers;
- We will always be fair and transparent when labelling and promoting our products, enabling our customers to make informed choices;
- We always take a responsible and inclusive approach to casting models;
- We always take a responsible approach when marketing children's products, for example we are signatories to the BRC Childrenswear Guidelines;
- We take promoting responsible drinking very seriously, for example we are signatories to Drink Aware;
- We take promoting healthy eating and a balanced diet very seriously—for example we were the first to introduce the traffic light labelling system and our Eat Well sunflower logo is displayed on over 1,200 products;
- We will never take part in any unsolicited marketing activities and will always alert customers if we are made aware of unsolicited marketing that uses the M&S brand without authorisation;
- We will never knowingly advertise in media or on websites that contain extremist views or explicit content;
- Our approach to cyber security always puts the customer first and we use the latest technology and advanced security systems to protect the data we hold.

includes "we always take a responsible and inclusive approach to casting models," thus creating a company-wide priority around diverse and inclusive imagery.

Company Policies, Procedures, and Advocacy

Globalization, workforce diversity, views and perspectives around valuing inclusiveness, and empowerment of employees have fostered the need for policies, procedures, opportunities, and advocacy around diversity, inclusiveness, and social justice. In addition, fashion brand companies are increasingly evaluated by those in the industry, current and future employees, and consumers around internal diversity initiatives and outcomes of these initiatives and around external advocacy around diversity and social justice issues. Companies have implemented a number of programs and initiatives to address the changing landscape around diversity and inclusiveness within the workplace and in external advocacy. Key to these initiatives is that acknowledgment that diversity and inclusiveness is not only the right thing to do but necessary for the company's success in innovation, productivity, and competitiveness.

Internal Diversity Programs

Many companies, including fashion brand companies, focus on diversity initiatives associated with their employees (Bush & Peters, 2016). Diversity initiatives and programs include

- Prioritization and articulation of diversity initiatives and goals by key organizational leaders
- Increasing the diversity of their workforce and being held accountable through hiring and retention goals
- Creating internal organizational policies and procedures that mandate equity for all employees including benefits and resources to be successful
- Implementing organizational training on cultural sensitivity with recognition of unconscious bias through ongoing and integrated programs

- Creating affinity groups ("place within an organization for like-minded people to gather, network, and share their experiences," Florentine, 2017), networking, and mentoring programs for all employees
- Initiating events and celebrations connecting employees from different backgrounds
- Building capacity through employee/team empowerment programs
- Supporting outreach and partnership efforts to increase diversity in the talent pipeline

"The Best Companies to Work for in Fashion in 2017," published by *The Business of Fashion* (2017), highlights the importance of diversity, equity, and inclusion initiatives in productivity and success of many fashion companies. For example, in Seattle, Washington, USA-based retailer Nordstrom, Inc. was celebrated as "a champion of diversity and inclusivity," noting their workforce diversity ("in 2016, of our company's total employment, 53% are people of color and 70% are women, while 40.7% of our management population is comprised of people of color and 69.4% are women.") and strategies to "encourage our employees and customers to recognize and celebrate the richness that diversity and culture bring to our communities" (Nordstrom, 2017) (see Figure 2.11).

Supplier/Vendor Diversity Programs

Fashion companies also recognize the importance of diversity programs for other companies within their supply chain, including their suppliers and vendors. For example, according to Nordstrom's Supplier Diversity Program: "We recruit and introduce vendors to all areas of our company, including merchandise, services and supplies. The program provides opportunities for businesses owned by minority, female, lesbian, gay, bisexual, transgendered, veteran, service-disabled veteran and disabled individuals to offer services and products to Nordstrom and our customers" (Nordstrom, 2017).

Swedish fashion retailer, Lindex, created the "WE Women by Lindex" initiative to "integrate gender

Figure 2.11 Fashion retailer Nordstrom, Inc. has committed to diversity and inclusiveness in their workforce.

equality into supplier management systems." Training and resources are provided to suppliers to improve gender equality in their business operations. In addition, suppliers to Lindex will be assessed as to their performance on gender equality. As AnnakKarin Dahlberg, production sustainability manager at Lindex, noted, "For many years we have worked to dive change in our supply chain through worker engagement and training. Now we will add a top-to-bottom approach, where we work to change the leadership and management style in factories to become more inclusive for women and aware of gender equality issues" (Russell, 2017, June 7).

External Policy Advocacy

In addition to their internal policies and procedures, fashion brand companies also serve as advocates for broader policies around diversity and inclusion. **Policy advocacy** refers to the strategies used to make changes in local, federal, and/or global policies and legislation. In the case of policies around diversity, equity, and inclusion, fashion brand companies advocate for policies that support diversity in the workplace and nondiscrimination. Strategies that fashion brand companies use for policy advocacy around community development and sustainability are discussed in Chapter 7. For example, San Francisco-based Levi Strauss & Co. notes the importance of their advocacy role on their website (Levi Strauss, 2017):

> As a company with a long history of standing up for equality, civil rights and social justice, we take a leadership role in advancing public policy initiatives in support of nondiscrimination and diversity

in the workplace. We led efforts to support same-sex marriage in California and continue to advocate for passage of the Employment Non-Discrimination Act and the Tax Equity for Domestic Partner and Health Plan Beneficiaries Act at the federal level.

Some fashion brands have created special collections or products donating all or part of the proceeds to efforts that promote social justice. For example, through San Francisco-based fashion brand Everlane's Human Initiative, for every "100% Human" unisex shirt sold, US$5 is donated to the Human Rights Campaign or the American Civil Liberties Union. In 2017, Finnish company Marimekko donated US$10 to the Equality Now organization for every Tasaraita striped shirt sold in their North American stores. Equality Now promotes "a just world for women and girls." Such advocacy reflects a fashion brand company's commitment to diversity, equity, and social justice beyond their own company to a larger community.

Summary

The fashion industry has faced challenges and issues around stereotyping and discrimination based on one's age, gender, culture, race, ethnicity, socioeconomic status, disability, and ideals of attractiveness. Because of systemic and institutionalized inequities within all sectors of the fashion industry, historically marginalized groups of individuals have not had equitable opportunities to succeed in the fashion industry. In addition, the results of non-inclusive fashion products and imagery of fashions include customers having limited options and limited exposure to diverse perspectives of what are considered fashion norms and ideals of attractiveness.

To address these challenges and issues, fashion brands have developed and implemented numerous strategies for creating more diverse, equitable, and inclusive workplaces, product lines, and product imagery. In addition, fashion brands have played a role in social justice by creating fashions that are part of solutions to larger societal, economic, health, and political problems. Universal design is one of the most common strategies associated with inclusive and equitable products. Using principles of universal design, fashion brands have created fashion products that are ability inclusive, size inclusive, and gender neutral or gender inclusive. Fashion brands have also advanced cultural and ethnic sustainability by creating fashions that appropriately use the symbolic elements (design of fabrics/materials, apparel, and/or accessories) found in traditional/national dress and/or appearance norms associated with a particular religious, ethnic, or cultural group.

Diverse and inclusive imagery and promotion of fashions is achieved through the use of models of multiple ages, ethnicities, physical abilities, genders, and ideals of physical attractiveness and through imagery that respects genders and does not perpetuate negative stereotypes. In recognizing and advocating for greater diversity of ideals of physical attractiveness and for the health of models, some countries have passed legislation that restricts images of very thin models. Within companies, decisions around diverse, inclusive, and equitable imagery in fashion promotions are typically the responsibility of individual fashion creatives employed by fashion brands, advertising firms, and media. These fashion creatives must prioritize diversity in the catwalks, advertising, and promotions.

In response to societal changes and acknowledgment of the benefits of diversity, companies have implemented a number of programs and initiatives to address the changing landscape around diversity and inclusiveness within the workplace and in external advocacy. Internal diversity programs focus on creating more diverse, inclusive, and equitable workplaces within their own company and with their suppliers and vendors. Advocacy of external policies around diversity, equity, and inclusion reflects a fashion brand company's commitment to diversity, equity, and social justice beyond their own company to a larger community.

Key Terms

adapted clothing
adaptive clothing
ageism
barrier-free design
big-and-tall clothing
cultural appropriation
cultural identity
culture
disability
diversity
equity
ethnic appropriation
ethnic identity
ethnicity
gender
gender expression
gender identity
gender inclusive fashions
gender neutral fashions
grade rules

healthwear
inclusion
inclusive design
national dress/clothing
petite clothing
plus-size clothing
policy advocacy
race
racial identity
size inclusive
social justice
socioeconomic status
solution-based design
sumptuary laws
tomboy brands
traditional dress/
    clothing
unisex fashions
universal design

References and Resources

Adams, Maurianne, Bell, Lee Anne, & Griffin, Pat (Editors) (2007). *Teaching for Diversity and Social Justice* (2nd ed.). New York: Rutledge.

All Walks Beyond the Catwalk (2017). "Who Are All Walks?" Retrieved on July 17, 2017, from http://www.allwalks.org/2012/05/who-are-all-walks/.

American Psychological Association (2017). "Socioeconomic Status." Retrieved on June 13, 2107, from http://www.apa.org/topics/socioeconomic-status/.

American Psychological Association & National Association of School Psychologists (2015). Resolution on Gender and Sexual Orientation Diversity in Children and Adolescents in Schools. Retrieved on July 13, 2017, from http://www.apa.org/about/policy/orientation-diversity.aspx.

Arewa, Olufunmilayo (2016, June 20). "Cultural Appropriation: When 'Borrowing' Becomes Exploitation." *The Conversation.* Retrieved on June 13, 2017, from http://theconversation.com/cultural-appropriation-when-borrowing-becomes-exploitation-57411.

Buck & Buck* (2017). "Adaptive Clothing Guide." Retrieved on July 13, 2017, from http://www.buckandbuck.com/adaptive-clothing-guide.html.

Burns, Leslie Davis, Mullet, Kathy K., & Bryant, Nancy O. (2016). *The Business of Fashion: Designing, Manufacturing, and Marketing.* NY: Fairchild Books/Bloomsbury.

Bush, Michael, & Peters, Kim (2016, December 5). How the Best Companies Do Diversity Right. *Fortune.* Retrieved on July 19, 2017, from http://fortune.com/2016/12/05/diversity-inclusion-workplaces/.

Calmese, Darío (2017, June 6). Op-Ed. "Fashion Does Not Need Cultural Appropriation." *Business of Fashion.* Retrieved on July 17, 2017, from https://www.businessoffashion.com/articles/opinion/op-ed-fashion-does-not-need-cultural-appropriation?utm_source=Subscribers&utm_campaign=2372e5c073-what-donna-karan-did-next-the-realreal-raises-50-m&utm_medium=email&utm_term=0_d2191372b3-2372e5c073-419443797.

Care + Wear (2017). "Care + Wear: Designed to Care." Retrieved on July 13, 2017, from https://www.careandwear.com/.

Centre for Excellence in Universal Design (2017a). "What Is Universal Design?" Retrieved on July 13, 2017, from http://universaldesign.ie/What-is-Universal-Design/.

Centre for Excellence in Universal Design (2017b). "Business Benefits for a Changing Market." Retrieved on June 7, 2017, from http://universaldesign.ie/What-is-Universal-Design/Benefits-and-drivers/.

Connell, Bettye Rose, Jones, Mike, Mace, Ron, Mueller, Jim, Mullick, Abir Ostroff, Elaine, Sanford, Jon, Steinfeld, Ed, Story, Molly, & Vanderheiden, Gregg (1997, April 1). *The Principles of Universal Design.* North Carolina State University, The Center for Universal Design.

Dictionary.com (2017). Culture, Definition. Retrieved on July 13, 2017, from http://www.dictionary.com/browse/culture?s=t.

Diderich, Joelle (2017, September 6). "Kering, LVMH Link for Models." *WWD*: 1, 12.

Disabled World (2017). "Disability: Definition, Types and Models." Retrieved on June 14, 2017, from https://www.disabled-world.com/disability/types/.

Florentine, Sharon (2017, March 14). "How to Get Diversity Initiatives Right." *CIO.* Retrieved on July 19, 2017, from http://www.cio.com/article/3180527/careers-staffing/how-to-get-diversity-initiatives-right.html.

Friedman, Vanessa (2016, July 19). "Fashion's Newest Frontier: The Disabled and the Displaced." *The New York Times.* Retrieved on July 13, 2017, from https://www.nytimes.com/2016/07/21/fashion/solution-based-design-disabled-refugees.html?_r=1.

Gayle, Damien (2017, May 6). "Fashion Models in France Need Doctor's Note before Taking to Catwalk." *The Guardian.* Retrieved on July 17, 2017, from https://www.theguardian.com/fashion/2017/may/06/fashion-models-france-doctors-note-thin-health-photographs.

Gee, Tabi Jackson (2017, April 26). "Is Fast Fashion A Class Issue?" *Refinery 29.* Retrieved on July 13, 2017, from http://www.refinery29.uk/2017/04/149877/fast-fashion-social-issue.

Gender Free World (2017). *About Us.* Retrieved on July 15, 2017, from https://www.genderfreeworld.com/pages/about-us.

Ghanem, Michel (2017, June 5). "Does the Fashion Industry Have a Gender Equality Issue? *Fashionista.* Retrieved on July 13, 2017, from https://fashionista.com/2017/06/gender-inequality-fashion-industry.

Janska® (2017). "Janska® Wellness Wear." Retrieved on July 13, 2017, from https://janska.com/wellness-wear.html.

Knoepp, Lilly (2017, March). These Brands Are Proving Gender-Fluid Is the Future of Fashion." *Forbes*. Retrieved on June 15, 2017, from https://www.forbes.com/sites/lillyknoepp/2017/03/22/these-brands-are-proving-gender-fluid-is-the-future-of-fashion/#704398b53fe9.

Levi Strauss & Co. (2017). "Who We Are." Retrieved on July 21, 2017, from http://www.levistrauss.com/who-we-are/.

Marks and Spencer (2017). "Responsible Marketing." Retrieved on July 21, 2017, from https://corporate.marksandspencer.com/plan-a/our-approach/business-wide/responsible-marketing.

Mau, Dhani (2017, February 14). "How, in 2017, Did This 'Vogue' Shoot of Karlie Kloss Dressed as a Geisha Happen?" *Fashionista.com*. Retrieved on June 22, 2017, from https://fashionista.com/2017/02/karlie-kloss-geisha-vogue-march-2017.

Nordstrom (2017). "Diversity at Nordstrom." Retrieved on July 21, 2017, from http://shop.nordstrom.com/c/diversity-at-nordstrom?origin=leftnav&cm_sp=Left%20Navigation-_-Diversity%20at%20Nordstrom.

Paget, Nick (2016, May 9). "Menswear and Gender Fluidity: Fashion Fad or Retail Reality?" *WGSN Insider*. Retrieved on June 15, 2017, from https://www.wgsn.com/blogs/gender-fluidity-in-fashion-menswear/#.

Park, Juyeon, Morris, Kristen, Stannard, Casey, & Hamilton, Wildrose (2014). "Design for Many, Design for Me: Universal Design for Apparel Products." *The Design Journal*, 17(2), 267–90.

Portland Community College (PCC) (2017). "PCC Diversity Definitions." Retrieved on July 13, 2017, from https://www.pcc.edu/about/equity-inclusion/definitions.html.

Rad Hourani (2017). *About*. Retrieved on July 15, 2017, from https://www.radhourani.com/pages/about.

Russell, Michelle (2017, June 1). "UK Plus-Size Market a Retail Growth Opportunity." *Just-style.com*. Retrieved on July 13, 2017, from http://www.just-style.com/news/uk-plus-size-market-a-retail-growth-opportunity_id130826.aspx?utm_source=daily-html&utm_medium=email&utm_campaign=01-06-2017&utm_term=id97679&utm_content=109033.

Russell, Michelle (2017, June 7). "Lindex Launches Supply Chain Gender Equity Programme." Retrieved on July 19, 2017, from http://www.just-style.com/news/lindex-launches-supply-chain-gender-equality-programme_id130876.aspx?utm_source=daily-html&utm_medium=email&utm_campaign=07-06-2017&utm_term=id97756&utm_content=109033.

Sherman, Lauren (2016, October 11). "3 Fashion Start-ups Tapping Tough Categories." *The Business of Fashion*. Retrieved on June 5, 2017, from https://www.businessoffashion.com/articles/intelligence/3-fashion-start-ups-tapping-tough-categories-hatch-universal-standard-black-tux.

The Business of Fashion (2017). "The Best Companies to Work for in Fashion in 2017." Retrieved on July 19, 2017, from https://www.businessoffashion.com/careers/best-fashion-companies-to-work-for.

Universal Standard (2017). "Universal Fit Liberty." Retrieved on June 6, 2017, from https://www.universalstandard.net/pages/ufl-universal-fit-liberty.

Weil, Jennifer with contributions from Diderich, Joelle (2017, May 8). "France Requires Labeling of Retouched Photos." *WWD*: 16.

Wildfang (2017). *Our Team*. Retrieved on June 15, 2017, from http://www.wildfang.com/our-team.

Case Study: Kowtow: Adding a Unisex/Gender Neutral Collection

Founded in 2007 by Gosia Piatek, Kowtow is a sustainable women's fashion brand with headquarters in Wellington, New Zealand, and a production factory in Kolkata, India. Kowtow fashions include knitwear, tops, pants, jackets, coats, dresses, and accessories. Styling is casual and over-sized. Kowtow is sold through their own online shop and through on-line and brick-and-mortar specialty stores around the world.

Kowtow fashions reflect values around environmental and social sustainability. Kowtow fashions are made using only 100 percent fair trade certified cotton as certified by the Fairtrade Labeling Organisations International and 100 percent organic certified cotton as certified by SKAL International. All fabric is dyed using Global Organic Textiles Standard (GOTS) approved dyes, which are free of hazardous elements. In addition, employees at the factory in Kolkata, India, receive a living wage and overtime pay as well as housing and transportation subsidies and medical and social benefits. Employees' children all receive free schooling. The factory itself is a spacious area with appropriate lighting and ventilation. The factory sponsors projects such as Girls Education, Cow Shed and Cow Donation programs in the farmers' villages.

Kowtow design and merchandising teams are considering adding a unisex collection that would follow the same design principles and price points as their women's wear collection. Team members will evaluate the advantages and disadvantages of adding this collection before making a decision.

Questions:

1. Go to the Kowtowclothing.com website and review the collection, design orientation, and retail outlets for the collection. Who is the target market for Kowtow?

2. From a design perspective, what are the advantages and disadvantages for Kowtow of adding a unisex/gender neutral collection? Give at least three advantages and three disadvantages.

3. From a merchandising perspective, what are the advantages and disadvantages for Kowtow of adding a unisex/gender neutral collection? Give at least three advantages and three disadvantages.

4. What recommendation would you give to the design and merchandising teams as to whether Kowtow should add a unisex/gender neutral collection? Provide support for your recommendation.

Reference

Kowtow (2017). Retrieved from https://www.kowtowclothing.com/ on April 12, 2017.

Note: The background for this case study is based on publicly available information. The business problem is speculative only and not based on the publicly available and/or documented information from Kowtow.

Call to Action Activities: Creating an Infographic around Diversity, Equity, and Inclusion

An infographic is an easily understandable visual image such as a chart or diagram with minimal words used to represent complicated or complex information or data. Infographics are effective in communicating data on issues, topics, and strategies. They are often used as an easily understood way of comparing data. They also focus on the content of the data rather than how the data were collected and analyzed. Infographics include

- Data—statistics, facts
- Visuals—chart, diagram, graphics—these can be used to chart data, compare data, show changes in data over time, or show relationships among data
- Insight into the data—what the data means

Select a topic or issue related to diversity, equity, and inclusion in the fashion industry. Research the topic and find valid and reliable data reflecting an aspect of the topic or issue.

Create a one-page infographic that communicates the issue and strategies for moving forward. The infographic must include at least one chart or diagram with minimal wording to convey the meaning of the chart or diagram.

Reference

Roy, Sneh (2009, November 18). "The Anatomy of an Infographic: 5 Steps to Create a Powerful Tool." *SpyreStudios*. Retrieved on July 12, 2017, from http://spyrestudios.com/the-anatomy-of-an-infographic-5-steps-to-create-a-powerful-visual/.

Call to Action Activities: Acknowledging Fashion Brands That Create Universal Designs

Fashion brands that create merchandise that can be worn by individuals regardless of their age, size, ability or disability are not often recognized for their work in this area. The objectives of this Call for Action Activity are to 1) identify fashion brands whose merchandise fulfills the principles of universal design and 2) acknowledge the fashion brand for creating this type of merchandise.

1. Find a fashion item (apparel or accessory) that fulfills the principles of universal design. Create an image (print, scan) of the fashion item noting the original citation/owner for the image.

2. Explain how the particular fashion item fulfills the principles of universal design.

3. Write to the fashion brand (you will be able to find their contact information from their website or Facebook page) acknowledging their use of universal design principles in the design of the fashion item.

Activate. Commentate. Motivate: **Conversation with Caryn Franklin**

Caryn Franklin, Cofounder, All Walks Beyond the Catwalk
http://www.allwalks.org/
http://franklinonfashion.com

Interview adapted from:
Size Matters, Episode 4 (2015, November 27). I-D https://www.youtube.com/watch?v=KwcUDy3we-I
Annaliese interviews Caryn Franklin (2013, January 11)
https://www.youtube.com/watch?v=0BDDv1CX8ts
The Big Issue. Manchester Metropolitan University—Hollings Faculty (June 25, 2014). https://www.youtube.com/
   watch?v=FZ8ifWwdFjE

Q: You have had an amazing career in the fashion industry. Please tell us about your career path and how fashion imagery has changed during this time.
A: After graduating from Central St. Martins, I worked for i-D magazine as fashion editor and co-editor. The emphasis was on individuality from the start for me. Fashion was never about following but about self-styling. I was influenced by lots of innovative emerging designers like Bodymap, who showcased their catwalk collection on a range of models as well as their friends along with mothers and aunties. I then moved to the BBC, where I worked for twelve years as host and contributing director of *The Clothes Show* and as a collaborator to fashion programs including BBC *Style Challenge*, ITV's *Fashion Tribute*, Discovery's *Fashion Academy*, Granada's *Frock and Roll Years,* and GMTV's *Planet Fashion*. During those years I really understood the impact of fashion on people's sense of self. I saw the power of fashion to influence self-image. I now work as a fashion commentator across media with particular focus on body image and diversity. I was always interested in identity at i-D but it was while working for such a large mainstream platform as the BBC that I was struck by the responsibility I had. Viewers looked to this platform and to the fashion industry as to the "right way" to appear. I don't subscribe to fashion rules and we always tried to showcase unique looks on a range of body types and racially diverse models on the show because we could all see how it was possible to shape people's views about themselves positively and negatively.

As a journalist, I note the process of communicating fashion imagery has changed tremendously and reflects the faster mass-market approach. In the past, as is still the case today, photographers are at every catwalk show.

However, back then, after the show, these photographers would hand rolls of film over to magazine editors and it wouldn't be till three months after the show, or even later, that the images appeared in print. I saw very few images of catwalk models in magazines back then. Today in addition to hard copy there is digital broadcast of the model body and everyone attending the catwalk records the imagery and promotes it on their own platform and social media outlet. Young women today see more images of unachievable beauty in one day than older women like me saw in their entire adolescence. When we are shown something over and over again we normalize it in our lives. So, we internalize the fashion normative body. But it's not normal, and high levels of body dissatisfaction are now rife amongst young women and increasingly men. Psychologists and mental health professionals are looking at fashion imagery and image makers as a contributing causal factor but also because fashion has power to impact on the wellbeing of women and increasingly men, it could be a powerful tool for positive change.

Another change has been the dependence upon post-produced images (that is, photoshopping) resulting in perfected exteriors to communicate falsified norms and ideals. For example, not only are there far less images of older models, but when they do appear they are photo-shopped to look younger. Younger consumers are encouraged to fear the signs of aging and to buy unnecessary products to prevent aging. They fear it because they have already noticed the invisibility of older women in mass media imagery—a fate they don't wish for themselves. Once again where companies have portrayed realistically aged women and women there is positive response. Britain's oldest super model Daphne Selfe is in her late 80s and is constantly working.

Q: What are the current issues in the fashion industry as they relate to diversity, equity, and inclusion?
A: The fashion industry's projection of the ideal or "right" way to look rarely changes—he or she is always young, thin, tall, and Caucasian; with a hairless body—men shave their chests. I'm not saying that a young thin white model is not beautiful or is unattractive, but I am saying that there is a much broader spectrum for beauty and attractiveness. Difference is exciting and so is ordinary life. I never use the term plus-size (my students call these models *life-size*) to reflect the fact that these models are not larger than normal.

Models themselves are also under great pressure to reflect this one ideal. It's a story I've heard many times that female models are told to "get down to the bone." This is unethical not just for the model but also for the consumer. These are young women who are dependent on adults with warped perspectives on the promotion of clothes. There are also challenges for models of color—being told "we already have a black model" or "you're too black for the brand image." This is of course something only a white art director would say. Racism is rife, and biased thinking around appearance and gender reflects the lackluster thinking of creatives in the field.

Fashion advertising has a narrative beyond clothes and creatives need to be better connected with the outcomes of their lazy thinking. Sexualized images are standard in fashion photography along with passive and perfected females, pre-orgasmic posturing even rape culture or women in pain and female models playing dead. Studies show these images disempower women.

The college curriculum needs to change with young creative being encouraged to take responsibility for their art direction, styling and of course design approach. In the United Kingdom, designers' sample size is a U.K. size 8–10. Many design students have never designed for a body that isn't a U.K. size 10. Even at the drawing stage, students in fashion illustration courses are not taught to draw life-size or older women. So, the elongated drawing sets up unrealistic proportions. It is important to think about a different way of doing things.

Q: How did *All Walks Beyond the Catwalk* get started? What is the mission of this voluntary organization?
A: *All Walks Beyond the Catwalk* is an initiative in which we challenge the fashion industry's dependence on

unachievable body ideals. This initiative was kick-started in May 2009, when Susan Ringwood, the chief executive of the eating disorders charity BEAT, asked, "Was it possible to show fashion on a range of inspiring bodies?"

My cofounders Debra Bourne (fashion consultant) and Erin O'Connor (model and founder of Model Sanctuary) and I came up with an initiative to showcase the work of eight cutting-edge designers on eight professional models aged between eighteen and sixty-five and size 8–16, as a celebration of individuality and diversity. With London Development Agency funding and British Fashion Council endorsement, we visualized a project that utilized high production fashion photography working with Kayt Jones and i-D magazine at a high-profile salon style presentation to present each designer's creations. *All Walks Beyond the Catwalk* was born and we could not have anticipated the huge response from industry, educators and ordinary women. What we thought might be a small voice to challenge the fashion industry's pre-occupation with a limited and unachievable body ideal soon turned into a much bigger thing!

The *All Walks* mission is simple: to expand upon the imagery coming out of our industry and mirror a more realistic range of women, in age, size, race and appearance than fashion standards currently offer. We also challenge growing hyper-sexualization of young women in fashion. The *All Walks* brand asks all fashion practitioners new and old to consider their own viewpoint on moral and ethical boundaries believing that positive messaging around self-esteem for young women and men is crucial.

Q: You often say that those in the fashion industry have a great deal of power. What strategies can those currently in the fashion industry take to address the issue of diversity in the fashion industry?
A: Yes, fashion creatives have great power and could change it "like that"! My question to creatives is: "Are you aware of how you integrate into the system and the impact that you have?" If we can move towards a space where we can all be vigilant about the imagery we are creating then we can begin to make choices and communicate with our viewers in a really impactful way. Fashion creatives need to recognize how influential they are to send positive messages about self-esteem and embolden consumers. Fashion creatives could prioritize

diversity in the catwalks, advertising, and promotions including

- Greater diversity in size, age, and skin tone

- Broader beauty ideal—young white thin models are beautiful but so are many other bodies

- Messaging that promotes positive self-esteem

- Less objectification of women

- Less hyper-sexualized imagery

One question that I am often asked is whether such diversity efforts have business currency? Companies are finding amazing feedback when they use a variety of models. Dr. Ben Barry's groundbreaking study showed that when consumers see models with whom they share characteristics, they show increased intention to purchase.

Q: What can consumers and students (those who will be the industry leaders of the future) do to contribute to these efforts?
A: I often wonder why consumers accept these post-produced images? Companies rely on us being compliant; it is easier to accept it than always questioning it. However, the power of the purse is massive. Consumers have the ability to choose or not to choose to purchase fashions that are portrayed in a way that is undermining. In addition, having consulted with the Advertising Standards Authority I know it only takes a few complaints from consumers to begin and investigation into offensive advertising. This can result in multi-million pound campaigns being brought down. The Diversity Network, which operates from the heart of Edinburgh College of Art and is run by Director Mal Burkinshaw, helps us support educators working to bring change. We underline the following strategies.

- That students can understand the power they have within the fashion and image-making industries to communicate to women and men about their bodies in a positive way, shifting from an objectified relationship with the use of bust stands and models to a more empathic position built on a multi-cultural society.

- To see diversity as a starting point for creativity, not an obstacle to impede it.

- To promote the business value and creative possibilities in the promotion of individuality and diversity.

- To encourage emotionally considerate design and practice in recognition that immovable and small size bust stands, do not represent the consumer. Enlightened image making in recognition that imagery of hyper-sexualized or infantalized bodies may not answer consumer need and writing for bodies in recognition of the need for discussion about wider variety of sizes, ages, skin tones, and physical difference.

- To introduce students to new academic research in the field of body-image, and the relationship between well-being and commerce and encouraging better understanding about the end user: the customer.

So far, we have engaged with thirty-three different colleges and universities. From these efforts six colleges have changed their curriculum to include Diversity as a module using our lecture and teaching aids. Edinburgh College of Art, The Arts University College Bournemouth, Nottingham and Trent University, Ravensbourne, Portsmouth University and Ryerson Institute in Toronto, Canada.

Creatives of the future must have an opinion. My message to students is: you have a voice and the power to use that voice. You don't need to think like me but you need to think—you are the change. Your generation is taking forward sustainability and making a positive impact on self-esteem. I would challenge you to question stereotypes around gender, design for a range of sizes, promote a range of skin tones, and cast a broader range of aspirational individuals. Because if fashion is about nothing else, it's about being human and expressing yourself.

Footnote: Caryn received an MBE in 2013 and stepped away from All Walks in 2015 to pursue and MSc in psychology. Now a professor of diversity for Kingston University, she is currently working on a book to empower the next generation of creatives with her findings.

Company Highlight

Adaptive Apparel That's Fashionable? ABL Denim Meets the Challenge

Reprinted by permission from Apparel Magazine.

Harnett, Liz (2016, September 15). Adaptive Apparel That's Fashionable? ABL Denim Meets the Challenge. Apparel. http://apparel.edgl.com/news/adaptive-apparel-that-s-fashionable—abl-denim-meets-the-challenge-106947?referraltype=newsletter

Innovation often begins with identifying a need. Stephanie Alves was aware of the need for custom clothing design for the disability community, thanks in part to watching family members cope with mobility challenges. She designed jeans for them that met their needs and were also fashionable and well made. This inspired her to launch ABL (Adaptive Brand and Lifestyle) Denim in 2013. According to the company, it is the only manufacturer of adaptive jeans for men, women and children. As CEO of ABL Denim, Alves applies twenty-five years of design experience to the task, having worked at prominent fashion houses including Ann Taylor Loft.

The company caters to a niche market that represents 56 million Americans. People of all ages can find dressing difficult due to a variety of conditions, including multiple sclerosis, spinal cord injury, stroke, autism, tactile sensitivities, and arthritis. Whatever their condition, says Alves, "they still want jeans, like everyone else." For people with such challenges, ABL Denim designs jeans and shorts using premium quality denim and then incorporates features that make them easier and more comfortable to use, including zipper access through either the front or both sides; longer zippers with larger pulls for greater access; hook and bar easy front closure; higher back waists with elastic that allows for stretching across the back; side pockets for catheter bags or personal items; and ultra-soft denim material and inside-out seams to provide for added comfort for people with sensory issues. One of the most popular designs is a skinny basic jean with inner leg zippers to assist in getting the foot though the leg opening and/or using a catheter. The company plans new designs based on requests that it receives, so customer loyalty and satisfaction is high. This makes the work very fulfilling, according to Alves, who said, "We often hear 'I haven't worn jeans in years and finally I can.'"

The future looks bright for ABL. A $250,000 Mission Main Street grant received in 2014 helped spur development of the company, which recently added dealers in Canada and the United Kingdom.

CEO Alves hopes to partner with rehabilitation centers and hospital shops to offer ABL products more widely. Walmart recently became the first mainstream retailer to offer ABL Denim products, available online and in stores. It carries a lower-priced men's jean designed specifically for those with limited mobility. The design incorporates strategic placement of zippers, pockets and seaming, simplifying daily tasks while still providing a fashionable fit. Thoughtful details include lasso-style pull loops on zippers—a boon to those with finger dexterity issues. ABL Denim is at the leading edge of this niche market, combining top quality materials with ingenious design to empower those with daily physical challenges (see Figure 2.12).

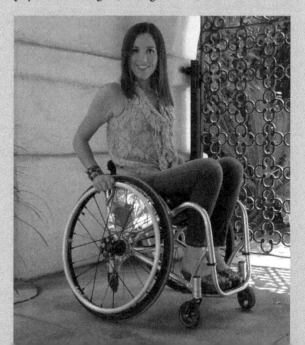

Figure 2.12 ABL Denim offers individuals with disabilities fashionable denim products that meet the needs of their physical challenges.

Product Life Cycle

Objectives

- Describe the role of product life cycle assessments in determining environmental footprints of products.

- Explain how decision makers for fashion brand companies use these assessments to develop initiatives and goals for reducing the environmental impact of their products.

- Assess strategies used by fashion brands to decrease the environmental impact of their products.

- Recognize laws, regulations, industry standards, and certifications as guidelines and tools for fashion brands and consumers to assure authenticity and transparency of design and merchandising for product life cycle.

Tonlé is a fashion brand of women's apparel and accessories headquartered in Phnom Penh, Cambodia. Not only can you go online and meet the team of Tonlé's workers in Phnom Penh, you can see photographs of the team sewing, knitting, screen-printing, and hand-weaving products. In addition, Tonlé merchandise combines two strategies for zero-waste fashion: "creative pattern making that uses 100% of a given material, and generating garments from remnant materials." Designers and production team members work side-by-side to create merchandise that results in only 2 to 3 percent waste fabric (which by any account is amazing!). However, they were not satisfied—they then take this waste fabric to create recycled paper (see Figure 3.1).

Figure 3.1 Designers for fashion brand Tonlé use zero waste fashion strategies such as using remnant fabrics to make merchandise.

The practices of Tonlé (2017) are great examples of a fashion brand company focusing on product life cycle when designing and manufacturing apparel, that is, taking into account the environmental sustainability of materials and end use practices, the ability for the materials/product to be recycled or upcycled, and reducing textile waste throughout the design and merchandising processes. This chapter focuses on design and merchandising for product life cycle. It starts with an overview of product life cycle and product life cycle assessment including self-assessment tools for fashion brand companies. Strategies for reducing the environmental impact of producing fashion products are then discussed. The chapter ends with an overview of laws, regulations, industry standards, and certifications around environmental sustainability relevant to the global fashion industry.

Product Life Cycle and Product Life Cycle Assessment

The phrase **product life cycle** has several definitions depending on the context or perspective to which it is applied: marketing and consumer demand perspective, supply chain management perspective, or environmental perspective. Although this chapter focuses on the environmental perspective of product life cycle, the other perspectives are briefly described to provide a general context of the phrase.

From a marketing and consumer demand perspective, product life cycle refers to the four marketing and consumer demand stages of a product:

1. Introduction—a new product is designed, created, and launched.

2. Growth—sales of the product grow and the business can benefit from economies of scale in production.

3. Maturity—the product becomes established and the business may make modifications to the product to assure continued sales.

4. Decline—over time the consumer demand for the product diminishes. Declining sales may be attributed to changes in consumers' wants and needs, new technologies, new competing products, or other factors.

From a supply chain perspective, product life cycle refers to the stages of a product from its inception, manufacturing, retail distribution, purchase or acquisition by a consumer, and its use and eventual disposition and disposal. The environmental perspective of product life cycle expands on the supply chain perspective by analyzing the environmental impact of a product from its inception through consumer use, disposition, and waste treatment. **Product life cycle assessment** or **life cycle assessment (LCA)** refers to the scientific analysis and measurement of the environmental footprint associated with a product through the "compilation and evaluation of the inputs, outputs and the potential environmental impacts of a product system throughout its life cycle" (ISO, 2016). The overall goal for a company to conduct LCA on products is to understand the environmental impact of their products, the result being an **environmental footprint**, a multi-indicator summary of the product's environmental impact. Companies can then use this multi-indicator analysis to make decisions, implement strategies, and develop operations to reduce the environmental impact of their products. Although many LCA are for proprietary use by a particular company or organization, the LCA for a few fibers and apparel products are publicly available. To give you a sense of the complexities of LCA, the LCA of cotton (comparing conventional and organic cotton) and the LCA of a pair of Levi's® 501® Jeans are described next.

Life Cycle Assessment of Cotton

Life cycle for cotton starts with the growing and harvesting of cotton fibers; moves through the creation of cotton yarns, fabrics, and products; continues through the use and recycling or re-purposing of products, and ends with the eventual disposal of the cotton product. Cotton fibers in the product are biodegradable. In 2014 Textile Exchange (2014, November) contracted with PE International AG to conduct a Life Cycle Assessment (LCA) of organic cotton. The LCA investigated the impact of organic cotton agriculture on climate change/global warming potential, soil erosion and acidification, water use, and consumption and energy demand. Data were analyzed from producer groups from the top five countries for organic cotton (India, Turkey, China, USA, and Tanzania make up over 95 percent of the organic cotton grown worldwide, with India producing almost 74 percent) to provide a multi-indicator product environmental footprint of the production of organic cotton. Data for organic cotton were compared with the LCA of conventional cotton conducted by Cotton Inc. and PE International AG in 2012.

Results indicated that organically grown cotton had the following potential impact savings (per 1,000 kg cotton fiber) over conventional cotton:

- 46 percent reduced global warming potential
- 70 percent reduced acidification potential
- 26 percent reduced eutrophication potential (soil erosion)
- 91 percent reduced blue water (fresh surface and ground water) consumption
- 62 percent reduced primary energy demand (non-renewable)

The differences were attributed to the lower amounts of mineral fertilizer and pesticides, less use of tractors and other machinery, and less irrigation necessary for organic agriculture (see Table 3.1).

Life Cycle Assessment of a Pair of Levi's® 501® Jeans

The life cycle of a pair of jeans starts with the growing of the cotton fiber, continues through the creation and production of the jeans, moves through

Table 3.1 LCA for Organic Cotton Production

- Global Warming Potential—analysis of greenhouse gases emitted from of the production of 1,000 kg organic cotton adds up to 978 kg CO_2 equivalents. This compares with 1,808 kg of CO_2 equivalents for producing 1,000 kg of conventional cotton.

- Acidification Potential—causing for example acid rain relates to the air, soil, and water quality around agricultural systems. Acidification Potential for organic cotton production was found to be 5.7 kg SO_2 equivalent for 1 metric ton of cotton fiber. This compares to 18.7 kg SO_2 for conventional cotton.

- Eutrophication Potential—over-fertilization is also relevant to air, soil, and water quality in agricultural systems. Eutrophication Potential of 2.8 kg PO_4 equivalent was found for organic cotton as compared to 3.8 kg PO_4 for conventional cotton production.

- Water Consumption—water consumption is water removed from but not returned to the same drainage basin. Water consumed can be either "green" or "blue–green" water is water from rainfall that is stored in the soil; "blue" water withdrawn from groundwater or surface water bodies (i.e., irrigation). The global average total water consumed to produce 1 metric ton of organic cotton fiber is 15,000 m^3 with almost all of the water used is "green" water (very little irrigation). When comparing the use of blue water to produce 1,000 kg organic lint cotton fiber is 182 m^3. This compares to 2,129 m^3/100 kg cotton fiber for conventional cotton.

- Primary Energy Demand (PED)—demand from non-renewable sources of energy (e.g., petroleum, natural gas, etc.). PED from non-renewable sources were ca. 5,800 MJ, per 1,000 kg of organic cotton. This compares to ca. 15,000 MJ per 1,000 kg cotton fiber.

Reference: Maxwell, McAndrew, and Ryan (2015).

use and care of the jeans by the consumer, continues through any repurposing or upcycling of the product, and ends with the disposal of the jeans by the consumer. In 2007 Levi Strauss & Co conducted an LCA of a pair of Levi's® 501® jeans (see Figure 3.2).

As a result of the LCA, Levi Strauss & Co. evaluated their production strategies to reduce the environmental impact of this classic product. Results of the LCA indicated that

- Water Consumption—Nearly 3,800 liters of water was consumed in the life cycle of a pair of jeans. Fiber production, predominantly cotton (68 percent), consumed the most water, followed by consumer care (23 percent).

- Climate Change—Of the 33.4 kg of carbon dioxide produced during the life cycle of a pair of jeans, consumer care (37 percent) and fabric production (27 percent) generated the most significant climate change impact and energy use.

The LCA evaluated water consumption by region of the world and noted that the amount of water used

to grow cotton varied significantly across the world. Based on this LCA, over the past ten years Levi's has implemented a number of strategies to reduce the environmental impact of their products. These and other examples of strategies are described later in this chapter.

Self-Assessment Tools for Fashion Brand Companies

Although fashion brand companies may not have the financial resources or time to conduct formal LCA for each of their products, self-assessment tools are available to assist product developers, designers, sourcing analysts, production engineers, merchandisers, and others in conducting self-assessments of their practices.

Higg Index

The **Higg Index**, developed by the Sustainable Apparel Coalition (2016), is a collection of self-assessment tools designed to empower "brands,

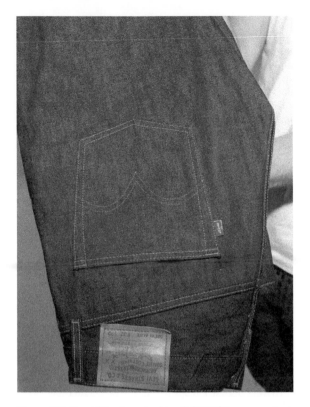

Figure 3.2 The LCA of a pair of Levi's® 501® jeans resulted in strategies to reduce the environmental impact of their production.

retailers and facilities of all sizes, at every stage in their sustainability journey, to measure their own environmental and social and labor impacts and identify areas for improvement" (see Figure 3.3). The environmental modules offer assessments that can be used by designers, product developers, and sourcing analysts in measuring the environmental impact of their decisions related to selection of fibers and fabrics, construction techniques from initial prototyping to final design. The Materials Sustainability Index (MSI) provides quantitative measures of commonly used materials. The Design and Development module provides designers and product developers with an assessment of the complete life cycle of a product to provide them with the information necessary for them to make more sustainable choices upfront in the design process.

Organic Cotton Sustainability Assessment Tool (OC-SAT)

OC-SAT, distributed by Textile Exchange (2014), builds on the findings of the Organic Cotton Life Cycle Assessment and provides a framework for self-assessment of the environmental, economic, and social impacts of organic cotton agriculture.

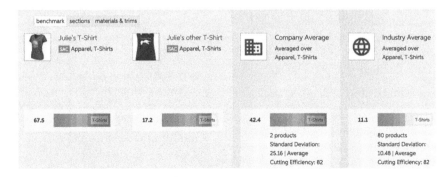

Figure 3.3 The Higg Index is a collection of self-assessment tools fashion brand companies can use to assess environmental and social/labor impact of decisions.

Water Risk Tools

Several tools are available to assist companies understand implications of business practices associated with water risk.

- WWF Water Risk Filter (WWF, 2016) is used to assess and quantify water risk by industry, country, province, and basin along with suggested strategies for reducing water risk. The results for a facility of ECOTEXTIL are provided as an example.

- World Resource Institute Aqueduct Water Risk Atlas (World Resources Institute, 2016) uses twelve indicators to help "companies, investors, governments, and other users understand where and how water risks and opportunities are emerging worldwide."

- Water Risk Monetizer (2014) is used to compare efficiency of water use of different cotton growing techniques to "help businesses around the world understand the impact of water scarcity to their business and quantify those risks in financial terms to inform decisions that enable growth."

Strategies to Decrease the Environmental Impact of Fashion Products

The overall goal of formal life cycle assessments (LCA) and self-assessment (e.g., Higg Index, WWF Water Risk Filter) are to determine the product environmental footprints of products as a baseline for subsequent initiatives to decrease the environmental impact of the products. LCA and self-assessments provide fashion brands with baseline data to assess improvements over time. Strategies used by fashion brands to decrease the environmental impact of their products include

- Use of environmentally responsible materials (fabrics, trims, buttons, etc.)

- Reduction in water consumption over the life cycle of the product

- Decreased use of energy from fossil fuels and increased use of renewable energy sources

- Reduced textile waste

These strategies are also implemented by fashion brands or organizations that have not conducted LCA or self-assessments on specific products but still want to decrease the environmental impact of their products. The only difference from those who have LCA or self-assessment data is that accurate documentation of the impact of the initiatives may be difficult. However, fashion brand companies that implement any or all of these strategies know that they are reducing the environmental impact of their products. It should be noted that these strategies are not mutually exclusive. In fact, many fashion brand companies employ several of the strategies simultaneously.

Use of Environmentally Responsible Materials

One of the most common strategies used by fashion brands to reduce the environmental impact of their products is the use of environmentally responsible materials (fabrics, trims, buttons, and other materials) in the creation of the product. Environmentally responsible materials include those that are

- Made from renewable resources (i.e., resources that can renewed naturally)

- Produced with recycled, limited amount of, or no chemicals

- Made from recycled materials that would otherwise be disposed

For many fashion brand companies, finding and using environmentally responsible materials is a routine practice. Many environmentally responsible materials have been developed by textile and/or chemical companies and available for purchase by any fashion brand. Fashion brand companies have also developed environmentally responsible materials either in-house or in partnership with other companies for proprietary use. The examples of fashion brand companies and their efforts around this strategy are numerous. As a sampling, fashion brand companies Indigenous Designs Corp and Patagonia source organic cotton. Fashion brand Nau sources recycled polyester. Tagua buttons, sourced by Ecuador-based fashion brand Winter Sun, come from the nuts of naturally renewable rainforest trees (see Figure 3.4). In addition, new developments in environmentally responsible materials continue to grow. A recent fabric challenge initiated by the international industry/government consortium LAUNCH (2013) resulted in innovations such as renewable bark cloth fleece, flax fiber that is grown with far less water than cotton but with the same comfort qualities as cotton, and fiber made from the proteins of surplus milk unfit for human consumption.

Commercially Available Materials

Textile and/or chemical companies have developed numerous environmentally responsible materials for commercial sale to fashion brands. As such, purchasing environmentally responsible materials is a common strategy used by fashion brands to be more environmentally sustainable. According to Textile Exchange's 2016 Preferred Fiber and Materials Market Report, recycled polyester, lyocell, bio-based synthetics, recycled cotton, recycled wool, and organic cotton are the preferred fibers among fashion brands/companies for environmental sustainability (Textile Exchange, 2016).

Recycled cotton, recycled wool, and organic cotton fibers and fabrics made from these fibers are

Figure 3.4 Fashion brand Winter Sun uses buttons made from tagua nuts, an environmentally responsible material.

generally sold to fashion brands as commodities (i.e., without a particular brand associated with the fibers/ fabrics). Environmentally responsible manufactured fibers (e.g., lyocell, recycled polyester) are generally sold under a brand name. For example, Lenzing's Tencel® lyocell is one of the most common of these commercially available environmentally responsible manufactured fibers.

Several online resources are available to designers, product developers, buyers, and sourcing analysts wanting to source environmentally responsible materials including

- Future Fabrics Virtual Expo (futurefabricsvirtual expo.com/sustainability/)—online showcase of sustainable fabrics and mills. Sustainability criteria include water, waste, energy, and biodiversity.
- Laura Chenoweth: Organic Fabrics (http:// laurachenoweth.com/)—Ethically sourced organic fabrics including GOTS certified organic cotton, organic linen, peace silk +recycled polyester, and peace silk.
- LeSouk (www.lesouk.co/)—Online showroom for materials searchable for sustainability qualities including certified organic and certified recycled.
- Material Connexion (www.materialconnexion. com/newyork/)—member-based organization with offerings that include a materials library and database searchable for sustainability qualities.
- Offset Warehouse (www.offsetwarehouse.com/)— Eco textiles for fashion and interiors.

Materials for Proprietary Use

Fashion brands have also conducted research and/ or partnered with textile/chemical companies to create environmentally responsible materials for their own proprietary use (in some cases, these materials are also available to other companies). For example, performance apparel brand, Patagonia, first started making recycled polyester from plastic soda bottles in 1993 to create Capilene®. In addition to plastic soda bottles, they also now use unusable manufacturing waste and worn-out garments into polyester fibers to produce clothing from Capilene® (Patagonia, 2013).

Reduced Water Consumption

According to a 2015 report produced for the Global Leadership Award in Sustainable Apparel (GLASA), responsible water management in the fashion industry is imperative for the future of the industry. Growth in the world's population, increased water pollution, and increased competition for freshwater have resulted in a number of water-stressed regions of the world (including India and China, two important regions for growing cotton) and in water scarcity worldwide. Fashion is a water-intense industry with water consumption occurring throughout the production of materials used for fashion products as well as consumer use. For example, as can be seen from the LCA of cotton fibers and jeans, ample water is necessary to grow, process, dye, and launder jeans made from cotton (Maxwell, McAndrew, & Ryan, 2015). In addition,

- Ninety-five percent of the water use by conventional cotton happens at the fiber growing stage.
- Eighty-six percent of water use for polyester happens at the fiber preparation stage.
- Seventy-seven percent of the water use for rayon happens at the dyeing and finishing stage.

The 2015 GLASA report offered several recommended strategies to address this critical environmental issue:

- Using less water to grow cotton
- Eliminating chemicals in wastewater and recycling water in fiber/fabric processing
- Using less water in fiber/fabric processing
- Reducing water use in laundering and care of apparel

Using Less Water to Grow Cotton

Using less water in fiber production, particularly growing cotton, can be achieved through improving efficiency of water use, reducing water pollution, and reducing the amount of irrigation needed to grow cotton. Because of improved efficiencies in

using water and less water pollution, producing 1 kilogram of cotton in the United States consumes 8,000 liters whereas producing 1 kilogram of cotton in India consumes 22,500 liters of water. With 73 percent of cotton produced in irrigated fields, improved irrigation technologies are important to water strategies. For example, moving to a drip-feed irrigation system was found to improve the efficiency of water use for growing cotton by 20 percent.

Another strategy used to reduce the amount of water needed is for fashion brands to use alternative materials to cotton that use less water. For example, fashion brands can blend cotton with other natural fibers such as flax or hemp that require less water to produce. Fashion brands also use regenerated manmade fibers such as Tencel® lyocell (using pulp from Forest Stewardship Council certified sources) that requires less water than cotton to produce.

Eliminating Chemicals in Wastewater and Recycling Water in Fiber/Fabric Processing

Conventional dyeing and finishing of fibers and fabrics not only consumes a great deal of water but also creates wastewater with residues of dyes and chemicals. This wastewater requires appropriate treatment before its release into the environment (Babu et al., 2007). Therefore, a key water stewardship strategy is to eliminate chemicals in wastewater and increase water recycling in textile dyeing and finishing processes. The industry consortium, Zero Discharge of Hazardous Chemicals (ZDHC) Program (2016), has a goal of zero discharge of hazardous chemicals throughout the supply chain for textile and footwear products. Contributors to ZDHC include Adidas Group, United Colors of Benneton, Burberry, C&A, Esprit, G-Star Raw, Gap Inc., H&M, Inditex, Levi Strauss & Co, Lbrands, Marks & Spencer, Nike, Puma, New Balance, and PVH.

Textile companies have also implemented technologies for recycling the water used in fiber/fabric finishing processes (Ethical Fashion Forum, 2015). For example, Pratibha Syntex (2016), a vertically integrated cotton producer in India, recycles 90 percent of water used in dyeing process. They also harvest rainwater to reduce overall water use (see Company Highlight: Pratibha Syntex and Responsible Water Management). Shyam Tex and Gupta Exim, also Indian textile companies, have established Effluent Treatment Plant (ETP) to treat wastewater. ETP purifies wastewater of chemicals so that the water can be recycled. Shyam Tex also harvests rainwater.

Using Less Water in Fiber/Fabric Processing

Because conventional dyeing, finishing, and other processes require large amounts of water, technologies to reduce or even eliminate water in fiber/fabric processing have been developed (Hepburn, 2015). A few examples of these technologies are

- ColorZen™ (2016) is a pre-treatment service for cotton that makes it more receptive to dye. "The result is cotton dyes three times faster, with 90 % less water, 75 % less energy and no toxic chemicals."
- Water<Less production processes developed by Levis Strauss & Co. (2014) eliminate up to 96 percent of the water used in the finishing process.
- DyeCoo (2015) uses super-charged liquid CO_2 to force dye into the fabric. With this process, almost all the dye is used and with no residue inks or chemicals. The only residue is used CO_2 which is separated from leftover dye. In 2013 Nike introduced DyeCoo technology in a contract factory in Taiwan to create a fabric used by Nike called ColorDry.
- AirDye® created by Japanese company Debs Textile Corporation (2016) transfers dye from paper to polyester using printing machines. This process "uses up to 95% less water, 86% less energy and 84% less greenhouse gases than conventional print and dye methods." AirDye recycles paper used in the process and the dyes area reused.
- Jeanologia G2 waterless washing machines for jeans being used by Artistic Milliners (2016), a vertically integrated denim and garment

manufacturer in Pakistan, results in a 67 percent reduction in water use.

Reducing Water Use in Laundering and Care of Apparel

As noted by the LCA of denim jeans conducted by Levi Strauss & Co., consumer care accounted for 23 percent of the water consumed in the life cycle of a pair of jeans. However, because of differing efficiencies of washing machines, detergents, and practices, the amount of water used in laundering and caring for apparel varies around the world. Fashion brand companies often encourage consumers to reduce the amount of water they use by investing in washing machines that use less water and reduce how often garments are laundered. For example, according to the Levi Strauss & Co. LCA of denim jeans, wearing jeans ten times before washing, U.S. consumers could reduce their water and climate change impact by 77 percent, U.K. and French consumers by 75 percent, and Chinese consumers by 61 percent.

In developed countries, public water treatment plants handle decreasing the toxicity of laundry detergents before the wastewater is returned to the environment; unfortunately, this is not always the case in developing countries. However, even in developed countries high levels of polyester and nylon have been found in wastewater treatment facilities caused by microfibers emitted through laundering procedures. Recommendations for consumers include avoiding use of detergents with high pH, powder detergents, and use of oxidizing agents. Research around creating fabrics that reduce fiber loss during laundering and machines that filter microfibers is underway. However, it is clear that additional research and consumer information initiatives are needed around this strategy (O'Connor, 2016).

Decreased Reliance on Fossil Fuels and Increased Use of Renewable Energy Sources

Another strategy used by fashion brand companies to reduce the environmental footprint of their products is to decrease their reliance on fossil fuels for materials and energy and increase their use of energy from renewable sources. Why is this strategy so important to reduce the company's environmental impact? It all has to do with emission and build-up of greenhouse gases that contribute to global climate change. Greenhouse gases such as carbon dioxide, methane, and nitrous oxide occur naturally in the environment and absorb infrared radiation produced by solar warming of the Earth's surface. According to the Environmental Protection Agency (2016, August 18), "as greenhouse gas emissions from human activities increase, they build up in the atmosphere and warm the climate, leading to many other changes around the world—in the atmosphere, on land, and in the oceans." The majority of the world's emissions of greenhouse gases result from production, burning, and combustion of fossil fuels (oil, natural gas, and coal) used for electricity and transportation. Emissions of greenhouse gases continue to increase worldwide and are a primary contributor to climate change. Worldwide, from 1990 to 2010, net emissions of greenhouse gases from human activities increased by 35 percent. Emissions of carbon dioxide, which account for about three-fourths of total emissions, increased by 42 percent over this time period. Methane and nitrous oxide are also emitted through agricultural practices (Environmental Protection Agency, 2016, August 10). Therefore, the environmental impact of creating, distributing, using, and disposing of fashion products is directly related to the amount of non-renewable energy used by fashion brand company's operations throughout the product's life cycle.

Carbon Footprint

The measurement used to assess and communicate the amount of fossil fuel consumed is a **carbon footprint** or **carbon intensity** metric. An entity's carbon footprint is the amount of carbon dioxide and other carbon compounds emitted due to the consumption of fossil fuels and is typically expressed in equivalent tons of carbon dioxide (CO_2) for a particular time period (usually per year).

Energy use in creating fashion products occurs throughout the life cycle of the products. For example, most of the energy use for a polyester

garment occurs at the production stage; most of the energy use for a cotton garment occurs at the use phase (washing, drying, and ironing the garment). Therefore, the interrelated strategies used by fashion brands to reduce their carbon footprint are

- Using materials that are not a by-product of fossil fuel production
- Reducing energy use from non-renewable fossil fuels throughout the life cycle (fiber/fabric processing, garment production, distribution and retailing, and in consumer laundering and care for the garment)
- Increasing the use of renewable energy sources throughout the product life cycle (fiber/fabric processing, garment production, distribution and retailing, and in consumer laundering and care for the garment)

Closed-Loop Recycling Systems

As a by-product of non-renewable petroleum resources, synthetic fibers contribute to the environmental impact of fashion products (Chen & Burns, 2006, p. 251; Lewin, 2006). In addition, synthetic fibers do not decompose and when disposed to landfills they release heavy metals and chemicals into the soil and groundwater. To address the negative environmental impact of synthetics, many fashion brand companies are now using materials such as recycled polyester, nylon, and other synthetic fibers in **closed-loop recycling systems** (Baugh, 2015). Closed-loop recycling refers to a production process in which postconsumer waste is collected, recycled, and used to make new products. For example, Eco-fi®, produced by Foss Manufacturing Company, LLC (2016) (formerly known as EcoSpun by Wellman Inc.), is made from recycled plastic (polyethylene terephthalate, PET) soda bottles. According to the company, twelve PET soda bottles are converted into 1 pound of fiber; that is, it takes seventeen PET soda bottles to make a sweatshirt. The bottles are collected from community recycling centers, sterilized, crushed and chopped into flakes, melted, and processed into spun fibers that are then knitted and woven into fabric.

Alternatives to Conventional Synthetic Fibers

Using alternatives to conventional synthetic fibers is another strategy used by fashion brand companies. For example, Patagonia (2016), in partnership with bio-rubber specialist Yulex Corporation, recently launched high performance non-neoprene wetsuits made with natural rubber from sources certified by the Forest Stewardship Council rather than synthetic fibers. The rubber is from heva trees grown on reclaimed farmland in Guatemala with impurities removed through the Yulex Pure™ process (see Figure 3.5). Because the polymer comes from trees instead of factories, the amount of CO_2 emitted during the manufacturing process is reduced by up to 80 percent.

Figure 3.5 The Yulex Pure™ process creates environmentally responsible natural rubber.

Energy Use

Many fashion brand companies also have goals to decrease their overall use of energy, decrease their use of energy from non-renewable sources, and increase their use of energy from renewable sources in their operations. For example, VF Corporation has pledged that by 2025 they will have converted all 2,000 of their owned and operated facilities in seventy-five countries (manufacturing plants, distribution centers, retail stores, and corporate offices) to 100 percent renewable energy. VF Corp is meeting this goal by converting facilities to renewable energy sources including solar panels, hydroelectric power, and wind energy (Russell, 2016, July 21). Similarly, Nike's European logistics campus in Belgium uses renewable energy (wind and solar) and transportation routes have been revised to reduce CO_2 emissions by 30 percent (Russell, 2016,

June 3). Crystal Denim, the denim division of Hong Kong-based apparel company, Crystal Group, reduced their carbon footprint by 20 percent simply through converting to high energy efficient equipment in their factories (Barrie, 2016). Strategies associated with environmental sustainability in operations are discussed in greater detail in Chapter 6.

Energy use in consumer laundering and care also contributes to the environmental impact of fashion. The areas in which consumers can make a more positive impact are reduced frequency of laundering, use of cold water for laundering, and decreasing the use or duration of tumble drying. Fashion brand companies often recommend laundering procedures that reduce energy use. For example, Patagonia's product care instructions recommend cold water wash and line drying. In addition, consumers worldwide are adopting technologies including high efficiency washing machines and dryers that reduce the amount of both water and energy use.

Reduced Textile Waste

Another strategy fashion brands use to reduce the environmental impact of their products is to reduce **textile waste** throughout the creation, use, and disposal of the textile product. What *is* textile waste and what are ways in which both consumers and companies are tackling the textile waste?

Types of Textile Waste

There are three types of textile waste:

1. **Pre-consumer textile waste** is created during the manufacturing process and includes fabric selvages, left over fabric from the cutting process, and other fabric scraps. Companies that use textile materials typically have a waste tolerance rate that they use when generating their production markers (pattern layout guides). In general, they want to waste as little fabric as is possible given their design parameters. For apparel companies, waste tolerance rates can be anywhere from 0 to 15 percent, although there are few companies that have a zero waste tolerance rate.

2. **Postconsumer textile waste** includes apparel and household textiles (e.g., towels, sheets, rugs) that are discarded by consumers. It also includes carpets, window coverings, hotel linens, upholstery and other textiles used in commercial settings and discarded. The U.S. Environmental Protection Agency (2015) estimated that in 2013 approximately 15 percent of all postconsumer textile waste (2.3 million tons) was recovered (i.e., recycled, reused, etc.). This means that approximately 85 percent (12.83 million tons) of all postconsumer textile waste was not recovered. Some have suggested that the amounts are higher; others lower. However, even with differing statistics, it is fair to say that a great deal of postconsumer textile waste is generated each year and most of it ends up in landfills.

3. **Industrial textile waste** is generated from industrial applications such as conveyor belts, filters, geotextiles, wiping rags, etc. It should be noted that some analysts also use the term *industrial waste* to describe *pre-consumer textile waste*.

In the past, most of the strategies to reduce textile waste have focused on reducing postconsumer textile waste that ends up in landfills. However, more recently fashion brand companies have are implemented strategies to address pre-consumer textile waste. Both pre- and postconsumer textile waste materials can be converted for use in industry applications (e.g., wiping rags, filters, spill absorption).

Strategies for Reducing Pre-Consumer Textile Waste

Strategies for reducing pre-consumer textile waste include

- Zero waste design
- Using materials made from reclaimed fibers and yarns
- Using materials made from regenerated fibers and yarns

Zero waste design or **zero waste fashion design** takes fabric utilization to the extreme—using all

scraps and remnants from the cutting or production process and/or creating patterns for a design that create a marker (pattern layout) that looks like a large jigsaw puzzle and results in 100 percent fabric utilization. Creating these types of patterns is very difficult to do—as the human body is both 3-dimensional and asymmetrical, front and back. In order to reduce fabric waste (or ultimately to have zero waste) designers and pattern makers must work together with marker making and pattern cutting as it is important to the design process as the design itself.

Designers focus on zero waste design for a number of reasons. Many do so specifically to reduce the amount of pre-consumer textile waste. Successful zero waste fashion designers such as Timo Rissanen, Tara St. James for Study NY, Rachel Faller for Tonlé, and Daniel Silverstein create unique and wearable apparel designs with zero fabric waste in the cutting process. Fashion designer Katherine Soucie for Sans Soucie takes pre-consumer hosiery waste to create materials and fashion products (see Figure 3.6). In an effort to assist designers and fashion brands in producing upcycled collections, Orsola de Castro and Fillippo Ricci founded Reclaim to Wear. The collaboration between UK fashion brand, Topshop, and Reclaim to Wear resulted in three collections. Still other designers implement aspects of zero waste design as a cost savings measure. Through improving fabric utilization in the pattern cutting process savings in the cost of fabric can be achieved. For example, a fashion brand may discover that they could increase fabric utilization, and reduce the cost of expensive fabric, for jackets with hoods by separating the hood pattern into two pattern pieces that would later be sewn together.

Timo Rissanen's advice to designers wanting to reduce fabric waste (2015, p. 201):

> When you next design or make a garment, examine the fabric. Try to see how the garment you want to create could use all of it. What is the relationship between the width of the fabric and garment? If you have a pattern, see where the largest gaps or waste occur between the pieces. How can you adjust the design by incorporating

Figure 3.6 The San Soucie collection, designed by zero waste designer, Katherine Soucie, is created from pre-consumer waste hosiery.

these gaps into the garment? Remember, your creativity and openness to possibility are your greatest asset. Remember also that these can be your greatest limitations. Try to identify what learned rules guide your practice. One useful advantage of rules is that they can help us make sense of things. Once we have learned a rule, breaking it may take us forward. Be brave.

Another strategy used by fashion brand companies to reduce pre-consumer textile waste is to use reclaimed fibers. **Reclaimed fibers** from pre-consumer textile waste are the result of collecting fabric scraps and cuttings left from the cutting and sewing processes and processing them to create a new fiber. For

example, Martex Fiber Company (2014) offers services for utilizing reclaimed cotton fibers using pre-consumer textile waste as part of their ZERO Landfill and No Fiber Left Behind campaigns. ECO2cotton™ (2016, in association with Jimtex Yarns) is made from processing pre-consumer cotton knit cuttings to create yarns and fabric. Denim North America (Levin, 2016) is currently using ECO2cotton™ for their R³ Denim collection. Thread International (2016) combines reclaimed cotton (from pre-consumer waste) and postconsumer polyester to create new fibers and fabrics. Their jersey knit, for example, is made from reclaimed U.S. cotton and recycled plastic bottles collected in Haiti.

Strategies for Reducing Postconsumer Textile Waste

Recovering postconsumer textile waste is a multi-billion dollar global industry. Numerous companies and organizations sort, reuse, repurpose, recycle, upcycle, and re-sell used clothing and other textile products. The term **recycle** refers to processes by which waste materials are made suitable for reuse. The term **repurpose** refers to the process of using waste materials/items again but with new purposes. The term **upcycle** refers to the process by which discarded materials/items are transformed to create products with a higher value than what was being discarded without changing the composition of the original material. The website for the association Secondary Materials and Recycled Textiles (SMART) has a wealth of information about this industry (www.smartasn.org).

The used clothing market is an important component for the postconsumer textile waste industry. Consumers are encouraged to donate all clothing and other household textiles (even worn or stained clothing) to organizations such as Goodwill® that have textile waste operations and/or to fashion brand retailers that have take-back programs (e.g., Eileen Fisher, Uniqlo). In the United States only about 5 percent of the textiles donated to charities ends up in landfills, with approximately 20 percent of donated clothing sold in charitable shops and 75 percent reused, repurposed, and/or recycled.

The Council for Textile Recycling (2017) website has great information around these efforts (www.weardonaterecycle.org).

Reclaimed fibers from postconsumer textile waste result from taking used clothing and textiles and processing them to reclaim their original fibers to be used again. For example, wool from Miller Waste Mills, Inc. (2016) is made from 100 percent postconsumer fibers. In addition, new technologies have emerged for reclaiming cotton fibers from postconsumer waste. For example, Evrnu™ (2015) technology purifies cotton garment waste by first stripping dyes and other contaminants. The waste is then converted to a pulp, breaking it down to fiber molecules. The molecules are then recombined and extruded as a new fiber. Evrnu™ recently partnered with Levi Strauss to create jeans from fabrics made with at least 50 percent postconsumer cotton waste. Most recently, Austrian fiber producer, Lenzing, is creating a new generation of Tencel® lyocell fibers based on waste cotton fabrics (Wright, 2016).

Repurposing and upcycling postconsumer waste into new products has become popular among fashion designers (Brown, 2013), as part of the do-it-yourself trend, and for artisans selling merchandise through specialty retailers, online boutiques, and sites such as Etsy.com. One only needs to type in recycled or upcycled in the search engine of Etsy.com to find hundreds of artisan-made items being sold—used/worn sweaters upcycled into mittens, pillows, and blankets; cotton and cotton blend fabric rags woven into rugs; used t-shirts made into dresses or quilts. Fashion industry initiatives related to repurposing and upcycling both pre-consumer textile waste and postconsumer textile waste are discussed in greater detail in Chapter 4 and fashion brand retailer take back programs in Chapter 6.

Laws, Regulations, Industry Standards, and Certifications

Designing, producing, and merchandising fashion goods that take product life cycle into consideration and are as environmentally responsible as possible are goals for many fashion brands. However, in achieving these goals fashion brand companies must address numerous challenges. LCA of products can be costly, time-consuming, and difficult to interpret. Authenticity of materials and processes must be verified and documented. That is, if a textile company advertises that they are using organic cotton, certifications must be verified. Companies must be assured that their strategies are not creating unintended consequences. For example, they may want to use environmentally responsible materials but find that the amount of fossil fuels used to ship the materials to their factories off sets the environmental advantages of the materials. Companies must also comply with laws and regulations around authentic marketing and advertising of the environmental qualities of their products. This section describes the laws, regulations, industry standards, and certifications to guide decision makers around design and merchandising for product life cycle.

Laws and Regulations

In the United States the U.S. Environmental Protection Agency and the Federal Trade Commission oversee laws and regulations regarding environmental stewardship and honesty in advertising the environmental qualities and impact of products. In the European Union, the Treaty on the Functioning of the European Union includes several principles around environmental standards and objectives, and the EU also has laws governing environmental stewardship including production and use of chemicals. The European Environment Agency of the European Union provides research and assessments on environmental policy issues such as air quality, climate change, and resource efficiency and waste. Other countries and regions have equivalent laws and regulations, although they will vary in the strictness of the standards and oversight.

The U.S. Environmental Protection Agency oversees a number of laws and regulations including

- Clean Air Act (1970, amended in 1990) regulates emissions of hazardous air pollutants through establishing and enforcing air quality standards. Fashion brands companies must comply with these regulations in all of their U.S. operations and facilities.

- Clean Water Act (1972) regulates discharges of pollutants into the waters of the United States and regulates quality standards for surface waters. Fashion brands companies must comply with these regulations in all of their U.S. operations and facilities.

- Federal Insecticide, Fungicide, and Rodenticide Act (1996) regulates all pesticides in the United States according the standard that the pesticide "will not generally cause unreasonable adverse effects on the environment." This law pertains most directly to the cultivation of natural fibers.

- Toxic Substances Control Act (1976, amended in 2016) addresses the production, importation, use, distribution, and disposal of specific chemicals.

Fashion brand companies must accurately label and use honest and accurate advertisements regarding the environmental impact of their products. Starting in 1992, the U.S. Federal Trade Commission (FTC) has issued *Guides for the Use of Environmental Marketing* ("Green Guides") to provide guidance to companies around legal aspects of labeling and claims around environmental impact of products, including textiles and textile products. In addition, a number of third-party certifications and labeling programs provide services to companies who wish to use one or more of many ecolabels on their products. These are discussed in the next section of this chapter.

Industry Standards, Certifications, and Labeling Programs

With the growth of international trade, multi-national corporations, and the need for common processes and procedures, standards, certifications, and labeling programs have been important to maintain authenticity around environmental initiatives and claims. Certifications and respective textile product labels around environmental sustainability were first introduced in Europe in the

early 1990s when the European Economic Council instituted the EU Eco-Label criteria for textiles (see description of this certification later in the chapter). According to the Ecolabel Index (2016) over 100 ecolabels now exist for textiles and textile products, including those that are

- Global in nature (e.g., ISO, Better Cotton Initiative, Global Organic Textile Standard)
- Country specific (USDA Organic)
- Specific to a company (e.g., Timberland's Green Index)

Following are brief descriptions (listed in alphabetical order) of a few of the most predominant international and national standards, certifications, and labeling programs for environmental sustainability of textile and apparel products. It should be noted that some of the standards go beyond environmental sustainability. These certifications will also be discussed in other chapters as they relate to other dimensions of socially responsible practices.

Better Cotton Standard System (bettercotton.org)

Overseen by the Better Cotton Initiative, the Better Cotton Standard System covers three areas of sustainability of cotton production: environmental, social, and economic. The system is designed to ensure the exchange of industry best practices among member companies of the Better Cotton Initiative and thus establish Better Cotton as a "sustainable mainstream commodity." Production principles include minimizing the use of pesticides and harmful chemicals, adopting practices to improve water efficiency, using strategies to maintain soil fertility, conserving natural habitat, and adopting practices that maximize the fiber quality.

Blue Angel (der Blaue Engel) (www.blauer-engel.de/)

Initiated by the German government, the Blue Angel certification is awarded to products and services that are beneficial for the environment and fulfill high standards of occupational health and safety.

bluesign® Standard and Certification (www.bluesign.com)

The bluesign® standard, managed by bluesign technologies, takes a holistic approach to enhance environmental sustainability through eliminating harmful substances before production starts with a focus on analyzing "input streams" including raw materials, chemicals, and resources. According the bluesign® standard website, "our goal is to link chemicals suppliers, textile manufacturers, and brands together to foster a healthy, responsible, and profitable textile industry." Applicants are certified against the following criteria established by bluesign technologies (bluesign, 2018):

- Resource productivity and optimization including the technologies and partnerships used to achieve cost savings in their use of resources.

- Air emissions—a substance emission factor is created during the audit that covers all aspects of emissions

- Occupational Health & Safety—looks at protection of workers from exposure to dangerous chemicals in the workplace during the execution of work duties

- Water Emissions—looks at biodegradability, bio-elimination, what happens with fish and other organisms when exposed to water containing sulfates, phosphates, heavy metals, and other restricted substances during the on-site evaluation.

- Consumer Safety—avoiding problematic substances (carcinogenic, mutagenic, irritants, toxic substances, etc.).

Eileen Fisher became bluesign® members in 2009. Since that time, the silk fabrics used by Eileen Fisher were bluesign® certified in 2012 and became the first U.S. fashion company to earn bluesign® certification (Eileen Fisher, 2017).

Cradle to Cradle Certified®

Published in 2002, the seminal sustainability book *Cradle to Cradle: Remaking the Way We Make Things* by architect William McDonough and chemist Michael Braungart challenged designers and manufacturers to upcycle resources in the design and manufacturing processes. Rather than disposing of products at the end of their intended purpose and then recycling the materials into a lesser grade resource, the cradle to cradle philosophy focuses on using perpetually cycling materials from one product into the next, creating circular or closed-loop industrial cycles. They created a framework for assessment of products that reflect this philosophy: the Cradle to Cradle Certified® Products Program which is administered by the non-profit organization, Cradle to Cradle Products Innovation Institute. Cradle to Cradle Certified® criteria include (2014)

- Material health—contextual assessment based on chemical hazard identification and qualitative exposure considerations during a product's final manufacture, use, and end-of-use

- Material reutilization including upcycling, recycling, and composting

- Renewable energy and carbon management

- Water stewardship

- Social fairness and strategies for social responsibility

The Fashion Positive website (www.c2ccertified. org/fashionpositivematerials) serves as the online resource for yarns, fabrics, dyes and finishes, thread, trims and notions, and apparel companies whose products have been assessed and met the either *Cradle to Cradle Certified®* certification standard (basic, bronze, silver, gold) and/or the Material Health Certificate (bronze, silver, gold, platinum). Currently, fourteen materials have received C2C certification and twelve materials have received Material Health certification. For example, Metawear® T-shirts received Material Health certification (see Figure 3.7). For additional information, see the Conversation with Annie Gullingsrud, Director of the Fashion Positive Initiative at the Cradle to Cradle Products Innovation Institute, at the end of the chapter.

Figure 3.7 Metawear® T-shirts are made with organic cotton and seaweed based dyes, earning them Material Health certification through Cradle to Cradle Certified® Products Program.

EU Ecolabel (ec.europa.eu/environment/ecolabel/index_en.htm)

As one of the first certification and labeling programs, the EU Ecolabel is used on products of European companies that meet the criteria, established by experts and stakeholders, to reduce harmful effects of each step of the manufacturing process and end use practices. The EU Ecolabel (aka Flower Label) is managed by the European Commission. Licenses have been awarded to twenty-nine textile companies offering over 1,000 products and eleven footwear companies offering more than 100 products.

Global Recycled Standard (textileexchange.org/integrity/)

Overseen by Textile Exchange, the Global Recycled Standard provides verification that recycled materials were used from input to final products and "ensures responsible social, environmental practices and chemical use through production." Companies must keep full records of the use of chemicals, energy, water consumption and waste water treatment including the disposal of sludge.

International Organization for Standardization (ISO) (www.iso.org/iso/home.htm)

The International Organization for Standardization (ISO) develops and publishes international standards designed to assure that "products and services are safe, reliable, and of good quality." Because countries and companies are using standardized guidelines and procedures, ISO standards facilitate communication and trade, minimize errors, and reduce costs. According to ISO, once a need for a standard has been established, a panel of experts negotiates a draft standard that is shared with ISO members for comment and vote. This process continues until a consensus is reached and the draft then becomes an ISO standard. The ISO standards most related to design and merchandising for product life cycle are ISO 14040 and ISO 14044 which are guidelines on Life Cycle Assessments. ISO 14040:2006 describes the principles and framework for life LCA; ISO 14044:2006 specifies requirements and provides guidelines for LCA. For example, the LCA of organic cotton commissioned by Textile Exchange (2014) used procedures outlined in ISO 14040 and ISO14044. ISO 14025 describes standards for environmental labels and declarations.

NSF Sustainability (www.nsf.org/)

NSF International is an independent non-profit organization whose mission is to develop "public health standards and certification programs that help protect the world's food, water, consumer products, and environment." In addition to developing standards and certifications, they provide auditing, education, and risk management services. With regard to textiles, the NSF Sustainability certification (conformant, silver, gold, or platinum) and labeling is applied to carpet, commercial furnishings fabrics, and other interior textiles and means that the product complied with the standards set for environmental and social impact. Certification to the Association for Contract Textiles "Facts" program and being able to use the "Facts" ecolabel is based on compliance with the NSF Sustainability standards. NSF is accredited by the American National Standards Institute and standards are often identified by both NSF/ANSI.

OEKO-TEX® (https://www.oeko-tex.com/en /business/business_home/business_home .xhtml)

The Oeko-Tex® Association is comprised of independent textile testing institutes that work toward enhancing product safety and sustainability throughout the textile supply chain. As one of the most prominent international standard setting groups for environmental labeling on textile products, the Association oversees several certification and labeling systems including

- *OEKO-TEX® Standard 100* testing and certification criteria for textiles and textile products (yarns, fabrics, clothing, and household textiles) include testing for illegal and/or harmful substances in all aspects of production and in actual use of the textile or textile product.

- *Made in Green by OEKO-TEX®* is an independent label that indicates that materials and products were tested for harmful substances throughout the manufacturing process. In addition, items certified with the Made in Green by Oeko-Tex® label have unique product ID or QR codes that provide full traceability and transparency regarding the production facilities throughout the supply chain for the items.

- *Sustainable Textile Production (STeP) by OEKO-TEX®* certification focuses on sustainable manufacturing processes throughout the textile product supply chain. Criteria include permanent

implementation of environmentally friendly production processes, optimum health and safety and socially acceptable working conditions.

Organic Certifications

A number of certifications exist to verify use of organic farming or production processes. In addition to the certifications listed here, several countries have their own certifications that follow or expand on the listed certifications.

- European Union Council Regulation (EC) No 834/2007 (eur-lex.europa.eu/homepage.html) describes technical rules for organic production and processing and detailed rules for labelling and control for European Union member countries.

- Introduced in 2006, the Global Organic Textile Standard (www.global-standard.org/) (GOTS) is a collaborative initiative of international organic standard setters using independent certification processes around environmental, health, and social compliance (International Labor Organization) in the processing, manufacturing, packaging, labeling, and distribution of textiles made from at least 70 percent certified organic natural fibers. Standards and criteria are established by the International Working Group of member organizations. Upon certification, companies can use the GOTS label on products.

- Organic Cotton Standard (OCS) (http:// textileexch.wpengine.com/integrity/) Textile Exchange oversees OCS providing third-party verification that a product contains the accurate amount of organically grown material. Once certified, companies can label products with the OCS label.

- USDA National Organic Program (http://www.usda.gov/wps/portal/usda/ usdahome?navid=organic-agriculture)

    The United States Department of Agriculture (USDA) oversees the USDA National Organic Program (NOP), one of the most common certifications in the United States. NOP outlines the rules and regulations by which the USDA Organic label can be used. Accredited certifying agents conduct annual audits of all production

Figure 3.8 Members of the Texas Organic Cotton Marketing Cooperative produce the majority of organic cotton grown in the United States.

handling systems including on-site inspections. In addition to these federal regulations, some states also have their own organic certification processes. For example, farms in Texas that are inspected by the Texas Department of Agriculture and comply with the USDA NOP standards can label fibers as Texas Certified Organically Produced and marketed through the Texas Organic Cotton Marketing Cooperative (see Figure 3.8).

Recycled Claim Standard (textileexchange.org/integrity/)

Overseen by Textile Exchange, the Recycled Claim Standard verifies that recycled materials were used from input to final product.

Responsible Down Standard (textileexchange.org/integrity/)

Overseen by Textile Exchange, the Responsible Down Standard "verifies responsible animal welfare practices on farms in the down supply chain and tracks down and feathers from input to the final product."

Responsible Wool Standard (responsiblewool.org/)

Overseen by Textile Exchange, the Responsible Wool Standard is a voluntary global standard that addresses the welfare of sheep and rangeland used for grazing.

Single Market for Green Products Initiative (http://ec.europa.eu/environment/eussd /smgp/index.htm)

When the European Union was established, member countries were using different assessment processes for LCA. The *Single Market for Green Products Initiative* establishes two methods to measure environmental performance throughout the life cycle: the Product Environmental Footprint (PEF) and the Organization Environmental Footprint (OEF) to be used by Member States.

SMaRT© (http://mts.sustainableproducts.com/ SMaRT_product_standard.html)

Overseen by The Institute for Market Transformation to Sustainability, Sustainable Materials Rating Technology© (SMaRT) provides a rating system (Sustainable, Sustainable Silver, Sustainable Gold, and Sustainable Platinum) for a variety of materials based on multiple environmental, social, and economic benefits across the supply chain. Environmental standards are based on several life cycle environmental performance indicators including use of renewable energy, product reclamation, use of postconsumer recycled or organic materials, and reduced or non-use of numerous pollutants.

USDA Certified Biobased Product Label (part of the BioPreferred Program)

Overseen by the U.S. Department of Agriculture, the USDA Certified Biobased Product Label set standards for renewable biobased elements from agricultural, forestry or marine materials. In 2011,

Austrian fiber producer, Lenzing, was awarded this certification for its lyocell fiber, Tencel®. In 2017, the certification was awarded for its Viscose and Moda fibers (Wright, 2017).

Navigating the numerous certifications and processes for certification can be a daunting task for fashion brands/companies. Through their "family of companies" OneCert® provides services for multiple certifications around the world (see Figure 3.9). For textiles, they provide certification to the US NOP and equivalency programs in Canada, European Union, Japan, Taiwan and Korea; Indian National Programme for Organic Production; GOTS; and several certifications through Textile Exchange (OneCert®, 2017).

Summary

Fashion design and merchandising for product life cycle focuses on strategies used by fashion brand companies to take into account the environmental sustainability of materials and end use practices, the ability for the materials/product to be recycled or upcycled, and reducing textile waste throughout the design and merchandising processes. To determine the environmental footprint of their products, companies and organizations conduct product life cycle assessments (LCA). Both LCA and self-assessments (using self-assessment tools) provide multidimensional metrics around environmental sustainability and are used to inform decision makers regarding revising and/or implementing initiatives and strategies to reduce their environmental footprint.

Fashion brand companies use a number of strategies to reduce their environmental footprint. These include use of environmentally responsible materials (fabrics, trims, buttons, etc.), reduction in water consumption over the life cycle of the product, decreased use of energy from fossil fuels and increased use of renewable energy sources, and reduced textile waste. One of the most common strategies used by fashion brand companies is to use environmentally responsible materials such as organic cotton, lyocell, or recycled polyester. Several

Figure 3.9 OneCert® is a "family of companies" that provides services for multiple certifications for organic cotton.

online resources exist for sourcing environmentally responsible materials. Fashion brand companies have also implemented strategies to reduce water consumption throughout the life cycle of their products. These strategies include using less water to grow cotton, eliminating chemicals in wastewater and recycling water in fiber/fabric processing, using less water in fiber/fabric processing, and encouraging the reduction of water use in laundering and care of apparel. Environmental footprints, specifically carbon footprints, of fashion products can also be reduced through fashion brand companies reducing their reliance on fossil fuels and increasing their use of renewable energy sources. Companies implement this strategy by using synthetics in closed-loop recycling systems (such as recycled polyester); using alternatives to synthetic fibers; converting facilities to renewable energy including solar panels, hydroelectric power, and wind energy; and encouraging the reduction of energy use during laundering and care of products. Another strategy fashion brand companies use to reduce environmental impact of their products is to reduce pre-consumer and postconsumer textile waste. Pre-consumer textile waste is reduced through implementing zero waste design practices and using materials made from reclaimed or regenerated fibers and yarns. Postconsumer waste is reduced through recycling, repurposing, upcycling, and reclaiming used textiles.

With the goal of designing, producing, and merchandising fashion goods that are as environmentally responsible as possible, decision makers in fashion brand companies rely on laws, regulations, industry standards, and certifications to guide their decisions. Laws designed to protect the environment are evident worldwide. In addition, with the growth of international trade, multi-national corporations, and the need for common processes and procedures, standards, certifications, and labeling programs have been important to maintain authenticity around environmental initiatives and claims. These include the Better Cotton Standard System, bluesign® Standard and Certification, and OEKO-TEX®.

Key Terms

carbon footprint
carbon intensity
closed-loop recycling systems
Higg Index
industrial textile waste
life cycle assessment (LCA)
postconsumer textile waste
pre-consumer textile waste
product environmental footprint
product life cycle
product life cycle assessment
reclaimed fibers
recycle
repurpose
textile waste
upcycle
zero waste design
zero waste fashion design

References and Resources

Artistic Milliners (2016). "The Green Imprint." Retrieved on September 19, 2016, from http://www.artisticmilliners.com/.

Babu, B.R., Parande, A.K., Raghu, S., & Kumar, T. P. (2007). Cotton Textile Processing: Waste Generation and Effluent Treatment. *Journal of Cotton Science*, 11: 141–53.

Barrie, Leonie (2016, April 11). "Crystal Denim Cuts Garment Carbon Footprint by 20%." Retrieved on September 15, 2016, from http://www.just-style.com/news/crystal-denim-cuts-garment-carbon-footprint-by-20_id127620.aspx.

Baugh, Gail (2015). "Fibers: Exploring Healthy and Clean Fiber," in J. Hethorn & C. Ulasewicz (eds). *Sustainable Fashion What's Next?* (2nd ed.): 313–45. NY: Fairchild Books.

bluesign (2018). "How Does It Work?" Retrieved on June 25, 2018, from https://www.bluesign.com/consumer/how-does-it-work.html.

Brown, Sass (2013). *Refashioned: Cutting Edge Clothing from Upcycled Materials*. London: Laurence King.

Chen, Hsiou-Lien, & Burns, Leslie Davis (2006). "Environmental Analysis of Textile Products," *Clothing and Textiles Research Journal*, 24(3): 248–61.

Colorzen LLC (2016). "What Is ColorZen?" Retrieved on September 9, 2016, from www.colorzen.com/.

Cotton, Inc. (2012). "Life Cycle Assessment of Cotton Fiber and Fabric." Available for download at https://cottontoday.cottoninc.com/lca-2016/.

Council for Textile Recycling (2016). "The Life Cycle of Secondhand Clothing." Retrieved on September 19, 2016, from http://www.weardonaterecycle.org/about/clothing-life-cycle.html.

Cradle to Cradle Products Innovation Institute (2014). "Get Certified." Retrieved on September 19, 2016, from http://www.c2ccertified.org/.

Debs Textile Corporation (2016). "Airdye Techology." Retrieved on September 9, 2016, from http://www.debscorp.com/eng/airdye-technology/.

DyeCoo (2015). "CO_2 Dyeing." Retrieved on September 9, 2016, from www.dyecoo.com/co2-dyeing/.

Eco2cotton (2016). *Home.* Retrieved on September 19, 2016, from http://www.eco2cotton.com/.

Ecolabel Index (2016). *Ecolabel Index.* Retrieved on September 15, 2016, from www.ecolabelindex.com.

Eileen Fisher (2017). "Business as a Movement." Retrieved on April 4, 2017, from http://www.eileenfisher.com//business-as-a-movement/business-as-a-movement/.

Environmental Protection Agency (2015, June). "Advancing Sustainable Materials Management: 2013 Fact Sheet." Available for download from https://www.epa.gov/sites/production/files/2015-09/documents/2013_advncng_smm_fs.pdf.

Environmental Protection Agency (2016, August 18). "Overview of Greenhouse Gases." Retrieved on September 19, 2016, from https://www.epa.gov/ghgemissions/overview-greenhouse-gases.

Environmental Protection Agency (2016, August 10). "Climate Change Indicators: Greenhouse Gases." Retrieved on September 19, 2016, from https://www.epa.gov/climate-indicators/greenhouse-gases.

Ethical Fashion Forum (2015, October 26). "5 Fashion Industry Manufacturers Tackling Water Consumption." *Ethical Fashion SOURCE.* Retrieved on September 9, 2016, from source.ethicalfashionforum.com/article/5-fashion-industry-manufacturers-tackling-water-consumption.

Evrnu™ (2015). *Home.* Retrieved on September 15, 2016, from http://www.evrnu.com/#intro.

Foss Manufacturing Company, LLC (2016). "Eco-fi." Retrieved on September 9, 2016, from http://eco-fi.com/.

Hepburn, Stephanie (2015, April 24). "Nike and Adidas Show Cautious Support for Eco-Friendly Dye Technology," *The Guardian.* Retrieved on September 9, 2016, from www.theguardian.com/sustainable-business/sustainable-fashion-blog/2015/apr/24/nike-and-adidas-show-cautious-support-for-eco-friendly-dye-technology.

International Organization for Standardization (ISO) (2016). ISO 14040:2006. Retrieved on June 27, 2018, from https://www.iso.org/standard/37456.html.

LAUNCH (2013, September). "Systems Challenge: Fabric." Retrieved on September 6, 2016, from http://www.launch.org/circular/fabrics/.

Levi Strauss & Co. (2007). "Life Cycle Assessment of Levi's® 501® Jeans." Retrieved on August 30, 2016, from http://www.levistrauss.com/sustainability/planet/lifecycle-assessment/.

Levi Strauss & Co. (2014, October 22). "How We're Squeezing the Water Out of Our Jeans." Retrieved on September 9, 2016, from http://www.levistrauss.com/unzipped-blog/2014/10/22/how-were-squeezing-the-water-out-of-our-jeans/.

Levin, Cleo (2016, June 21). "Denim North America Debuts Sustainable Collection." Retrieved on September 19, 2016, from http://www.denimna.com/blog/newspress/newspress.aspx.

Lewin, Menachem, Editor (2006). *Handbook of Fiber Chemistry* (3rd ed.). Boca Raton, FL: CRC Press/Taylor & Francis Group.

Martex Fiber Company (2014). "360° Recycling Process." Retrieved on September 19, 2016, from http://www.martexfiber.com/about/360-recycling-process/.

Maxwell, D., McAndrew, L., & Ryan, J. (2015, August). "State of the Apparel Sector Report—Water: A Report for the Global Leadership Award in Sustainable Apparel." Retrieved on September 8, 2016, from http://glasaaward.org/wp-content/uploads/2015/05/GLASA_2015_StateofApparelSector_SpecialReport_Water_150624.pdf.

McDonough, William, & Braungart, Michael (2002). *Cradle to Cradle: Remaking the Way We Make Things.* NY: North Point Press.

Miller Waste Mills, Inc. (2016). *Home.* Retrieved on September 19, 2016, from http://www.millerwastemills.com/.

O'Connor, Mary Catherine (2016, June 20). "Patagonia's New Study Finds Fleece Jackets Are a Serious Pollutant." *Outside.* Retrieved on September 20, 2016, from http://www.outsideonline.com/2091876/patagonias-new-study-finds-fleece-jackets-are-giant-pollutant.

Patagonia (2013). "Recycled Polyester." Retrieved on September 8, 2016, from https://www.patagonia.com/recycled-polyester.html.

Patagonia (2016). "Yulex." Retrieved on September 19, 2016, from https://www.patagonia.com/yulex.html.

Pratibha Syntex (2016). "Green Steps." Retrieved on September 8, 2016, from http://www.pratibhasyntex.com/.

PeoplewearSF® (2012, June 19). "Table Cloth Project." Retrieved on August 30, 2016, from http://peoplewearsf.wgarnsey.com/2012/06/19/the-tableclothproject/.

Rissanen, Timo (2015). "Zero Waste Fashion Design," in J. Hethorn and C. Ulasewicz (eds). *Sustainable Fashion What's Next?* (2nd ed.): 179–203. NY: Fairchild Books.

Russell, Michelle (2016, June 3). "Nike Expands Eco-Friendly European Logistics Campus." *Just-style.com.* Retrieved on September 15, 2015, from http://www.just-style.com/news/nike-expands-eco-friendly-european-logistics-campus_id128021.aspx.

Russell, Michelle (2016, July 21). "VF Corporation Confident on 'Solid' Sustainability Roadmap." *Just-style.com.* Retrieved on September 15, 2016, from http://www.just-style.com/news/vf-corp-confident-on-solid-sustainability-roadmap_id128402.aspx.

Secondary Materials and Recycled Textiles Association (SMART) (2017). *Home.* Retrieved on June 7, 2017, from http://www.smartasn.org/.

Sustainable Apparel Coalition (2016). "The Higg Index." Retrieved on September 19, 2016, from http://apparelcoalition.org/the-higg-index/.

Textile Exchange (2014). "Organic Cotton Sustainability Assessment Tool." Retrieved on September 19, 2016, from http://textileexchange.org/organic-cotton-sustainability-assessment-summary-of-findings-download-and-link-to-self-assessment-tool/.

Textile Exchange (2014, November). "The Life Cycle Assessment of Organic Cotton Fiber." Available for download at https://textileexchange.org/downloads/the-life-cycle-assessment-of-organic-cotton-fiber-summary-of-findings/.

Textile Exchange (2016). "Preferred Fiber and Materials Market Report: Overview." Retrieved on July 22, 2016, from http://textileexchange.org/downloads/2016-preferred-fiber-materials-benchmark-sector-overview-report/.

Thread International (2016, May 25). Introducing: Reclaimed Jersey. Retrieved on June 25, 2018, from https://threadinternational.com/products/introducing-reclaimed-jersey/.

Tonlé (2017). "What Is Zero Waste Fashion?" Retrieved on June 7, 2017, from https://tonle.com/pages/zero-waste.

Water Risk Monetizer (2014). Retrieved on September 19, 2016, from https://tool.waterriskmonetizer.com/.

World Resources Institute (2016). "Aqueduct Global Water Risk Map." Retrieved on September 19, 2016, from http://www.wri.org/our-work/project/aqueduct.

Wright, Beth (2016, July 22). "New Tencel Fibre Based on Cotton Waste Fabrics." *Just-style.com*. Retrieved on September 7, 2016, from http://www.just-style.com/news/new-tencel-fibre-based-on-cotton-waste-fabrics_id128409.aspx?utm_source=daily-html&utm_medium=email&utm_campaign=22-07-2016&utm_term=id94100.

Wright, Beth (2017, February 17). "Lenzing Viscose and Moda Fibres Earn Biobased Certification." Retrieved on June 7, 2017, from http://www.just-style.com/news/lenzing-viscose-and-moda-fibres-earn-biobased-certification_id130040.aspx?utm_source=daily-html&utm_medium=email&utm_campaign=17-02-2017&utm_term=id96306&utm_content=109033.

WWF (2016). "WWF The Water Risk Filter: Water Risk Assessment." Retrieved on September 19, 2016, from http://waterriskfilter.panda.org/en/Assessment#WaterRiskAssessmentTab/facility/1354.

Zero Discharge of Hazardous Chemicals (ZDHC). (2016). *About*. Retrieved on September 19, 2016, from http://www.roadmaptozero.com/.

Case Study: Strategies for Lululemon Athletica Inc. to Decrease Their Environmental Impact

Founded in 1998 in Vancouver, British Columbia, Canada, lululemon athletica® is a "technical athletic apparel company for yoga, running, training and most other sweaty pursuits" for women, men, and female youth. Starting out as an apparel company specifically for yoga, the company has grown to include apparel for other healthy lifestyle activities including running, cycling, and training. Lululemon Athletica Inc. is publicly traded on NASDAQ under LULU. The company describes its core values as "quality, product, integrity, balance, entrepreneurship, greatness and fun are lived by our people every day and are at the heart of our unique company culture."

Facilities include the corporate headquarters in Vancouver; four distribution centers; two guest education centers; four store support centers; and nearly 500 lululemon and ivivva stores, showrooms, and factory outlets. The company has a Code of Conduct and Ethics that centers on the values of the organization; integrity of business practices; compliance with all laws around business and trade; avoiding conflicts of interest; compliance with rules and regulations around environmental sustainability, workplace safety and labor practices; and maintaining inclusive employee and guest relationships.

The lululemon athletica® website identifies "sustainability" as a key value of the organization with the following vision: "We embrace social, environmental, and economic health in every part of our organization and our global communities. We're working to be part of an elevated world that operates within nature's boundaries and provides for human needs—creating opportunities for people to lead happy and fulfilling lives."

Current initiatives around environmental sustainability are in two areas:

• Energy and carbon—an environmental carbon footprint analysis was conducted in 2011. Results indicated that the two largest areas for improvement in reducing energy use were 1) supplier energy use and 2) consumer energy use in laundering and drying the garments. They have been working on reducing energy use through energy reduction in their stores and distribution centers and more effective shipping strategies.

- Waste—in 2014 an assessment of the company's waste footprint was conducted. Based on this assessment, the company has increased efforts around recycling at the company's facilities. They are exploring options that make their packaging and shopping bags to have reduced waste. They are also exploring ways of reducing the textile waste created through the production of their products and with products returned by consumers.

Whereas these are important initiatives, management and employees are now eager to expand on these initiatives as well as address additional meaningful, effective, and systematic initiatives around environmental sustainability throughout the organization and throughout the supply chain. Initiatives must focus on both the organizational values but also the values of the target customer to whom they serve. Given the numerous options for enhancing environmental sustainability throughout the supply chain and the desire for the initiatives to be meaningful and intentional, lululemon athletica® needs to develop a plan for expanding and/or implementing initiatives over time. You have been hired as a consultant to assist the lululemon athletica® sustainability team to create this plan.

1. Who is the target customer for lululemon athletica® merchandise? What aspects of environmental sustainability are important to this target customer?

2. Write a 100 word "vision" for environmental sustainability for lululemon athletica®.

3. Identify and describe four initiatives that you would recommend lululemon athletica® expand/implement to achieve this vision for environmental sustainability. Include specific strategies in which the impact can be measured over time.

4. Describe the advantages and disadvantages of each of the initiatives for lululemon athletica®.

5. Write a three-page ($1^1/_2$ spaced, 1 inch margins, times roman font) report to the sustainability team for lululemon athletica® including

    - The vision for environmental sustainability
    - Recommended initiatives
    - Advantages/disadvantages of these initiatives
    - A plan of action for expansion/implementation of the initiatives
    - How the effectiveness of the initiatives will be assessed
    - References

Note: The background for this case study is based on publicly available information. The business problem is speculative only and not based on publicly available and/or documented information from lululemon athletica®.

Call to Action Activity: "I Pledge _____" Activity

The goals of this call to action activity are for you to

- Identify a consumer issue related to product life cycle
- Inform and incentivize individuals to take action around this issue for at least two weeks
- Reflect on their actions for future work around the identified issue

1. Identify a consumer issue related to design and/or merchandising for product life cycle. That is, how can consumers contribute to reducing the environmental impact of fashion through purchasing, wearing, or caring for fashion items?

2. Create a "pledge" that will be signed by at least ten individuals, that reflects an action that they will do for a minimum of two weeks. Be sure it is an action they are not already doing. For example, if the issue is to reduce energy and water use in caring for apparel, the pledge may be to launder their jeans only after wearing them at least ten times.

3. Create a one-page information sheet that describes the issue and what individuals can do help in addressing the issue. Solicit the assistance of at least ten individuals (e.g., friends, family, colleagues) to read the information and sign the "pledge."

4. After the two weeks, follow up with the individuals who signed the pledge to see if they carried it out, what they learned from the activity, if they will continue with the activity, and your suggestions for ways in which consumers may be incentivized to address the issue in the future.

5. Turn in

- Description of the issue and pledge
- One-page information sheet provided to the individuals (include appropriate references)
- Signatures of the ten individuals who signed the pledge
- Reflection paper (minimum of two pages) of the follow up with the individuals who signed the pledge, what they learned from the activity, if they will continue with the activity, and your suggestions for ways in which consumers may be incentivized to address the issue in the future

Fashion Positive: Conversation with Annie Gullingsrud

Annie Gullingsrud, Director of the Fashion Positive Initiative at the Cradle to Cradle Products Innovation Institute. Author of Fashion Fibers: Designing for Sustainability (2017, NY: Fairchild Books).

Conversation based on Conscious Chatter podcast S 01 Episode 19, Cradle to Cradle + Fashion Positive
Kestrel Jenkins, Founder/Host Conscious Chatter, kestrel@awearworld.com
July 3, 2016 – posted July 4, 2016
http://consciouschatter.com/podcast/2016/7/3/s01-episode-19-cradle-to-cradle-fashion-positive

Q: What is your background and how did you get involved with Cradle to Cradle Products Innovation Institute?
A: My first career was in the advertising industry. I was working for a great advertising company when I decided to return to school to study fashion design. I have always loved and have been passionate about clothing and fashion. I was going to thrift stores and sewing and so I decided to focus on sustainability in fashion design. As a designer, the focus on sustainability set me apart from the other students and gave my work depth. My design work was rooted in sustainable fibers and fabrics and zero waste design. The entire time I was in school I worked with mentors who were a source of creative energy and inspiration. I also did an internship at a sustainable textile factory in India. I knew I had found my purpose in life and knew where I was going—to focus on sustainability in the fashion industry. I had something special. It was a bit difficult to find the right position when I graduated. When the Cradle to Cradle Products Innovation Institute launched the Fashion Positive initiative, it fit with my approach and my naturally positive outlook on life. I felt like I was coming home.

Q: The Cradle to Cradle Products Innovation Institute advances the circular economy. What does that mean?
A: Very simply, Cradle to Cradle (C2C) is a methodology based on the principle that there is no such thing as waste. Instead, designers and producers are intentional about what happens next with the

materials they use. When we're thinking about textiles, the C2C methodology goes beyond recycled textiles by maximizing materials in intelligent ways. For example, when we create the first generation of product, we pay attention to what's going in, what types of labor, water discharge, and what happens next. Are they designed for disassembly? Is there a pathway for reuse, renewal or resell? What will happen to the materials if the fashion garments cannot be resold? Can the materials be turned into fiber that is virgin-quality (upcycling)? Or are the products or materials built to be biodegradable? With upcycling, we see beyond a pair of jeans becoming insulation. Given the time, effort, and resources in the jeans—the next generation product or materials need to be of equal or higher value. That is, we design the products with the intent of passing off an equal or higher quality product or material.

The Cradle to Cradle Products Innovation Institute oversees Cradle to Cradle Certification in which this methodology is used to assess and verify the inputs of products and materials, production process, and practices of companies. Certification of products provides verified information to designers and merchandisers. C2C certification provides me with the information I need that the products and materials are verified and meeting rigorous cradle to cradle standard requirements.

Q: What is Fashion Positive?
A: In 2013, Lewis Perkins, president of the Cradle to Cradle Innovation Institute, was excited about having discussions about fashion. He had a passion for fashion and saw that the fashion industry needed a positive approach to C2C methodology. C2C Certification and standards had been around for over ten years but had not been applied to the fashion industry. He knew the standard could be applied to fashion materials. However, apparel has a short shelf-life. The C2C Certification is a very rigorous standard with both time and cost investments. Was it feasible for apparel brands to go through the certification process for specific fashion items? What would make the most impact in the fashion industry? Therefore, we started first with the building blocks of fashion that have an influence on the entire industry—yarns, dyes, fabrics, trims. The potential for impact was greatest as these products are used across the industry. We then raised funds to build a library for C2C Certified materials. I was hired to make that happen. Currently, we have over fifty products

(buttons, elastics, dyes, fabrics, yarns) in the C2C Certified product registry.

Starting in 2016, I worked to evolve the strategy of Fashion Positive to focus our efforts on creating cradle to cradle, circular materials in a collaborative of large and small brands and designers. We are working with companies through our PLUS membership, including H&M, Eileen Fisher, and Kering, to identify shared material needs, such as yarns, dyes, fabrics, zippers, trims, finishing, and more—creating a growing collective of "positive" materials with which to design from the beginning. We are focussing on pre-competitive, building block materials, so these brands can share time, effort and cost of material improvement and innovation. The result will be Cradle to Cradle Certified materials available in our public library.

Q: How do we keep the movement going forward? What are the biggest challenges?
A: The only way to keep moving forward is to start where you're at and keep going. Collaboration among fashion brands is key—we have to do it together through shared leadership. Asking competing fashion brand companies to collaborate in improving materials was a little bit uncomfortable. Therefore, starting with shared base materials has facilitated moving forward. In my experience, large and small fashion companies and designers are using a lot of the same base materials and suppliers. Through our PLUS membership we are enabling acceleration of cradle to cradle materials through the acknowledgment of these shared materials.

Another challenge is creating an infrastructure to advance the circular nature of resources that go into fashion. For example, fashion garments are made with multiple materials—fabrics made with three fibers, thread made from another fiber, buttons made from another material—and we do not have the infrastructure to separate the materials to be used as the resource for the next generation of products. Fortunately, emerging technologies are addressing this issue. New technologies in chemical recycling can create materials of virgin quality to the input.

Q: How do we do a better job of telling the story?
A: We are still exploring the best way of telling the story. There is a great deal of excitement among designers and fashion brands and so we want to build on that passion.

Our team has been "out there"—telling the story and forming relationships with the fashion brands. We also need accurate information and data to demonstrate the impact. I saw lots of conflicting information about sustainable fibers which is one of the reasons why I wrote the book, *Fashion Fibers: Designing for Sustainability*.

Q: All of us can play a role. How can we, as consumers, support a circular economy?
A: We need to be aware of the waste around us and take the effort to learn about reducing waste. First, let's agree to stop shaming people for the bad choices they make and instead celebrate people for the good choices they make. Second, and this one is super easy: when you are done wearing your clothes put them in a take back bin, such as the ones at H&M. And if you want to go further, get interested companies who are creating beautiful clothes that have been made with a sustainable approach. To me, these types of clothes, whether they are priced

liked Stella McCartney or H&M Conscious Collection, are of a higher quality because I know that there has been consideration made to the planet and people making them.

Q: There currently appears to be a positive energy in the fashion industry around sustainability. What advice do you have for others moving into the industry with this focus?
A: Yes, you can feel the positive energy! The positivity does not surprise me—positivity and abundance. That perspective is so important to motivate people. This so refreshing! Let's focus on all of the things we are doing as an industry! My duty is to encourage others particularly those who feel it's a challenge to focus on sustainability in the fashion industry. I do see a growing number of positions and people with this passion. There are so many roles and so much positive change to be made—and each one of us are needed!

Company Highlight

Pratibha Syntex and Responsible Water Management

Pratibha Syntex, headquartered in India, is a large vertically integrated manufacturer of knitted textile products with operations ranging from growing cotton to finished products. It produces yarns, fabrics, knitted sleep and lounge wear, and knitted athleisure wear and thermal underwear. Pratibha Syntex employs 10,000 people and engages with 30,000 farmers. It works with global fashion brands in twenty countries including Nike, C&A, and Patagonia. The company was recognized for its sustainability practices with the "Best Global Supplier of the Year Award" for 2016 by C&A.

With operations based in water stressed regions of India, water stewardship is not only a responsibility but also an imperative for the company. Pratibha Syntex's responsible water management approach focuses on reducing its impact in cotton growing regions and in the production supply chain. In total, Pratibha Syntex reduced its blue water footprint by 53 percent in 2014–15 from the base year 2010-11. Key activities included

- Providing training and technology including drip irrigation to farmers and reducing the need for irrigation to every two weeks versus every week

- Growing sustainable cotton (Organic, Better Cotton Initiative, and Fair Trade)

- Using rainwater harvesting for ground water discharge and replenishment.

- Upgrading technology in fiber, fabric and dyeing/finishing techniques to reduce water use
- Enhancing water treatment capabilities to recycle 92 percent of water for reuse
- Using spun-dyed viscose rayon fibers that eliminates the need for dyeing and saves 85percent water and 35 percent energy
- Increasing use of preferred fibers (e.g., recycled polyester, lyocell)
- Implementing strict chemicals management standards including Bluesign and GOTS.
- Optimizing the color palette of offerings by pro-actively engaging with business partners in reducing color shades from fifty-two to eighteen.

Longevity of Use

4

Objectives

- Describe the fashion process and forms of obsolescence and their relationship to fashion design and merchandising for longevity of use.
- Describe the characteristics of fashion brand companies that use the slow fashion philosophy in their approach to design and merchandising.
- Describe and explain strategies fashion brands use to design and merchandise fashion products for potential longevity of use.
- Explain consumer/user attitudes and behaviors that affect longevity of use of fashion products.

In the webinar "The Future of Textiles: Creating Fashion Through Cradle to Cradle Design" (SustainableBrands.com, 2016), William McDonough, Chief Executive of McDonough Innovation, speaks about circular models in the fashion industry—specifically around innovations in textiles that foster a circular economy and more environmentally sustainable fashion industry. In addition, he speaks to other sustainability strategies such as design and merchandising for longevity of use, often initiated by fashion brand companies and then carried out by consumers/users of the fashion brand. He tells the story of a Filson brand jacket, originally purchased and worn by his grandfather, which he still owns and wears. This heirloom jacket embodies not only durable materials but also history and personal attachment. Filson is a Seattle, WA, USA-based apparel and accessories heritage brand company that started in 1897 as the C.C. Filson's Alaska Clothing and Blanket Manufacturers. First catering to men who were heading north from Seattle to Alaska during the Gold Rush, Filson products were/are designed and manufactured for durability, comfort, and longevity of use. Indeed, the intent of Filson was/is to design and sell quality products that can be worn over a long period of time with the hope that items will be passed on to others to wear (see Figure 4.1). However, it took consumers/users, in this case William McDonough and his grandfather, to carry through with the intent of the company by wearing and caring for the jacket over time and across generations.

This chapter explores design and merchandising strategies for **longevity of use**, or extending the life of fashions. Longevity of use reflects the lengthening of the *use* of fashion products through strategies incorporated *throughout the life cycle* of the products—from design and product development, through manufacturing, and ending with users wearing and caring for the product over time.

From an environmental sustainability perspective, extending the life of fashions results from fashion products being viewed as valued resources. According to this perspective, when fashions are valued and worn over time, consumers will purchase fewer but higher quality fashions, materials used in fashions will be used for a longer period of time either as the original item or as repurposed or upcycled products, and less postconsumer textile waste will be generated. In fact, a report of the U.K. Waste and Resources Action Programme (WRAP), titled "Valuing Our Clothing" (WRAP, 2016, p. 5), concluded that

> Extending the life of clothing by an extra nine months of active use would reduce carbon, waste and water footprints by around 20-30 % each and cut resource costs by 20% (£5 billion). This is a key opportunity to make a difference, and encompasses changes in design (e.g. to increase durability), getting existing clothes out of the wardrobe more often, repair and greater reuse of clothing by UK consumers.

Figure 4.1 Doug Williams, former CEO of C.C. Filson, holds a classic Filson jacket, designed and manufactured for durability, comfort, and longevity of use.

Creating fashions for longevity of use requires intentional behaviors from *both* the creator/manufacturer of the fashion brand and the ultimate consumer/user. That is, simply creating and producing physically durable and adaptable fashions is not enough, consumers/users must value and have a connection with the fashions for them to wear and care for the fashions for an extended time. This connection may be, in fact, beyond the control of the designer and/or fashion brand (Chapman, 2010) although strategies exist for enhancing the potential for this connection by the designer and/or fashion brand.

This chapter discusses longevity of use or extending the life of fashions including

1. The design and merchandising of fashion products that consumers have a connection to with the intention of the products to be worn over time and
2. Using/wearing fashion products over time until the items become the resources for the next generation of products or become waste materials.

The chapter starts with overviews of the ready-to-wear fashion industry, the fashion process, and forms of obsolescence that serve as motivators for discarding of fashion products and/or purchasing new fashions. Strategies implemented by fashion brand companies for intended longevity of use and consumer/user attitudes and behaviors that affect their purchasing, care of, and valuing fashion products are then discussed.

Historical Perspective

As described in Chapter 1, until the Industrial Revolution (starting in the mid-1700s in England and continuing through the late 1880s in Europe and the United States) handmade textiles and clothing were valued resources rarely thrown away. Reusing clothing and textile products to maximize their value over time was commonplace—clothing items were altered to reflect changes in the size of wearers or latest fashion trends; worn clothing was patched for extended use; and fabrics from clothing no longer wearable were used for quilts, rugs, or other textile products.

With the advent of the Industrial Revolution came mass-produced **ready-to-wear** clothing. Some of the first mass-produced clothing in the United States included less expensive and readily available clothing for working-class men. For example, in 1849 Brooks Brothers, the oldest men's apparel retailer in the United States, introduced men's ready-made suits targeting men headed to the California Gold Rush (Brooks Brothers, 2017). By the early 1900s, ready-to-wear clothing was available for men, women, and children and was often less expensive than custom made by a tailor (for men's clothing) or seamstress/dressmaker (for women's and children's clothing). However, from the mid-1850s when the first sewing machine was invented until the early 1960s, **home sewing** was still a popular and economic activity. Home sewing was typically a role of women who had the resources to purchase a sewing machine (typically purchased by males for females in the family), time, and skills to perform this role for one's family (Putnam, 1999; Schofield-Tomschin, 1999). Motivations for home sewing included the creation of less expensive, higher quality, better-fitting, and more creative garments. However, during the last half of the twentieth century, cultural shifts resulted in fewer individuals (particularly women) having the time, skills, and resources to meet their own or their family's needs for clothing.

In this same time frame, the ready-to-wear industry continued to grow and purchasing ready-to-wear became the norm—ready-to-wear with simple designs were often less expensive than home-sewn clothing, reflected ever-changing fashion trends, and could be easily discarded or given to charity when they no longer fit or went out of style. With the rise of ready-to-wear and most recently, fast fashion, consumers are now accustomed to and purchase large quantities of readily available inexpensive trendy apparel made with low quality materials and workmanship. Designed and constructed to be worn only a few times before discarding with little, if any, attachment to the fashion by the consumer, low-quality fast fashions are typically not durable and become "worn out" with only a few launderings. As such, fashion products no longer carry value for the consumer/user. As noted in earlier chapters, the throwaway mentality of fast fashion is one reason for the increase in and alarming amount of postconsumer textile waste (The True Cost, 2015). However, attitudes and behaviors of consumers/users play an important role in design and merchandising for longevity of use. Consumers decide how and what type of clothing to acquire whether it be purchasing new clothing, making new clothing, purchasing used clothing, having clothing altered or remodeled, and/ or upcycling used clothing.

The Fashion Process and Forms of Obsolescence

Whereby other strategies for sustainability and social change in fashion are dependent on intentional decisions and behaviors by those who work for the fashion brand which can be reinforced by consumer behavior, extending the life of fashions is dependent on *both* the decisions and behaviors of those in the fashion industry and of consumers and users of fashions. Therefore, fundamental to understanding strategies for design, merchandising, and consumption for longevity of use is an understanding of the fashion process, consumer desire for new fashions, and forms of obsolescence that spur the discarding of fashions.

The Fashion Process

The **fashion process** or **fashion cycle** is the "dynamic mechanism of change through which a potential new fashion is created and transmitted from its point of creation to public introduction, discernible public acceptance, and eventual obsolescence" (Sproles & Burns, 1994, p. 13). **Fast fashion** accelerates the fashion process as new fashions are introduced on a regular (in some cases, weekly or monthly) basis. Both fashion brands and consumer behavior have contributed to the acceleration of the fashion process—wearing current fashions is the norm for consumers, purchasing new fashions is less expensive than repairing or altering current fashions, and inexpensive fashions are readily available.

It should be noted that the debate between purchasing and wearing inexpensive lower quality clothing for a short period of time and purchasing and wearing more expensive higher quality clothing for a longer time period is not a recent phenomenon. From the beginning of the ready-to-wear industry, socially conscious fashion brand companies have made decisions to create products for longevity of use and encouraged consumers to reflect their values by purchasing such merchandise. For example, this quote from the 1914 catalog of heritage brand, Filson (the same brand described in the introduction of this chapter), represents a common theme for fashion brands that design and merchandise products for longevity of use:

> The goods we quote must not be confounded with the cheap and vastly inferior grade with which the market is over-run. Such goods are not only useless for the purpose for which they are intended, but the person wearing them would be better off without them (Clinton C. Filson, 1914 Filson catalog).

Forms of Obsolescence

With an accelerated fashion process, consumers obtain new fashions and/or discard of current fashions because of one or more forms of obsolescence (WRAP, 2013). **Obsolescence** is "the significant decline in the competitiveness, usefulness, or value of an article or property. Obsolescence occurs generally due to the availability of alternatives that perform better or are cheaper or both, or due to changes in user preference, requirements, or styles" (businessdictionary.com, 2017). When applied to fashion, several forms of obsolescence motivate consumers to add to their wardrobe, replace fashion items, or discard fashion items (Burns, 2010; Fletcher, 2012).

- *Technical obsolescence*—Consumers may purchase new fashions when new technologies become available; or they may discard fashions if materials fail, stain, or become damaged. For example, a consumer may purchase new athletic/sports clothing when new items become available that are perceived as being technically better than current items. On the other hand, consumers may discard a jacket if the zipper breaks, buttons are lost, or the fabric becomes stained or worn.

- *Style or aesthetic obsolescence*—Consumers may stop wearing a fashion if it is no longer perceived as "in fashion" within the larger fashion context and/or within the individual's social groups. Similarly, consumers may purchase new clothing to represent fashion norms within the larger fashion context or within their social groups.

- *Fit obsolescence*—One of the most common reasons why consumers discard clothing is that it no longer fits (WRAP, 2013) because of changes in body size or the fashion items have changed sizes because of laundering.

- *Psychological obsolescence*—Consumers may stop wearing a fashion if it no longer projects the individual's self-image or may purchase new clothing to convey a new social role or self-image. For example, if projecting a self-image of being "fashionable" is important to a consumer, then wearing the latest trends in fashion may be an important motivator for purchasing new clothing and/or discarding older clothing. Similarly, an individual may be motivated to purchase new clothing when the individual wants to project a new image associated with a new job or other social role. Lastly, tastes in styles may change with changes in age, social group affiliation, or location of residence.

- *Economic obsolescence*—Consumers may discard fashion items when it is less costly to purchase a new item than to repair and/or alter a worn fashion item. In our era of inexpensive fast fashion options, purchasing a new fashion item is often less expensive that repairing or altering a fashion item that is no longer being worn.

Forms of obsolescence in fashion are not mutually exclusive. Indeed, several forms contribute to consumers' motivation to discard current fashions and purchase/acquire new fashions. For example, a consumer may purchase an inexpensive and poorly constructed but trendy shirt. After a few washings the shirt is not only worn out but also no longer fashionable. This may then lead the consumer to discard the shirt. Consumers may save clothing (but may not wear it) that needs repair and/or does not fit in **temporary inactive storage** (Cluver, 2008) with the intent of mending the clothing and/or hopes that the clothing may fit again in the future. However, what generally happens is that the consumer eventually discards or donates the clothing often when the clothing is no longer sellable. Fortunately, many consumers are showing a growing interest in learning about ways to extend the life of their fashions. This trend affords opportunities for fashion brands to provide information and education to consumers about informed choices and decisions from purchasing longer lasting fashions to learning to repair or mend fashions (WRAP, 2016).

Slow Fashion Movement

In response to the accelerated fashion process and the resulting increase in postconsumer textile waste, many fashion industry professionals have increased intentional decisions, behaviors, and marketing around fashions designed and merchandised for as valued resources for longevity of use. This philosophy, known as the **slow fashion** movement (Fletcher, 2008), countered the perspective of fashions only being characterized by mass-produced, poorly constructed, standardized products made from inexpensive materials that are sold quickly and worn a short period of time (Fletcher, 2008, 2010). Instead, slow fashion brands approach the supply chain through systems thinking with goals of extending product life, enhancing consumer/user connections, and addressing all aspects of sustainability.

The slow fashion movement is patterned after the slow food movement that focuses on food that is "good, clean, and fair" including local sourcing, traditional methods of production, experiential connection, ecosystem diversity, and responsibility (Slow Food, 2017). Similarly, the slow fashion movement includes designers and fashion brands that have the following characteristics:

- Use of small-scale, traditional techniques
- Local sourcing
- Environmental, social, and cultural sustainability
- Economic sustainability
- Designing for durability

Use of Small-Scale, Traditional Techniques

Although fashions designed and produced as "slow fashion" may use mass-production techniques, many brands have focused on using small-scale traditional techniques of design and production. Traditional textile and apparel design and production techniques include hand-weaving, hand-dyeing, hand-printing, zero-waste design, and construction techniques that focus on durability. Using such techniques increases the connection with culture, history, and value of the resources uses. For example, artisans in Jaipur, India, use traditional dyeing and printing techniques to create small-scale textiles for use in apparel and home décor (see Figure 4.2).

Local Sourcing

When applied to fashion, **local sourcing** refers to the business strategy of purchasing materials and producing fashion merchandise within a close proximity to either the ultimate consumer or the company's distribution center. When possible, slow fashion brands use local materials and labor. As noted by Cataldi et al. (2010) local sourcing is often a challenge for fashion brands as socially responsible materials or manufacturing may not be available on a local or even regional basis. In some cases, fashion brands within the slow fashion movement create a localized infrastructure to support the design, production, and distribution of the fashion brands. For example, Softstar Shoes, a company that produces and sells minimalist footwear, created their own production infrastructure and designs and manufactures their merchandise in a remodeled roller-skating rink in Philomath, Oregon, USA (see Figure 4.3).

Co-creation/Co-production

To enhance the consumer's connection to the product and the product's perceived value, the consumer is brought into the supply chain as a **co-creator** or **co-producer**. This characteristic is demonstrated in several ways:

Figure 4.2 Sustainable textile distributor Laura Chenoweth works with artisans in India who create hand-blocked printed fabrics.

Figure 4.3 Slow fashion footwear brand Softstar Shoes focuses on local production of their footwear.

- Collaborating on the design or fit of the product, building trusting and lasting relationships. For example, designer Shari Noble of La Macón by Shari Noble works with clients in ensuring customized fit of the leather jackets she creates. Clients also connect with the production process as the jackets are handsewn in her Seattle, WA, USA, studio.

- Creating personal narratives through customization and personalization. For example, a grandparent may purchase clothing as a gift for a grandchild with the child's name on it, thus creating a personal connection with clothing.

- Collaborating on the environmental and social aspects of the product. For example, Recreation Equipment, Inc. (REI), an outdoor apparel and gear co-op retailer headquartered in Kent, WA, USA, sponsors a number of community stewardship projects that build community collaborations. Projects include bike drives at REI stores, training hiking trail volunteers to assist with building and repairing hiking trails, and organizing volunteers to build and repair mountain bike trails.

Environmental, Social, and Cultural Sustainability

Fashion brands carrying out the slow fashion philosophy are aware of their connections with the environmental, social, and cultural systems and strive to enhance their connections as well as the consumers' connections with these systems. This characteristic is exhibited through use of environmentally responsible materials, paying living wages, and enhancing the quality of life for all involved in the supply chain (Cataldi et al., 2010). For example, slow fashion brand Sudara (2017) "is a benefit corporation that exists to advocate on behalf of and empower women who have escaped from, or at the highest risk of, human trafficking by providing dignified employment opportunities." They achieve this goal through sewing center partnerships in India (see Figure 4.4).

Economic Sustainability

Slow fashion designers and fashion brands strive to de-accelerate the fashion process. Rather than multiple collections per year, these fashion brands may have only one or two with the collections designed to be worn across seasons and for many years. Their economic foundation is to sell fewer but higher priced items and they encourage consumers to purchase fewer but higher prices (and consequently higher quality) items. For example, rather than following the traditional fashion calendar of showing collections to buyers six months before

Figure 4.4 Slow fashion brands such as Sudara create social change through their employment and empowerment strategies.

the fashion season, slow fashion brand, Study NY, creates seamless capsule collections of three to four styles each month. This allows both designers and consumers greater flexibility in their decisions, with a goal to "re-educate the consumer about consumption" (study-ny.com, 2013).

Designing for Durability

According to Fletcher (2012, p. 235), the goal of **designing for durability** is to "foster and amplify the skills, habits of mind, and abilities of users to create and engage with fashion from within a context of satisfaction and resourcefulness." In this way, we come to "recognize the social and experiential dimensions to fashion, which, facilitated by a garment's materials, design, and construction, influence how long clothing lasts" (p. 236). Thus, designing for durability integrates the previous characteristics to promote the connection between fashions and the consumer/user resulting in increased perceived value of the product and increased satisfaction by the consumer.

Whereas the slow fashion movement is an overarching philosophy toward fashion design and merchandising, the characteristics associated with slow fashion are generally limited to smaller fashion brands. In addition, fully achieving all of the goals of slow fashion can be difficult (Cataldi et al., 2010). For example, designer Matthew Tobeck (2013) designed a men's jacket using the slow fashion philosophy (good, clean, fair, coproduction) as a sustainability filter in the apparel design process (see Figure 4.5). He employed House of Quality model (customer requirements, technical requirements, planning matrix, interrelationship matrix, technical correlation matrix, and priorities and target section) to identify, organize and evaluate consumer needs as they were translated into design specifications. In this process, challenges included local sourcing of sustainable materials and local production. Therefore, in addition to adhering to the slow fashion philosophy, fashion brands have utilized a variety of strategies in moving toward designing and merchandising for longevity of use.

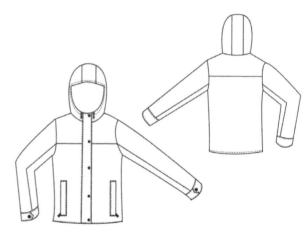

Figure 4.5 A men's jacket was designed using the slow fashion philosophy and House of Quality design model.

Strategies for Design and Merchandising for Longevity of Use

According to the online resource and platform *Design for Longevity* (2017):

> As designers and product developers, we have the power to change things for the better. The decisions we make in the design phase mean all the difference in terms of style. But they also determine so much more—like the environmental impact of production, how long clothes will remain wearable, and whether they may be reused or recycled.

Fashion brands that design and merchandise fashion products for longevity of use employ one or more of the following strategies:

- High quality and durable fabrics and construction techniques
- Classic design or design for style adaptability
- Fewer and trans-seasonal collections/lines
- Modular and/or multifunctional design
- Size, style, and technical alterability

- Upcycling
- Creating an emotional and/or experiential connection between the item and the wearer

These strategies are dependent on a mindset around designing with longevity of use that aligns with a business model that supports these strategies (Design for Longevity, 2017). In addition, these strategies are not mutually exclusive and optimal strategies depend on product category. For example, when designing children's wear for extended use, fashion brands would want to incorporate the following strategies (WRAP, 2013, p. 18):

- Selecting fabrics and components that are proven to offer durability and colorfastness (quality and durable fabrics)
- Applying fabric finishes to reduce the likelihood of staining (quality and durable fabrics)
- Reinforcing weak areas, or areas liable to extra stress such as elbows and knees (durable construction)
- Designing-in a growth allowance (size alterability)
- Designing garments for multi-functionality such as reversible coats (multi-functionality)

When designing denim products for extended use, fashion brands would want to incorporate the following strategies (WRAP, 2013, p. 36):

- Enhancing fabric strength and surface quality by applying sustainable dyeing, bleaching and surface treatments (quality and durable fabrics)
- Reduce the number of seasonal lines (fewer and trans-seasonal collections/lines)
- Applying traditional manufacturing methods and mass customization strategies to products (create an emotional or experiential connection)
- Educating consumers about the unique characteristics of denim and how to care for it and repair, reuse or repurpose it (create an emotional or experiential connection)
- Creating emotional attachment through ethical sourcing and production, no waste and craft design approaches (create an emotional or experiential connection)

In addition, fashion brand companies often combine a number of the strategies in their design principles. For example, New Zealand-based Icebreaker, known for their high quality merino wool products, use four design principles in guiding their work:

1. Simplicity: With elegant simplicity comes timelessness that doesn't date.
2. Versatility: Our clothes transcend single usage—we make multifunctional pieces that adapt to your life and style, on the mountain, in the city and at home.
3. Longevity: Icebreaker is the polar opposite of fast fashion; through high quality performance our goal is to thrive in your wardrobe and during your activities for many seasons.
4. Purpose: We make purposeful clothing that responds to your body's active needs. Our zoned merino base layers have layers for both heat retention and heat dumping. Our t-shirts come in a casual cut for travel and an athletic cut for working out (Icebreaker, 2017).

High Quality and Durable Fabrics and Construction Techniques

For a fashion to last, it must be made to last. This requires physical durability—high quality and durable materials and high quality and durable construction techniques. Selecting and using fibers and fabrics that are appropriate for the end use is important to maximize durability and extended use. This requires knowledge of fibers, fabrics, and textile testing standards and understanding the requirements of the intended end use. That is, selecting optimal materials for man's work clothing requires a different set of requirements than selecting optimal materials used for women's eveningwear. In addition, selecting and sourcing quality and durable materials appropriate for an end use goes beyond fiber content and fabric structure. For example, simply knowing that a t-shirt is made from 100 percent cotton knit tells the designer or product developer nothing about the quality or durability of the material.

A number of physical and chemical tests are used to assess durability of fabrics and materials. These include strength testing, abrasion resistance, elasticity, pilling, color fastness, and stain resistance. For example, ASTM International (2017) offers numerous standard test methods for assessing the durability of fabrics and materials (see Table 4.1 for selected examples).

In addition to using high quality and durable fabrics, using high quality and durable construction techniques appropriate for the intended end use are also important for extending the life of a fashion. Aspects of the garment itself can be tested for physical durability including seam strength, strength of buttonholes, and seam slippage. ASTM International also offers standard test methods for assessing the durability of garment features (see Table 4.1 for selected examples).

In addition, understanding user behavior in caring for the fabric is necessary in designing for longevity of use. For example, using a high quality fine wool for trousers requires appropriate care by the consumer to have an extended use. Fashion brands use wearer trials to determine consumer/user issues that may affect the longevity of use. Such trials with actual wearers inform the designers and product developers about issues including laundering practices, understanding care instructions, and appropriateness for intended use. ASTM International (2017) outlines standard procedures for conducting wear tests (ASTM D3181-15e1: Standard Guide for Conducting Wear Tests on Textiles).

Although using quality fabrics and workmanship/construction appropriate for the end use is a necessary characteristic of longevity of use, it is not a sufficient characteristic for longevity of use. The assumption that if one makes durable fashions then consumers will purchase fewer fashions and wear them for a longer time may not be true (Fletcher, 2012). As stated so well by designer and author Kate Fletcher (2012, p. 227) "making a garment last is very different to making a long-lasting garment." Therefore, in addition to being durable through quality materials and construction, fashions that are worn for extended periods of time must have other characteristics that relate to the consumer's relationship with the fashion and their intentional

Table 4.1 Selected ASTM Test Methods Related to Durability of Fabrics and Garment Features

ASTM Test Method	Durability Characteristic
ASTM D4850-13e1	Standard Terminology Relating to Fabric and Fabric Test Methods
ASTM D5034-09 (2013)	Breaking Strength and Elongation of Textile Fabrics (Grab Test)
ASTM D5035-11 (2015)	Breaking Force and Elongation of Textile Fabrics (Strip Method)
ASTM D6644-01 (2013)	Tension Strength of Sew-Through Flange Buttons
ASTM D2059M-03 (2014)	Resistance of Zippers to Salt Spray (Fog)
ASTM D2061-07 (2013)	Strength Text for Zippers
ASTM D5278/D5278M-09 (2013)	Elongation of Narrow Elastic Fabrics (Static-Load Testing)
ASTM D7747/D7747M-11e1	Determining Integrity of Seams Produced Using Thermo-Fusion Methods
ASTM D4846-96 (2016)	Resistance to Unsnapping of Snap Fasteners
ASTM D7142-05 (2016)	Holding Strength of Prong-Ring Attached Snap Fasteners
ASTM D5170-98 (2015)	Peel Strength of Hook and Loop Touch Fasteners
ASTM D3181-15e1	Standard Guide for Conducting Wear Tests on Textiles

Reference: ASTM International (2017).

behaviors toward the products. As noted in the WRAP report (2013, pp. 14–15):

> Product design has been identified as pivotal to determining the longevity of the garment. Designers are able to specify many relevant characteristics of the final garment. Some of these characteristics are physical and can be tested for compliance; others, such as "fashionability" or styling, are subjective and cannot be objectively tested. They are nonetheless crucial in determining garment longevity.

Classic Design or Design for Style-Adaptability

One of the most important features of fashions designed for extended use is the styling of the fashions in terms of versatility and reflecting fashion trends over time (WRAP, 2013). Therefore, products are designed for extended use through incorporating classic styles or styles that can be easily adapted to reflect current fashions. A **classic fashion** is defined as (Calasibetta, 1988, p. 113):

> Apparel in such simple good taste and of a design appropriate to so many individuals that it continues to be in style over a long period of time, returning to high fashion at intervals. It retains the basic lines but is sometimes altered in minor details, e.g., trenchcoat, polo coat, chemise, shirtwaist dress, cardigan, blazer.

Classic styles identified as extending the life of fashions (WRAP, 2013) include tailored or semi-tailored items (e.g., blazers, tailored shirts, tailored trousers), styles with simple lines (e.g., chemise dress, pencil skirt, bomber jacket) especially when using core colors (e.g., black, white, gray, navy blue), and versatile knitwear (e.g., cardigan sweater/jumper, V-neck sweater/jumper, oversized knits that could be belted).

From a business perspective, incorporating classic and fashion-adaptable designs allows designers to focus on and enhance expertise in key areas, build lasting relationships with vendors and production facilities, and create a brand identity around classic styling. For example, a fashion brand may be known for designing classic little black dresses that can be updated across fashion seasons with the use of accessories (e.g., belts, scarfs) but remains "in style" for an extended period of time. All Myn, an Australian brand, creates classic apparel designs that are "designed to fit" using a combination of basic measurements of customers with high quality materials and construction. "All Myn works on a 'slow fashion' business model, . . . designing, producing and supplying garments for quality and longevity" (All Myn, 2017).

Heritage brands are typically older fashion brands characterized by quality materials, classic styling, and potential for longevity of use. Whereas most heritage brands have a long history some newer brands are marketing themselves as heritage as a means of conveying these characteristics to consumers. Filson, Brooks Brothers, Woolrich, Timberland, and Pendleton Woolen Mills in the United States and Pringle, Burberry, and Liberty of London in the United Kingdom, chose to distinguish themselves based on the quality and longevity of use. Heritage brands take pride in their business longevity, commitment to durable and long-lasting fashions, and relationships with consumers (see Table 4.2).

Fewer and Trans-Seasonal Collections/Lines

Over the history of ready-to-wear, the speed of the fashion cycle has increased, resulting in shorter lead times from design to retail. The original two fashion seasons (spring/summer, fall/winter) transformed to six fashion seasons (spring, summer, pre-fall, fall, holiday, resort) which with the advent of fast fashion has transformed to weekly or monthly fashion "mini-seasons." Indeed, fast fashion brands can create fashions from design sketch to retail delivery in as little time as fourteen days. In the context of high competition, fashion brands and retailers strive toward fast turnaround marking down merchandise within a few weeks, or in the case of fast fashion not at all, to make room for new lines of merchandise.

Table 4.2 Selected Examples of Heritage Brands

Brand Name	Headquarters	Year Founded	Signature Product
Arrow	USA	1851	Men's dress shirts
Balthazar Merz	Germany	1911	Knitwear
Barbour	UK	1894	Jackets for shooting & boating
Barrie Knitwear	UK/Scotland	1903	Cashmere knitwear
Brooks Brothers	USA	1818	Men's tailored clothing
Bruno Magli	Italy	1936	Footwear
Burberry	UK	1856	Classic trench coats
Canada Goose	Canada	1957	Down-filled jackets
Charvet	France	1838	Men's dress shirts, ties
Cole Haan	USA	1928	Footwear
Devold	Norway	1853	Knit sweaters
Dunhill	UK	1893	Men's leather accessories, fountain pens
Fendi	Italy	1925	Fur and leather goods
Filson	USA	1897	Cruiser jacket
Finollo	Italy	1912	Men's tailored shirts, ties
Gucci	Italy	1921	Leather goods
Hermes	France	1837	Leather goods
Himel Brothers	Canada	1927	Leather goods
Hunter	UK/Scotland	1856	Rubber boots
Hush Puppies	USA	1958	Leather footwear
James Lock & Co	UK	1676	Hats
Levi Strauss	USA	1853	501 jeans
Liberty	UK	1875	Cotton fabrics
L.L. Bean	USA	1912	L.L. Bean boot
London Fog	USA	1923	Trench coats
Louis Vuitton	France	1854	Travel trunks, leather goods
Mackintosh	UK	1846	Rubberized coats and accessories
Pendleton Woolen Mills	USA	1909	Wool blankets, clothing
Prada	Italy	1913	Leather goods
Pringle	UK/Scotland	1815	Cashmere knitwear
Red Wing	USA	1905	No. 875 boot
Salvatore Ferragamo	Italy	1914	Leather footwear
Sanita	Denmark	1907	Wooden clogs
S.N.S Herning	Denmark	1931	Knit sweaters
Timberland	USA	1918	Waterproof boots
Woolrich	USA	1830	Wool fabric, outdoor wear

References: Brannigan (2015), Cox (2013), Styles (2014).

As such, aesthetic or style obsolescence is a familiar characteristic in today's fashion industry (Connor-Crab et al., 2016; Parry, 2014). Consumers are now accustomed to and expect seeing new merchandise available whenever they shop. Rather than purchasing a few high quality more expensive fashion items designed to last over time, consumers often purchase a high quantity of inexpensive low-quality fashion and simply throw them away after a few wearings (Bhardwaj & Fairhurst, 2010).

To counter this throw-away mentality, some fashion brands are creating fewer and more trans-seasonal collections (Parry, 2014). Eileen Fisher, a certified B Corporation headquartered in Irvington, NY, USA, utilizes a number of strategies to create sustainable and long-lasting fashions. One of these strategies is the creation of high-quality items to be worn across seasons. The designs utilize materials such as linen, organic cotton, light-weight wool, and Tencel® lyocell in classic styles and complimentary colors so that the items can be layered for weather changes.

However, changing the consumers' mindset around purchasing fewer items that can be worn across seasons is not necessarily easy. For example, Paul Dillinger, Head of global Product Innovation at Levi Strauss & Co (as quoted in Segran, 2017), noted:

> We're choosing not to participate in the fashion cycle. Instead, we're choosing to cultivate long-term relationships with the consumer and deliver against their needs. And hopefully that participates in the recalibration of consumption broadly, though that is a lofty goal.

Modular and/or Multi-Functional Design

Another strategy used by fashion brands to design merchandise with extended life is to create modular and/or multi-functional garments that allow for adaptation and change (Connor-Crab et al., 2016). **Modular design** is the "strategy to build systems of complex products from small individual subsystems/modules that work as an integrated whole" (Ribeiro

et al., 2014). When applied to fashion, modular design is a design solution when (Ribeiro et al., 2014)

- Replacement of a specific part of the fashion that receives repeated use is needed (e.g., detachable pockets);
- Changes in seasons, weather, or activity require adding or reducing apparel (e.g., detachable hoods, detachable jacket linings);
- The consumer desires changes in color, fabrics, or shapes (e.g., reversible jackets, changeable handbag handles);
- The design itself is made of modular pieces which allows for varying styles (see Figure 4.6);
- Choice of fabric is based on a specific end use (e.g., waterproof cape attached to a jacket);
- Adaptations are needed for various occasions or end uses (e.g., detachable sleeves or attachable skirt that changes a business dress to a cocktail dress, zip-off trouser bottoms to change long pants to shorts);
- Parts of the design need to be removed for easy maintenance and/or effective recycling (e.g., removable collar for cleaning, removable trims for recycling).

An early example of creating modular designs is the heritage brand Arrow, which now produces men's and women's tailored shirts but started out making detachable collars for men's shirts (Arrow, 2017). These detachable collars allowed for laundering the collar separately from the shirt, improving the efficiencies of caring for the shirt and extending the life of the shirt since the collar was typically the first garment feature to wear out. Currently, fashion brands include a number of modular design features that allow for multi-functionality of the product and, similar to Arrow shirt collars, allow the consumer to replace or change particular aspects of the garment. For example, performance apparel brand Sugoi (2017), headquartered in Burnaby, British Columbia, Canada, creates apparel for cycling and running that can be easily changed with changing weather conditions or activity level. Fashion brand Calzico creates reversible and adaptable pieces for the female

Figure 4.6 Modular design includes fashions made from modular pieces.

Figure 4.7 Fashion brand, Calzico, extends the life of apparel through adaptable styles for tweens.

tween (six to fourteen years) customer. These include zipskirts with removable layers and reversible jackets that can be worn multiple ways allowing for greater versatility and function (see Figure 4.7).

Size, Style, and Technical Alterability

According to fit, style, technical, and economic obsolescence, clothing is discarded because it no longer fits, is out of style, or needs repair and it is easier to replace the item rather than alter or fix it to be wearable again. We can all think of a favorite fashion that may have been thrown away or donated because it needed to be repaired, altered, or re-styled.

Historically, discarding clothing because of fit, style, technical, and/or economic obsolescence was not always the case. For example, in the midst of World War II, the Ministry of Information in Great Britain created a pamphlet "Make Do and Mend" (1943) with countless possibilities for altering the sizes or styles of clothing and giving "new life" to worn clothing. Even today, do-it-yourself websites and YouTube videos offer instructions on altering and fixing clothing items to extend their use.

Therefore, to extend the life of fashions, altering, fixing, or mending items for further use is an optimal solution. However, the question remains, how can fashion brands encourage consumers to alter and mend clothing, particularly when most consumers do not have the skills to do so? To counter this challenge, designers are creating innovative fashions that easily adapt to size changes; fashion brands are offering services to both consumers and fashion brand partners for altering, fixing, or mending fashion items to extend their use; and fashion brands are providing consumer education and do-it-yourself tools/kits to enhance the skills of consumers. Strategies include creating designs for fit or size adaptability, offering components and/or services for fixing or mending items, and providing educational tools for consumers to learn the necessary skills. As a result of these strategies they are also creating lasting relationships with consumers.

Creating Designs for Fit or Size Adaptability

Although the ready-to-wear industry is based on "standardized sizing," in reality consumers are not standardized in terms of size and shape, consumers' shapes and sizes change over time, and consumers have different preferences with regard to sizing and comfort (WRAP, 2013). And whereas the fit of apparel and subsequent comfort are highly important criteria used by consumers when purchasing apparel, perceived fit is highly subjective and is affected by both individual (e.g., personal preferences, changes

in size) and product characteristics (e.g., fabric, style). According to Waste Resources Action Plan (WRAP, 2013) "around 30% of clothing in the average wardrobe [of UK consumers] has not been worn for at least a year, most commonly because it no longer fits." Examples of design strategies used by fashion brands to facilitate adjustments to accommodate changes and differences in size and shape include

- Larger seam allowances to allow for "letting out" garments
- Fastenings that allow for increasing or decreasing the length of side seams or hems
- Waistbands that expand or contract to adjust to different waist sizes
- Collar bands that expand or contract to adjust to different neck sizes
- Multiple belt loops on coats and jackets to accommodate higher or lower waist height
- Hems that allow for raising or lowering

A great example of size adaptability is The Shoe That Grows footwear (TheShoeThatGrows.org,

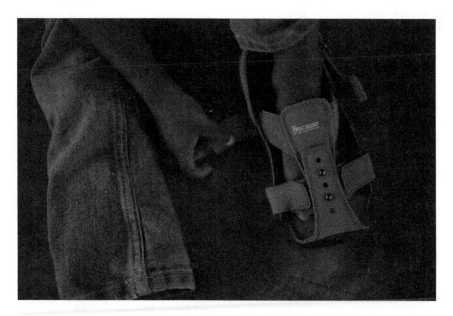

Figure 4.8 The design of The Shoe that Grows allows for adjustable sizing.

2017). The design of this shoe adjusts and expands up to five sizes; thus, the child or adult always has a pair of shoes that fits (see Figure 4.8). In addition, the organization that oversees the production and distribution of The Show That Grows is Because International (becauseinternational.org), which uses innovations to improve resources used in daily life. As they noted "The sole purpose for our first project is to help kid stay healthy through sustainable and solid footwear."

Offering Components and/or Services to Fix or Mend Items

According to technical obsolescence, clothing is discarded because materials fail, zippers no longer work, or buttons fall off. Therefore, to extend the life of fashions, fixing or mending items for further use is an optimal solution. Fashion brands often include components and/or services that allow for fixing or mending the fashions. Examples include the following.

- *Extra trims*. A fashion brand may provide the consumer with extra trims (buttons, shoe laces, buckles) that may become lost or worn. One of the most common strategies used by fashion brands is attaching extra buttons to a garment in case one loses a button a spare is available. However, if these are attached externally to the garment (e.g., as part of a hangtag), it is important that the consumer save the extra buttons. To avoid the extra buttons being lost or thrown away, attaching the extra buttons onto a sewn-in tag or seam is a better strategy.

- *Repair and educational services*. A number of fashion brands/companies offer repair services and do-it-yourself (DIY) educational services to encourage consumers to repair clothing rather than discarding items.

  - Patagonia's Worn Wear (https://wornwear.patagonia.com/) program encourages repairing garments for extended life. According to their website "Patagonia employs 45 full-time repair technicians at our service center in Reno, Nevada. It's the largest repair facility in North America—completing about 40,000 repairs per year. We've also teamed up with the repair experts at iFixit to create care and repair guides so you can easily do it yourself." They also offer maintenance and repair guides including how to install a zipper in a Patagonia fleece jacket, repairing a hole in Patagonia waders, and patching a Patagonia down jacket with repair tape.

- Birkenstock, a German footwear company, has been encouraging their customers to repair worn shoes and sandals for years. On their website, they provide information on a variety of stores that offer repair services. Type in your zip code and find authorized Birkenstock repair retailers near you. Many offer both in-store and mail order repair. Birkenstock also has several YouTube videos for do-it-yourself resoling and recorking directions.

- Nudie Jeans, a Swedish apparel denim brand, has a "Repair and Take Care of Your Jeans" section to their website. If your Nudie jeans need repair you can take them to a Nudie jeans store where they will repair the jeans for free (see Figure 4.9) or you can order a free Nudie jeans repair kit and do it yourself.

- Coach, based in New York City, offers free repairs on their handbags, briefcases, and small leather goods for one year after purchase. After that, they offer repair services for a fee. You can take your coach leather goods in need of repair to selected retail stores or send them to their centralized repair assessment location in Florida. For simple repairs such as replacing a turnlock, they will send you a new one with instruction for DIY repair. Their website also provides information about repairing other Coach merchandise.

Companies That Offer Services to Alter, Fix, Resize, and/or Restyle Fashions

Although, as noted earlier, several fashion brands offer their own services for repairing or mending fashion items, most fashion brands do not. In

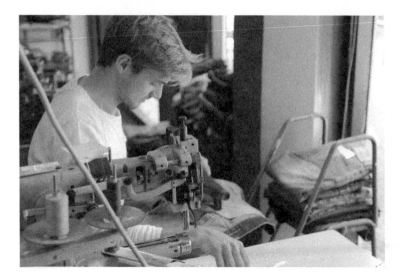

Figure 4.9 Nudie jeans offers repair services through their retail stores.

addition, as noted earlier, most consumers do not have the time and/or skills to alter or fix apparel. Therefore, to fill this gap, a growing number of companies are offering services to alter, fix, or mend fashions. These companies, once known best for altering heirloom or ready-to-wear wedding dresses, have expanded their services to include resizing, restyling, and other alterations to extend the life of all types of fashions. For example, The Zip Yard (2017), with franchises in Ireland and the United Kingdom, offers professional tailoring and garment alterations including relining jackets, tapering trouser legs, resizing garments, and restyling garments. As they note: "Whether you've inherited some vintage items from a relative and want to modernise them, or simply want to refresh your existing clothing collection, we can help" (thezipyard.com, 2017).

Upcycling

As introduced in Chapter 3, **upcycling** pre-consumer and postconsumer textile waste materials is a process by which discarded materials or items are transformed to create products with a higher value than what was being discarded without changing

the composition of the original material. Once limited to items such as patchwork quilts, bags made from worn jeans, and children's wear made from worn adult clothing, upcycled fashions have become more sophisticated and commercially viable. Fashion brands and companies are using a number of material sources to commercially create and sell upcycled merchandise including pre-consumer waste (e.g., scraps from cutting floors), **deadstock fabric** (flawed fabrics/materials or fabrics left over from textile mills), and postconsumer waste (e.g., worn/used textile products). Examples include

- Sans Soucie (http://www.sanssoucie.ca): Designer Katherine Soucie uses pre-consumer waste hosiery purchased by the pound from hosiery mills to create fabrics for apparel and accessories. San Soucie is headquartered in Vancouver, B.C., Canada (see Figure 4.10). See Conversation with Katherine Soucie at the end of this chapter.

- Sword & Plough (https://www.swordandplough.com/): Military fabrics are upcycled to create a variety of bags. "By recycling and repurposing military fabrics with a fashionable touch, and working with veterans at each stage (from product

Figure 4.10 Designer Katherine Soucie upcycles pre-consumer waste hosiery to create unique fabrics and apparel.

conception to order fulfillment), we create sturdy and sophisticated products." Sword & Plough is headquartered in Denver, CO, USA.

- An innovative business-to-business service that takes unsellable or returned merchandise and excess inventory and turns them into "renewed apparel, material for upcycling, or feedstock for recycling" is The Renewal Workshop (2017), headquartered in Cascade Locks, OR, USA (see Figure 4.11). Working with fashion brand partners including PrAna, Ibex, Toad&Co, Mountain Khakis, and Indigenous, The Renewal Workshop collects products from these brands that were unsold, damaged, or returned by customers to create one-of-a-kind apparel sold through their website (renewalworkshop.com).

- TRMTAB (http://www.trmtab.com/): In partnership with Prachi Leathers in Kanpur, India, TRMTAB takes leather scraps, dead stock, and naturally spotted leathers and turns them into limited edition collections of leather tote bags, backpacks, wallets, sandals, and other small leather goods. The upcycling feedstock leather scraps are either woven or chevron stitched to create the merchandise. "Our collections and making methods continue to be inspired by the power of creating small changes."

Figure 4.11 The Renewal Workshop partners with fashion brands including PrAna to create renewed apparel.

- Looptworks (https://www.looptworks.com/): With the motto "use only what exists," Looptworks, headquartered in Portland, OR, USA, uses worn airline leather seat covers and excess and deadstock materials caused by order changes or cancellations to create a variety of merchandising including apparel, backpacks, duffle bags, and other accessories. For example, partnering with Alaska Airlines/Horizon Airlines and Southwest Airlines, they upcycled leather from airline seats into bags and small leather accessories. They have also partnered with the NBA team, Portland Trailblazers, to upcycle 4,000 obsolete game jerseys into backpacks, scarfs, and jackets.

Creating an Emotional and/or Experiential Connection between the Item and the Wearer

Fashion items serve as physical reminders of special connections with family members/friends and/or memories of individuals and/or past events. Therefore, when a wearer of a fashion item has an emotional and/or experiential connection to the fashion item, the item is more likely to be saved and/or worn over time. The phrase **emotionally durable design** (Chapman, 2015) describes this emotional and experiential relationship between a consumer and the products they purchase. In his study of consumption of electronic products, Chapman (2009) found that consumers retain products when they remain meaningful to them over time; thus concluding that reduction in electronic waste would occur through increasing the resilience of the relationship between consumer and product. That is, the product can adapt in ways that retain the meaningfulness to the consumer. And whereby a designer or creator may attempt to contribute to this attachment (e.g., co-created, handmade); ultimately, the user determines the attachment or connection and its implications for extended use (Chapman, 2015; Fletcher, 2012). When applying the concept of emotionally durable design to fashion items, fashion brands use several strategies to create an intentional connection and relationship with the consumer/user:

- Creating heirlooms
- Co-creation/co-production
- Narratives around shared values
- Creating shared experiences

Creating Heirlooms

Heirloom garments or accessories are designed and created with the intent or hope that they will be shared and worn across generations. Heirlooms are

- Associated with special occasions or events such as christenings, baptisms, or weddings
- Custom-made or handmade, and/or
- Items worn by a relative or someone with whom the current wearer has a strong attachment

For an heirloom to continue to be worn over time, the fashion must reflect changing styles and user preferences and lifestyle, fit, and not being saved for posterity's sake (e.g., wedding gown that will never again be worn). Fashion brands that intentionally create heirlooms focus on the quality, care, exclusivity, and often, handmade, aspects of the items. For example, established in 1978 Granted Clothing, headquartered in Vancouver, B.C., Canada, designs and makes handmade sweaters. The company uses quality of process, tradition, and care in creating the products. As it notes on its website (Granted Clothing, 2017):

- "Due to the lengthy process of hand-knitting, production is limited. However, this allows for an attention to detail and quality that has become synonymous with the brand."
- "We believe handmade sweaters have a touch of magic in them—they're rooted in tradition, and no two are ever truly identical."
- "With care and love, our hand-knit woolen clothing will keep you warm through a lifetime of daily adventures."

Co-Creation/Co-Production

As noted in the section on the slow fashion movement, to enhance the consumer's connection to the product and the product's perceived value, the consumer is brought into the supply chain as a co-creator or co-producer. Custom-made and personalized fashion products create immediate connections between the consumer and the product. Whereas once limited to working with local seamstresses and tailors, with the advent of online resources, consumers can easily be part of the creation and production of apparel made around the world. Etsy.com, for example, offers close to 50,000 custom-made and personalized clothing items. Heritage brand Brooks Brothers offers customized shirts and suits through their website. To design a customized shirt, customers select from one of four general types of fit; fabric type, color, pattern, and weave; one of eight collar options; one of four cuff options; pockets, back style; and monograph. Collar size and sleeve length are entered and the custom shirt is ordered.

Narratives around Shared Values

Fashion brands create connections with consumers through narratives around shared values. In this context, values are ideas and behaviors that are important to individuals. Socially conscious fashion brands create narratives (e.g., blogs, videos, images, etc.) that reflect the impact of their socially responsible work. Consumers who share the same values identify and connect with the brand around these values. For example, Krochet Kids intl. produces and sells men's, women's, and children's apparel and accessories and in the process provides jobs, education, and mentorship to women in Uganda and Peru. Every product they make is hand-signed by the person who made it and they encourage consumers to write notes of thanks and encouragement to the individual, thus creating opportunities to directly engage with the individual who made the product you purchased. The Krochet Kids intl. website includes images, videos, and blogs about the impact of their work (see Figure 4.12).

In their goal to refocus Levi Strauss & Co around values of sustainability, creating and sharing narratives around their goals has become an important strategy. In fact, when asked the

Figure 4.12 Krochet Kids Intl. creates narratives around shared values, thus creating strong connections with consumers.

question "You're tasked with creating a product that is fairly timeless and less subject to trends. Are you intentionally changing the narrative about consumption?" (Segran, 2017), Paul Dillinger, Head of Global Product Innovation at Levi Strauss & Co, answered:

> Yes. In my wildest dreams, we'd be helping to cultivate a Levi's consumer who values durability and demonstrates a real attachment to an object. We'd be nurturing the person who doesn't purchase because of immediate seasonal change, but who purchases for lasting value. This would mean there are shared values between our brand and our consumer.

Creating Shared Experiences

Fashion brand companies also create connections with consumers through brand communities (Muniz & O'Guinn, 2001). A **brand community** is "a group of ardent consumers organized around the lifestyle, activities, and ethos of the brand" (Fournier & Lee, 2009). As an effective business strategy, companies provide support for brand communities through their product offerings, sponsorship of events, online social networks, physical spaces for activities, and employee engagement/volunteerism. In return, consumers in the brand community have an extraordinary connection with the brand through the shared experiences. Examples include

- Vancouver, B.C.-based athletic apparel brand, lululemon athletica, creates brand communities by offering its retail spaces for complimentary yoga classes.
- In addition to creating an online community, Vans® footwear brand, headquartered in California, USA, sponsors skate parks, music festivals, and skateboard and bicycle motocross (BMX) events that connect their consumers.
- Rapha performance bicycling brand, headquartered in London, UK, offers Rapha clubhouses that serve not only as retail spaces for Rapha products but also as meeting places for cyclists including a café as well as programs of live racing, rides and events. Clubhouses also sponsor chapters of the Rapha Cycling Club.

Although it is unclear if being part of brand community results in wearing the brand for a longer period of time, consumers who are part of a brand community do feel a strong attachment to and have positive attitudes toward the brand's products.

Consumer/User Attitudes and Behavior

Whereas fashion brands can create durable and adaptable fashions with an intended emotional and/or experiential connection to the consumer, the user ultimately determines any attachment or connection to the item as well as how long to keep and wear the item. People save and adapt clothing for longevity of use for a variety of reasons (Fletcher, 2012), asking questions such as: Do I consider the item to be an heirloom that will be saved but not worn? Will the item be worn until it is "worn out"? Do I have the skills, time, and incentives to remodel, repair, or mend the item? Do I have the space to store or keep the item? Consumers vary in the degree to which they value clothing as a

resource and therefore vary in behaviors including purchasing fewer and higher quality items, taking care of the clothing they purchase, wearing the item until it is worn out, acquiring and using the skills to fix or alter clothing, and/or engage in fashion-sharing activities. Strategies used by consumers to extend the use of their clothing include

- Reducing consumption and buying fewer and higher quality items
- Caring of fashion items
- Repairing and/or altering fashions
- Sharing fashions

Reducing Consumption and Buying Fewer and Higher Quality Items

Many consumers choose to purchase fewer and high quality fashion items with the intent that these items will be worn over time. Purchasing classic styles and heritage brands and limiting shopping activities are typical behaviors. In some cases, consumers may view these purchases as **investment dressing**, particularly around business attire. To be an effective strategy for consumers, this type of behavior is dependent on the consumer's knowledge of fibers, fabrics, construction, and styling.

Caring for Fashion Items

Fashion items are worn for a longer period of time when the items continue to look good. Therefore, the use and care of fashion items affects the items' longevity of use (WRAP, 2016). Users prolong the life of their fashions by

- Wearing layers to protect clothing including aprons, T-shirts worn under shirts, or dress shields protecting from perspiration.
- Washing items less frequently.
- Following washing and/or care information. Laundering items at the wrong temperature or not following the care information provided for the item can shorten the lifespan of the garment.

Repairing and/or Altering Fashions

Some people may have the ability to sew on a button but fewer have the skills to alter or fix their clothing, particularly among younger people (WRAP, 2013). Likewise, those who may have the skills may not have the time to mend or alter their clothing. In addition, wearing clothing with visible repairs may not be socially acceptable (Gwilt, 2014). Regardless of reason, clothing that needs mending or altering are either stored or discard items. If owners had the time and skills, these items might be more likely to be worn for a longer period of time. The growing number of repair fairs, DIY tools, YouTube videos, and Pinterest boards dedicated to mending, altering, and refashioning clothing is evidence of the growing interest in learning and executing the skills to extend the life of garments (Lewis-Hammond, 2014). For example, in addition to creating heirloom products, lifestyle apparel and home fashions company, Alabama Chanin, offers books and workshops to build sewing skills. (See Figure 4.13 and Company Highlight at the end of this chapter.) With a goal of generating a "repair revolution," The Edinburgh Remakery (in Edinburgh, UK) provides individual training for sewing and mending skills in addition

Figure 4.13 Alabama Chanin creates heirlooms and offers books and workshops for customers to build sewing skills.

to classes and training to repair a variety of other products and workstations equipped with sewing machines and tools.

Sharing Fashions

The **sharing economy** or **collaborative consumption** are broad terms that describe activities in which goods and/or services are shared between private individuals, either for free or for a fee. When there is a fee, the terms **performance economy** or **functional service economy** are used to describe that the consumer pays for only the performance or service of the product rather than the product itself. Such activities reflect the ability for and often the preferences of individuals to rent, share, or borrow goods rather than buy and own them. The internet has facilitated consumers' willingness and ability to engage in one or more aspects of the sharing economy (e.g., Airbnb, Lyft, and Uber). The sharing economy has also resulted increased services whereby consumers can borrow or rent apparel. Men's tuxedo rentals have been commonplace. However, the common belief was that women would not want to borrow or rent apparel or that men would not want to rent apparel beyond tuxedos. With the growth in apparel and accessory rental companies such as Rent a Runway (rentarunway.com), Le Tote (letote.com), The Ms. Collection (themscollection.com), Bag Borrow or Steal (bagborroworsteal.com), Gwynnie Bee (closet. gwynniebee.com), and Lena the Fashion Library (lena-library.com) for women's apparel and The Mr. Collection (themrcollection.com) and Fresh Neck (freshneck.com) for men, that belief is no longer the case. Although this strategy feeds on consumers' desire to have quickly ever-changing fashions, it allows consumers to rent better quality merchandise and return the apparel after wearing just a few times instead of donating or discarding the apparel.

Summary

With the rise of the ready-to-wear industry came an associated rise in textiles and clothing no longer viewed as valued resources. Instead, in today's fast fashion context, consumers are accustomed to readily available inexpensive trendy apparel made with low quality materials and workmanship meant to be worn only a few times and then discarded. However, extending the life of fashions has a direct impact on environmental sustainability. Extending the useful life of fashions is dependent on both the decisions and behaviors of those in the fashion industry and of consumers and users of fashions. Therefore, fundamental to understanding strategies for design, merchandising, and consumption for longevity of use is an understanding of the fashion process, consumer desire for new fashions, and forms of obsolescence that spur the discarding of fashions. Forms of obsolescence include technical, style, fit, psychological, and economic obsolescence. Forms of obsolescence are not mutually exclusive and several can contribute to consumers' motivation to discard current fashions and purchase/acquire new fashions.

In response to the accelerated fashion process and the resulting increase in postconsumer textile waste, many fashion industry professionals have increased intentional decisions, behaviors, and marketing around fashions designed and merchandised for as valued resources for longevity of use. This philosophy, known as the slow fashion movement, includes designers and fashion brands that use small-scale; traditional techniques; local sourcing; co-creation/co-production; environmental, social, and cultural sustainability; economic sustainability; and design for durability.

Fashion brands that design and merchandise fashion products for longevity of use employ one or more of the following strategies: high quality and durable fabrics and workmanship/construction, classic design or design for fashion-adaptability, fewer and trans-seasonal collections/lines, modular and/or multi-functional design, design for size or style alterability, upcycling, and creating an emotional and/or experiential connection between the item and the wearer. Optimal strategies depend on the product category.

Whereas fashion brands can create durable and adaptable fashions with an intended emotional and/or experiential connection to the consumer, the user ultimately determines any attachment or connection

to the item as well as how long to keep and wear the item. People save and adapt clothing for longevity of use for a variety of reasons. In addition, consumers vary in the degree to which they value clothing as a resource and therefore vary in behaviors including purchasing fewer and higher quality items, taking care of the clothing they purchase, wearing the item until it is worn out, acquiring and using the skills to fix or alter clothing, and/or engage in fashion-sharing activities.

Key Terms

aesthetic obsolescence	heritage brand
brand community	home sewing
classic fashion	investment dressing
co-creator	local sourcing
collaborative consumption	longevity of use
	modular design
co-producer	obsolescence
deadstock fabric	performance economy
designing for durability	psychological obsolescence
emotionally durable design	ready-to-wear
fashion cycle	slow fashion
fashion process	shared economy
fast fashion	style obsolescence
fit obsolescence	technical obsolescence
functional service economy	temporary inactive storage
economic obsolescence	upcycling
heirloom	

References and Resources

All Myn (2017). *Our Ethos*. Retrieved on July 21, 2017, from https://www.allmyn.net/pages/our-products.

Arrow (2017). "Arrow: An American Classic." Retrieved on March 16, 2017, from http://www.arrowlife.com/heritage.

ASTM International (2017). "Standards and Publications: Textiles." Retrieved on March 22, 2017, from https://www.astm.org/.

Brannigan, Maura (2015, June 30). "From Levi's to L.L. Bean, American Heritage Brands are Enjoying a Renaissance." Retrieved on February 15, 2017, from http://fashionista.com/2015/06/american-heritage-brands.

Bhardwaj, Vertica & Fairhurst, Ann (2010, February). "Fast Fashion: Response to Changes in the Fashion Industry." *The International Review of Retail, Distribution and Consumer Research*, 20(1): 165, 173.

British Library (2017). "Make Do and Mend 1943." Retrieved on March 23, 2017, from http://www.bl.uk/learning/timeline/item106365.html.

Brooks Brothers (2017). "About Us: A Company with a History of Value." Retrieved on February 27, 2017, from http://www.brooksbrothers.com/about-us/about-us,default,pg.html.

Burns, Brian (2010). "Re-evaluating Obsolescence and Planning for It," in Tim Cooper (ed). *Longer Lasting Products: Alternatives to the Throwaway Society* 39–60). Farnham: Gower Publishing.

Business Dictionary (2017). Obsolescence, Definition. Retrieved from on February 19, 2017, from http://www.businessdictionary.com/definition/obsolescence.html.

Calasibetta, Charlotte M. (1988). *Fairchild's Dictionary of Fashion* (2nd ed.). NY: Fairchild Books.

Cataldi, Carlotta, Dickson, Mareen, & Grover, Chrystal (2010). *Slow Fashion: Tailoring a Strategic Approach towards Sustainability*. Thesis submitted for completion of Master of Strategic Leadership towards Sustainability, Blekinge Institute of Technology, Karlskrona, Sweden. Retrieved on June 7, 2017, from http://www.diva-portal.org/smash/record.jsf?pid=diva2%3A832785&dswid=-3996.

Chapman, Jonathan (2009, autumn). Design for (Emotional) Durability. *Design Issues*, 25(4): 29–35.

Chapman, Jonathan (2010). Subject/Object Relationships and Emotionally Durable Design," in Tim Cooper (ed). *Longer Lasting Products: Alternatives to the Throwaway Society* 61–76. Farnham: Gower Publishing.

Chapman, Jonathan (2015). *Emotionally Durable Design: Objects, Experiences and Empathy* (2nd ed). London: Routledge.

Clark, Hazel (2008). Slow + fashion—an oxymoron—or a promise for the future. . .? *Fashion Theory*, 12(4): 427–46.

Cluver, Brigitte Gaal (2008). "Consumer Clothing Inventory Management." Unpublished dissertation Oregon State University. Retrieved on November 1, 2016, from http://ir.library.oregonstate.edu/xmlui/bitstream/handle/1957/9507/Brigitte_Cluver.pdf?sequence=1.

Connor-Crabb, Anja, Miller, Karen, & Chapman, Jonathan (2016). "Design Strategies for the Eternal Reoccurrence of the New." *Fashion Practice*, 8(1): 22–43.

Cooper, Tim (2013). "Sustainability, Consumption and the Throwaway Culture," in Stewart Walker & Jacques Giard (eds). *The Handbook of Design for Sustainability*, 137–55. London: Bloomsbury Academic.

Cox, Caroline (2013). *Luxury Fashion: A Global History of Heritage Brands*. London: Bloomsbury Publishing.

Design for Longevity (2017). *About*. Retrieved on October 5, 2017, from https://designforlongevity.com/page/about.

Fletcher, Kate (2012). "Durability, Fashion, Sustainability: The Processes and Practices of Use." *Fashion Practice*, 4(2): 221–38.

Fletcher, Kate (2010). "Slow Fashion: An Invitation for Systems Change." *Fashion Practice*, 2(2): 259–65.

Fletcher, Kate (2014). *Sustainable Fashion and Textiles: Design Journeys*. London: Earthscan.

Fletcher, Kate (2014). "Local Wisdom." Retrieved on June 7, 2017, from http://www.localwisdom.info.

Fletcher, Kate, & Tham, Mathilda, editors (2015). Routledge Handbook of Sustainability and Fashion. London: Routledge

Fournier, Susan, & Lee, Lara (2009, April) "Getting Brand Communities Right." *Harvard Business Review*. Retrieved on June 7, 2017, from https://hbr.org/2009/04/getting-brand-communities-right.

Granted Clothing (2017). *Our Story*. Retrieved on April 6, 2017, from https://www.grantedclothing.com/pages/our-story.

Gwilt, Alison (2014). What Prevents People Repairing Clothes? An Investigation into Community-Based Approaches to Sustainable Product Service Systems for Clothing Repair. *Making Futures Journal*, 3: 331–37.

Gwilt, Alison (2014). *A Practical Guide to Sustainable Fashion*. London: Bloomsbury.

Icebreaker (2017). "The Icebreaker Way." Retrieved on September 1, 2017, from https://www.icebreaker.com/en/our-story/philosophy.html.

Lewis-Hammond, Sarah (2014, May 10). "The Rise of Mending: How Britain Learned to Repair Clothes Again." *The Guardian*. Retrieved on June 7, 2017, from http://www.theguardian.com/lifeandstyle/2014/may/19/the-rise-of-mending-how-britain-learned-to-repair-clothes-again .

Muniz, Albert M., Jr. & O'Guinn, Thomas C. (2001, March). "Brand Community." *Journal of Consumer Research*, 27(4): 412–32.

Niinimäki, K. (2010). "Eco-Clothing, Consumer Identity and Ideology." *Sustainable Development*, 18(3): 150–62.

Parry, Carrie (2014, September 17). "Traditional Fashion Calendar Fuels Overconsumption and Waste." *The Guardian*. Retrieved on June 7, 2017, from http://www.theguardian.com/sustainable-business/sustainable-fashion-blog/2014/sep/17/fashion-calendar-sustainable-climate-change-london-fashion-week.

Putnam, Tim (1999). "The Sewing Machine Comes Home," in Barbara Burman (ed). *The Culture of Sewing: Gender, Consumption, and Home Dressmaking*, 269–83. Oxford, UK: Berg.

Riberio, Liliana, Miguel, Rui, Pereira, Madalena, Barata, João, Trindade, Isabel, & Lucas, José (2014). *Modular Design: Development of Fashion Accessories*. Presentation at the 9th Conference of the International Committee for Design History and Design Studies. Blucher Design Proceedings, 5(1): 60–61. Retrieved on March 22, 2017, from http://pdf.blucher.com.br.s3-sa-east-1.amazonaws.com/designproceedings/icdhs2014/0130.pdf.

Schofield-Tomschin, Sherry (1999). "Home Sewing: Motivational Changes in the Twentieth Century," in Barbara Burman (ed). *The Culture of Sewing: Gender, Consumption, and Home Dressmaking*, 97–110. Oxford, UK: Berg.

Segran, Elizabeth (2017, February 9). "Levi's Is Radically Redefining Sustainability." Retrieved on February 19, 2017, from https://www.fastcompany.com/3067895/moving-the-needle/levis-is-radically-redefining-sustainability.

Slow Food (2017). *Our Philosophy*. Retrieved on February 27, 2017, from www.slowfood.com.

Styles, Isabella Redmond (2014, February 17). "London's Top 10 Heritage Brands." *Global Blue*. Retrieved on February 15, 2017, from http://www.globalblue.com/destinations/uk/london/london-top-10-heritage-brands/.

Sproles, George, & Burns, Leslie Davis (1994). *Changing Appearances: Understanding Dress in Contemporary Society*. NY: Fairchild Books.

St. James, Tara (2013, April 9). "The Anti-(fashion)-Calendar." Retrieved on May 30, 2017, from http://study-ny.com/blog/2013/4/5/the-anti-fashion-calendar.

Sudara (2017). *Our Story*. Retrieved on March 15, 2017, from https://www.sudara.org/pages/our-story.

Sugoi (2017). "Modular Technology." Retrieved on May 30, 2017, from http://www.sugoi.com/en-US/modular-technology.

SustainableBrands.com (December 2, 2016). "The Future of Textiles: Creating Sustainable Fashion Through Cradle to Cradle Design." Retrieved on December 9, 2016, from http://www.sustainablebrands.com/digital_learning/webinar/products_design/future_textiles_creating_sustainable_fashion_through_cradle.

The Renewal Workshop (2017). *Our Story*. Retrieved on March 30, 2017, from https://www.renewalworkshop.com/en/home.

The Zip Yard (2017). "The Zip Yard Garment Alterations. Services." Retrieved on March 30, 2017, from http://thezipyard.com/.

Tobeck, Matthew (2013). *Slow Fashion Development: A Model for Sustainability*. Unpublished master's thesis, Oregon State University. Retrieved on June 1, 2017, from https://ir.library.oregonstate.edu/xmlui/handle/1957/40075.

WRAP (2016, May 4). *Valuing Our Clothes: The True Cost of How We Design, Use, and Dispose of Clothing in the UK*. Based on data from 2012 Report. Retrieved on February 20, 2017, from http://www.wrap.org.uk/sites/files/wrap/VoC%20FINAL%20online%202012%2007%2011.pdf.

WRAP (2017). "Love Your Clothes Campaign—Sustainable Clothing Action Plan." Retrieved on February 20, 2017, from https://www.loveyourclothes.org.uk/.

WRAP (2013, May). "Design for Longevity: Guidance for Increasing the Active Life of Clothing." Retrieved on February 20, 2017, from http://www.wrap.org.uk/sites/files/wrap/Design%20for%20Longevity%20Report_0.pdf.

Case Study: Heritage Brand Collaborations: Pendleton Woolen Mills

Pendleton Woolen Mills exemplifies the characteristics of a heritage brand. As stated on their website, "For more than 153 years, Pendleton has set the standard for American style. With six generations of family ownership, the company remains dedicated to its American heritage, authenticity and fabric craftsmanship" (Pendleton Woolen Mills, 2017). In 1909, three brothers, Clarence, Roy, and Chauncy Bishop, opened a woolen mill in Pendleton, Oregon, at the time a major wool shipping center for sheep growers in the Columbia River Plateau region. The products first produced included blankets and robes for Native Americans. The Pendleton blankets "were used as basic wearing apparel and as a standard of value for trading and credit among Native Americans. The blankets also became prized for ceremonial use." With the opening of an additional mill, Pendleton added men's apparel, specifically men's woolen shirts and sportswear, to their line of products; and later (after WWII) added a line women's apparel to its offerings.

With corporate headquarters in Portland, Oregon, USA, Pendleton remains a vertically integrated company—owning and operating five production facilities that process raw wool into finished materials, designing apparel and home products, and selling merchandise through specialty and department store retailers in addition to direct sales through fifty Pendleton retail and outlet stores, apparel and home direct catalogs, and the Pendleton-usa.com website. They are well-known for wool blankets and other home products and for both woolen and non-woolen apparel with classic styling and consistent color stories. They market their merchandise as "It Lasts," highlighting the resiliency and durability of wool and high-quality product construction. As heirlooms, "Pendleton blankets, shirts, 49er jackets and pleated skirts and many other signature products are passed from generation to generation."

In recent years, Pendleton has collaborated with fashion brands including UGG® Australia, Timberland, Canada Goose®, and Nike® to create merchandise that incorporates Pendleton textiles. For example, Canada Goose X Pendleton hat, scarves, and blanket combine Pendleton wool with Canada Goose® white goose down.

These exclusive and limited edition products have proven to be successful in expanding the product lines without compromising the integrity of the Pendleton brand. Pendleton is considering future collaborations with appropriate and relevant fashion brands. Such brands must share Pendleton's values as a company and commitment to designing for longevity of use while at the same time, expanding Pendleton's reach to new consumers.

Questions

1. Describe Pendleton Woolen Mills as a company including an analysis of their current product lines. Who is the target customer for Pendleton products?

2. What are the advantages and disadvantages for Pendleton in collaborating with other fashion brands?

3. What fashion brands are currently collaborating with Pendleton? Why do you think these brands have agreed to collaborate with Pendleton? Why do you think Pendleton has agreed to collaborate with these fashion brands?

4. What criteria should Pendleton use in selecting fashion brands for future collaborations? Based on this list, what three fashion brands would be appropriate brands for future collaborations with Pendleton? Why? How would each brand continue Pendleton's commitment to designing for longevity of use?

Reference

Pendleton Woolen Mills (2017). *Company History*. Retrieved on April 11, 2017, from https://www.pendleton-usa.com/custserv/custserv.jsp?pageName=CompanyHistory&parentName=Heritage.

Note: The background for this case study is based on publicly available information. The business problem is speculative only and not based on publicly available and/or documented information from Pendleton Woolen Mills.

Call to Action Activity: Longevity of Use: Cost-Per-Wearing Analysis

Learning Objectives

- Determine cost-per-wearing of selected apparel and accessory items.
- Evaluate the strategies for longevity of use in lowering cost-per-wearing of clothing and accessories.
- Recommend optimal strategies for lowering cost-per-wearing of personal clothing and accessories.

Procedure

1. Select five items from your wardrobe (clothing or accessories) that you
   - Know the purchase price
   - Know how long you have had the item and can estimate the number of times you have worn it since you purchased it
   - Can document the number of times you will wear the item over the next six months

2. Determine the cost-per-wearing of each item. Divide the purchase price of the item by the number of times you have worn the item since you purchased it. This will give you the cost-per-wearing for each item.

3. Estimate the number of times you plan to wear the item over the next six months. Re-calculate the cost-per-wearing including the number of times you plan to wear the item over the next six months.

Analysis Paper

Write a paper that includes the following:

1. Original and re-calculated costs-per-wearing for each item

2. Explanation of the different between the two calculations for each item

3. Listing and description of five strategies a consumer might use to reduce the cost-per-wearing of items in their wardrobe. Include the advantages and disadvantages of each

4. Recommendation of the two strategies that you personally will use to reduce the cost-per-wearing of the selected items from your wardrobe over the next 6 months. Address the question—why did you select these two strategies?

Slow Fashion Zero Waste Design: Conversation with Katherine Soucie

Katherine Soucie, Owner and Designer
Sans Soucie Textile + Design
Vancouver, B.C., Canada

Q: You were introduced to textiles, apparel, and fashion at an early age. What were your influences?
A: I grew up in southern Ontario, just across the border from Detroit, Michigan. My mother was a seamstress and embroiderer and made my clothing when I was young. I grew up with the values of being resourceful and not wasting resources. In addition, I come from a very multicultural background and I explored clothing as a form of cultural expression early on.

Q: How did you first become aware of textile waste and the possibilities of zero-waste fashion design? For example, were there particular projects or courses that influenced you?
A: My high school years were very influential for setting the foundation for my current work. The school I attended taught entrepreneurship and had a mini-mall with boutiques where we could sell merchandise. From grades 9 through 12 I took the initiative to learn about sewing through the classes offered. I was influenced by 90s grunge music and I was always looking at fashion magazines to see the newest trends. This was also the beginning of the cultural movement of recycling. During that time, I was shopping at the Salvation Army where they sold seconds from Ralph Lauren and other companies that had manufacturing factories in the area. I started modifying them to create unique designs.

After graduating from high school, I moved to Toronto to study fashion design and to be closer to the Canadian fashion industry. After earning my design degree there was a natural progression for me to learn more about textiles. I was working for a buyer at Fabricland and seeing the waste that occurred in textile mills. In order to feel empowered within this sphere, I knew I needed to know more about dyeing and printing processes. I also became aware of the tremendous amount of waste, in general. At the time, my boyfriend worked as a truck driver for a company in Toronto that would haul trash to the state of Michigan to dump into landfills. While accompanying him on one of these trips to the landfills I experienced the surreal realization that these were "graveyards of stuff." I knew I needed to be part of a different process for our society.

I then moved to Vancouver, British Columbia, and pursued a graduate degree at Capilano University. I explored the use of waste materials and materials designed to be disposable, such as hosiery, in my design work. Even though nylon hosiery is a by-product of the petroleum industry, the materials exist in the here and now. Therefore, I wanted to capture the circular nature of these finite resources used to create hosiery. I finished my graduate degree in 2003 and received two scholarships that I used in setting up my studio in Vancouver, British Columbia. In Vancouver, I am away from the competitive distractions of New York City and the east coast. I can be self-reflective and pursue my creative work without being told "you can't do that." From 2003 to 2008 was an amazing time for me. I was traveling extensively, showcasing my designs, receiving awards, and gaining exposure, thus laying the foundation for my business.

Q: You are currently using pre-consumer nylon waste hosiery. How did you form the partnerships with mills to obtain their waste textiles?
A: My original prototype was made from hosiery purchased at the Dollar Store. There was a RN (registration number) on the package and labeled as Made in Canada. I contacted the mill to see if I could purchase seconds. At the time, I did not know there was a term, "waste hosiery." I worked with two Canadian hosiery companies, Reliable Hosiery and Doris Hosiery Mill. I now also work with a mill located in North Carolina. I purchase the waste hosiery by the pound and pay for freight. I generally purchase 150 to 300 pounds at a time. I receive the waste hosiery either as tubes or as finished hosiery. The hosiery has a flaw of some sort and I am never sure as to what I am going to get from the mills.

Q: How does your design process reflect slow fashion and the use of pre-consumer textile waste? What are the inspirations for your designs?
A: After receiving the bales of waste hosiery, I first sort them—they are all usable but for different applications. Some are suitable for draping dresses; others are best for accessories. The color palettes I use are influenced by my travel. Travel, to me, includes visiting nature, experiencing culture, observing art, and listening to music. I am also influenced by art history and how it communicates today's environment. As I am determining the color palettes, I continue to assess the materials for different applications. I continue to conduct research on textiles and dyeing. I use a hot water dye process. However, none of the water is discarded; once the dyes are used, they get stored until the next time I need them. Because I use a drip dry process, I only dye materials from April to October so that the material can dry during the warmer and drier months of the year.

Printing the materials happens year round. The materials are printed in either tube form or flat. Fabric print designs are influenced by whatever is going on in my life. I want the eye to meander. I also want to tell the story of the resources through reimagining the resource. Hosiery is designed to be a second skin but the hosiery I use is a pre-consumer waste material, an interruption in the story. Some of the prints are abstractions. For others I get "really nerdy." For example, I printed the nylon chemical structure on nylon fabric.

I use metal free acid dyes and water soluble inks and natural pigments. Once the materials are dyed and printed, they are heat set—I use a mangle iron to heat set the materials. The materials are then ready to be made into fabric. Throughout this process I continue to assess the materials for fabric and garment applications. Fabrics are created using a visible mending/hemming process. In creating the fabrics, I use historical and cultural elements as well as decisions about the application. Applications will include a combination of successful silhouettes as well as new silhouettes (see Figure 4.14).

Q: What are your marketing and distribution strategies? How have they changed over time?
A: Producing, marketing, and selling a line of clothing were a challenge for me. I always wanted to be self-employed. I knew what I could bring to the table in terms of design and creating fabrics but I had to learn

Figure 4.14 Katherine Soucie's unique designs are created from waste hosiery.

about production, brand positioning, and channels of distribution. I first distributed my products through Mighty Flirt, an early online shop, and sold through this site until the early 2000s. Starting in 2005, I showed and sold my work at trade shows, craft fairs, and fashion weeks. At that time, buyers did not care about the sustainability aspect of the collection. That has definitely changed over time.

However, in honoring and reflecting the process, there is only so much I can produce. Now my primary distribution channel is through direct sales from my website, updated twice per year to highlight seasonal collections. I do custom (made-to-order) designs. I am also a member of Circle Craft, a very successful artist cooperative in British Columbia, and continue to distribute through their gallery and Christmas Market.

Q: Where do you see your design work moving in the future? How do you see Sans Soucie Textile + Design as a design studio and business moving forward?
A: There is always going to be textile waste. In fact, I use the shavings from the production of my fabrics to create Christmas wreaths. In 2012, a local rug maker asked to purchase shavings for use in creating her rugs. Another textile artist purchases scraps for use in her own artwork. Through word of mouth, I am now selling yarns and scraps to other artists. Thus, a new business model has evolved whereby artists purchase these pre-consumer waste materials from me. When I set out to create new

materials from pre-consumer waste, I had no idea I would now be providing materials to other designers.

In addition, I continue to move forward with partnerships with the industry in North Carolina. I recently held an exhibition there. The story of the life of hosiery was very compelling and spoke to those whose lives centered on the creation of these products and materials. I would love to partner with larger mills who share the vision of valuing the circular nature of resources and materials and re-thinking the industry.

Q: Anything else that you would like to share about your passion and work as a zero-waste designer and entrepreneur?
A: My background and training continue to inform my design process. For example, I still use inspiration boards. In my opinion, fashion design teaches you a different way of thinking and problem solving than do other design processes. In fashion design, you cannot skip a step. This skill is often undervalued but imperative. As such, education and mentorship have become important to me and I take seriously the contributions I make towards inspiring the next generation of designers.

In addition, being self-reflective as a designer is critical. It is easy to get caught up in an antiquated system and so one must constantly question the status quo. What are the larger questions we need to be addressing? How can we keep manufacturing in Canada and the United States? How can craft and design influence the overall industry?

Company Highlight

Alabama Chanin: Thoughtful design. Responsible production. Good business. Quality that lasts.

Headquartered in Florence, Alabama, USA, Alabama Chanin is a lifestyle company that produces heirloom apparel and home fashions and provides educational resources for those who want to create their own heirlooms. Natalie Chanin started the company in 2000 with a commitment to slow fashion philosophy and techniques including traditional techniques, sustainable materials, and production by local artisans (see Figure 4.15). As noted on their website (Alabama Chanin, 2017), "We are a leader in elevated craft due to a strong believe in tradition and dedication to locally sewn garments and goods—both hand and machine-sewn. We maintain sustainable practices—across the disciplines—and creating sustainable products, holding ourselves to the highest standards for quality."

But Alabama Chanin does more than create heirloom fashions in the luxury price zone (dresses can cost up to $3,000, skirts up to $1,400, and trenchcoats up to $2,000), "at Alabama Chanin, we preserve traditions of community, design, producing, and living arts by examining work and life through the acts of storytelling, photography, education, and making." They do this through a variety of initiatives of "The School of Making" including

- Studio Book Series including pattern books and books that provide hand-stitching and sewing instruction
- Workshops including one-day, three-day, and two-week immersion hands-on experiences that provide participants with opportunities to learn and experiment with hand- and machine sewing techniques and create customized garments.
- Subscriptions to "Build a Wardrobe" series whereby four times per year individuals receive a new DIY garment pattern, instructions, and enough fabric and thread and notions to make basic versions of each garment in their chosen colors.
- Maker supplies including kits for DIY projects from the Alabama Studio Book Series that include everything you need to make it yourself, Fabrics (organic cotton jersey), embroidery thread, notions, and sewing kits

Thus, you can purchase an heirloom Alabama Chanin item, you can attend a workshop to make an heirloom, you can purchase a kit with everything you need to make an heirloom, or you can purchase a pattern book and make it yourself.

References

Alabama Chanin (2017). *About Alabama Chanin*. Retrieved on April 10, 2017, from http://alabamachanin.com/about-alabama-chanin.

Alabama Chanin (2017). *The School of Making*. Retrieved on April 10, 2017, from https://alabamachanin.com/the-school-of-making.

Figure 4.15 Alabama Chanin creates (a) machine-sewn fashions with (b) hand-created details maintaining a heritage of quality and longevity of use.

Supply Chain Assurance and Transparency

Objectives

- Discuss issues in the global fashion industry supply chain that introduce risks for fashion brand companies.
- Define and explain supply chain management strategies associated with supply chain assurance, traceability, and transparency.
- Describe strategies for implementing effective social compliance programs by fashion brand companies.

Fashion brand company Patagonia is primarily known for its environmentally sustainable merchandise (see Figure 5.1). However, the company is also a leader in supply chain transparency. Patagonia's The Footprint Chronicles® includes an interactive world map with links to each of the farms (tier three suppliers), textile mills (tier two suppliers), and factories (tier one suppliers) used by the company . Information is provided on each supplier including location and photograph of the facility, length of time Patagonia has used them as a supplier, a description of the company and why Patagonia sources with them, certifications achieved by the vendor, number and gender mix of workers, language(s) spoken, and what is produced for Patagonia at the factory. For example,

Youngone Namdihn Co., Ltd.
Textile Mill and Sewing Factory
A Patagonia supplier since 2005
Lot O-R, Road N6, My Xa Commune
Hoa Xa Industrial Zone
Nam Dinh City, Nam Dinh, Vietnam
Number of Workers: 7456
Gender Mix: 84 percent Female, 16 percent Male
Languages Spoken: Vietnamese and English
Produced Here: Outerwear, Sportswear, and Knitwear

Based in Vietnam, Youngone Nam Dinh produces a variety of technical garments, ranging from lightweight trail running jackets to high-pile fleece sportswear. They recently received Global Traceable Down Certification from NSF International—a critical step toward Patagonia's goal of tracing their down products from farm to factory. As a service to their employees and surrounding community, Youngone brings trainees from Seoul Medical University to provide free public health services for people in the villages of Nam Dinh Province who do not have access to regular medical care (Patagonia, 2017).

Figure 5.1 Fashion brand company, Patagonia, is a leader in supply chain transparency through its The Footprint Chronicles®.

Patagonia's The Footprint Chronicles® is an excellent example of supply chain/supplier transparency, providing information about suppliers of materials used in making their products as well as suppliers of their finished goods. Why is providing this type of information important? Three general issues are prompting companies to put a priority on supply chain assurance, traceability, and transparency.

1. Because of the continued issues of human trafficking, modern slavery, and worker exploitation, fashion brands are increasingly being held accountable by governments, stakeholders, and consumers for legal and ethical sourcing strategies and supply chain management.

2. Legal and ethical supply chains are also good business strategies. Companies realize that good working conditions create healthier and, therefore, more productive work environments; ones where employees create, produce, and distribute higher

quality merchandise. In addition, consumers are increasingly purchasing merchandise from fashion brands that are transparent about their supply chains and their strategies for improvement.

3. Many fashion brands hold values around human rights as core to their overall business strategy. Such values guide sourcing philosophies and supply chain decisions.

Supply chain assurance, traceability, and transparency are imperative for fashion brand companies to be socially, environmentally, economically, and culturally sustainable. This chapter begins with an overview of supply chain and risk management in the global fashion industry. Next is a discussion of the primary risks found in fashion brand company supply chains. The chapter ends with strategies that are part of a fashion brand company's social compliance program and used to address these risks by assuring social, economic, environmental, and cultural sustainability.

Sourcing and Supply Chain Management in the Fashion Industry

Before discussing the strategies used by fashion brand companies around supply chain assurance, traceability, and transparency, an overview of factors that form the foundation for these strategies is provided. These factors include sourcing decisions made by a company and their resulting supply chain management activities.

Supply Chain and Sourcing

The term **supply chain** encompasses three general functions related to a company's production and distribution of merchandise (Canadian Supply Chain Sector Council, 2017):

1. Supply of materials to a manufacturer
2. The manufacturing process
3. The distribution of finished goods through a network of distributors and retailers to a final customer

The term **value chain** is also used to describe these functions and is often preferred by companies to reinforce a process-orientation and the valued-added aspects of each step in creating a fashion product.

Throughout its supply or value chain, a company makes **sourcing decisions** around procuring materials, production systems, and distribution pipelines. Sourcing decisions include "(1) who will design your products; (2) how, when, and where materials will be purchased; and (3) how, when, and where the merchandise will be produced and distributed" (Burns, Mullet, & Bryant, 2016, p. 256). Sourcing decisions are guided by

- Internal operations, including the company's overall sourcing philosophy; materials, labor, and equipment requirements; and factory capacity and capability requirements
- Political and geographic constraints, external to the company, including trade regulations, political and economic risks in particular countries, country infrastructure, and risks of natural disasters (Burns, Mullet, & Bryant, 2016)

A company's overall sourcing philosophy provides the framework for many of the other decisions related to supply chain assurance and transparency. Many fashion brands provide public statements about sourcing philosophies and related strategies that align with their philosophy. For example, as noted on Patagonia's (2017) Corporate Social Responsibility website:

> When considering new factories, or evaluating current ones, we take a fourfold vetting approach—one that includes social and environmental practices equally with quality standards and business requirements like financial stability, adequate capacity and fair pricing.

Supply Chain Management

"**Supply chain management** encompasses the planning and management of all activities involved in sourcing and procurement, conversion, and all logistics management activities. Importantly, it also includes coordination and collaboration with channel partners, which can be suppliers, intermediaries, third-party service providers, and customers" (Council of Supply Chain Management Professionals, 2017). For fashion brand companies, effective supply chain management (SCM) is based on the "philosophy of sharing and coordinating information across all segments of the soft goods industry" (Burns, Mullet, & Bryant, 2016, p. 17) and is dependent on trust and communication among a company's suppliers and customers. In the fashion industry, SCM is organized around tiers of suppliers:

- Tier one suppliers—direct suppliers to the fashion brand company, e.g., a factory that manufactures the apparel and accessory products.

- Tier two suppliers—suppliers to tier one suppliers, e.g., textile mills, zipper producers, button producers.

- Tier three suppliers—suppliers to tier two suppliers, e.g., yarn suppliers, fabric print or dye producers, producers of plastics and metals for zippers and/or buttons.

Fashion brand companies use two general approaches to SCM to achieve effective and efficient management of their production and distribution processes across tiers: vertical integration and contracting.

Vertical Integration

Fashion brands may be vertically integrated, in which the same company is engaged in more than one segment within the supply chain. **Vertical integration** provides advantages to fashion brand companies. Single ownership of companies within the supply chain allows fashion brands to control the availability and quality of a variety of materials and services, reducing risks associated with procuring materials and contracting services from other companies.

Very few fashion brands have fully integrated supply chains. However, aspects of vertical integration within segments of the fashion supply chain are common. For example, many fashion brands own and operate their retail stores in addition to their design and marketing operations. Large fashion brands such as Nike, Tommy Hilfiger, and Adidas all operate retail outlets (online and brick-and-mortar). In addition, most department and discount store retailers create and offer **private label brands** (brands unique to the retailer). For example, Macy's private label brands include I.N.C., Alfani, Charter Club, Karen Scott, and Style & Co. Target's private label brands include Cat and Jack, A New Day, C9 Champion, Joy Lab, and Goodfellow & Co. **Specialty store retailers of private label apparel (SPA)** offer only their own private label brands. Examples include Banana Republic, GAP, and Ann Taylor and fast fashion companies Uniqlo, Zara, and H&M.

Although it is less common for fashion brands to own their own production factories or textile mills (e.g., tier one and tier two suppliers), some fashion brands have traditionally focused on this type of vertical integration. Small fashion brands such as Softstar Shoes, headquartered in Philomath, Oregon, manufactures all of their footwear within a production facility which also houses their brick-and-mortar retail outlet, although most of their sales are through their online retail website (see Figure 5.2). As another example, Creytex®, headquartered in Medellín, Colombia, uses two business models as a vertically integrated textile and apparel company. The first model is as a **full-package contractor** (offers design, pattern making, and manufacturing services) to fashion brands including Champion, Under Armour, and VF Corp. The second model is in the development of their own brands, Belife and Baby Planet. For both models, Creytex® produces knit fabrics, dyes the fabrics, designs and develops the fashion products, cuts and sews garments, and provides embellishment services such as embroidery and screen printing (Creytex, 2017).

Luxury fashion brands have increasingly turned to vertical integration acquiring key suppliers to assure the longevity, stability, and security of their supply chains (The Fashion Law, 2017). For example, luxury brand Chanel (see Figure 5.3) owns and operates the companies that produce its buttons (Desrues),

Figure 5.2 Softstar Shoes owns and operates their own production facility.

provide embroidery services (Lesage), supply materials (Barrie cashmere, Richard Tannery), and specialize in feathers (Lemarie). Similarly, LVMH Moët Hennessy Louis Vuitton owns Heng Long, a key crocodile tannery and supplier.

Contractors

Despite advantages of vertical integration in the supply chain, most fashion brands do not own and operate tier one, two, or three suppliers; but, instead focus on design, marketing, and distribution/retailing while using **contractors**, factories owned and operated by other companies, as their suppliers. This affords them greater flexibility without the costs and management challenges associated with owning production facilities. Tier one suppliers for fashion brands include both **domestic contractors** and **off-shore contractors** (i.e., those not located in the same country as the headquarters of the company or as the ultimate consumers of the fashion products). When using contract production, fashion brands must take into account costs and logistics of transporting materials and finished products, often across country borders, thus creating complex supply chain management decisions (see Figure 5.4). **Subcontractors** are hired by contractors to complete orders or perform specific tasks (e.g., embellishments, embroidery) needed to complete

Figure 5.3 Chanel owns and operates companies that provide the brand with embroidery and other services.

orders from fashion brand companies. The use of subcontractors further complicates a fashion brand company's supply chain.

Supply Chain Management Issues in the Fashion Industry

Within supply chains come risks for fashion brands—are suppliers/contractors in compliance with laws and codes of conduct around wages, hiring standards, workplace safety, and/or environmental requirements? Are they honest and ethical in their business activities and do they have high integrity? If contractors (and subcontractors) within a fashion brand company's supply chain are not legal, compliant, or ethical, the fashion brand company can be sued, fined, and/or publicly admonished resulting in legal sanctions, tarnished brand image, lost contracts, lost sales, stock price reduction (for

Figure 5.4 Most fashion brand companies utilize contract production factories.

corporations), and/or stakeholder withdrawal. In these cases, costly legal actions and public relations strategies may be necessary.

Risk Management

Fashion brand companies have the responsibility to ensure that their business activities are legal, are ethical, respect human rights, and promote stewardship of resources. To avoid or eliminate the risks associated with complex supply chains, fashion brand companies engage in **risk management** strategies, "the identification, analysis, assessment, control, and avoidance, minimization, or elimination of unacceptable risks" (Business Dictionary, 2017) associated with their business activities. One of the primary strategies for a fashion brand company's risk assessment and management is exercising supply chain **due diligence**, the "pro-active assessment of risks and investigation of incidences of abuse anywhere in the supply chain, remedying those situations and publicly reporting on how they are addressed" (ETI, 2017, p. 14). Through supply chain due diligence:

- Care is taken in creating and implementing policies, processes and procedures for sourcing decisions including codes of conduct (described later in this chapter).

- Actual and potential internal and external risks associated with one's supply chain are identified. These risks include illegal hiring of workers, employee and worker health and safety, worker compensation, product integrity, and environmental impact of business activities.

- Risk assessments are conducted and the company determines if risks can be avoided and/or eliminated.

- Any adverse impacts of business activities are mitigated and/or remedied.

One of the most basic forms of supply chain due diligence is around human rights. According to the United Nations Guiding Principles for Business and Human Rights (2011), businesses have the responsibility to "respect human rights" and exercise due diligence in assuring **human rights** are protected in their business activities. Human rights include (United Nations, 2017):

- civil and political rights (e.g., right to life, equality before the law)

- economic, social, and cultural rights (e.g., rights to work, social security, and education)

- collective rights (e.g., rights to development and self-determination)

Risk Management Issues

A number of risk management issues are part of the supply chain for fashion products. These include:

- Human trafficking and modern slavery
- Child labor
- Workplace standards, safety, and compensation
- Product integrity
- Environmental sustainability

Human Trafficking and Modern Slavery

Issues of **human trafficking** and **modern slavery** are prevalent in many industries, including the global fashion industry. According to a guide for businesses published by Anti-Slavery International and the Ethical Trade Initiative (ETI) (Skrivánková,

2017) "modern slavery is an umbrella term that includes forced labour, debt bondage, servitude and trafficking for the purposes of labour exploitation." The guide further defines the following terms.

- **Forced labor** is "any work or services which people are not doing voluntarily and which is exacted under a threat of some form of punishment, including the loss of rights or privileges."
- **Bonded labor** is "demanded as a means of repayment of a debt or a loan and can apply to a whole family and be inherited through generations."
- **Involuntary prison labor** is "prison labour that violates international labour standards. It includes situations where prisoners are required to work for the benefit of a private company or an individual" (Skrivánková, 2017).

When applied to the fashion industry, modern slavery can occur in any part of the supply chain and in any country and abuses have been found worldwide in all segments of production and distribution. For example, forced labor has been found in the cotton industries in Turkmenistan, Uzbekistan, Pakistan, India, and China (Responsible Sourcing Network, 2017). Human trafficking and forced labor are also found in the apparel manufacturing factories throughout the world, particularly in countries with high numbers of migrant workers. Risk of forced labor is also higher in industry segments and with companies that use subcontractors and when **recruitment fees** (fees paid by individuals to secure work) are paid.

Child Labor

According to the International Labour Organization (2017), **child labor** is "work that deprives children of their childhood, their potential and their dignity, and that is harmful to physical and mental development. It refers to work that is mentally, physically, socially or morally dangerous and harmful to children; and interferes with their schooling by: depriving them of the opportunity to attend school; obliging them to leave school prematurely; or requiring them to attempt to combine school attendance with

excessively long and heavy work." From a human rights perspective, a child is an individual under the age of 18 years (United Nations, 1989); although laws and standards around minimum age of employment vary across countries and across standards set by particular organizations and companies. For example, certification criteria of the Worldwide Responsible Accredited Production (WRAP) prohibits certified facilities from hiring employees under the age of 14 or under the legal minimum age of the country, whichever is greater or "any employee whose employment would interfere with compulsory schooling" (WRAP, 2017). Child labor is against the law in most countries and the United Nations Convention on the Rights of the Child (1989) stipulates that it is the right of the child is to be protected from child labor.

Despite legal mandates, child labor exists throughout the fashion industry supply chain. For example, child labor has been found in cotton seed production, in harvesting cotton, and in spinning mills. In the garment production industry, children have been put to work clipping threads, sewing on buttons, doing embroidery work, and folding and packing garments (SOMO, 2014). The cycle of poverty plays an important role in this issue. In many cases, children are forced to work to contribute to family's income. Because of their work, they may not be able to achieve the level of education needed for other jobs, thus, continuing the cycle of poverty. Lastly, factory audits as part of social compliance programs often miss child labor, workers may not have proof of age, have false documents or children may lie about their age.

Worker Compensation and Workplace Standards and Safety

The history of the ready-to-wear industry is full of examples of factories with contract labor who work long hours for low pay in poor and unhealthy and unsafe working conditions. Indeed, the term **sweatshop** became associated with factories in the apparel industry with such characteristics. Sweatshops within the fashion industry are a result of the proliferation of contractors and subcontractors, lack of oversight and factory inspections, and the desire for low-cost, low quality and quickly produced fashions. Risks occur when laws associated with workplace health and safety are not upheld, non-compliance with codes of conduct lead to lawsuits and/or negative publicity and media exposure.

Product Integrity

The safety and integrity of product quality can also pose risks for fashion brand companies. Consumer laws require that clothing meet certain safety standards, particularly in relation to children's clothing and protective clothing. For example, the U.S. Consumer Product Safety Commission (CPSC) set safety standards around design aspects of children's clothing that may pose a risk for choking (see Figure 5.5) and around the flammability for children's sleepwear to protect children from injuries if they come in contact with ignition sources such as a space heater. Consumers also hold fashion brands accountable for creating and producing quality merchandise that meet their expectations. Risks occur if faulty products do not meet standards or expectations, cause harm or dissatisfaction, and leave the fashion brand liable for any damages, product recalls, and/or negative publicity.

Figure 5.5 The U.S. CPSC recalled this children's pant set because the fabric at the end of the sleeves, hem, and pockets could be torn off and pose a choking hazard.

Environmental Sustainability

In many countries, fashion brand companies are, like all companies, required to meet country/regional standards associated with environmental sustainability including standards around air emissions, proper waste management (solid/hazardous waste and water discharge), and continuous improvement around environmental sustainability. Many companies have additional and/or higher environmental standards as part of their codes of conducts. Risks occur when standards are not met resulting in possible lawsuits, negative publicity, and/or stakeholder disengagement.

Reasons for the Existence of These Issues

Why do these supply chain issues exist? In general, modern slavery, child labor, worker exploitation, unsafe products, and environmental harm are caused

by unethical businesses wanting to drive higher profits by exploiting vulnerable populations of people (Skrivánková, 2017) and/or environmental resources. When people (including children) are in poverty, lack decent work, are in unsafe living conditions, are refugees or migrants, and/or whose rights are restricted or suppressed, they are at increased risk of modern slavery and exploitation. In many cases, these individuals are not aware of their labor rights and/or strategies for breaking away from abusive situations. In addition, contractors in the fashion industry may resort to modern slavery, worker exploitation, fraudulent products, and environmental harm because of pressures associated with expectations of fashion brands for very lost cost production with short lead times and fast turnaround often resulting in their use of subcontractors, homework, faster but possibly illegal business practices, and poor record-keeping. Varying laws and lack of accountability across legal systems among countries within a supply chain also contributes to abuses.

Supply Chain Assurance

Supply chain assurance is achieved through management systems designed to guarantee the integrity of suppliers that constitute the fashion brand company's supply chain and mitigate risks of modern slavery, faulty products, and worker and environmental resource exploitation. These systems, which are reflected in a fashion brand company's social compliance program, include legal assessments, risk assessments, supplier verification and auditing, and product testing and quality assurance. The ultimate goal of the systems is to create trustworthy products, healthy environments, and ethical, equitable, fair, and transparent conditions for all workers within the global fashion industry.

Three aspects of supply chain assurance are discussed in this section:

- Responsible sourcing
- Responsible production
- Responsible purchasing practices

Responsible distribution to the ultimate consumer is discussed in Chapter 6. Responsible sourcing, production, and purchasing practices are assured through the fashion brand company's social compliance program including codes of conduct, factory auditing and certification, and through their membership and/or commitment to industry-wide responsible sourcing organizations, certifications, and/or initiatives.

Responsible Sourcing

Responsible sourcing (or **ethical sourcing**) reflects sourcing decisions that result in socially, environmentally, economically, and culturally sustainable fashion products. Fashion brands that use responsible sourcing strategies create

and document a comprehensive set of policies and criteria for managing purchasing decisions throughout their supply chains that take into account environmental, social, cultural, and economic sustainability. Risks associated with sourcing decisions (e.g., in what country production may occur) are assessed by buyers, sourcing analysts, or production mangers within a fashion brand company and decisions made accordingly. As noted earlier, sourcing decisions are based on a number of factors. Responsible sourcing prioritizes social, environmental, economic, and cultural sustainability in these decisions. For example, based on their assessments, a fashion brand company may decide not to source production in a particular country because of the country's documented human rights violations, or may decide to source materials as close to production facilities to reduce the environmental impact of production, or may decide to simplify their supply chain, reducing the number of contractors and building longer term relationships with their contractors.

Responsible Production

Responsible production or (**ethical production**) reflects standards association with workers' rights, compensation, and workplace health and safety. Closely aligned with responsible sourcing decisions, risks associated with production are assessed and decisions about workers' rights, compensation, and workplace health and safety are made. Responsible production decisions prioritize the following:

- Employees' rights of free association and collective bargaining.
- Workplace is free of discrimination
- Workplace is free of physical, sexual, or psychological harassment or abuse
- Working hours per day and per week are legal and are not excessive
- Employment conditions (e.g., acquiring employment, length of employment) are legal and consensual
- Workplace is safe, clean, and healthy.

- Workplace is proactive in addressing health and safety issues.
- Adequate training is available to for employees to perform jobs to reduce risk of injury or accidents.
- **Personal protection equipment** (PPE), designed to protect the worker from injury or illness are provided. These include gloves, safety glasses, face masks, and helmets (see Figure 5.6).
- Compensation meets the legal minimum wage, overtime work is legally compensated, and other personnel benefits (e.g., health insurance) are assured.

Responsible Purchasing

Responsible purchasing or (**ethical purchasing**) reflects internal decisions that mitigate negative effects on employees throughout the fashion brand company's supply chain. Decisions that may have a negative effect on production factory workers (resulting in the employees of a production factory working excessive overtime and/or not

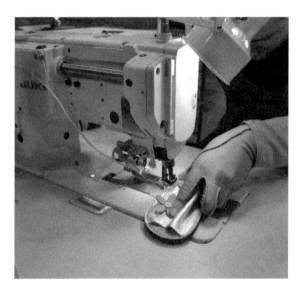

Figure 5.6 Personal protection equipment (PPE) includes hand protection for sewing operators.

fairly compensated or unethical/illegal workplace practices) include unethical negotiations, late orders, late changes in orders, late changes in style or design specifications, and late payments. Therefore, responsible purchasing practices assures that all decisions throughout the design, sales, and marketing of fashion products prioritize the health, safety, and compensation of workers throughout the supply chain.

Supply Chain Traceability and Transparency

Supply chain assurance are the management systems by which responsible sourcing, production, and purchasing are achieved. Providing evidence of these systems and their effectiveness, thus assuring governments, stakeholders, and consumers of a company's social, economic, and environmental sustainability, is achieved through supply chain traceability and transparency.

Supply Chain Traceability

Supply chain traceability is the ability of a fashion brand company to track and identify the entire supply chain for each product it distributes. The United Nations defines traceability as "the ability to trace and identify the history, distribution, location and application of products, parts and materials; to ensure the reliability of sustainability claims in the areas of human rights, labour (including health and safety), the environment and anti-corruption" (United Nations Global Compact Office, 2014). Traceability is imperative for both supply chain assurance and transparency—if a fashion brand cannot trace its sources of materials and production, then it cannot assure its legal and ethical compliance nor can it be transparent in communicating its supply chain or make claims about the sustainability of its products.

Effective traceability includes all tiers of suppliers—production factories, textile mills, and raw material providers. For example, fashion brand companies who are signatories to the Responsible Sourcing Network's commitment to not use Uzbek cotton in any of their products must be able to trace the source of the cotton used in their products. Fashion brands with relatively simple supply chains may have very strong knowledge of suppliers throughout their supply chain. Those with more complex supply chains often find tracing suppliers beyond tier-one suppliers difficult. For example, in a study of tracing child labor in cotton production found it was difficult to trace the cotton beyond the cotton farms because of the frequent use of agents (Russell, 2017). Therefore, fashion brands with large and complex supply chains often utilize industry-wide systems and certifications to assure traceability. Examples include:

Figure 5.7 The Global Organic Textile Standard assures traceability of the materials.

- Eileen Fisher sources fabrics made from Tencel® lyocell produced by Lenzing which has a Wood and Pulp Sourcing Policy assuring purchasers that the wood and pulp used in making Tencel® lyocell is from sustainable sources including wood certified by the Forest Stewardship Council®.

- Textile Exchange's Global Recycled Standard certifies products with recycled content assuring the traceability of the recycled materials in fashion products. The standard can be used in certifying any product that contains at least 20 percent recycled materials. "Each stage of production is required to be certified, beginning at the recycling stage and ending at the last seller in the final business-to-business transaction" (Textile Exchange, 2014, p. 6). Additional certifications for raw materials used for fashion products include Textile Exchange's Organic Content Standard, Recycled Claim Standard, Responsible Down Standard, and Responsible Wool Standard; and the Global Organic Textile Standard (GOTS) (see Figure 5.7).

- The Leather Working Group (LWG) promotes environmental sustainability by assessing the environmental compliance of leather manufacturers/tanners. The Leather Working Group Environmental Stewardship Protocol for auditing tanneries includes a Guidance Note for

Hide Traceability that helps leather manufacturers fully understand their supply chain. Through this protocol, member companies of LWG can assure purchasers of the traceability of the hides and skins (LWG, 2017).

Supply Chain Transparency

Supply chain transparency is achieved when information about suppliers within the supply chain are readily available and publicly shared. Transparency of supply chains is increasingly important for compliance with government regulations and pressures from stakeholders and consumers. Governments are requiring evidence that no human trafficking and modern slavery are found in a company's supply chain and stakeholders and consumers want evidence of authenticity of claims, want to know about the raw materials used in our fashion products, and want to know where and by whom fashion products are made.

International Standards and Legal Mandates for Transparency

A number of international standards and legal mandates around transparency of supply chains have been enacted in an effort to eradicate human trafficking and modern slavery throughout supply chains. Through these standards and mandates, companies (particularly large multinational corporations) are being held accountable for legal and ethical business practices throughout their supply chain.

These include:

- Several ILO conventions are associated with preventing human trafficking and forced labor. These date back to 1930 with the C29 Forced Labour Convention and continue to the 2014 Protocol to the Forced Labour Convention, which updated and expanded on previous conventions. The signatories to the conventions agree to prohibit the use forced labor.

- The United Nations Global Compact provides both a "policy platform and a practical framework for companies that are committed to sustainability and responsible business practices" including *A Guide to Traceability: A Practical Approach to Advance Sustainability in Global Supply Chains* (UN Global Compact, 2014).

- The California Transparency in Supply Chains Act of 2010 (implemented January 1, 2012) by the state of California, USA, requires "retail sellers and manufacturers doing business in the state [with annual worldwide gross receipts that exceed US$100,000,000] to disclose their efforts to eradicate slavery and human trafficking from their direct supply chains for tangible goods offered for sale" (Becerra, 2018).

- European Union Non-Financial Reporting Directive of 2014 are the rules for European Union member countries for disclosure of non-financial and diversity information by large companies (more than 500 employees). Companies must publish reports on their business policies and due diligence processes around respect for human rights, anti-corruption and bribery, environmental protection, social responsibility and treatment of employees, and diversity on company boards (European Commission, 2017).

- UK Modern Slavery Act 2015 requires "businesses, or part of businesses, with annual global turnover of £36 million or more to publish a statement confirming the steps they have taken to ensure that modern slavery and human trafficking are not taking place in their supply chain or to confirm that no steps have been taken to confirm the existence of slavery or human trafficking" (UK Legislation, 2017).

- 2017 French Corporate Duty of Vigilance law is a binding legal mandate that requires large French companies (with at least 5,000 employees) to identify and address any adverse impacts of their business activities on human rights or the environment. This includes impacts resulting from their own activities, those of companies they control, and those of subcontractors and suppliers with whom they have an established commercial relationship. Companies failing to comply can be fined (Lopez, 2017).

Company Reporting for Supply Chain Transparency

Fashion brand companies use a number of strategies to communicate information about their supply chains including mandatory reports and reports/public disclosures of their suppliers, producers, and prices. Depending on their size and complexity of their supply chains, fashion brand companies may engage in several of these strategies or focus on specific aspects of their supply chain.

Mandatory Reporting

In compliance with legal mandates described above, fashion brands, particularly large companies, post their mandatory reports on their websites and as part of registries. For example, the California Transparency in Supply Chains Act of 2010 requires businesses to include on the business' website homepage, in a manner which is "easily understood and conspicuous" the extent to which the business verifies their suppliers, conducts audits, certifies materials, maintains internal standards for accountability, and provides employee training.

According to the Modern Slavery Act, the business must publish the statement in a "prominent" place on its website and the Modern Slavery Registry is a publicly available database of the statements. The Modern Slavery Registry includes statements from 125 companies in the Consumer Durables and Apparel Sector (Modern Slavery Registry, 2017). Statements provide evidence of how the company addresses the risk of human trafficking and modern slavery in their supply chain. Typical processes and procedures include country assessments, codes of conduct and third-party audits of suppliers, trainings, and support of international organizations that focus on human rights.

Figure 5.8 The individual who created the Tonlé product signs the item's hangtag and label.

Supplier Transparency

Many fashion brand companies provide information about the location of their tier one suppliers—addresses of their contract factories often with images and/or videos of the factories. In some cases, fashion brands also provide information about their tier two and tier three suppliers. Large international fashion brand companies with complex supply chains such as Nike, C&A, Marks and Spencer, and H&M use interactive maps, updated on a periodic basis, to disclose their suppliers. For example, Dutch fashion retailer, C&A's sustainability report includes an interactive global map that lists names and addresses of all 788 global suppliers who run over 2,000 tier one suppliers (cut and sew factories) and tier two suppliers (embroiders, launderers, printers), and a number of tier three suppliers (fabric mills, spinning mills, dye houses) in 40 countries (C&A, 2017).

Worker/Producer Transparency— Who Made Your Clothes?

Fashion brand companies put a face to fashion and connect with consumers through information about specific individuals who were involved with their production processes. Photographs, videos, and interviews with workers throughout their supply chain allow consumers to "get to know" the people who produced the merchandise. For example, Tonlé, using factories in Cambodia, includes the names of individuals who created the product on the item's hangtag/label (see Figure 5.8). Images of these individuals can be found on their website. Products made by Krochet Kids intl., headquartered in California, USA, are also hand-signed by the individuals who created them. Profiles of these individuals are on the company's website where you can send a message to thank the person.

Fashion Revolution, a social enterprise headquartered in the UK, sponsors Fashion Revolution Week that includes the #whomademyclothes campaign. During this week, consumers are empowered to ask fashion brands "who made my clothes?" and fashion are encouraged to respond with greater worker/producer transparency. Many brands post images of their workers with the sign "I made your clothes." In addition, Fashion Revolution's website includes images, diaries, and videos of garment workers throughout the world (Fashion Revolution, 2017).

Price Transparency

One of the newest forms of transparency is price transparency whereby fashion brand companies publish a breakdown of the actual costs of producing and distributing products (Stevenson, 2017). For example, San Francisco, California, USA-based Everlane includes price transparency as part of their Radical Transparency philosophy (see Company Highlight at the end of this chapter). For example, the price breakdown for an Everlane Twill Weekender bag made in Dongguan, China, that retails for US$115 is: Materials: $18.31, Hardware: $7.55, Labor: $10.74, Duties: $2.81, and Transportation: $4.85. Similarly, USA-based accessory brand Oliver Cabell includes a price breakdown for each of their products (Oliver Cabell, 2017). For example, the price breakdown for an Oliver Cabell Kennedy Weekender bag that retails for US$285 is Canvas: $16.02, Leather: $11.58, Lining: $5.68, Webbing: $0.78, Nylon: $2.61, Reinforcement: $4.35, Zipper: $4.27, Hardware: $3.70, Cutting/Manufacturing/Quality Control: $48.12, Transit: $5.84, Duties: $7.40, Packaging: $7.24, and Shipping: $9.89. Honest By, headquartered in Antwerp, Belgium, markets themselves as "the world's first 100% transparent company." For each product available through their online store, detailed information is provided about the material (e.g., fiber content, certification, spinner location, knitter location, supplier, printing ink, sewing thread, woven brand label, security seal), garment and components manufacturing, and price calculation (Honest By, 2017).

Social Compliance Programs

A **social compliance program** "is a continuing process in which the involved parties keep on looking for better ways to protect the health, safety, and fundamental rights of their employees, and to protect and enhance the community and environment in which they operate" (Business Dictionary, 2017).

Social compliance programs include systems to assure that companies' supply chains are legal and ethical to ensure social, economic, environmental, and cultural sustainability. Specifically, social compliance programs of fashion brand companies include:

- sourcing guidelines
- codes of conduct
- processes for auditing and regular inspection of contractors' (and subcontractors') facilities
- membership in and/or engagement with industry-wide efforts
- strategies for public disclosure of these efforts
- identification of areas of improvement
- strategies for continuous improvement.

For example, Patagonia's Social and Environmental Responsibility Program includes a number of strategies "to ensure that Patagonia products are produced under safe, fair, legal and humane working conditions throughout the supply chain" (Patagonia, 2017) including:

- Strategies that promote and sustain fair labor practices such as a Supplier Workplace Code of Conduct, pre-screening process for factories, Responsible Purchasing Practices Program, multi-stakeholder initiatives such as Fair Trade Certified™ products, and supply chain transparency (The Footprint Chronicles®).
- Strategies that build relationships with suppliers of high quality technical materials that reduce environmental and social impact. This is accomplished by "evaluating performance [of suppliers] in four key areas: quality, traceability, environmental health and safety, and social responsibility."

Codes of Conduct

Organizational and company **codes of conduct** are written principles, policies, and rules as the minimum standards a company requires of its suppliers in relation to human resources, employee health and safety, and labor and environmental laws. Codes of conduct include:

- General principles or statements that describe the company's values, objectives, and commitments.
- Management philosophy statements that include the CEO or company leadership's personal philosophy and commitment to enforcing the code.
- Compliance statement or directives regarding mandatory and/or prohibited conduct. For example, a compliance statement may prohibit forced labor.

Companies either develop their own codes of conduct or abide by or adapt published organizational codes of conduct (examples are discussed later in this chapter). Effectiveness of codes of conduct depend on companies' commitment to communicating and enforcing the codes and providing educational and remediation as needed for supplier to meet the standards set in the code. Most codes of conduct reflect standards associated with responsible sourcing and production; some also reflect standards associated with responsible purchasing practices. As part of social compliance programs and efforts toward transparency, fashion brand companies post their codes of conduct on their websites. For example, Nike's website "Nike Aims to Transform Manufacturing" includes their code of conduct/compliance statements, general principles, industry-wide auditing protocols, future goals, and an interactive map of their suppliers (http://about.nike.com/pages/transform-manufacturing).

Factory Auditing

A fashion brand company's social compliance program also includes **factory auditing** (also called **factory monitoring**) and/or use of factories that have been certified by an outside organization. Historically, factory auditing began, in earnest, in the 1990s and have evolved over the years. They were instituted because:

- large fashion brand companies had moved away from vertical integration whereby they owned their own production factories or never owned their own factories,

- contract factories were more often than not located in developing countries with individuals from vulnerable populations as the primary workers
- poor working conditions of contract factories were made public resulting in negative publicity and lost sales for the fashion brands who were contracting with the factories.

Therefore, the goals of factory auditing and facility certification programs are to:

- evaluate the efficiency and capacity of the factory
- assure a voluntarily work environment and payment of any hiring brokerage or recruitment fees
- improve the health and safety of working conditions
- assure that workers do not work excessive hours and are compensated fairly and timely, including appropriate overtime pay
- ensure that workers have opportunities for freedom of association and collective bargaining
- verify compliance with appropriate labor laws and/or standards
- verify compliance with appropriate environmental laws and/or standards
- verify that product safety and quality assurance standards are being met
- ensure the security of the brand name and merchandise
- ensure that all subcontractor arrangements are in alignment with factory standards

A number of processes are used in conducting factory audits including observations during tours of the factory and subcontractors, analysis of human resource and financial documents, examination of products throughout the manufacturing process, interviews with management and workers, and review of government certifications and reports (see Figure 5.9). Determining the right factory that meets the needs, values, and standards of the fashion brand critical to the successful production of merchandise as well as the success of a fashion brand's social compliance program. Therefore, audits are first conducted as part of the vetting process for new contractors (Leffman, 2017). Once a contractor is in place, audits are conducted on a regular basis and if any problems arise. Building relationships with suppliers through the auditing process fosters a collaborative approach in achieving efficient and effective workplace—one that benefits both the supplier and fashion brand. This includes face-to-face meetings, open communications, and team building.

Depending on who conducts the audit, factory audits are categorized as first-party, second-party, or third-party audits.

- **First-party** or **internal audits** are conducted by employees of the factory or company that owns the factory. For example, a vertically integrated fashion brand company may have employees who audit the factories for which they own.

- **Second-party audits** are conducted by employees of the fashion brand company for contractors with whom they are vetting for possible contracts or with whom they already have a contract. For example, prior to signing a contract with a factory, sourcing analysts for the fashion brand company may conduct an audit of the factory.

- **Third-party audits** are conducted by individuals who work for a company or organization that is separate from either the fashion brand company or the contract factory. Organizations that conduct third-party audits in the fashion industry include Intertek, WRAP, and Verité. WRAP, for example, provides factory certification assuring fashion brands that the facility meets WRAP's 12 Principles (see Table 5.1).

Factory audits are also conducted by organizations for their members. For example, the Fair Labor Association and Worker Rights Consortium conduct audits for their member companies.

The effectiveness of factory audits is dependent on their alignment and consistency with sourcing philosophies, principles of sourcing, and codes of conduct; the quality and accuracy of the data collected; and how the results of the audit are used for continuous improvement for both the contract factory and fashion brand company. However, as factory auditing processes have evolved, fashion brand companies faced challenges with conducting authentic and effective factory auditing. Auditors were often met with resistance at both the factory and government levels as assessments were conducted, results analyzed, and factories were asked to make changes. Large fashion brand companies with complex supply chains had difficulty managing the processes across countries. In addition, the workers and management of contract factories were often overwhelmed by the number and frequency of audits by different fashion brand companies with different codes of conduct, resulting in a process referred to as **audit fatigue**. Even worse, when codes of conduct were not enforced through

Figure 5.9 Factory audits include observations made during tours of factories.

Table 5.1 Worldwide Responsible Accredited Production (WRAP) 12 Principles

WRAP Principle	Description
1. Compliance with Laws and Workplace Regulations	Facilities will comply with laws and regulations in all locations where they conduct business.
2. Prohibition of Forced Labor	Facilities will not use involuntary, forced or trafficked labor.
3. Prohibition of Child Labor	Facilities will not hire any employee under the age of 14 or under the minimum age established by law for employment, whichever is greater, or any employee whose employment would interfere with compulsory schooling.
4. Prohibition of Harassment or Abuse	Facilities will provide a work environment free of supervisory or co-worker harassment or abuse, and free of corporal punishment in any form.
5. Compensation and Benefits	Facilities will pay at least the minimum total compensation required by local law, including all mandated wages, allowances & benefits.
6. Hours of Work	Hours worked each day, and days worked each week, should not exceed the limitations of the country's law. Facilities will provide at least one day off in every seven-day period, except as required to meet urgent business needs.
7. Prohibition of Discrimination	Facilities will employ, pay, promote, and terminate workers on the basis of their ability to do the job, rather than on the basis of personal characteristics or beliefs.
8. Health and Safety	Facilities will provide a safe and healthy work environment. Where residential housing is provided for workers, facilities will provide safe and healthy housing.
9. Freedom of Association and Collective Bargaining	Facilities will recognize and respect the right of employees to exercise their lawful rights of free association and collective bargaining.
10. Environment	Facilities will comply with environmental rules, regulations and standards applicable to their operations, and will observe environmentally conscious practices in all locations where they operate.
11. Customs Compliance	Facilities will comply with applicable customs laws, and in particular, will establish and maintain programs to comply with customs laws regarding illegal transshipment of finished products.
12. Security	Facilities will maintain facility security procedures to guard against the introduction of non-manifested cargo into outbound shipments (i.e. drugs, explosives biohazards and/or other contraband).

Reference: WRAP (2017).

factory audits, workers became less willing to voice concerns. The integrity of audits was questioned by the fashion brand companies, consumers, and stakeholders. Fortunately, in recent years changes in auditing process have resulted in more collaborative and inclusive processes with a focus on continuous improvement, increased communications, and capabilities for mutual problem-solving. For example, Levi Strauss & Co implemented Worker Well-being programs within its contract factories. Funded by the

Levi Strauss Foundation, these programs focus on listening to and identifying high-impact programs within each factory that address the workers' most critical needs such as health or financial literacy. Both business and social objectives of the programs are measured and used in Levi's sourcing decisions (LS&Co, Unzipped Team, 2016, 2017).

Industrywide Initiatives, Organizations, and Certifications

Social compliance programs also include the fashion brand's commitment to industrywide initiatives; membership in organizations whose goals are to enhance responsible sourcing, production, and purchasing; use of suppliers who have been certified as meeting standards associated with social compliance; and/or public disclosure of these efforts. Public commitment to, membership in, and engagement with these initiatives and organizations offer fashion brand companies opportunities to leverage resources around research, advocacy, education, best practice strategies, and communications around supply chain assurance, traceability, and transparency. Below are a few examples (in alphabetical order) of these initiatives, organizations, and certifications.

Accord on Fire and Building Safety in Bangladesh and Alliance for Bangladesh Worker Safety. As a result of the collapse of the Rana Plaza building in Bangladesh and the death of over 1,100 people, two industry initiatives were created:

- The Accord on Fire and Building Safety in Bangladesh ("the Accord," primarily European brands, 2017). Signatory companies of the Accord (over 200 in total) include Adidas, Benneton, C&A, Carrefour, Esprit, Fast Retailing, G-Star, H&M, Hugo Boss AG, Inditex, Mango, Marks & Spencer, Primark, PVH, and Tesco. Work of the Accord will extend to 2021.

- Alliance for Bangladesh Worker Safety ("the Alliance," primarily US brands, 2017). Signatory companies of the Alliance include Carter's Inc., The Children's Place Retail Stores Inc., Fruit of

the Loom, Inc., Gap Inc., J.C. Penney Company Inc., L.L. Bean, Macy's, Nordstrom, Target, VF Corporation, and Wal-Mart Stores, Inc. Work of the Alliance will start transitioning out of Bangladesh in 2018.

Both are agreements among fashion brand companies to create safe and healthy working environments in Bangladesh including public listings of factories, inspections, corrective action plans, eliminating unauthorized subcontracting, worker empowerment, training programs, and commitments to fund necessary programs.

Better Buying Project. With a goal of enhancing responsible purchasing by fashion brand companies, Better Buying seeks to "to support industry-wide transformation of buyer purchasing practices so that business relationships support suppliers in providing decent workplace conditions" (Better Buying, 2017). To learn more about the Better Buying project, see Conversation with Marsha Dickson at the end of this chapter (see Figure 5.10).

Figure 5.10 Better Buying project focuses on responsible purchasing practices in the apparel industry.

Better Cotton Initiative. The Better Cotton Initiative (BCI) is a non-profit organization with member companies committed to enhancing the global cotton industry from environmental, social and economic perspectives (Better Cotton Initiative, 2017). The Better Cotton Standard System includes principles around production practices, worker training, continuing assessment, and communication. Members of BCI can communicate their involvement and use the Better Cotton logo. Members include

Levi Strauss & Co, Adidas, Inditex, H&M, Burberry, Ikea, Nike, Tommy Hilfiger, Marimekko, and VF.

Better Work. "As a partnership between the UN's International Labour Organization and the International Finance Corporation, a member of the World Bank Group, Better Work brings diverse groups together—governments, global brands, factory owners, and unions and workers—to improve working conditions in the garment industry and make the sector more competitive" (Better Work, 2017). Better work promotes compliance with international core labor standards and national labor laws by companies in the global fashion industry by assisting companies in assessments and workplace improvements, providing financial incentives, and disclosing serious non-compliance of labor laws and standards.

Partner companies include Asics, Gap Inc., H&M, Inditex, J.Crew, Levi Strauss & Co., Li & Fung, Marks & Spencer, Nike, Patagonia, Puma, PVH, REI Co-Op, Muji, and Target.

Ethical Trading Initiative. Headquartered in London, UK, the Ethical Trading Initiative (ETI) is an "alliance of companies, trade unions and NGOs that promotes respect for workers' rights around the globe. Our vision is a world where all workers are free from exploitation and discrimination, and enjoy conditions of freedom, security and equity" (ETI, 2017). Members include Burberry Group Plc, C&A, Gap Inc., Stella McCartney, Marks & Spencer, Melrose Textiles, H&M, and Inditex (Zara). Working in a number of industries, including the global fashion industry, ETI accomplishes this goal through activities including commitments from member companies to address issues within their supply chain (ETI Base Code), stakeholder working groups, providing funding for worker training, and to advocate for workers' rights in government policies.

Fair Labor Association. Headquartered in Washington, DC, USA (with regional offices in Geneva, Switzerland and Shanghai, China), the Fair Labor Association conducts and commissions research and implements projects associated with improving the lives of workers and conducts supply chain assessments for member companies. In addition, FLA accredits social compliance programs of companies. Companies who are members of FLA commit to FLA Principles of Fair Labor and Responsible Sourcing and Production in their owned and contract factories and to uphold the FLA Workplace Code of Conduct in their supply chain (FLA, 2017).

Fair Factories Clearinghouse. The Fair Factories Clearinghouse (FFC) is a non-profit organization that strives to improve factory working conditions and supply chain assurance and transparency by providing member companies, trade associations, and other industry initiatives with supply chain management tools, compliance and auditing tools, and access to factory profiles. Members of FCC can research factories, collaborate with other brands, share audit reports, and track workers' grievances and trainings (FFC, 2017).

Fair Trade Certifications. Fair trade focuses on partnerships among producers, brands, and retailers that support social, economic, and environmental sustainability. Fair trade certification assures consumers that the products they purchase have met standards set to achieve the goals of fair trade.

- FLOCERT is the independent third-party certifier for Fairtrade International. FLOCERT conducts audits of producers and trade throughout the world to determine if Fairtrade standards and price premiums are met. If so, the producer can market themselves using the international FAIRTRADE Marks (Fairtrade International, 2017, FLOCERT, 2017).

- Fair Trade USA is a third-party auditor and certifier of fair trade products in the United States. Auditors certify that transactions between U.S. companies and their international suppliers meet the standards set for prices/wages, working conditions, environmental sustainability, and economic development. They also provide educational tools for companies that want to utilize fair trade practices. Fashion brand partners of Fair Trade USA include Patagonia, prAna, Outerknown, BGreen, and Oliberte (Fair Trade USA, 2017).

- World Fair Trade Organization Guarantee System is an accountability and development tool for organizations. WTFO members that passed the GS self-assessment, monitoring audit, peer visit and Fair Trade Accountability Watch may use the WFTO label on their products (WFTO, 2017).

Fair Wear Foundation. Headquartered in Amsterdam, the Netherlands, the non-profit organization Fair Wear Foundation (FWF), "works with brands and industry influencers to improve working conditions where your clothing is made" (Fair Wear Foundation, 2017). FWF membership is open to any European garment company with a minimum annual turnover of €2.5 million and produces merchandise in one of the eleven production countries where they believe they can make the most impact (e.g., Bangladesh, China, India, Indonesia, Turkey, Vietnam). Member companies commit to the FWF Code of Labour Practices and FWF assists them in their improving workplaces and meeting this code, thus demonstrating their "due diligence under the UN Guiding Principles on Business and Human Rights" (Fair Wear Foundation, 2017; see Figure 5.11).

Figure 5.11 Fair Wear Foundation is one of several industry initiatives to improve working conditions within the global fashion industry.

Goodweave. With goals on eliminating child labor in the international carpet and rug industries and supporting children's rights, Goodweave is a certification program that partners with brands, importers/exporters, and retailers to assure consumers that child labor was not used in the carpet/rug supply chain (Goodweave, 2017). The GoodWeave label on products indicates that no child, forced, or bonded labor were used and that workplace standards were met through annual audits of facilities.

Intertek. Headquartered in London, UK, Intertek is a "Total Quality Assurance" provider offering auditing, product testing, and certification services worldwide. Intertek works with clients across their unique supply chains to provide supply chain assurance services to meet standards and certifications associated with product quality, health and safety, environment, and social compliance" (Intertek, 2017).

MADE-BY. Headquartered in Amsterdam, the Netherlands, Made-By is a non-profit organization that partners with fashion brands and retailers to "make sustainable fashion common practice" (Made-by, 2017). One of their offerings is MODE Tracker, a tool to support tracking and communicating sustainability performance and progress around topics including labor standards and human rights in the supply chain, manufacturing impacts, and supply chain transparency. Fashion brands (six, so far) publicly publish their results.

Responsible Sourcing Network. With a focus on the raw materials used for products, including clothing, the Responsible Sourcing Network "champions human rights with vulnerable communities" (e.g., "forced labor in the cotton fields of Uzbekistan") to "create positive change for brands, consumers, and the impacted communities" (Responsible Social Network, 2017). Over 270 brands and companies have signed a commitment to assure that forced and child labor are not used in their supply chain and specifically not to use Uzbek cotton in any of their products. RSN works with these fashion brands and retailers to fulfill that commitment. The YESS (Yarn Ethically and Sustainably Sourced) initiative of the RSN is an "industry-wide due diligence system for yarn spinning mills to identify and eliminate forced labor" (YESS/RSN, 2016).

Higg Index

Figure 5.12 The Higg Index includes self-assessment modules related to facility and workforce standards.

Sustainable Apparel Coalition. The Sustainable Apparel Coalition is an alliance of companies around sustainable production with a focus on building the Higg Index, a standardized supply chain measurement tool (see Figure 5.12). Through the use of the Higg Index, brands, retailers, and facilities can measure social and labor impacts (in addition to environmental impacts) and identify areas for improvement (SAC, 2017). The Social and Labor Module assesses facility workforce standards, external engagement on social-labor issues, and community engagement.

Worker Rights Consortium. With a focus on labor rights in the factories that produce university-licensed apparel products, the Worker Rights Consortium conducts independent audits and investigations, issues public reports of these investigations, and assists workers in the factories (WRC, 2017). As of 2017, 190 colleges and universities had affiliated with the WRC.

Worldwide Responsible Accredited Production (WRAP). WRAP is an independent factory-based social compliance certification and education organization for the sewn products industries. The over 2,400 certified WRAP factories worldwide received certification by complying with the WRAP 12 Principles as demonstrated through on-going factory audits. WRAP also conducts numerous trainings and educational programs including factory fire safety education (WRAP, 2017).

Hierarchy of Social Compliance Programs

As noted earlier, a company's social compliance program typically includes strategies such as implementation of a code of conduct or standards of compliance, auditing programs, and engagement with industry initiatives and/or organizations. A fashion brand company's social compliance program typically starts with a code of conduct and auditing program. However, a number of fashion brands are going "beyond auditing" in their social compliance programs towards the ideal situation of self-directed continuing improvement. The following hierarchy of social compliance programs describes the evolution of social compliance programs (see Figure 5.13).

- Code of Conduct and Supplier Auditing Checklist—at the basic level a buyer/brand has a code of conduct or standards of compliance and relies on first, second, or third party audits for risk management assessment associated with sourcing.

- Building a Relationship with the Supplier/Factory Management—at this next level, relationships are built between the buyer/brand and supplier/factory management. This partnership between the brand/buyer and supplier/factory results in increased communications and capabilities for mutual problem-solving. At this level, social compliance programs are considered to be more than a risk management assessment strategy for the buyer/brand.

- Capacity Building—at this next level, workers are brought into the process through increased worker education and worker-management communications. The buyer/brand becomes involved with the community and strives to improve conditions outside the walls of the factory. The use of mobile technologies for worker feedback may be incorporated.

- Self-Directed Continuing Improvement—at the highest level, suppliers/factories would engage in self-directed continuing improvement strategies to the point where audits would no longer be needed. In addition, 360-degree feedback processes would allow suppliers/factories to rate

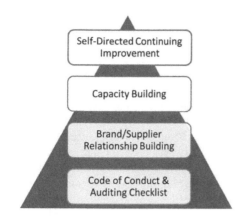

Figure 5.13 The evolution of social compliance programs.

and provide feedback on buyers/brands just as buyers/brands to rate and provide feedback on suppliers/factories.

In many cases, aspects of several levels are being implemented at once. Indeed, even at the highest level, a fashion brand company may not eliminate audits but utilize them for new factories and/or suppliers. To move "beyond auditing" requires accurate data from multiple sources, strong relationships with suppliers, and an understanding of suppliers beyond tier one (Russell, 2017).

Summary

A fashion brand company's supply chain includes the supply of materials to a manufacturer, the manufacturing process and the distribution of finished goods to the ultimate consumer. Throughout its supply or value chain, a company makes sourcing decisions around procuring materials, production systems, and distribution pipelines. These planning and management decisions reflect the company's supply chain management (SCM) strategies. Fashion brand companies use two general approaches to SCM to achieve effective and efficient management of their production and distribution processes: vertical integration and contracting. Fashion brands may be vertically integrated, in which the same company is engaged in more than one segment within the supply

chain. Very few fashion brands are fully integrated but many have aspects of vertical integration within their supply chain. The use of contractors and subcontractors for the manufacturing operations is typical in today's global fashion industry creating complex supply chains.

Within supply chains come risks for fashion brands including human trafficking and modern slavery, child labor, workplace safety, worker compensation, product integrity, and environmental sustainability. Fashion brand companies use risk management strategies to avoid or eliminate the risks within their supply chains. Through supply chain due diligence, fashion brand companies pro-actively assess risks, investigate any abuses, and publicly report their activities.

Supply chain assurance is achieved through management systems designed to guarantee the integrity of suppliers that constitute the fashion brand company's supply chain and mitigate risks of modern slavery, faulty products, and worker and environmental resource exploitation. Supply chain assurance is achieved through responsible sourcing, responsible production, and responsible purchasing practices. Supply chain traceability is the ability for a fashion brand company to track and identify sources of materials and production throughout the supply chain for each product it distributes. Supply chain transparency is achieved when information about suppliers within the supply chain are readily available and publicly shared. A number of international standards and legal mandates around transparency of supply chains have been enacted in an effort to eradicate human trafficking and modern slavery throughout supply chains. Supply chain transparency reporting by companies includes mandatory reporting, supplier transparency, worker/producer transparency, and price transparency.

Responsible sourcing, production, and purchasing practices are assured and communicated through the fashion brand company's social compliance program. Social compliance programs include codes of conduct, factory auditing programs, commitment to and/or membership in industry-wide social compliance initiatives and organizations, and reporting/disclosure strategies. As social compliance programs evolve, fashion brands strive towards self-directed continuous improvement strategies.

Key Terms

audit fatigue	responsible sourcing
bonded labor	risk management
child labor	second party audits
codes of conduct	social compliance
contractor	program
domestic contractor	sourcing decisions
due diligence	specialty store retailers
ethical production	of private label apparel
ethical purchasing	(SPA)
ethical sourcing	subcontractor
factory auditing	supply chain
factory monitoring	supply chain assurance
first party audits	supply chain
forced labor	management
full-package contractor	supply chain traceability
human rights	supply chain
internal audits	transparency
involuntary prison labor	sweatshop
off-shore contractor	third-party audits
personal protection	tier one suppliers
equipment	tier three suppliers
private label brands	tier two suppliers
recruitment fees	value chain
responsible production	vertical integration
responsible purchasing	

References and Resources

Accord (2017). "Accord on Fire and Building Safety in Bangladesh. About the Accord." Retrieved on August 3, 201,7 from http://bangladeshaccord.org/about/.

Becerra, Xanier (2018). The California Transparency in Supply Chains Act. Retrieved on June 25, 2018, from https://oag.ca.gov/SB657.

Better Buying (2017). *About Us.* Retrieved on August 10, 2017, from http://www.betterbuying.org/Home/about-us.

Better Work (2017). *Better Work.* Retrieved on August 3, 2017, from https://betterwork.org/.

Business Dictionary (2017). Risk Assessment, Definition. Retrieved on July 25, 2017, from http://www.businessdictionary.com/definition/risk-assessment.html.

Business Dictionary (2017). Risk Management, Definition. Retrieved on July 30, 2017, from http://www.businessdictionary.com/definition/risk-management.html.

Business Dictionary (2017). Social Compliance, Definition. Retrieved on July 11, 2017, from http://www.businessdictionary.com/definition/social-compliance.html.

C&A (2017). *C&A Supplier List/Map.* Retrieved on August 11, 2017, from http://sustainability.c-and-a.com/supplier-map/.

Canadian Supply Chain Sector Council (2017). Supply Chain, Definitions. Retrieved on July 18, 2017, from http://www.supplychaincanada.org/en/supply-chain.

Council of Supply Chain Management Professionals (2017). Supply Chain Management Definitions and Glossary. Retrieved on July 18, 2017, from http://cscmp.org/CSCMP/Educate/SCM_Definitions_and_Glossary_of_Terms/CSCMP/Educate/SCM_Definitions_and_Glossary_of_Terms.aspx?hkey=60879588-f65f-4ab5-8c4b-6878815ef921.

Creytex (2017). *Who We Are.* Retrieved on July 25, 2017, from http://www.cicreytex.com.co/index.php?option=com_content&view=article&id=86&Itemid=592&lang=en.

Ethical Trading Initiative—ETI (2017). *About ETI.* Retrieved on August 2, 2017, from http://www.ethicaltrade.org/about-eti.

European Commission (2017). "Non-Financial Reporting." Retrieved on August 7, 2017, from https://ec.europa.eu/info/business-economy-euro/company-reporting-and-auditing/company-reporting/non-financial-reporting_en.

Everlane (2017). *About.* Retrieved on August 10, 2017, from https://www.everlane.com/about.

Fair Factories Clearinghouse (2017). "What Do We Offer?" Retrieved on August 10, 2017, from http://www.fairfactories.org/Home/Solutions-Overview.

Fair Labor Association (2017). "Principles of Fair Labor and Responsible Sourcing and Production." http://www.fairlabor.org/our-work/principles.

Fair Trade USA (2017). *Who We Are.* Retrieved on August 4, 2017, from http://fairtradeusa.org/about-fair-trade-usa/who-we-are.

Fair Wear Foundation (2017). About. Retrieved on June 25, 2018, from https://www.fairwear.org/about/#.

Fairtrade International (2017). *About Fairtrade.* Retrieved on August 4, 2017, from https://www.fairtrade.net/about-fairtrade.html.

Fashion Revolution (2017). *About.* Retrieved on August 11, 2017, from http://fashionrevolution.org/.

Fashion Revolution CIC (2017). "Fashion Transparency Index 2017." Downloaded on June 23, 2017, from https://www.fashionrevolution.org/about/transparency/.

Goodweave (2017). *About.* Retrieved on August 11, 2017, from https://goodweave.org/about/our-vision/.

Honest By (2017). *About.* Retrieved on October 12, 2017, from http://www.honestby.com/.

Human Rights Watch (2017, April 20). "Follow the Thread: The Need for Supply Chain Transparency in the Garment and Footwear Industry." Retrieved on August 7, 2017, from https://www.hrw.org/report/2017/04/20/follow-thread/need-supply-chain-transparency-garment-and-footwear-industry.

International Labour Organization (2017). "What Is Child Labour?" Retrieved on July 28, 2017, from http://www.ilo.org/ipec/facts/lang—en/index.htm.

International Labour Organization (2017). "What Is Forced Labour, Modern Slavery and Human Trafficking?" http://www.ilo.org/global/topics/forced-labour/definition/lang—en/index.htm.

Intertek (2017). *About Us*. Retrieved on August 5, 2017, from http://www.intertek.com/about/.

Kansara, Vikram Alexei (2016, March 21). "Michael Preysman on Iterating Everlane and 'Fixing' Fashion Retail." Retrieved on August 10, 2017, from https://www.businessoffashion.com/articles/founder-stories/michael-preysman-on-iterating-everlane-and-fixing-fashion-retail.

KnowTheChain (2016). "Apparel & Footwear Benchmark Findings Report." *San Francisco: KnowTheChain*. Retrieved on August 2, 2017, from https://knowthechain.org/wp-content/plugins/ktc-benchmark/app/public/images/benchmark_reports/KTC_A&F_ExternalReport_Final.pdf.

Leffman, Liz (2017, July 11). "Top Tips for Choosing and Evaluating Your Suppliers." Retrieved on July 18, 2017, from https://www.just-style.com/analysis/top-tips-for-choosing-and-evaluating-your-suppliers_id131112.aspx?utm_source=daily-html&utm_medium=email&utm_campaign=11-07-2017&utm_term=id98214&utm_content=109033.

Leather Working Group—LWG (2017). *Who We Are*. Retrieved on August 7, 2017, from https://www.leatherworkinggroup.com/who-we-are.

Levi Strauss & Co. Unzipped Team (2016, June 22). "Defining Well-Being for Apparel Workers Globally." Retrieved on August 29, 2017, from http://www.levistrauss.com/unzipped-blog/2016/06/defining-wellness-for-apparel-workers-globally/.

Levi Strauss & Co. Unzipped Team (2017, January 30). "Investing in the Health of Factory Workers." Retrieved on August 29, 2017, from http://www.levistrauss.com/unzipped-blog/2017/01/investing-health-factory-workers/.

Lopez, Edwin (2017, March 2). "France Passes Law Requiring Supply Chain Due Diligence." *Supply Chain Dive*. Retrieved on August 11, 2017, from http://www.supplychaindive.com/news/France-supply-chain-human-rights-reporting-audits/437191/.

MADE-BY (2017). "MODE Tracker." Retrieved on August 10, 2017, from http://www.made-by.org/modetracker/.

Marks and Spencer Global Sourcing Principles (2018, March). Retrieved on June 25, 2018 from https://corporate.marksandspencer.com/documents/plan-a-our-approach/global-sourcing-principles.pdf.

Marks and Spencer (2017). "Responsible Sourcing." Retrieved on July 18, 2017, from https://corporate.marksandspencer.com/plan-a/our-approach/business-wide/responsible-sourcing.

Modern Slavery Registry (2017). "Consumer Durables and Apparel." Retrieved on August 11, 2017, from http://www.modernslaveryregistry.org/.

Nike, Inc. (2017). "Nike Aims to Transform Manufacturing." Retrieved on July 31, 2017, from http://about.nike.com/pages/transform-manufacturing.

Nimbalker, Gershon, Mawson, Jasmin, Lee, Hsu-Ann, & Cremen, Claire (2017, April 19). "The 2017 Ethical Fashion Report: The Truth Behind the Barcode." *Baptist World Aid and Tearfund New Zealand*. Retrieved on August 7, 2017, from https://www.tearfund.org.nz/getmedia/135135c5-9701-4245-964b-e50864170bff/EthicalFashionReport_2017.pdf.aspx.

Oliver Cabell (2017). "Kennedy Weekender." Retrieved on August 11, 2017, from https://olivercabell.com/products/heathrow-weekender?variant=7662480517.

Patagonia (2017). "The Footprint Chronicles." Retrieved on July 28, 2017, from http://www.patagonia.com/footprint.html.

Project JUST (2017, March 8). "Deconstructing Radical Transparency: An Interview with Michael Preysman, Founder and CEO, Everlane." Retrieved on August 10, 2017, from https://projectjust.com/specialfeature_everlane-interview/.

Responsible Sourcing Network—RSN (2017). *About*. Retrieved on August 4, 2017, from https://www.sourcingnetwork.org/about/.

Responsible Sourcing Network (2017). "Cotton Program Overview." Retrieved on August 11, 2017, from http://www.sourcingnetwork.org/cotton/.

Russell, Michelle (2017, June 8). "Supply Chain Mapping Key to Tackling Child Labour." *Just-style.com*. Retrieved on August 7, 2017, from https://www.just-style.com/news/supply-chain-mapping-key-to-tackling-child-labour_id130892.aspx?utm_source=daily-html&utm_medium=email&utm_campaign=08-06-2017&utm_term=id97774&utm_content=109033.

Russell, Michelle (2017, July 12). "Are Supply Chains Ready to Go "Beyond" Audits?" *Just-style.com*. Retrieved on August 4, 2017, from https://www.just-style.com/news/are-supply-chains-ready-to-go-beyond-audits_id131142.aspx?utm_source=daily-html&utm_medium=email&utm_campaign=12-07-2017&utm_term=id98232&utm_content=109033.

Skrivánková, Klára (2017, July). "Base Code Guidance: Modern Slavery." *Anti-Slavery International and Ethical Trade Initiative*. London: Ethical Trade Initiative.

SOMO (2014, March). "Fact Sheet: Child Labour in the Textile and Garment Industry." *Centre for Research on Multinational Corporations, Amsterdam, the Netherlands*. https://www.somo.nl/wp-content/uploads/2014/03/Fact-Sheet-child-labour-Focus-on-the-role-of-buying-companies.pdf.

Stevenson, Iman (2017, June 7). "How Much Did That Zipper Cost? With Transparency Pricing You Know Everything." *The New York Times*. Retrieved on July 12, 2017, from https://www.nytimes.com/2017/06/07/business/smallbusiness/transparency-pricing-retail-clothing.html?smid=fb-share&_r=0.

Sustainable Apparel Coalition (2017). "The Higg Index." Retrieved on August 10, 2017, from http://apparelcoalition.org/the-higg-index/.

Textile Exchange (2014). "Global Recycled Standard 4.0." Retrieved on August 5, 2017, from http://textileexchange.org/wp-content/uploads/2017/06/Global-Recycled-Standard-v4.0.pdf.

The Fashion Law (2017, April 15). "Chanel and Co. Are Snapping Up Suppliers to Solidify Their Supply Chains." *The Fashion Law*. Retrieved on July 28, 2017, from http://www.thefashionlaw.com/home/chanel-acquires-yet-another-tannery-in-aim-to-control-supply-chain.

UK Legislation (2017). "Modern Slavery Act of 2015." Retrieved on August 11, 2017, from http://www.legislation.gov.uk/ukpga/2015/30/part/6/enacted.

United Nations (2011). "Guiding Principles on Business and Human Rights." New York and Geneva: United Nations Human Rights Office of the High Commissioner. Retrieved on August 1, 2017, from http://www.ohchr.org/Documents/Publications/GuidingPrinciplesBusinessHR_EN.pdf.

United Nations (2017). "What Are Human Rights?" United Nations Human Rights Office of the High Commissioner. Retrieved on August 1, 2017, from http://www.ohchr.org/EN/Issues/Pages/WhatareHumanRights.aspx.

United Nations (1989). "Convention on the Rights of the Child." United Nations Human Rights Office of the High Commissioner. Retrieved on August 1, 2017, from http://www.ohchr.org/EN/ProfessionalInterest/Pages/CRC.aspx.

United Nations Global Compact Office (2014). "A Guide to Traceability: A Practical Approach to Advance Sustainability in Global Supply Chains." Retrieved on August 5, 2017, from https://www.unglobalcompact.org/docs/issues_doc/supply_chain/Traceability/Guide_to_Traceability.pdf.

Worker Rights Consortium—WRC (2017). *Mission*. Retrieved on August 4, 2017, from http://www.workersrights.org/about/.

World Fair Trade Organization (WFTO) (2017). "Standard and Guarantee System." Retrieved on October 12, 2017, from http://wfto.com/standard-and-guarantee-system/guarantee-system.

WRAP (2017). "Worldwide Responsible Accredited Production. WRAP's 12 Principles." Retrieved on August 1, 2017, from http://www.wrapcompliance.org/en/12-principles.

YESS/RSN (2016, August 31). "Overview YESS: Yarn Ethically and Sustainably Sourced." *Responsible Sourcing Network*. Retrieved on August 4, 2017, from http://www.sourcingnetwork.org/yess/.

Case Study: Picture Organic Clothing: Supply Chain Assurance and Transparency

French company, Picture Organic Clothing (Picture), offers lines of men's, women's, and children's active and technical sportswear for snowboarding, skiing, surfing, skateboarding, and other outdoor activities. The company was launched in 2008 by three friends, Julien Durant, Jeremy Rochette, and Vincent Andre, who envisioned a new type of technical product—one that was environmentally sustainable, high quality, and competitively priced. They first started selling merchandise in France and Switzerland and then expanded distribution to other European countries, Russia, and eventually to North America.

The company's success is based on three principles (Picture Organic, 2017):

- A product conception that is eco-friendly.
- Unique creations that you notice easily thanks to fresh and colorful designs and are appreciated for their technical innovation and quality.
- Street prices that are monitored, so that our products are a possible alternative to products that are non-eco-friendly thanks to aligned prices.

To achieve their environmentally sustainable products, Picture focuses on sourcing materials with global certifications including the Global Organic Textile Standard (GOTS), OEKO-TEX® 100 certified materials, Bluesign® approved fabrics, and the Taiwan Green Mark. Their efforts have paid off—their designs have been recognized with several ISPO Awards (honoring sports product innovations) including ISPO Award Gold for their 100 percent recyclable Welcome Jacket composed of recycled polyester (2013) and their Iceland Proknit Jacket (2017). In 2013, they also earned the "Environmental Excellence" of the year award by ISPO.

Picture would like to expand their corporate social responsibility efforts to include supply chain assurance and transparency initiatives. Specifically, they want to assure key stakeholders that their tier one and tier two suppliers meet social compliance standards. Key initiatives around these efforts need to be researched, adopted, and implemented. As a social compliance consultant, you have been asked to develop a plan of action and goals for Picture around supply chain assurance and transparency.

Questions

1. Who is the target customer for Picture Organic Clothing?

2. What is Picture's sourcing philosophy and how is this philosophy achieved?

3. What four initiatives to assure that their supply chain meets social compliance standards might Picture implement? Describe each initiative with metrics for measuring success. Which two of these four initiatives do you believe Picture should implement first? Why?

4. What four initiatives around supply chain transparency might Picture implement? Describe each initiative with metrics for measuring success. Which two of these four initiatives do you believe Picture should implement first? Why?

5. Once these initiatives are implemented, do you believe Picture should market themselves as a socially conscious brand in addition to being an environmentally conscious brand? Why or why not?

References

Picture Organic Clothing (2017). *About Picture*. Retrieved on July 29, 2017, from http://www.picture-organic-clothing.com/about-picture/.

Transworld Business (2013, November 13). "Catching Up With: Picture Organic Clothing on Launching in the U.S. Transworld Business." Retrieved on July 29, 2017, from http://www.grindtv.com/transworld-business/features/picture-organic-clothing/.

Note: The background for this case study is based on publicly available information. The business problem is speculative only and not based on publicly available and/or documented information from Picture Organic Clothing.

Call to Action Activity: Consumer Perceptions of Supply Chain Transparency

Is the transparency of a fashion brand important to consumers? To answer this research question, develop and implement a marketing research protocol (e.g., focus group protocol, online survey, observational strategy) to determine consumers' perceptions of transparency initiatives/efforts of a fashion brand appropriate to the consumers being studied (i.e., the sample should be the target customers of the fashion brand selected).

1. Select a fashion brand for which you have access to its target customer.

2. Research the fashion brand regarding its level of transparency around policies, governance, traceability, supply chain assurance, and collaborations (see the Fashion Transparency Index for additional information on these areas).

3. Develop and implement a marketing research protocol that provides information to answer the research question "Is the transparency of this fashion brand important to consumers who are the target customer for the brand?" This protocol might be a focus group, online survey, observational study, or interviews?

4. Using this protocol, collect data from at least 10 individuals. Analyze the data collected.

5. Write a report that includes an introduction, research question, description of the method used to answer this question, summary and analysis of the results, conclusions that can be drawn, limitations of the study, and next steps for further research.

Better Buying: Conversation with Marsha Dickson

Marsha Dickson, Ph.D., Irma Ayers Professor of Human Services
Department of Fashion and Apparel Studies, University of Delaware
Better Buying
Founders, Marsha Dickson and Doug Cahn
Technical Support from Fair Factories Clearinghouse
Funded by the C&A Foundation and Humanity United

Resource: http://www.betterbuying.org/

Q: Before discussing Better Buying, a question about your background. How did you become interested in corporate social responsibility in the apparel industry?
A: After graduating from college, I was employed as a clothing designer. When I went back to graduate school at Iowa State University I thought I would be a professor of clothing design focusing on studio design work. However, during graduate school I became interested in consumer behavior and the global fashion industry. I was in Mexico on an international study tour with Mary Littrell (a professor at Iowa State University). We were in the backyard of a woman's house where she was creating beautiful weaving using a backstrap loom. The house had dirt floors and chickens and children were playing in the dirt. It struck me—how could someone be making something so beautiful while living in poverty? This experience changed my thinking about clothing design and the global fashion industry. I knew I wanted to focus on initiatives that would help people. I first focused on consumer behavior and fairtrade initiatives. In the early 1990s, conditions in apparel factories were in the news and consumers were recognizing the impact that companies have on workers. The emphasis of my research at the time was on consumers. If we could understand why consumers purchase socially responsible apparel then we could possibly shift consumption patterns. However, I learned that even the most socially conscious consumers who care about these issues do not necessarily act on that care (although there have been changes in consumer behavior, particularly in Europe). Therefore, I shifted my emphasis to working on industry initiatives—affecting those who are directly making the company decisions about design and production in the apparel industry.

Q: What do you see as the important issues surrounding corporate social responsibility in the apparel industry?
A: Our current business model does not work for people. Because of pressure from investors, many fashion brands and retailers focus on short term profits. In addition, consumers continue to want something new on a continual basis and as cheap as possible. Therefore, suppliers are pressured to produce unreasonably fast, sometimes at a financial loss, to meet the demands of the fashion brands and retailers (buyers). The day-to-day decisions and actions of staff responsible for buying, planning, design, development and other functions are root causes contributing to the inability of suppliers to comply with codes of conduct and laws. At the brand/retail level, individual buyers are paralyzed by data and are making decisions based on minutia in the data. Their ability to have that level of data creates a reliance on it and they are fearful that they will make a mistake. Product development professionals are afraid to make decisions and, in fact, they may not have the expertise to make decisions around how their work impacts suppliers. The irony is that there is a high correlation between good working conditions and financial sustainability. So, the question remains—how do we change how the full industry works?

Q: You have recently launched Better Buying. How did this project come about?
A: Better Buying focuses on buyer (fashion brand or retail company) purchasing practices. Several aspects of my work came together in launching Better Buying. I became involved with the Fair Labor Association (FLA) serving on their Board of Directors for 14 years. In 2003

the FLA was contacted by Oxfam, a "global movement of people working together to end the injustice of poverty" (Oxfam, 2017) who was working on a new purchasing project. When I became aware of this project, I realized this was the missing link. I pushed the FLA to include purchasing practices as part of its Principles of Fair Labor and Responsible Sourcing in addition to Principles of Fair Labor and Responsible Production. At the same time, I was working on creating a new graduate program at the University of Delaware with a focus corporate social responsibility within the full supply chain. We know that decisions that affect factory workers happen throughout the supply chain and throughout the organization. However, when we would ask companies about what design and merchandising students needed to know, companies would say—"not much"—we have our division of corporate social responsibility to handle that. Therefore, it was important for the graduate program to empower designers and merchandisers throughout the organization to focus on corporate social responsibility. I also worked with the Sustainable Apparel Coalition in the development of measures of purchasing practices in the Higg Index.

My work with apparel companies revealed that purchasing practices are key but that basic business practices related to purchasing were inefficient and responsible sourcing and purchasing initiatives were lacking. My colleague, Doug Cahn, and I approached the C&A Foundation about conducting research to create and implement a rating system whereby suppliers (e.g., factories) would anonymously rate buyers (e.g., fashion brand companies) on the purchasing practices of the fashion brand companies. We believed that with credible data fashion brand companies could make better decisions around purchasing practices. However, reforming purchasing practices is a sensitive topic for apparel companies that are successfully developing and sourcing products—these activities, after all, result in their primary source of revenue. However, the persistence of wage violations, excessive hours of work, unauthorized subcontracting, and precarious work in apparel supply chains demand that brands and retailers understand their impacts and take action where necessary.

Q: According to the Better Buying website, a goal of the initiative is to create a means by which suppliers could provide input to buyers' regarding their buying processes (i.e., purchasing practices) that may result in non-compliance with the buyers' code of conduct. Why is this goal needed in today's apparel industry? That is, why aren't buyers already asking suppliers for this input?

A: Some fashion brand companies do get feedback from their suppliers. For example, some fashion brand companies have "supplier summits"—a time when they ask their suppliers to tell them what they are doing wrong and how they might improve. However, factory management is not necessarily going to reveal problems or complain about a fashion brand company in front of other suppliers as they worry about consequences. In other cases, suppliers inform a fashion brand company about problems or issues related to purchasing practices through the fashion brand company's CSR person. However, this may not be the right person to initiate changes and the information may not be shared with the actual purchasing agents. Power structure and lack of trust is evident in these relationships. Suppliers often feel they are at the mercy of the buyer for fast cheap production—which can prevent supplier compliance with the codes of conduct of fashion brand companies and can put at risk the lives and dignity of factory workers.

Q: A pilot test of the Better Buying rating system was recently conducted? What were the preliminary findings?

A: A total of 51 ratings from 30 different suppliers from eight countries were used for the pilot test. Suppliers were located in Bangladesh, Brazil, China, Hong Kong, South Korea, Sri Lanka, the United States, and Vietnam. Suppliers rated buyers according to seven categories of buyers' purchasing practices:

- Planning and forecasting
- Design and development
- Cost and cost negotiation
- Sourcing and order placement
- Production management
- Payment and terms
- Management of purchasing practices

Although there were a range of scores for buyers in each category, results of the pilot test revealed that buyers received the highest average score was in the area of Payment and Terms and the lowest average score was in the area of Sourcing and Order Placement. As more data are collected, we will be providing the public, summaries of specific buying companies' scores and buyers with detailed analyses of their own ratings relative to an emerging industry benchmark. Based on data we provide to buyers about their "score" from suppliers they will then need to figure out how to solve the issue. In addition, in partnership with other initiatives pursuing improved purchasing practices, we intend to ignite a "race to the top" where buyers that are improving their purchasing practices are highlighted. On the flip side, suppliers will be able to compare their experience in the seven categories with other suppliers in their region and globally. As buyer-specific data become available, they will be able to use it to evaluate their existing customer base and make decisions about which customers they should continue to work with.

Company Highlight

Everlane: Radical Transparency

Everlane, founded by Michael Preysman, and headquartered in San Francisco, CA, USA, is "a mission-driven designer brand that's relevant to the entrepreneurial-spirited person who wants to make the world a better place and is looking for a place to specifically go and buy good quality and well-fitted designer basics."

Everlane calls their approach towards supply chain assurance and transparency *Radical Transparency* which encompasses three aspects (Everlane, 2017):

- Know Your Factories
- Know Your Costs
- Always Ask Why

Know Your Factories

Everlane is committed to finding the best factories around the world. They visit them often and build strong personal relationships with the owners. According to Project JUST, Everlane shares stories and photographs of their tier one and some of their tier two suppliers. In an interview with Natalie Grillon, Project JUST Co-Founder (Project JUST, 2017), Preysman noted:

> We have five buckets: labor, wages and hours, health and safety management

systems, and environment. What we've done, which is a bit different, is we looked at it and thought about it from fully unannounced, semi-unannounced and completely unannounced visits. Fully unannounced, although that's ideal, is very disruptive for factories. To go to them and say, hey we're here today, let's do everything—it's disruptive. So, we give them a two-week period on that level, where we come in for an annual audit. And then on top of that, we do a completely unannounced half-day audit, and that half-day audit looks at mostly environmental and labor issues: is there anything going on that we wouldn't like to see? So, we get a total of four audits per facility a year, and then on top of that the production team visits three times a year, per factory.

Know Your Costs

Everlane believes customers have the right to know what their products cost to make. Therefore, the true cost, including markup, of each product is available on the company's website (Everlane, 2017). For example, a men's 100 percent cotton Reverse French Terry shirt made in Ho Chi Minh City, Vietnam, by Nobland Vietnam Co., Ltd. (image of factory) with a retail price of $45 has the following costs: materials: $10.20, hardware: $.44, labor: $5.60, duties/tariffs: $2.38, transportation: $.75, and Everlane markup to cover their expenses: $25.

Always Ask Why

According to Preysman, "Everlane really started with this idea that if you had a blank slate, how would you do it? Our blank slate was 'Why don't we create that t-shirt at an affordable price point?' Well, if we want to do that, we can't have an entire selection, we really need to focus on a t-shirt and do that well" (Kansara, 2016). With this general philosophy, Everlane is known for constantly challenging the status quo—analyzing "every single decision we make at every level of the company" (Everlane, 2017).

Sustainable Business Logistics and Retailing

Objectives

- Describe the goals and implementation strategies fashion brand companies use to achieve sustainable business logistics.
- Describe the strategies fashion brand companies use to enhance the environmental sustainability of their packaging.
- Describe the strategies fashion brand companies implement to enhance the environmental sustainability of their operations.
- Describe the business strategies of sustainable fashion retailers to promote environmental, social, economic, and cultural sustainability.

A socially responsible fashion brand company creates jackets with organic cotton and recycled polyester using zero waste design techniques to produce high-quality, long-lasting garments. The company values supply chain assurance and transparency utilizing codes of conduct and engagement with their production facilities and providing public information about where and by whom their products are made. In addition, the company offers numerous well-being programs for their employees and factory workers. Consumers who purchase fashion products from this company do so because the company promotes environmental, social, and economic sustainability. But, think about the logistics system necessary to get the products to these consumers. The organic cotton is grown in India, the recycled polyester is manufactured in Japan, the zippers used in the jackets are manufactured in Vietnam. All of these component parts are shipped to the production facilities in China. Before shipping, each garment is placed in a plastic bag and then into cardboard boxes that are put into larger cartons for shipping. Cartons of finished goods are then shipped to the United States where they are transported to a distribution center, unpackaged, have labels attached, sorted, and trucked to retail outlets throughout the county. The ultimate consumer in the United States drives to the fashion retailer to purchase the product. Or if the consumer ordered the product over the internet, the merchandise is trucked to the consumer's home from the distribution center. Packaging and moving the components and finished products around the world takes away from the environmental sustainability of the products. Is it possible for this socially responsible company to extend its philosophy throughout its production, distribution, and sale to the ultimate consumer? The answer is "yes"!

This chapter examines the sustainability of business logistics, packaging, operations, and retail distribution strategies for fashion merchandise. These aspects of the business of fashion brand companies are often overlooked but are critical to the overarching sustainability goals of fashion brand companies. The chapter begins with an overview of business logistics and the importance of accuracy of their sales forecasting, minimizing amount and distance of transporting components and finished goods, and using environmentally sustainable modes of transportation. The chapter then describes strategies fashion brand companies use to enhance the environmental sustainability of packaging. The chapter ends with an overview of sustainable fashion retailing, business strategies of fashion retailers that promote environmental, social, economic, and cultural sustainability to improve the health and well-being of customers, employees, and communities.

Business Logistics

All fashion brand companies handle business logistics associated with the creation, production, distribution, and retailing of their fashion products. For small fashion brand companies, these processes may be relatively simple and streamlined; for larger companies, these processes may be complex and global in nature. Regardless of size of company, effective and efficient business logistics are imperative for the sustained profitability of the company. **Business logistics** involves the coordination of forecasting need; purchasing materials, trims, and findings; and moving materials, semi-finished and finished products from the product's inception and distribution to the ultimate consumer. The terms **distribution** or **physical distribution** refer to the "outbound flow of goods from the end of the production process to the consumer" (Encyclopedia of Business, 2017).

When applied to the fashion industry, the overarching goal of business logistic systems is directly aligned with goals of the company's merchandising strategies; that is, getting the right product, at the right price, at the right time, to the right consumer. Business logistics starts with the customer (retailer or ultimate consumer) placing an order. The product is then either produced or shipped from existing inventory to the customer. As products are sold, raw materials are acquired from suppliers and made available to production factories. Products are sewn/manufactured to fill demand and/or replenish inventories. The system used by the fashion brand company determines how and when the customer receives the product. For example, some fashion brand companies ship to retail clients or ultimate consumers directly from production factories. Others move finished goods to a distribution center for sorting and distribution to customers.

Fashion brand companies have always focused on the cost and efficiency of business logistics systems. Now, many fashion brand companies are taking a more comprehensive examination of the design, development, and implementation of their systems from environmental and social sustainability perspectives. In doing so, fashion brand companies examine the accuracy of their sales forecasting, minimize the amount and distance of transporting components and finished goods, and use environmentally sustainable modes of transportation.

Figure 6.1 Inaccurate sales forecasting can result in merchandise being sold at discount prices and increases in pre-consumer textile waste.

Accurate Sales Forecasting

Sustainable business logistics for fashion brand companies relies on accurate sales forecasting. **Sales forecasting** is an ongoing process companies use for estimating future sales. Sales forecasts are based on sales from previous sales forecast periods (monthly, quarterly, annually) and on an understanding of and any future changes in marketing, products, customers, and/or business environment (e.g., economy, industry trends). Fashion brand companies strive to have the most accurate sales data possible as inaccurate forecasting of consumer demand for products can result in a number of issues related to both environmental and social sustainability. Inaccurate forecasting can result in overproduction of merchandise and surplus of inventory necessitating products to be sold at discount prices and/or disposed/sold as textile waste (see Figure 6.1). Inaccurate forecasting can also lead to last minute changes in product specifications resulting in factories requiring workers to extend their working hours, often without additional pay.

Minimal Transportation

Transportation is an important aspect of fashion brand companies' business logistics. Global supply chains for fashion products involve shipping and transporting materials, trims and findings, semi-finished products, and finished products. Components for fashion goods are often produced in multiple countries. Materials management systems assure that the materials and components needed to produce the finished goods arrive at the production facility in alignment with the production schedule. Transporting materials, components, and finished goods adds to both costs and environmental impact of the fashion products. Therefore, fashion brand companies strive to minimize the amount and distance components and finished goods must travel.

Through their business logistics systems, transport distances are analyzed and sourcing decisions are made to minimize transportation requirements. For example, a fashion brand company may source materials as close to production facilities as possible and source production facilities as close to distribution centers as possible. A fashion brand company may also source production as close to the ultimate consumer as possible to minimize shipping requirements.

Environmentally Sustainable Modes of Transportation

Fashion brand companies also strive to use the most environmentally sustainable modes of transportation for the distance and type of material and/or product they are moving. As part of their sourcing decisions, fashion brand companies assess transportation companies or carriers and modes of transportation to achieve effective, efficient, and environmentally sustainable processes. Across modes of transportation, carrier options for fashion brand companies include

- Private carrier in which the fashion brand company owns the transportation methods. Because of the investments required, in the fashion industry private carriers are typically trucks owned by large companies who maintain their own distribution centers.

- Contract carrier that is hired by a fashion brand company to supply shipping services. Contract carriers often customize services to meet the specific needs of the company.

- Common carrier whose services are offered to the general public or on a for-hire basis.

In the fashion industry, the modes of transportation most commonly used include ocean or sea freight, air freight, rail, and truck (see Table 6.1). Each transportation mode has advantages and disadvantages depending on the needs and priorities of the company and the products it produces (Carnarius, 2017; Roos, 2012). Optimal decisions depend on type of merchandise, source of merchandise, destination, and time requirements for delivery. Ocean, sea, and air freight are most common for shipping long distances across large bodies of water; rail and trucking are most common for shipping across land. In rare cases are inland barges used to move fashion merchandise on rivers. In 2004, the United State Environmental Protection Agency (EPA) launched the SmartWay program that "helps companies identify and select more efficient freight carriers, transport modes, equipment, and operational strategies to improve supply chain sustainability and lower costs from goods movement" (EPA, 2017). Currently, 3,500 companies partner with the EPA through the SmartWay to "measure, benchmark, and improve their logistics operations so that they can reduce their environmental footprint" (EPA, 2017).

Ocean or Sea Freight

Ocean or sea freight is the most common mode of transportation for global trade with broad coverage around the world. Compared to air freight, container ships used for ocean of sea freight emit lower amount of polluting gases. That said, large container ships require a large amount of fuel and can cause ocean pollution. New technologies that allow for the use of wind and solar energy for part of the power needs or the use of liquefied natural gas improve the environmental sustainability of ocean or sea freight. However, ocean or sea freight is relatively slow mode of transportation. For example, moving goods between Asia and the European Union can take anywhere from twenty-three to forty-three days (Center for Climate and Energy Solutions, 2010).

Air Freight

Air freight is a reliable and speedy mode of transportation, moving finished goods from Asia to the European Union in one to ten days (Center for Climate and Energy Solutions, 2010). Therefore, air freight is often used by fashion brand companies who demand speed for inventory replenishment. Air freight is also relatively expensive along with weight and size limitations for cargo. As mentioned earlier, air freight emits more polluting gases than does ocean or sea freight.

Rail Freight

Trains are more fuel-efficient mode of transportation for shipping goods across land. Moving goods from Asia to the European Union by train takes anywhere from fourteen to nineteen days (Center for Climate and Energy Solutions, 2010). New technologies such as trains that tailor horsepower needs to terrain and cargo and hybrid electric-diesel trains resulting in more environmentally sustainable mode of transportation. However, rail transportation is often limited and trucks are typically needed to move goods from trains to final destinations.

Trucks

Trucks are commonly used to get finished products to distribution centers and retail outlets as quickly as possible. In some cases, trucks are the only viable mode of transporting merchandise and allow for flexible service and deliveries at a moderate cost (see Figure 6.2). Trucks rely on highway/road systems and speed can be affected by any problems with weather or road conditions. In addition, most freight trucks run on conventional diesel fuel resulting in greenhouse gas emissions. Technologies that allow for the use of biodiesel or blend of diesel and biodiesel create a more environmentally sustainable freight truck. Many large pick-up and delivery services, including FedEx, UPS and United States Postal Service (USPS), have programs that focus

Figure 6.2 Trucks are the best mode of transportation for flexible services and deliveries.

on enhancing environmental sustainability of their trucking services. In addition, pick-up services are recommended as these companies optimize fuel efficiency in their service routes.

Intermodal transportation or **multimodal transportation** refers to using different modes of transportation for different needs within the supply chain. For example, a fashion brand company may transport finished products from their factories in

Table 6.1 Modes of Transportation Used by Fashion Brand Companies

Mode of Transportation	Distance less than 400 kilometers (approximately 250 miles)	Distance more than 400 kilometers (approximately 250 miles)	Large loads	Speed	Cross-border	Overseas
Ocean or Sea		X	X		X	X
Air		X		X	X	X
Rail		X	X		X	
Truck	X			X	X	
Intermodal		X	X	X	X	X

Adapted from Carnarius (2017).

southeast Asia to the United States by ship and use trucks to get finished products from distribution center to retail outlets or ultimate consumer, thus taking advantage of the environmental advantage of ocean freight along with the flexibility of trucks.

Packaging

Packaging is the "wrapping material around a consumer item that serves to contain, identify, describe, protect, display, promote and otherwise make the product marketable and keep it clean" (Entrepreneur, 2017). Packaging used by fashion brand companies includes labels, polybags, cardboard boxes, packing materials (such as paper or airbags), and cartons (see Figure 6.3). Finished goods of fashion brand companies are typically packaged for shipping and to create **floor-ready merchandise** (merchandise with all hangtags, labels, and pricing information affixed so that the merchandise can be directly moved to retail selling floor or shipped directly to the ultimate consumer) by the factory and/or by the distribution center. When deciding on the appropriate packaging materials, fashion brand companies take into consideration a number of factors (Entrepreneur, 2017):

- Labeling requirements
- Brand identity
- Product information
- Needed protection of the product in shipping and distribution processes
- Weight and size of the materials
- Cost of packaging materials
- Ease of unpackaging processes
- Ease of product display
- Environmental sustainability of the materials

Fashion brand companies use a number of strategies to enhance the sustainability of their packaging, rethinking what is absolutely necessary to protect the products and communicate brand identity (Jarvi, 2015; Pullen, 2012). These strategies focus on reducing the amount of packaging, changing the type

Figure 6.3 Fashion brand packaging serves a number of functions including brand identity and product protection.

of packaging used, recycling packaging materials, and considering environmental sustainability throughout the life cycle of packaging (including product returns). Unfortunately, most fashion brands do not publicly describe their packaging strategies. One exception is the zero waste fashion brand, Tonlé, which describes their strategies on their website (Tonlé, 2017):

> Packaging might not seem like a big deal, but wasteful packaging is a huge contributor to our environmental problems. By contrast, we ship all of our products in bags made from 100% recycled materials, and our hang tags are made with recycled cardboard that is hand printed with our logo. For wholesale, we do not pack our products in individual plastic bags unless requested, preferring to group sizes and colors together in our signature recycled packaging materials. In our workshop, we even make tote bags made from recycled

materials when we do market shopping trips, and store our fabric in re-usable totes made from rice sacks. All of this enables us to minimize the waste that we are creating and distributing at the tonlé workshops.

Labels

Fashion brand companies use a variety of labels for brand identity, product information, care instructions, sizing information, security and brand protection, and required information about the product's country of origin, fiber content, and manufacturer. Labels used by fashion brand companies include those printed onto the products themselves, printed material labels sewn into the product, and printed hangtags. Fashion brand companies use a number of strategies to enhance the environmental sustainability of their labels, including using scrap materials, using recycled materials, and printing labels using thermal printers that do not need ink. Using less ink in printed labels is also recommended. In fact, brands can often reinterpret their logos to use less ink when printing (Wilson, 2017). Small fashion brand companies also use labels to convey and reinforce brand values to the consumer, thus enhancing their narrative around environmental and social sustainability (see Figure 6.4).

Product Protection

In the fashion industry, polyethylene bags or **poly bags** are used extensively to protect products from dirt, dust, and moisture during processing, shipping, and distribution. If products are dirty or damaged while processed or shipped, then they are typically disposed of by the fashion brand company. In fact, in a study of processing and shipping systems conducted by Patagonia (2014), 30 percent of garments that went through their system without poly bags were damaged or had physical signs of dirt, thus making them unsellable. In addition, use of paper mailers in their processing and shipping systems was not found to be satisfactory. Fashion brand prAna (2017) found that over 75 percent of their products could be safely

Figure 6.4 Labels on Indigenous brand merchandise reflect their commitment to social and environmental sustainability.

shipped without poly bags; thus from 2011 through 2016 they eliminated over 10.6 million poly bags used in shipping. When using poly bags, recommendations are to (Cohen, 2014)

- Source and use recycled poly bags.
- Reduce the size of poly bags needed to protect the finished goods through the processing and shipping systems thus possibly requiring new folding and packaging guidelines.
- Recycle poly bags at the distribution center and retail outlets; and provide education and encourage consumers to recycle poly bags if the products are delivered to them with this protective packaging.

Shipping Container Materials

Shipping containers used by fashion brand companies include the variety of large strong boxes used in freight

Figure 6.5 Using recycled corrugated cardboard for appropriately sized boxes enhances the environmental sustainability of shipping containers.

handling and shipping. In many cases the containers are reusable, such as the large metal intermodal containers in standardized sizes to be used across modes of transportation. For shipping cartons, boxes, and envelopes recommendations include using materials that are recycled, from sustainably managed forests certified by Forestry Stewardship Council, and/or certified by Cradle to Cradle. Corrugated cardboard is one of the most recycled materials and is a popular choice for many companies for cartons and boxes (see Figure 6.5). Large delivery services, including UPS, FedEx, and USPS, use recycled materials in their shipping boxes. A number of other companies offer recycled boxes, envelopes, and mailers including Treecycle, Ecobox, and Globe Guard.

Shipping Container and Packaging Size and Volume

Using the appropriate size of shipping containers and packaging can also affect their environmental sustainability. Using a one-box-size-fits-all often results in increased waste, shipping weight, and costs. Recommendations include reducing the size and volume of packaging and shipping containers, thus using fewer materials and reducing shipping weight and volume.

Packaging Filler

When shipping products, **packaging filler** is used to fill the "void" between the product package and shipping container to protect the merchandise during shipping. In the past, non-recyclable expanded polystyrene foam (Styrofoam™) peanuts were a favorite packaging filler. However, in recent years, more environmentally sustainable materials are being used including biodegradable fillers such as starch-based packing peanuts, recycled and/or recyclable materials, and inflatables that reduce shipping weight and are made with recycled plastics. For example, Ecovative's Mushroom® packaging is grown from mycelium, the root structure of mushrooms. The customizable packaging material is not made from petroleum and is compostable, contributing to its environmental sustainability features.

Return Plan

Increases in online sales have resulted in increases in packaging and shipping of returned merchandise. Thus, a **return plan** that takes environmental sustainability into consideration is recommended. Fashion brand companies typically require consumers to return defective or unwanted products either to a retail outlet or through a delivery service (e.g., mail, UPS). However, if the product is relatively low cost, fashion brand companies may consider sending a new product (e.g., new size, non-defective) to the consumer without requiring that they send the old one back. This eliminates the pollution caused by return shipping. If the fashion brand does accept the merchandise back, repairing it so as not to waste the materials is recommended. For example, The Renewal Workshop partners with several fashion brand companies, including Indigenous, prAna, and Mountain Khakis, to repair returned merchandise to be sold as "renewed apparel" (see Figure 6.6).

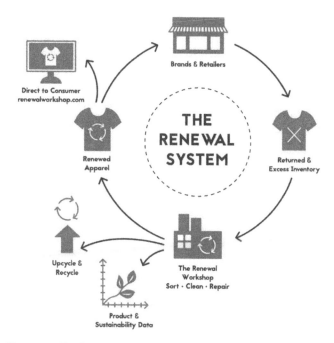

Figure 6.6 The Renewal Workshop repairs returned merchandise as part of the return plan of their fashion brand partners.

Sustainable Operations of Fashion Brand Companies

Operations of fashion brand companies are the strategies, activities, and management systems required for a fashion brand company to operate on a day-to-day basis including human resource management, inventory management, facility and store design and maintenance, and merchandising strategies (e.g., buying, pricing, display). Operations of fashion brand companies includes these activities at any of the facilities in which they own and operate including

- Design and marketing headquarters
- Manufacturing facilities
- Distribution centers
- Fashion retailing operations (brick and mortar stores and/or non-store operations)
- Any other facility owned and operated by the fashion brand company

Sustainable operations involve taking into account economic, environmental, social, and cultural sustainability in all aspects of the company's operations. Economic sustainability of fashion brand companies has always been a priority when determining effective and efficient operational systems. However, more fashion brand companies are incorporating environmental, social, and cultural sustainability into the operations of the company. Social and cultural sustainability strategies are incorporated into many operational systems of fashion brand companies. Many of these were discussed in Chapter 2.

Fashion brand companies also incorporate environmental sustainability into their operations using a number of strategies including creating environmentally sustainable building and store designs, reusing and recycling resources used in company operations, and creating incentives for employees and customers to be more environmentally sustainable.

One of the most common ways for fashion brand companies to enhance their environmental sustainability is by designing, maintaining, and refurbishing buildings, facilities, and retail stores. A few examples include

- Use of environmentally sustainable building materials such as timber certified by the Forest Stewardship Council, reclaimed bricks, and recycled aggregate
- Use of heat pump technology
- Use of renewable energy such as solar and wind
- Use of LED and natural lighting
- Harvesting rainwater to use for flush toilets and irrigation systems
- Low maintenance landscaping with native plants

The Leadership in Energy and Environmental Design (LEED) certification developed by the U.S. Green Building Council assesses six areas in building design and awards certifications (basic, silver, gold, and platinum) based on these assessments:

- Sustainable plots
- Water efficiency
- Energy and atmosphere
- Materials and resources
- Environmental quality of the interior
- Innovation in processes and technology

In addition, fashion brand companies have enhanced the environmental sustainability of their operations through reusing and recycling resources. Examples include

- Reusing and recycling boxes and other shipping materials
- Recycling poly bags and other product packaging (see explanation above)
- Reusing and repurposing hangers and retail fixtures

Providing incentives to employees to reduce energy use and waste are important strategies for fashion brand companies. For example, employees may be educated and incentivized to turn off machinery and lights when not in use and recycle and reuse office supplies. Employees can also be provided with incentives to carpool, ride a bike, or take public transportation to and from their place of employments. For example, Patagonia's "Drive-Less Program" pays U.S. and Canadian employees $2 per trip when they do not drive alone to work. "As a collective result, in that first year we drove 690,000 fewer miles, cut CO_2 emissions by 500,000 pounds and saved 25,700 gallons of fuel" (Patagonia, 2017).

Similarly, customers can be incentivized to reduce energy and waste through programs and consumer education. For example, online consumers may be educated and encouraged to reuse and recycle shipping materials. Brick-and-mortar stores can provide recycling and reuse opportunities for product packaging and shopping bags, electric car charging points in the parking lots, and access to public transportation. Many fashion brand companies (e.g., Eileen Fisher, The North Face, Levi Strauss & Co., H&M, Uniqlo, Columbia Sportswear) offer a "take back" or recycling programs—incentivizing customers to bring used clothing to their stores and in some cases receiving a voucher for discounts in future purchases for doing so. Examples of these take back and recycling programs include the following.

- Eileen Fisher Renew Program (https://www.eileenfisherrenew.com/): Customers who bring worn or damaged Eileen Fisher clothing to any Eileen Fisher or Renew retail store receive a $5 Rewards Card for each item. The clothes are renewed and sold online and through their Renew retail outlets. A portion of the profits for Reworn clothes will go to programs that support positive change for women, girls, and the environment.
- Columbia Sportswear ReThreads Program (http://www.columbia.com/en_en/productsd-view/About-Us_Giving-Back_Rethreads.html): Dry and clean clothing, shoes, or other textiles (any brand) can be dropped off at any U.S. Columbia Sportswear retail locations. Columbia Sportwear has partnered with the Switzerland-based company, I:CO, who sorts the clothes for a variety of purposes including resale, shredding, and recycled yarns.

- Levi Strauss & Co (http://www.levistrauss.com/ sustainability/planet/#recycling-reuse): Clean and dry clothing and shoes (of any brand) can be dropped off at any U.S. Levi's store. As with other fashion brand companies, I:CO handles the reuse/ recycle/upcycle sorting processes. Or customers can download a free shipping Goodwill label, fill a box with any brand of clean, dry clothing or shoes, affix the label and ship to Goodwill.

- UNIQLO: All Product Recycling Initiative (http:// www.uniqlo.com/en/csr/refugees/recycle/): UNIQLO clothing is collected from customers at UNIQLO stores. The collected clothing is either distributed to those in need in over fifty countries or recycled for industrial reuse. UNIQLO currently partners with local agencies and nonprofit organizations for distribution and recycling efforts (see Figure 6.7).

Sustainable Fashion Retailers

The term **fashion retailing** refers to the process of selling fashion merchandise to ultimate consumers. **Sustainable fashion retailing** reflects business strategies of fashion retailers that promote environmental, social, economic, and cultural sustainability to improve the health and well-being of customers, employees, and communities. Sustainable fashion retailing includes two overarching areas:

- Environmental and social sustainability of the retail operations of fashion brand companies (as described earlier)

- Retailers of fashion brands who promote social, environmental, economic, and cultural sustainability through the products they sell

Socially responsible fashion retailers often combine the two areas; that is, they sell sustainable merchandise through retail outlets whose operations are also sustainable. Sustainable fashion retailers can be classified according to whether they sell new merchandise or previously owned merchandise (Burns, Mullet, & Bryant, 2016). In both cases, retailers may offer merchandise through brick-and-mortar stores and/or through a variety

Figure 6.7 Uniqlo's All Product Recycling Program is an example of a fashion brand company's "take-back" program.

of non-store retail outlets, the most common being online stores.

Sustainable Retailers of New Fashion Products

Sustainable fashion retailers may sell new merchandise that is produced using materials, production techniques, and distribution strategies that promote environmental, social, economic, and cultural sustainability. Such retailers include department stores and specialty stores who sell specific products, lines, and/or collections of socially responsible fashion brands. These retailers may be large multi-unit and omnichannel international companies, small single unit brick-and-mortar retailers, or retailers that are exclusively online. Most of the fashion brand companies used as examples throughout this book have online retail outlets. In some cases they offer their merchandise through their own brick-and-mortar stores also (e.g., Patagonia, Eileen Fisher) as specialty retailers of private label apparel (SPA). Other examples of sustainable retailers who sell new merchandise include

- UK-based Marks and Spencer department stores offer private label merchandise that meet strict standards around environmental and social sustainability.

- Headquartered in Akron, Pennsylvania, USA, Ten Thousand Villages, a nonprofit social enterprise, offers only fair trade merchandise in their stores across the United States and Canada.

- Sassafras, in Seattle, Washington, retails lines and collections of socially responsible independent designers in the northwest United States (see Figure 6.8 and Conversation with Amy Tipton at the end of this chapter).

- Many small fashion brands with primarily an online presence may offer merchandise through pop-up brick-and-mortar stores. For example,

Figure 6.8 Specialty store, Sassafras, retails socially responsible fashion collections.

Ramblers Way, headquartered in Kennebunk, Maine, USA, participated in a pop-up store of organic cotton and wool products in New York City (see Figure 6.9).

Sustainable Retailers of Previously Owned Fashion Products

Sustainable retailers also sell fashion products that were previously owned, although the merchandise may not have actually been worn and/or used. Selling merchandise a second time is referred to as **resale**. The goals of **fashion resale** are to

- Extend the life of the fashion product through multiple owners
- Keep waste textiles out of landfills
- Employ individuals in resale stores who may have limited opportunities

One of the key aspects of business plans for fashion resale retailers is acquiring the merchandise. Fashion resale retailers acquire the merchandise using one or more of the following:

- Re-commerce
- Consignment
- Charitable donations
- Upcycling

Re-commerce

Re-commerce is a general term used to describe the process of merchants buying used (pre-owned) merchandise from consumers and then reselling, recycling, or reusing the merchandise. Interestingly, re-commerce of fashion merchandise is common for a variety of fashion merchandise, functional apparel, and accessories—from low end to high end. At the low end is merchandise that was donated to charity and/or thrift store and cannot be sold to consumers and therefore sold to waste textile companies by the pound who then recycle or reuse the merchandise. For example, headquartered in Seattle, Washington, USA, Buffalo Export LLC purchases waste textiles by the pound from charitable organizations and thrift stores and sells mixed rags as well as used

Figure 6.9 Pop-up stores, such as this Ramblers Way pop-up in New York City, increase consumer awareness of the brand.

clothing throughout the world. At the high end of re-commerce are luxury brands that are purchased for resale to other consumers. Although some consumers choose to sell used luxury brands directly online (e.g., through online auction sites such as Ebay), purchasers cannot necessarily be guaranteed the authenticity of the merchandise. Thus, re-commerce retailers will purchase the luxury brands, guaranteeing their authenticity, and reselling them. For example, WatchUWant.com sells pre-owned luxury watches (Adams, 2014). In between are a variety of used specialty products that are purchased or acquired through donations that are then sold. For example, resale retailers may sell pre-owned medical scrubs, maternity wear, performance and sports apparel, and well-known brands.

Consignment

In the **consignment** process used by some resale fashion retailers, the seller of the used fashion merchandise (consignor) contracts with a consignment retailer (consignee) to sell the fashion products for them. The consignor does not get paid for the fashion goods until they are sold in the consignment shop. After the goods are sold, the consignee will then take a percentage of what the consignor's item sold for as their fee. Consignment shops are common for a variety of fashion merchandise, particularly well-known and luxury brands, expensive tailored or classic apparel, evening wear, and merchandise that has not been worn or only worn a few times (see Figure 6.10). Consignment shops often combine re-commerce and consignment processes for acquiring merchandise. For example, a retailer of **vintage clothing and accessories** (clothing and/ or accessories that are at least twenty years old) may acquire merchandise through purchasing vintage clothing and consigning the resale of the merchandise.

Figure 6.10 Consignment shops are a form on resale fashion retailers, selling pre-owned fashion merchandise.

Charitable Donations

Resale fashion retailers may also acquire merchandise through charitable donations, individuals and companies donating pre-owned and/or new fashion merchandise to be processed and sold through brick-and-mortar and online **thrift stores**. Heightened consumer awareness and increased retail sophistication of thrift stores has led to a growth in the number and type of resale fashion retailers who sell donated merchandise. These retailers include Goodwill Industries International, headquartered in Rockville, Maryland, USA, that has more than 3,200 stores and an online auction site, shopgoodwill.com. Goodwill® also employs individuals in their stores and operations who may not otherwise have employment opportunities (Goodwill, 2017). Savers, Inc (known as Value Village in the Pacific NW, USA, and Village Des Valeurs in Quebec, Canada) is a for-profit thrift retailer that acquires merchandise by purchasing merchandise donated to their nonprofit partners; thus combining re-commerce and charitable donation strategies. Headquartered in Bellevue, Washington, USA, and operating in over 330 locations in Canada, United States, and Australia, Savers/Value Village promotes the advantages of "the power of reuse" and their impact on keeping textile and other waste out of landfills (Value Village, 2017). Using a similar business

model, online thrift store thredUP Inc. collects pre-owned merchandise from consumers who ship their clothing to threadUP. Sellers can either "donate" their merchandise to a nonprofit, or sell the merchandise to thredUP for site credit or cash payout (Apparel, 2017). For more information about thredUP, see the Company Highlight at the end of this chapter.

Upcycle

As discussed in Chapter 4, the term **upcycling** refers to the process by which discarded materials/items are transformed to create products with a higher value than what was being discarded without changing the composition of the original material. In many cases, pre-owned fashion products are upcycled to create merchandise to be sold through resale fashion retailers. Brick-and-mortar and online retailers that sell upcycled merchandise typically promote the positive environmental impact of the upcycled merchandise. Moving this trend forward, ReTuna Återbruksgalleria (https://www.retuna.se/) is a shopping center in Sweden devoted entirely to upcycled and repaired merchandise including home fashions, furniture, and accessories (Williams, 2017).

Connecting Consumers with Sustainable Fashion Brands

Nonprofit organizations whose missions are to foster and promote sustainable fashion often include online marketplaces for these products, thus serving as a vehicle for connecting consumers with sustainable fashion brands. For example, Fair Trade USA (2017), a nonprofit organization and third-party certifier of Fair Trade products, includes an online marketplace with links to twenty-five fashion brands that create and sell Fair Trade USA certified apparel and home fashions. Fashion brands include Patagonia, Obey, Outerknown, Senda, Threads for Thought, and Gallant International.

Summary

Business logistics involves the coordination of forecasting need; purchasing materials, trims, and findings; and moving materials, semi-finished and finished products from the product's inception and distribution to the ultimate consumer. All fashion brand companies handle business logistics associated with the creation, production, distribution, and retailing of their fashion products. In fact, business logistic systems is directly aligned with goals of the company's merchandising strategies of getting the right product, at the right price, at the right time, to the right consumer. Fashion brand companies have always focused on the cost and efficiency of business logistics systems. Now, many fashion brand companies are taking a more comprehensive examination of the design, development, and implementation of their systems from environmental and social sustainability perspectives. In doing so, fashion brand companies strive to have accurate sales forecasts, minimize the amount and distance of transporting components and finished goods, and use environmentally sustainable modes of transportation (sea/ocean, air, rail, truck, or intermodal depending on the products, destination, and distance).

Packaging used by fashion brand companies includes labels, polybags, cardboard boxes, packing materials (such as paper or airbags) and cartons. Finished goods of fashion brand companies are typically packaged for shipping and to create floor-ready merchandise (merchandise with all hangtags, labels, and pricing information affixed so that the merchandise can be directly moved to retail selling floor or shipped directly to the ultimate consumer) by the factory and/or by the distribution center. Fashion brand companies use a number of strategies to enhance the environmental sustainability of their packaging. These strategies focus on reducing the amount of packaging, changing the type of packaging used, recycling packaging materials, and considering environmental sustainability throughout the life cycle of packaging (including product returns).

Operations of fashion brand companies are the strategies, activities, and management systems required for a fashion brand company to operate on a day to day basis including human resource management, inventory management, facility and store design and maintenance, and merchandising strategies (e.g., buying, pricing, display). Sustainable operations involve taking into account economic, environmental, social, and cultural sustainability in all aspects of the company's operations. Fashion brand companies incorporate environmental sustainability into their operations using a number of strategies including creating environmentally sustainable building and store designs, reusing and recycling resources used in company operations, and creating incentives for employees and customers to be more environmentally sustainable.

Sustainable fashion retailing reflects business strategies of fashion retailers that promote environmental, social, economic, and cultural sustainability to improve the health and well-being of customers, employees, and communities. Some sustainable fashion retailers sell new merchandise that is produced using materials, production techniques, and distribution strategies that promote environmental, social, economic, and cultural sustainability. Other sustainable retailers sell fashion products that were previously owned, although the merchandise may not have actually been worn and/ or used. One of the key aspects of business plans for fashion resale retailers is acquiring the merchandise. Fashion resale retailers acquire the merchandise through re-commerce, consignment, charitable donations, and/or upcycling. Nonprofit organizations can also serve as a vehicle for connecting consumers to sustainable fashion brands.

Key Terms

business logistics	physical distribution
consignment	poly bags
distribution	re-commerce
fashion resale	resale
fashion retailing	return plan
floor-ready merchandise	sales forecasting
intermodal transportation	sustainable fashion retailing
multimodal transportation	sustainable operations
operations	thrift stores
packaging	upcycling
packaging filler	vintage clothing and accessories

References and Resources

Adams, Ariel (2014, April 30). "The Booming Market for Selling Your Timepiece Online: How Recommerce Is Dominating the Pre-Owned Watch World." Retrieved on September 6, 2017, from https://www.forbes.com/sites/arieladams/2014/04/30/the-booming-market-for-selling-your-luxury-timepiece-how-recommerce-is-dominating-the-watch-world/#5d5e2ff4370c.

Apparel (2017, May). "thredUP Inc. 2017 Top Innovators." *Apparelmag.com.*, 30.

Brannon, Evelyn (2010). *Fashion Forecasting* (3rd ed.). NY: Fairchild Books.

Carnarius, Joseph (2017, June 20). "Modes of Transportation Explained: Which Type of Cargo and Freight Transporation Is the Best?" Retrieved on September 5, 2017, from https://freighthub.com/en/blog/modes-transportation-explained-best/.

Center for Climate and Energy Solutions (2010). "Freight Transportation." Retrieved on September 5, 2017, from https://www.c2es.org/technology/factsheet/FreightTransportation.

Cohen, Nellie (2014, July 11). "Footprint Chronicles. Patagonia's Plastic Packaging—A Study on the Challenges of Garment Delivery." Retrieved on September 1, 2017, from https://www.patagonia.com/blog/2014/07/patagonias-plastic-packaging-a-study-on-the-challenges-of-garment-delivery/.

Encyclopedia of Business (2017). *Business Logistics.* Retrieved on September 3, 2017, from http://www.referenceforbusiness.com/encyclopedia/Bre-Cap/Business-Logistics.html.

Entrepreneur (2107). "Packaging. Small Business Encyclopedia." Retrieved on September 2, 2107, from https://www.entrepreneur.com/encyclopedia/packaging#.

Entrepreneur (2017). "Packaging." Retrieved on September 5, 2017, from https://www.entrepreneur.com/encyclopedia/packaging#.

Environmental Protection Agency (EPA) (2017). "Learn About SmartWay." Retrieved on October 3, 2017, from https://www.epa.gov/smartway/learn-about-smartway.

Fair Trade USA (2017). "Apparel and Home Goods." Retrieved on October 3, 2017, from http://fairtradeusa.org/products-partners/apparel.

Goodwill (2017). *About Us.* Retrieved on October 2, 2017, from http://www.goodwill.org/about-us/.

Jarvi, Erika. (2015, April 22). "The Easiest Way to Go Green That You're Overlooking: Green and Sustainable Shipping Practices." *Kabbage.* Retrieved on September 28, 2017, from https://www.kabbage.com/blog/Green+and+Sustainable+Shipping+Practices.

Patagonia (2017). "Becoming a Responsible Company." Retrieved on September 5, 2017, from http://www.patagonia.com/resource-use.html.

prAna (2017). "Thinking Outside the Bag." Retrieved on September 1, 2017, from http://www.prana.com/about-us/sustainability/polybag-reduction.html.

Pullen, John Patrick (2012, October 11). "7 Ideas for 'Greening' Your Shipping Strategy." *Entrepreneur.* Retrieved on August 16, 2017, from https://www.entrepreneur.com/article/224626.

Roos, Dave (2012, August 29). "5 Green Methods of Transporting Goods." *HowSTuffWorks.com.* Retrieved on September 3, 2017, from http://science.howstuffworks.com/environmental/green-science/5-green-methods-transporting-goods3.htm.

Tonlé (2017). *Packaging.* Retrieved on October 3, 2017, from https://tonle.com/pages/production.

Value Village (2017). *About Us.* Retrieved on October 2, 2017, from https://www.valuevillage.com/about-us.

Williams, Jeremy (2017, March 22). "The World's First Mall for Recycled Goods. Make Wealth History." Retrieved on April 6, 2017, from https://makewealthhistory.org/2017/03/22/the-worlds-first-mall-for-recycled-goods/amp/?utm_content=buffer31ecd&utm_medium=social&utm_source=facebook.com&utm_campaign=buffer.

Wilson, Mark (2017, September 25). "Ecobranding: Famous Corporate Logos, Redesigned to Use Less Ink." Retrieved on October 3, 2017, from https://www.fastcodesign.com/90144121/ecobranding-famous-corporate-logos-redesigned-to-use-less-ink?utm_source=postup&utm_medium=email&utm_campaign=Fast%20Company%20Daily&position=7&partner=newsletter&campaign_date=09252017.

Case Study: Sustainable Packaging for Icebreaker

Icebreaker, headquartered in Wellington, New Zealand, creates and sells merino wool (and wool blend) performance clothing and accessories. The brand was created in 1995 by Jeremy Moon who wanted "to provide garments for outdoor adventures with less reliance on petrochemical fibers" (Icebreaker, 2017a). In 2005, Icebreaker opened their first retail outlet in Wellington, New Zealand, offering a variety of men's and women's base layers, hats, scarves, and gloves; Icebreaker Kids collection was added in 2007. From their beginning, the company built long-term relationships with merino wool growers with common philosophies around animal welfare and the environment. They also focus on ethical sourcing of production and operations that are environmentally responsible. The three principles that guide Icebreaker are (Icebreaker, 2017b)

- Adaptation: adapting wool fibers into a clothing system that "lets humans return to nature"

- Symbiosis: working together with wool growers and manufacturers who share the values of Icebreaker is mutually beneficial

- Sustainability: considering environmental impact in all areas of the business including transportation, packaging, factories, and facilities

As a leader in innovative packaging, Icebreaker has launched a number of unique packaging strategies. For example, in 2010, Icebreaker introduced the "baacode" on garments labels, allowing customers to input a number into the Icebreaker website to trace the lineage of their products back to the wool grower. The also introduced packaging for their children's line that can be repurposed or "re-magined." That is, the boxes for younger children can be disassembled into "finger friend" toys; the boxes for older children are meant to be reused as containers for school or art supplies (Greenberg, 2009). Icebreaker also introduced environmentally responsible packaging for socks that eliminated the use of plastic pins, reduced the amount of paper needed, and was printed using vegetable-based ink on paper accredited by the Forest Stewardship Council. In-store retail fixtures for the socks were redesigned to use 30 percent less material and hold twice as much merchandise. Fixtures are also shipped flat to use less space when shipping (Portland Business Journal, 2010).

The time is right for Icebreaker to continue its leadership in sustainable packaging, implementing strategies that are in alignment with their principles and values as a fashion brand company.

1. Describe the principles and values of Icebreaker as a fashion brand company. How are these principles and values implemented in Icebreaker's product design and marketing strategies?

2. Describe the target customer for Icebreaker.

3. Describe four innovative strategies Icebreaker could implement to enhance the sustainability

of their packaging. What are the advantages and disadvantages of each of the strategies?

4. What metrics or measurements could Icebreaker report for each strategy described in question #3 to provide information to consumers about the impact of the strategy in enhancing the sustainability of their packaging?

5. Of the four strategies described in question #3, what strategy would you recommend Icebreaker implement first? Why?

Note: The background for this case study is based on publicly available information. The business problem is speculative only and not based on publicly available and/or documented information from Icebreaker.

References

Greenberg, Rebecca (2009, July 17). "Re-Imagining: A New Approach to Sustainable Packaging." *Triple Pundit*. Retrieved on October 4, 2017, from http://www.triple pundit.com/2009/07/re-imagining-a-new-approach -to-sustainable-packaging/.

Icebreaker (2017a). *History*. Retrieved on October 4, 2017, from https://www.icebreaker.com/en/our-story/history .html.

Icebreaker (2017b). *The Icebreaker Way*. Retrieved on October 4, 2017, from http://www.icebreaker.com/en/our-story /philosophy.html.

Portland Business Journal (2010, March 11, updated 2014, June 20). "Icebreaker Rolls Out Plastic-Free Packaging." Retrieved on October 4, 2017, from https://www .bizjournals.com/portland/blog/sbo/2010/03/icebreaker _rolls_out_plastic-free_packaging.html.

Call to Action Activity: **Volunteer at a Local Thrift Store**

Many local nonprofits have thrift stores that are used to raise money for their programs and services. For example, local/community chapters of nonprofits include The Arc, Humane Society, The Salvation Army, Goodwill, religious organizations, and others. Volunteers play essential roles in these operations by assisting customers, receiving donations, and sorting and pricing items. Volunteering at local thrift stores provides individuals with opportunities to contribute to the organization's fund-raising efforts, learn new skills, and receive hands-on experience.

1. Find a local nonprofit that has a thrift store and welcomes volunteers to assist with their thrift store operation.

2. Apply to volunteer at the thrift store, committing to the orientation, training, and time required by the organization.

3. After volunteering at the thrift store for at least twenty hours, reflect on your experience. What roles did you play as a volunteer? What did you learn about the organization? What did you learn about thrift store operations? What do you view as the most important benefit of this type of volunteer activity? Why? If you could make two suggestions to the thrift store as to how to improve their operations, what would they be? Why?

Retailing Slow Fashion and Independent Designer Collections: **Conversation with Amy Tipton**

Conversation with Amy Tipton, Owner
Sassafras
www.sassafras-seattle.com
Sassafras supports and promotes independent designers in Seattle and the Pacific Northwest. According to the Sassafras Web site (2017):
  Shop high-quality garments made by independent designers in Seattle and the Pacific Northwest. Our retail shop in Belltown also houses the fashion design studios of familiar local lines including Parallel Jewelry, La Macón by Shari Noble, Other Peoples Polyester, Bartle B., Stone Crow Designs, Perilous Activity, Katy Flynn Seattle, and Boho Republic.

Q: How did you get involved in the fashion industry? When and how did Sassafras get started?
A: I have always been interested in fashion design. Although I have a bachelor's degree in philosophy, I have been sewing since I was a child. My grandmother was a seamstress by trade and she taught me to sew. After graduation, I found myself in a career at Microsoft. Although there was some degree of creativity in the positions I held, after twelve years I knew I wanted to focus on sewing again. In the beginning of 2012, I started out with my own line of clothing, selling my line at local markets and craft fairs. I noticed other fashion designers doing the same. For a fashion designer, there is a long way between starting a line and selling the line at Nordstrom. Therefore, I wanted to provide a space for new designers to be able to launch a line and to make and sell limited edition lines. For some designers this is never the goal and they was to produce small batches of originals.

Sassafras opened its doors in December of 2012. I started working with one designer and now I work with over fifty designers. Initially I attracted designers with whom I had personal contacts. I also attended craft markets looking for fashion designers selling quality items. I also contact instructors at local fashion academies and attend their senior fashion shows. I enjoy working with these young designers on creating and producing seasonal collections. Now designers approach me about developing and selling their merchandise lines.

Q: Sassafras is known for supporting and promoting independent designers in Seattle and the Pacific Northwest through on-site fashion design studios and both brick-and-mortar and online retail. Tell me about the designers you work with. What is it like to have designers on-site?
A: As I mentioned, I work with over fifty designers. About 40 percent of the designers I work with sell

their merchandise exclusively through Sassafras. Other designers sell their lines through both Sassafras and other specialty retailers. For example, the clothing line Texture is sold online, at a variety of festivals/craft shows, through over seventy specialty stores, and online. Jewelry designers generally have the widest reach since the merchandise is often less expensive and the logistics of selling merchandise through a number of retailers is easier. The studio space accommodates six designers working onsite. Having designers on-site, creating and making their lines, defines the brand and identity of the Sassafras business. When customers discover that designers are making merchandise on-site, it is magical (see Figure 6.11).

Q: Building a sustainable business such as Sassafras is difficult. What is the general business model for Sassafras? What support do you provide to designers and brands to make this business model successful?
A: The on-site designers rent the space at a very reasonable rate. They provide their own equipment and in some cases share the space. They learn about the space through

Figure 6.11 Specialty retailer, Sassafras, also has onsite studio space for independent designers.

word of mouth. These designers consign the merchandise through the Sassafras retail boutique that is upstairs from the studio. The on-site designers may sell through other outlets, but they all consign with Sassafras. Most of the on-site designers work at least four days per week; some also have other jobs. Sassafras also carries lines from a number of other local Pacific Northwest designers and brands. Therefore, the merchandise sold through Sassafras is a combination of consignment and direct purchases.

I interact with all the designers and brands, giving them feedback and providing support. I do not require designers to sell a certain amount of merchandise. However, I conduct a quarterly review with each on-site designer. We talk about what has and has not sold, who the customer is for the line, and any feedback received about the line. I encourage designers to create and sell full lines and I require that they complete a full range of sizes rather than one-of-a-kind pieces. I also encourage the use of environmentally responsible materials. This is important not only to our customers but to me personally. Fortunately, designers also share this value. For example, the designer for Other People's Polyester finds and uses bulk fabrics at estate sales. The designer for Twig and Snip hand dyes materials with natural dyes from plants collected from area forests. Other lines such as Stone Crow Designs use organic cotton. The designers use different production processes but most will create and produce two to three lines per year. If a designer needs additional production capabilities, others will assist. Because the merchandise is either produced on-site or in small runs, creating the line closer to the fashion season is possible.

We welcome customer feedback on the lines we carry and I get excited when customers try on the designs and offer suggestions. In some cases a customer may want a special size or a slight variation to a design. Customers can then work directly with a designer. Designers are not creating one-of-a kind pieces, at least not through the retail shop, but may do size customization. On the other hand, the jewelry designers may do custom work and I coordinate the conversations and connect the designer with the customer.

Q: Who is the primary target customer for merchandise sold by Sassafras? How do you promote Sassafras to this customer?
A: The Sassafras customer is a professional woman who values shopping local, supporting women-owned businesses, and does not want to wear the same as everyone else. She is looking for high quality, timeless, and classic silhouettes. We cater to a wide age range (ages of our Facebook fans range from twenty-six to sixty-eight

years) but my guess is that most are in their thirties and forties. About 40 percent of our customers are repeat customers and another 30 percent are tourists who are in Seattle for various events, conferences, or vacations—mostly during the summer months.

With regards to promotion, we utilize Facebook, Instagram, and Twitter. In addition, we hold a number of events each year including trunk shows and collection openings. We also participate in the Belltown art walks that provide us with an important connection to the art community in Seattle. Write-ups in the *Seattle Times* newspaper has also brought individuals to the store. We also advertise in a magazine available to tourists through local hotels. We also allow nonprofit organizations to borrow clothing for fund-raising event fashion shows. We offer several plus-size lines that allow these organizations to have a variety of sizes of models to be in the shows. Lastly, designers have their own websites and business cards that indicate that their lines are available at Sassafras.

Q: In reading the interviews of designers posted on the Sassafras website, they are passionate about the creative process and many have been "makers" from an early age. However, the business side of creating a collection appears to be a sharp learning curve for them. How does Sassafras assist in building this community of designers to be financially sustainable?
A: One of the most important aspects of the business side of creating and selling a line of apparel is providing them with data on what is selling and what is not selling. I also help them with pricing of merchandise. Young designers are often afraid to price their merchandise too high. They know they need to pay for their materials and overhead, but they are sometimes reluctant to pay themselves for their design work. Designers also receive feedback and suggestions from me and from customers about their lines. I also push student interns on them if they let me. My experience is that this is a win-win situation. Interns force the designer to think about what needs to be accomplished and they learn from teaching others. Student interns gain valuable experience about both design and business. Lastly, I share templates for lookbooks and feature them on the Sassafras website.

Q: What do you perceive to be the biggest challenges for independent designers who sell their merchandise through Sassafras?
A: The biggest challenges for the designers I work with are

- Upfront costs of starting or expanding a line—Designers have difficulty securing the funds needed to buy fabric, trims, and studio space. In addition, designers are often hesitant to expand their wholesale business because they cannot afford to purchase the necessary materials.

- Sourcing materials—Many designers want to source materials locally but finding the appropriate fabrics and trims locally is difficult. Therefore, they often need to travel to purchase materials or order materials online.

Q: Anything else you would like to share about running a business like Sassafras and contributing to the community of independent fashion designers in the Pacific NW?
A: One of the reasons we became involved with the Belltown art walks in Seattle is to be intentionally connected with the Seattle art community. Fashion design is an art and yet it has not received the same support as other forms of art. People do not think about what goes into designing and creating the lines carried in Sassafras and it is important to bring those who support art into Sassafras. Having design studios on-site helps individuals fully understand the creative process of fashion designers. Over the holiday season we opened a pop-up shop in a local mall. In general, those who came into the shop were confused. Why would they pay for these limited edition designs when they could purchase inexpensive brand name apparel next door? They did not have a connection with the apparel they were purchasing. It is my belief that only when customers understand the resources and talent it takes to create a fashion line will then feel a connection to the fashions they wear.

Company Highlight

thredUP Inc.

Headquartered in San Francisco, CA, USA, thredUP has upped the image and services of the traditional thrift store experience. Founded in 2009, the company indicates it is now "the world's largest marketplace" to buy and sell pre-owned women's and children's apparel. Building on the trends of sustainability and sharing economy, they want people to "Think Secondhand First[SM]" and "discover the magic of secondhand." As stated by cofounder and chief technology officer, Chris Homer "We know that shopping secondhand helps the world in some small way, and we're proud to be a part of that. Being a conscious consumer matters. It matters to you, it matters to us, it matters in the whole big picture of the world" (Apparel, 2017).

Here's how it works. Consumers order a "Clean Out Bag" kit from thredUP. They fill it with women's and children's clothing and ship it (free of charge) to thredUP. Sellers have the option of "donating" the merchandise to one of thredUP's nonprofit partners or receiving site credit or a cash payout for a small fee that covers shipping and processing costs. For example, the payout for a quality Patagonia brand casual skirt would be approximately US$4.20. For items being sold on consignment, individuals can re-claim unsold items within a particular number of days. thredUP accepts approximately 40 percent of the clothing they receive and sellers can have unaccepted items returned to them for a processing and mailing fee. If unaccepted merchandise is still wearable, it is sold to third party sellers. If it is not wearable, it is passed to a textile recycler (thredup, 2017). This process, very similar to other thrift store operations, has often confused sellers who assume everything they "sell" to thredUP will be sold online and paid accordingly.

For the merchandise accepted, thredUP photographs and prices the items and enters it into their data base which includes a proprietary algorithm. Once online, shoppers can browse and filter searches by category, size, brand, color, and price. The online fashion resale retailer also uses computer technology to recommend products based on a customer's previous purchase history, style preferences, and the products that a customer is browsing.

Sustainable Communities

Objectives

- Describe the role the fashion industry plays in creating and maintaining sustainable communities.
- Describe and compare the strategies used by nonprofit and for-profit social enterprises to advance their social objectives.
- Explain and differentiate types of social enterprises in the fashion industry.
- Provide examples of fashion brand companies whose social objectives are equally or even more important than their business objectives.

The Shoe That Grows started in 2007 when Kenton Lee, the organization's founder, was living and working in Nairobi, Kenya. As the story goes . . . "one day while walking with the kids . . . he noticed a little girl in a white dress next to him who had shoes that were way too small for her feet. That led to questions about why. 'Wouldn't it be great if there was a shoe that could adjust and expand—so that kids always had a pair of shoes that fit?' Kenton and his team had the idea but they struggled through rejection from shoe companies and failed attempts at prototypes. But they believed it was a good idea that could help a lot of kids and so they kept going. Finally, after 5 years of hard work, it went from an idea to reality. The Shoe That Grows was born!" The Shoe That Grows is the first project of Because International, an organization founded in 2009 with a focus on "listening to those living in extreme poverty to hear their thoughts, ideas, and dreams for better life—and then working together to make those ideas into a reality." The sole purpose of the first project, The Shoe That Grows, was to help kids stay healthy through sustainable and solid footwear (The Shoe That Grows, 2017).

Can the global fashion industry and the fashion products created in this industry be a vehicle for making the world a better place? Kenton Lee and his team, as social entrepreneurs, founding organizations such as Because International with projects like The Shoe That Grows believe they can (see Figure 7.1). This chapter reviews the strategies that fashion brand companies take in creating, enhancing, and maintaining sustainable communities throughout the world—with a focus on companies whose social objectives are equally or even more important than their business objectives. Fashion brand companies whose social objectives focused on environmental sustainability as it relates to community health were discussed in Chapter 3, Product Life Cycle. Therefore, this chapter discusses fashion brand companies whose social objectives relate to other aspects of sustainability as they relate to community health and well-being.

Figure 7.1 The Shoe That Grows is a social enterprise that provides size-adaptable shoes to children in Africa.

What Are Sustainable Communities?

"A **sustainable community** is one that is economically, environmentally, and socially healthy and resilient. It meets challenges through integrated solutions rather than through fragmented approaches that meet one of those goals at the expense of the others. And it takes a long-term perspective—one that's focused on both the present and future, well beyond the next budget or election cycle" (Institute for Sustainable Communities, 2017). The sustainability of a community depends on several factors (Sustainable Communities, 2017):

- Economic health and security with sustainable job creation
- Public services and infrastructure
- Environmental health (water, air, biodiversity, energy, and ecosystems)
- Civic engagement and participation in planning and implementing community initiatives
- Educational opportunities
- Culture and art
- Justice, equity, and social well-being

A sustainable community "manages its human, natural, and financial resources to meet current needs while ensuring that adequate resources are equitably available for future generations" (Institute of Sustainable Communities, 2017). In other words, sustainable communities thrive, create environments for the individuals living in them to also thrive, and provide the same opportunities for the next generation of community members.

Fashion brand companies are involved with enhancing community sustainability:

- Where they do business and/or have employees. Economic, environmental, and social health of communities where they do business and/or have employees results in long term viability of human and natural resources to support the business enterprise.

- Where there are needs to be met. Fashion can be used as a vehicle for improving community sustainability, thus contributing to efforts beyond where the fashion brand company does business.

In both cases, strategies used by fashion brand companies in creating and maintaining sustainable communities focus on improving the health and well-being of individuals and the communities they live in around the world.

Social Enterprise and Social Entrepreneur

Fashion brand companies engaged with creating and maintaining sustainable communities are part of a global system. Governments, non-government organizations (NGOs), and businesses all create and fund community development initiatives that benefit the individuals living in the community for sustained economic, environmental, and social growth of the community. Because this chapter focuses on the roles of fashion brand companies in creating and maintaining sustainable communities, the discussion focuses on strategies that businesses and organizations with commercial activities use for this purpose. The term **social enterprise** describes these businesses and organizations "that address a basic unmet need or solve a social problem through a market-drive approach" (Social Enterprise Alliance, 2017). That is, social enterprises combine commercial business objectives and activities with social objectives and activities.

Many fashion brand companies are social enterprises. The social objectives of these companies address problems including poverty, hunger, environmental issues, and/or social injustice through creating and selling fashion products. In many cases, these companies are led by **social entrepreneurs** who "work to solve critical social problems and address basic unmet needs through innovation" (Social Enterprise Alliance, 2017). Social entrepreneurs identify opportunities for marketable innovations to address social objectives. Both social entrepreneurs and social enterprises serve as change agents to create, enhance, and maintain sustainable communities; social entrepreneurs change the way social needs are addressed and social enterprises create positive social change through their business activities (Luke & Chu, 2013). Fabric of Change, "a global initiative to support innovators for a fair and sustainable apparel industry" sponsored by the C&A Foundation and Ashoka, funds social entrepreneurs and social enterprises in the apparel industry (C&A Foundation, 2017).

Examples of social entrepreneurs in the global fashion industry include

- Kenton Lee, founder of The Shoe That Grows, is an example of a social entrepreneur who created a social enterprise, addressing the health of children through the innovative design of footwear that can be adapted to fit a child's foot over time.

- Rebecca Van Bergen, founder and executive director of Nest, a nonprofit organization committed to the social and economic advancement of global artisans and homeworkers. Through the Nest Artisan Guild, artisan businesses are provided with a "support network of peers, philanthropists, brands, and professional volunteers who are able to provide the resources, education, and tools" for success in building scalable solutions that are often a challenge for small businesses. With more than 350 artisan businesses across fifty countries, Nest is "building a new handworker economy to increase workforce inclusivity, improve women's wellbeing beyond factories, and preserve important cultural traditions around the world" (Nest, 2018).

- Indigenous Designs cofounders Scott Leonard and Matt Reynolds started their fashion brand in 1994 with the commitment to a combination of fair trade, environmentally sustainable materials such as organic cotton, and "to elevate artisans in economically marginalized communities to world renowned states in the global textile market" through free trainings and workshops, steady year-round work, investments in local schools, and zero interest loans for education (Indigenous Designs, 2017) (see Figure 7.2).

Financial Stability of Social Enterprises

One challenge faced by all social enterprises is financial stability: from launching a start-up to maintaining economic sustainability over time to scalability and growth of the enterprise. Social enterprises may be nonprofit or for-profit entities but either way, they must secure funds to launch the business and then make enough money to cover their costs of doing business and fulfill their social objectives to be economically sustainable (Bugg-Levine, Kogut, & Kulatilaka, 2012).

Return on Investment

Traditional fashion brand companies guided primarily by commercial **business objectives** (e.g., profit, business growth) create and sell goods to customers with proceeds used to fulfill their business objectives. These companies typically rely on financial institutions and private funders and investors to launch, sustain, and grow their business. These investors calculate their **return on investment**, calculated as (net profit/cost of investment) x 100, as a metric to inform their decision whether to invest in or loan money to the company. **Net profit** or **net income** for these companies is the actual profit of the business—the money left after all of the expenses

Figure 7.2 Indigenous Designs is a social enterprise committed to enhancing the lives of the artisans who create their merchandise.

have been paid. Unlike traditional fashion brand companies, social enterprises balance their business objectives and **social objectives** (e.g., reducing poverty, improving health). Therefore, the return on investment for social enterprises is different than of traditional companies. Return on investment for social enterprises is in terms of the social objectives *and* the business objectives of the company being met. That is, funders of and investors in social enterprises want to know if/how the social objectives are being fulfilled and how the company is meeting its business objectives at the same time. Therefore, as either nonprofit or for-profit organizations, social enterprises use a variety of fund-raising strategies to launch, sustain, and grow their business or organization.

Nonprofit Organizations

A social enterprise may be a **nonprofit organization** (or **not for profit organization**) whereby any revenues of the social enterprise available after all expenses are paid are completely reinvested into the work of the organization. Registered and approved nonprofit organizations may also receive tax exemptions and donations are often tax deductible. **Non-government organizations** (NGOs) are nonprofit voluntary citizens' groups that operate independent of governments. NGOs, such as World Wildlife Fund and Oxfam, may partner with nonprofit social enterprises that have a common mission. Although the social objectives of nonprofit social enterprises are clearly evident, nonprofit social enterprises still need to raise or earn enough to cover the expenses of the organization and fund the organizations' programs. When applied to fashion, the social objectives of a nonprofit social enterprise are achieved through commercial activities—creating and selling fashion merchandise. In fact, identification of nonprofit social enterprises by consumers may not be immediately evident since these nonprofit organizations create and sell fashion merchandise as do for-profit organizations. However, any surplus revenue of the organization is used to further the mission of the organization rather than distributed among owners. In addition to these commercial activities, opportunities for funding and investing in nonprofit organizations include

- Charitable donations from individuals or other organizations who share the mission of the nonprofit organization
- Private investors, including crowd-sourcing, who share the mission of the nonprofit organization
- Grants from foundations or governments specifically for nonprofit organizations to meet social objectives
- Loan guarantees from foundations so that nonprofit organizations can secure loans from traditional lending institutions such as banks
- Membership fees if the nonprofit organization is a member-based organization
- Government subsidies such as tax exemptions

Headquartered in Nampa, Idaho, USA, Because International is the nonprofit organization whose first project, The Shoe that Grows, was highlighted at the beginning of this chapter. According to their website, the mission of Because International is to "listen to those living in extreme poverty to hear their thoughts, ideas, and dreams for a better life— and then work together to help make those ideas into a reality (see Figure 7.3). The sole purpose for our first project is to help kid stay healthy through sustainable and solid footwear" (The Shoe That Grows, 2017). Another example of a nonprofit organization is the Open Arms Shop (see description later in this chapter).

For-Profit Organizations

Social enterprises may also be **for-profit organizations**, commercial entities whose profits are shared among owners. Fashion brand companies that are for-profit social enterprises fulfill their social objectives in a number of ways:

- Create and sell merchandise as the means for beneficiaries to gain employment and training
- Create and sell merchandise to beneficiaries at a reduced rate but still make a profit to fund growth and development
- Create and sell socially responsible merchandise with proceeds used to expand socially responsible activities of the company

Figure 7.3 Because International is a nonprofit organization whose mission is to advance the health of children in poverty.

- Create and sell merchandise with a percentage of the profits given to the charity of choice by the company
- Create a foundation that is the philanthropic arm of the company and the sale of merchandise subsidizes the operation of the foundation
- Private investors, including crowd sourcing, who share the mission of the organization
- Grants for social enterprise start-ups such as the Fabric of Change initiative
- Create and sell merchandise with financial returns that make them attractive to investors including foundations and traditional financial institutions (e.g., banks)

Types of Social Enterprises in the Fashion Industry

To reflect the strategies used by companies and organizations to enhance community sustainability, they are categorized by degree of alignment between their social objectives and the business objectives: directly aligned, overlapping, or unrelated. The

social and business objectives of a fourth category, corporate foundations, may be directly aligned, overlapping, or unrelated.

Social Objectives and Business Objectives Are Directly Aligned

Fashion brand social enterprises whose social objectives and business objectives are directly aligned include

- Social objective driven companies (social firms) whereby the social enterprise trains and employs beneficiaries to build capacity and economic sustainability
- Employee well-being programs including social objective driven companies that sell products at discounted prices to its beneficiaries
- Organizations that connect beneficiaries (e.g., small businesses) with their consumer markets
- Organizations that operate as cooperatives

Social Firms: Social Objective-Driven Companies and Organizations

Social firms are social objective-driven companies and organizations that employ individuals who might otherwise find it difficult to find jobs or that create jobs in areas where the individuals may not have alternative employment. In these cases, the purpose of the social enterprise is to provide sustainable work for individuals to alleviate poverty, improve lives, and create a more sustainable community. In many cases, the social firms' commercial aspects also directly fund programs for their employees and communities such as educational scholarships and financial and career planning support.

Many fashion brand companies are committed to providing steady employment in production facilities for individuals who may not have alternative employment including refugees, women who are at the highest risk of or have escaped human trafficking and modern slavery, individuals transitioning from homelessness, and former inmates. Following are a few examples:

- Founded in 2006, Sudara, headquartered in Oregon, USA, is a "mission-driven lifestyle

Figure 7.4 U.S.-based fashion brand Sudara partners with India-based Freeset that employs at-risk women.

- Lazlo, headquartered in Detroit, Michigan, USA, employs men who were previously incarcerated to produce organic cotton T-shirts. Using 100 percent Organic Supima® Cotton, grown in the American southwest, spun in Georgia and milled in California, each T-shirt in made in the production facility in Detroit. Workers are paid a living wage of at least $15 per hour (Lazlo, 2017).

- Raven + Lily, a certified B Corporation headquartered in Austin, Texas, USA, employs marginalized and at-risk women at fair trade wages in safe environments with sustainable income, health care, and education. With a focus on alleviating poverty, Raven + Lily partners with artisan groups in Africa, Malaysia, USA, Pakistan, Cambodia, India, and Peru to empower women to earn a living that can support themselves and their families (Raven + Lily, 2017) (see Figure 7.5).

- Sseko Designs, headquartered in Portland, Oregon, USA, with production facilities in Uganda, Africa, creates and sells sandals, handbags, and accessories. Sseko employs women from all walks of life. Proceeds from the sale of these products are used for scholarships for young women in Uganda to attend the university. "Every woman who has graduated from Sseko is currently pursuing her college degree or has

brand" that creates and sells loungewear and yoga apparel. Partnering with Freeset, located in Kolkata, India, they employ women in India who are at risk or have escaped human trafficking (Freeset, 2017). As they state on their website, our "success is not just measured or defined in sales and revenue, but in our positive social impact and creating long-term, sustainable change" (Sudara, 2017). Stories about the women can be found on their website (see Figure 7.4).

- The Open Arms Shop, a nonprofit social enterprise of the Multicultural Refugee Coalition, creates living wage employment opportunities for refugees in the Austin, Texas, USA area. The Open Arms Shop is a contract sewn products manufacturing facility that partners with fashion brands to make a variety of fashion merchandise. "By becoming a partner, companies can not only add the value of local USA-Made manufacturing to their brand, but simultaneously can help empower refugee women through employment." The Open Arms Shop also creates and sells upcycled pillow case covers (Multicultural Refugee Coalition, 2017).

Figure 7.5 With a focus on alleviating poverty, Raven + Lily partners with artisan groups several countries, including Cambodia.

graduated from university and is on her way to making our world a more beautiful place." The Sseko website includes the stories of these women. "Sseko Designs provides the opportunity for women in East Africa to end the cycle of poverty and create a more equitable society" (Sseko Designs, 2017).

- The Giving Keys creates and sells necklaces and other jewelry items with purchases supporting job creation and support services for individuals living in the Los Angeles, CA, are who are transitioning out of homelessness. In partnership with Chrysalis, a workforce development agency for homeless individuals, LIFT LA, and Downtown Women's Center, The Giving Keys provides individuals transitioning out of homelessness with full-time living wage jobs to engrave inspirational words on recycled metal keys that are made into necklaces, bracelets, earrings, and keychains. In addition, employees are provided benefits; paid time off for housing, education and case management appointments; and financial, goal-setting, and career assistance (The Giving Keys, 2017).

Fashion brand companies whose social objectives and business objective are directly aligned are also committed to providing employment in their warehouse and distribution facilities to individuals who may not have alternative employment. For example, Toad&Co, headquartered in California, USA, partnered with Search, Inc, to co-found Planet Access Company (PAC), a nonprofit organization whose mission is to positively change the lives of adults with developmental disabilities by providing them with job training and work opportunities. The Toad&Co warehouse serves as employment for individuals with developmental disabilities with 100 percent of Toad&Co's inventory picked, packed, and shipped by the PAC warehouse crew (Toad&Co, 2017).

Employee Well-Being Programs

Objectives of social enterprises also include well-being programs designed specifically for employees, including health care, family/child care, and selling products at discounted prices to employees. When the mission of the social enterprise is for the purpose of creating and implementing these programs, the social objectives are directly aligned with the business objectives. For example, APON Bangladesh, started by social entrepreneur, Shaikh Saif Rashid, works with garment factories, health service providers, and insurers in Bangladesh to ensure worker well-being. APON retail outlets inside factories sells quality household products to employees at discounted prices and also offers free healthcare and medical insurance which is paid for through commissions on the sales of the household items (McLean, 2017). APON has the potential to increase a worker's annual real income by 7 percent. The "direct benefits of the initiative go to the worker but factories save by reducing staff turnover and stemming illness" (Batist, 2017).

In addition to those that are social enterprises, many fashion brand companies offer programs related to health and well-being for their employees and factory workers including access to on-site family/child care, exercise programs, health screenings, financial literacy programs, paid leave, and short-term sabbatical leaves. For example, since 1983 Patagonia has offered corporate-sponsored on-site child care. As noted by Rose Marcario, Patagonia's president and CEO, "It's true, there are financial costs to offering on-site child care, but the benefits—financial and otherwise—pay for themselves every year. As a CEO, it's not even a question in my mind. Business leaders (and their chief financial officers) should take note" (Byars, 2016).

Organizations That Connect Beneficiaries with Consumer Markets

Social enterprises whose social and business objectives are aligned also serve the function of connecting beneficiaries, typically individuals and small businesses, with consumer markets. Through the services of these enterprises, individuals and small businesses receive marketing, retailing, financial, and distribution assistance. For example, Global Goods Partners (GGP) is a nonprofit social enterprise with a focus on alleviating poverty and promoting social justice. Through GGP, artisans earn incomes through the sale of jewelry, accessories, apparel, home décor, and gift items. GGP connects these artisans with the consumer market for fair trade, handmade products through their online stores. Working with more than forty community-based producer partners (many of which are social enterprises and artisan cooperatives) in twenty countries, GGP provides product development, operational expertise, capacity-building grants, and technical assistance (Global Goods Partners, 2017). For example, one of their producer partners, Streetwires, provides opportunities for 120 artisans in Cape Town and Johannesburg, South Africa, to sell their wire and bead creations.

Another organization that connects artisans with consumer markets is ClothRoads, headquartered in Colorado, USA. ClothRoads creates connections between indigenous textiles artisans and cooperatives from around the world with consumer markets. Their online global textile marketplace provides market opportunities to artisans so that they can sell their handmade textiles and weavings, including specialty dyeing, weaving, spinning, printing, and embroidering (see Figure 7.6). They also sponsor international gatherings of textile artisans, and sponsor artisans for the Santa Fe Folk Art Market (ClothRoads, 2017).

Cooperatives

Social enterprises, organized as **cooperatives**, are owned and operated by their members for the benefit of their members. Thus, the social objectives of cooperatives focus on the members/owners of the businesses themselves who share in the running and control of the business, all of whom have a say in how the business operates. When applied to fashion-related social enterprises, cooperatives are typically worker cooperatives, owned and operated by those who also work in the business with a primary goal of protecting the economic interests of the members of the cooperatives. Fashion-related cooperative businesses provide a way for individuals come together to create and produce fashion merchandise and share in the proceeds. Production cooperatives

Figure 7.6 ClothRoads creates connections between indigenous textiles artisans and cooperatives from around the world with consumer markets.

focus on providing services to fashion brands in the cutting and sewing of merchandise. Artisan cooperatives focus on creating and selling handmade jewelry, accessories, home fashions, and gift items (ClothRoads, 2017).

Social Objectives and Business Objectives Overlap

In the cases of social enterprises whose social objectives and business objectives overlap, the business sells products to an external market and uses revenue to provide services to the beneficiaries in an area related to the company. When applied to fashion brand companies, the company sells fashion merchandise for the distinct purpose of addressing a social issue related to the merchandise. One of the most common models used by fashion brand companies is the **one-for-one model**. Made famous by Los Angeles-based footwear brand TOMS' one-for-one model, every time a consumer buys one of its products, the company donates a related product or service (e.g., shoes) to someone in need. As TOMS grew as a company, their one-for-one program was often criticized for creating dependency and offering humanitarian aid rather than economic development. Indeed, as the company expanded and scaled their production, the company itself found that their social objectives were being overshadowed by their commercial business objectives. To address these concerns, since 2013 TOMS has strived to make an impact on sustainable communities including local manufacturing in Haiti, Kenya, India, and Ethiopia; products and services; and logistical support (TOMS, 2017).

Another fashion brand company that uses the one-for-one model is Bombas. Based in New York City, Bombas creates and sells a wide variety of men's, women's, and childrens' fashion and performance socks. Bombas' focus is to draw attention to and support the homeless community. Because, "socks are the #1 most requested clothing item at homeless shelters," for each pair of socks purchased, Bombas donates a pair of socks to a homeless shelter. Bombas works with over 600 giving partners across the United States to distribute socks needed by those in homeless shelters. Working closely with their partners, Bombas created a sock specifically designed to meet the needs of individuals who do not have the privilege of a clean pair of socks every day. Thus, the socks distributed have an anti-microbial treatment, are darker colors, and have reinforced seams (Bombas, 2017).

Using strategies other than the one-for-one model, fashion brands whose social objectives and business objectives overlap include companies who directly support nonprofit organizations that are related to their business objectives. For example, eyewear company, Warby Parker, believes "everyone has the right to see." The company creates and sells prescription fashion eyewear through direct marketing distribution channels. For each pair of glasses sold, the company makes a contribution to their primary nonprofit organization partner, VisionSpring, which enables individuals in developing countries access to affordable prescriptions glasses. Contributions are made on a monthly basis based on the number of glasses Warby

Figure 7.7 Warby Parker partners with VisionSpring enabling individuals in developing countries access to affordable prescriptions glasses.

Parker sells. VisionSpring trains men and women in developing countries to give basic eye exams and sell glasses to their communities at affordable prices (see Figure 7.7). Since Warby Parker started in 2010, approximately 2.5 million pairs of glasses have been distributed to those in need (Warby Parker, 2017).

Social Objectives and Business Objectives Are Unrelated

Fashion brand companies may fulfill social objectives by creating and selling fashion merchandise to raise money for causes and issues that are marginally or unrelated to the fashion products they create and sell. In many of these cases, the fashion brand company would not technically be considered a social enterprise since their social objectives are not equal to or more important than their business objectives. However, a review of the good work these companies perform is worth comment. Charitable giving programs are prevalent in the fashion industry whereby the fashion brand companies sell fashion products and use a portion of the proceeds or share of the profits to fund a charity organization that focuses on a cause or social service of interest to the company. Programs are often implemented to benefit 1) employees, families, or communities where the company operates and/or 2) causes or social services that are also of interest to the consumers of their products. In many cases, the charitable gift programs include employee matching gifts (the company will match any monetary contributions made by an employee) and in-kind gifts (contributions other than money, e.g., products, services) (Foundation Center, 2017).

Fashion brand companies use a number of strategies with regard to their charitable gift programs. The most common of the strategies is a fashion brand company donating a percentage of their sales to charities in locations where they do business and/or to charities that are of interest to their target customer. Examples include

- Nau, headquartered in Oregon, USA, contributes 2 percent of every sale to their nonprofit Partners for Change: Conservation Alliance, Mercy Corp and People for Bikes (Nau, 2017).

- SiiZU, headquartered in New York City, donates 10 percent of their profits to American Forests, a nonprofit organization that "advances the conservation of forests" with a goal of planting 2.7 million trees across forty-four projects nationally and to restore and protect critical wildlife habitat (American Forests, 2017; SiiZu, 2017).

- For every pair of socks purchased from Conscious Step, headquartered in Brooklyn, New York, they donate to one or more of their nonprofit organization partners including Action Against Hunger, Global Citizen, and Water.org. Socks are packaged around the issues addressed by these organizations including poverty, water, hunger, and disaster relief.

- 1% for the Planet is a nonprofit organization started in 2002 by Yvon Chouinard (founder of Patagonia) and Craig Mathews (founder of Blue Ribbon Flies). Member businesses commit to giving at least 1 percent of their annual sales to the organization which provides funding for approved nonprofit partners that focus on environmental sustainability. Member companies can use the 1% for the Planet logo on their merchandise (1% for the Planet, 2017). Numerous fashion brand companies are members of 1% for the Planet including Arnhem Clothing (Australia), Belle and Beau Clothing (US), CleoDesign (Italy), Cotton Leaf (Hong Kong), Cursor & Thread (Canada), Grown Clothing (UK), Nuu-Muu (US), Oliberté (Canada), Patagonia (US), SAOLA (France), and Woodlike (Germany).

Another strategy used by fashion brand companies as part of their charitable gift program is selling limited edition or exclusive collections, specifically created for the purpose of the proceeds funding a charity or cause. Luxury brands such as Fendi, Marc Jacobs, Alexander Wang, Aquatalia Boots & Shoes, and Dior have created capsule collections with a percentage of proceeds benefiting particular causes. For example, Alexander Wang released a new collection with proceeds from sales benefiting the nonprofit organization, Do Something, which promotes positive environmental and social change for youths. Aquatalia Boots & Shoes collaborated with American actress, Kerry Washington, to create a line of handbags with proceeds of the sales benefiting the Purple Purse Initiative which focuses on ending domestic violence (Cotton, 2017).

(RED), a division of The ONE campaign, is a nonprofit organization founded in 2006 by Bono and Bobby Shriver to engage businesses and people in the fight against AIDS. (RED) partners with a variety of for-profit companies including fashion brands and licensors that create specific (RED)-branded goods and contribute up to 50 percent of their profits from these goods to the Global Fund to fight AIDS, tuberculosis and malaria. (RED) was initially launched with fashion brands Giorgio Armani and Gap. Recently, Nickelodeon and (RED) partnered with Moschino to create a SpongeBob (RED) capsule collection. Global Fund grants, supported by (RED), focus on prevention, treatment, counseling, HIV testing, and care services. Over 90 million people have benefited from these grants ((Red), 2017).

As part of their charitable gift programs, fashion brand companies also implement grants programs whereby nonprofit organizations apply to receive funding from the fashion brand company. For example, Eileen Fisher grants program supports nonprofit organizations whose missions are to 1) empower women and girls, 2) expand innovative women-owned companies for "positive social and environmental impact," and 3) local nonprofit organizations that focus on the needs of their local communities (Eileen Fisher, 2017). As part of Nike's charitable gifts program, the Nike Community Impact Fund supports community organizations in Europe and the United States through a variety of community grants, donations, partnerships with organizations, and awards, all with a focus on getting children active. Their community grants programs provide funding to community organizations that support sport and physical activities for youth in selected communities in Belgium, Netherlands, and the United States. The Nike N7 Fund specifically focuses on sports activities for Native American and Aboriginal youth (Nike, 2017).

Corporate Foundations

In addition to furthering social objectives and business objectives within the company operations, fashion brand companies have also created separate entities, called **corporate foundations** (or **company-sponsored foundations**), to further their social objectives. According to the Council on Foundations (2017), a **foundation** is an "entity that supports charitable activities by making grants to unrelated organizations or institutions or to individuals for scientific, educational, cultural, religious, or other charitable purposes." Corporate foundations are created and financially supported by a company and, as with other strategies, are established to address specific issues or problems. Corporate foundations are set up as private foundations

(financially supported by an individual, family, or small number of sources) or as public foundations or charities (financially supported by multiple sources including corporate giving programs, individuals, other foundations, non-government organizations, governments, and fees). In both cases, the corporate foundation relies on the support of the company that oversees its operations to build the foundation's endowments and distribution of resources to beneficiaries (Foundation Center, 2017). Following are a few examples of corporate foundations created by fashion brand companies.

C&A is a Dutch fashion retail company with stores throughout Europe, Asia, and Americas (Mexico and Brazil). The C&A Foundation (2017) (originally with three regional organizations) was created to improve the lives through educational, health, and disaster relief initiatives in locations where C&A operated. In 2014, the C&A Foundation reorganized into a single corporate foundation with a vision to "transform the fashion industry" around the values and approach to sustainability held by the C&A corporation. Current work of the foundation focuses on several signature initiatives: accelerating the growing and use of sustainable cotton, improving working condition of garment workers, eradicating forced labor, fostering circular fashion, and strengthening communities by enabling volunteer programs and supporting local charities in communities where they have retail and sourcing operations. The C&A Foundation also fund grants that move these initiatives forward, partnering with universities and organizations including the Better Cotton Initiative, Fashion Revolution, Goodweave, Anti-Slavery International, International Labor Rights Forum, and Textile Exchange.

The Obakki Foundation is the philanthropic counterpart to the Obakki fashion brand, headquartered in Vancouver, B.C., Canada. Launched in 2009, the focus of the Obakki Foundation's projects is providing clean water and education in Cameroon and South Sudan Africa (see Figure 7.8). Through the work of the Obakki Foundation, twelve schools have been built and 900 water wells have been drilled. Obakki absorbs all administrative fees for the charity, allowing 100 percent of the Obakki Foundation's

Figure 7.8 Obakki Foundation, founded by Treana Peake, focuses on projects in Africa.

public donations to go directly to its charitable initiatives. In addition, 100 percent of the proceeds Obakki capsule collections go to projects (Obakki Foundation, 2017). For additional information about the Obakki Foundation, see the Conversation with Treana Peake at the end of this chapter.

The Gandys Foundation is the registered charity of fashion brand company, Gandys® (2017) that creates and sells travel-inspired men's and women's apparel. Two brothers, Rob and Paul Forkan, launched Gandys in 2012 and the Gandys Foundation in 2013. Ten percent of the profits of Gandys and gifts from other sources supports the primary program of the Gandys Foundation, the Orphans for Orphans program which assists underprivileged children in Sri Lanka. The Forkan brothers (then ages fifteen and seventeen) were traveling in Sri Lanka in 2004 when the tsunami off the Indian Ocean hit and killed their parents. Being orphans themselves, they set out to create a product and brand that would help parentless children, specifically orphans affected by the tsunami. The first Orphans for Orphans facility opened in Sri Lanka in 2014. Programs offered include academic support, woodwork lessons, and various sports activities.

Social Awareness and Policy Advocacy

Fashion brand companies also advance social objectives through heightening awareness for and advocating policies around the issues or problems they seek to address. Whereas the fashion brand companies themselves may not be considered social enterprises, the work that the companies have furthered is worth reviewing.

Heightening Social Awareness

Fashion brand companies often use their social visibility to heighten public awareness of a cause or issue. For example, since the 1980s, Kenneth Cole has raised awareness of HIV and AIDS through his brand name recognition, using both personal and business resources. In 1987, he joined the board of the American Foundation for AIDS Research (amfAR) and publicly sponsored a series of public service advertisements for amfAR. Some included supermodels of the day such as Paulina Porizkova, Christie Brinkley, Kelly Emberg, Beverly Johnson, and others with young children shot by Annie Liebovitz and the tagline "For the future of our children. . . Support the American Foundation for AIDS Research. We do" along with "sponsored by Kenneth Cole." Other ads with the tagline "We All Have AIDS If One of Us Does" included celebrities such as Will Smith, Tom Hanks, Elizabeth Taylor, Sharon Stone, Elton John, and others. In 2002, Cole became vice chairman of amfAR and two years later became chairman. The name of the organization was changed to The Foundation for AIDS Research (to reflect its global reach) but continued to use the acronym amfAR. In 1996 Kenneth Cole received the Dom Perignon Award for Humanitarian Leadership and in 2017 received the CFDA's inaugural Swarovski Award for Positive Change (Iredale, 2017; Kenneth Cole, 2017). (see Figure 7.9).

Policy Advocacy

Fashion brand companies have also been involved with advocating for policies that support their social

Figure 7.9 Kenneth Cole is chairman of the board of amfAR, which focuses on AIDS research.

objectives. For example, Patagonia refers to itself as *The Activist Company* around environmental issues. As they note, "At Patagonia, the protection and preservation of the environment isn't what we do after hours. It's the reason we're in business and every day's work." They support this activist approach through their sustainability mission, environmental grants, corporate partnerships, employee activism, and environmental campaigns. Their environmental campaigns include advocacy for policies to protect national monuments, restrict development in wilderness areas, prevent risky oil development on sensitive coasts, and restore the Snake River. Individuals can go on their website to learn how to "take action" around these efforts (Patagonia, 2017) as well as how to "vote our planet" (Patagonia, 2017).

Industry associations with fashion brand company members also have advocacy agendas to support issues of relevance to their member companies. For example, the American Apparel and Footwear Association, "representing more than 1,000 world famous name brands, we are the trusted public policy and political voice of the apparel and footwear industry, its management and shareholders, its nearly four million U.S. workers, and its contribution of $384 billion in annual U.S. retail sales" (AAFA, 2017). Areas in which they advocate with policymakers include brand protection, supply chain, and trade. Similarly, the Outdoor Industry Association's (OIA) mission to "drive change in policy, sustainability, and

outdoor participation" focuses on preserving natural areas, advocating for sustainability, and increasing participation in outdoor activities (OIA, 2017).

Fashion as a Vehicle to Advance Philanthropic and Advocacy Efforts

Since the time when women's philanthropic organizations sponsored fashion shows, using local models and retailers, as charity fund-raisers, fashions have provided a means to raise money for philanthropies and/or organizations focused on policy advocacy. Using fashion as a vehicle to advance philanthropic efforts is still the case today. For example, the Super Saturday fundraiser for the Ovarian Cancer Research Fund Alliance (OCRFA) sells donated fashion merchandise with proceeds going to OCRFA (OCRFA, 2017). The annual event, chaired by Donna Karan, Kelly Ripa, Gabby Karan de Felice, Molly Sims, and Rachel Zoe, features merchandise from over 150 fashion brand companies, including Alice + Olivia, Carolina Herrera New York, Donna Karan, Karl Lagerfeld, and Urban Zen (see Figure 7.10).

Delivering Good is a nonprofit organization that collaborates with hundreds of companies in the fashion, home, and children's industries who donate new excess products to the nonprofit which distributes them kids, adults, and families facing poverty and disaster around the world. Product donors have included Camuto Group, Coach, Disney, Eddie Bauer, Easy Spirit, Gap, H&M, HanesBrands, PVH, and Ralph Lauren Corp (Delivering Good, 2017).

Because of their visual nature and reflection of social norms, throughout history fashions have served as symbols of social change communicating solidarity around issues and causes. Individuals marching for rights, protesting the status quo, and/or supporting causes often wear a fashion symbol that reflects the cause and/or issue. As noted earlier, the selling of these items is often used to raise money for the issue or cause. In the early 1900s, suffragettes used a variety of fashion symbols to demonstrate solidarity and challenge gender roles. Women of color wore denim overalls as a symbol of commitment to civil rights during the 1963 March on Washington.

Figure 7.10 Fashion designer Donna Karan and Gabby Karan de Felice attend OCRFA's 20th Annual Super Saturday to Benefit Ovarian Cancer.

Figure 7.11 The pink pussy hat has become a symbol of support and solidarity for women's rights and political resistance.

Varying colored ribbons are worn to reflect the wearer's support for particular issues and/or groups. These fashion symbols may be predetermined as seen in slogan T-shirts or arise because of their symbolic association with a particular issue such as the hoodie becoming a symbol of injustice in 2012 after the tragic death of Trayvon Martin who was wearing a hoodie when he was shot. More recently the pink pussy hat became a symbol of "support and solidarity for women's rights and political resistance" (Pussy Hat Project, 2017). Worn by thousands of women in women's marches around the world and at events celebrating and advocating for women's rights (see Figure 7.11).

Summary

With a focus on economic, environmental, and social health and resiliency, sustainable communities thrive, create environments for the individuals living in them to also thrive, and provide the same opportunities for the next generation of community members. Strategies used by fashion brand companies in creating and maintaining sustainable communities focus on improving the health and well-being of individuals and the communities they live in around the world both where they do business and have employees and where there are needs to be met. Social enterprises are businesses or organizations that address unmet needs or social problems through commercial and market-driven approaches; thus, social enterprises combine business objectives and activities and social objectives and activities. Many are started and/or led by social entrepreneurs who address unmet needs or social problems through innovations.

Social enterprises may be nonprofit or for-profit entities, but either way, they must secure funds to launch the business and then make enough money to cover their costs of doing business and fulfill their social objectives to be economically sustainable. Unlike traditional fashion brand companies, companies that are social enterprises balance their business objectives and social objectives with both contributing to their abilities to launch, sustain, and grow their business or organization.

Social enterprises in the fashion industry are organized by degree of alignment between their social objectives and the business objectives: directly aligned, overlapping, or unrelated. The social and business objectives of a fourth category, corporate foundations, may be directly aligned, overlapping, or unrelated. Fashion brand social enterprises whose social objectives and business objectives are directly aligned include social firms whereby the social enterprise trains and employs beneficiaries to build capacity and economic sustainability, employee well-being programs, organizations that connect beneficiaries with their consumer markets, and organizations that operate as cooperatives. In the cases of social enterprises whose social objectives and business objectives overlap, the business sells products (i.e., fashion merchandise) to an external market and uses revenue to provide services to the beneficiaries in an area related to the company. Fashion brand companies also fulfill social objectives by creating and selling fashion merchandise to raise money for causes and issues that are marginally or unrelated to the fashion products they create and sell. Corporate foundations are created and financially supported by a company and, as with other strategies, are established to address specific issues or problems.

Fashion brand companies also advance social objectives through heightening awareness for and advocating policies around the issues or problems they seek to address. In addition, fashions can be used as a vehicle to advance philanthropic and advocacy efforts. As such, fashions often emerge as symbols of social change around important issues of the day.

Key Terms

business objectives
company-sponsored
    foundations
cooperatives
corporate foundations
for-profit organizations
foundation
non-government
    organizations (NGOs)
nonprofit organization

not for profit
    organization
one-for-one model
return on investment
social enterprise
social entrepreneurs
social firms
social objectives
sustainable community

References and Resources

1% for the Planet (2017). *Home*. Retrieved on August 30, 2017, from https://www.onepercentfortheplanet.org/index.php.

American Apparel and Footwear Association (AAFA) (2017). *Home*. Retrieved on August 30, 2017, from https://www.aafa global.org/.

American Forests (2017). *Our Story*. Retrieved on August 30, 2017, from https://www.americanforests.org/discover-american -forests/our-story/.

Batist, Danielle (2017, February 28). "Incentivizing Sustainable Fashion: Lessons from Social Entrepreneurs." *Forbes*. Retrieved on August 30, 2017, from https://www.forbes.com/sites /ashoka/2017/02/28/incentivizing-sustainable-fashion-lessons -from-social-entrepreneurs/#19c908247d3e.

Bombas (2017). *Giving Back*. Retrieved on August 30, 2017, from https://bombas.com/pages/giving-back.

Bugg-Levine, Antony, Kogut, Bruce, & Kulatilaka, Nalin (2012, January–February). "A New Approach to Funding Social Enterprises." *Harvard Business Review*. Retrieved on August 9, 2017, from https://hbr.org/2012/01/a-new-approach-to -funding-social-enterprises.

Byars, Tessa (2016, August 9). "Patagonia Releases New Book, 'Family Business: Innovative Child Care Since 1983.'" Retrieved on September 6, 2017, from http://www.patagoniaworks.com /press/2016/8/8/patagonia-releases-new-book-family-business -innovative-on-site-child-care-since-1983.

C&A Foundation (2017). *C&A Foundation*. Retrieved on August 18, 2017, from http://www.candafoundation.org/.

ClothRoads (2017). *Home*. Retrieved on August 26, 2017, from https://www.clothroads.com/.

ClothRoads (2017, August 10). "A Moroccan Button Takes on New Forms." Retrieved on August 26, 2017, from https://www .clothroads.com/moroccan-button-takes-new-forms/.

Cotton, Jasmine (2017, March 29). "Top Ten Celebrity and Fashion Collaborations for a Good Cause." *Fashion Industry Broadcast*. Retrieved on August 30, 2017, from https:// fashionindustrybroadcast.com/2017/03/29/top-10-celebrity fashioncharity-collaborations/.

Council on Foundations (2017). *Foundation Basics*. Retrieved on August 18, 2017, from https://www.cof.org/content /foundation-basics.

Delivering Good (2017). *Home*. Retrieved on August 30, 2017, from http://www.delivering-good.org/.

Eileen Fisher (2017). *Grants Overview*. Retrieved on August 18, 2017, from https://www.eileenfisher.com/grants/grants -overview/.

Foundation Center (2017). *Grantspace: Knowledge Base*. Retrieved on August 8, 2017, from http://grantspace.org/tools/knowledge -base/Funding-Research/Definitions-and-Clarification /corporate-foundations-vs-giving-programs.

Freeset (2017). *Who We Are*. Retrieved on August 30, 2017, from http://freesetglobal.com/who-we-are.

Gandys (2017). *Gandys Foundation*. Retrieved on August 30, 2017, from http://www.gandyslondon.com/gandys-foundation.

Global Goods Partners (2017). *Our Story*. Retrieved on August 30, 2017, from https://globalgoodspartners.org/pages/our-story.

Indigenous Designs (2017). *Impact Report*. Retrieved on February 21, 2018, from https://cdn.shopify.com/s/files/1/1814/2399/files/Indigenous_Designs_Impact_Report_2017_2_96ppi_dec17.pdf?4848433388766832882.

Institute for Sustainable Communities (2017). *Definition of Sustainable Community*. Retrieved on August 4, 2017, from http://www.iscvt.org/impact/definition-sustainable-community/.

Iredale, Jessica (2017, June 5). "Kenneth Cole: Staying Woke After All These Years." *WWD*, 7.

Kenneth Cole (2017). "Making AIDS History." Retrieved on August 29, 2017, from https://www.kennethcole.com/lgfg-making-aids-history.html.

Lazlo (2017). *Lazlo*. Retrieved on August 26, 2017, from https://lazlo.co/.

Luke, Belinda G. & Chu, Vien (2013). "Social Enterprise versus Social Entrepreneurship: An Examination of the 'Why' and 'How' in Pursuing Social Change," *International Small Business Journal*, 31(7): 764–84.

McLean, Felicity (2017, February 3). "Saif Rashid Weaves Together Benefits for Bangladesh Garment Workers." *Changemakers*. Retrieved on August 30, 2017, from https://www.changemakers.com/fabricofchange/blog/saif-rashid-weaves-together-benefits-bangladesh-garment.

Multicultural Refugee Coalition (2017). *Open Arms Shop*. Retrieved on August 26, 2017, from http://www.mrcaustin.org/open-arms/.

Nau (2017). *Partners for Change*. Retrieved on August 30, 2017, from https://www.nau.com/partners-for-change.

Nest (2018). *About*. Retrieved on June 26, 2018, from https://www.buildanest.org/about/.

Nike (2017). *How We Give*. Retrieved on August 18, 2017, from https://communityimpact.nike.com/how-we-give.

Ovarian Cancer Research Fund Alliance (OCRFA) (2017). *Super Saturday*. Retrieved on August 30, 2017, from https://ocrfa.org/events/super-saturday/about/.

Outdoor Industry Association (OIA) (2017). *Home*. Retrieved on August 30, 2017, from https://outdoorindustry.org/.

Patagonia (2017). "The Activist Company." Retrieved on August 18, 2017, from http://www.patagonia.com/the-activist-company.html.

Patagonia (2017). "Vote Our Planet." Retrieved on August 18, 2017, from http://www.patagonia.com/vote-our-planet.html.

Pussy Hat Project (2017). *Home*. Retrieved on August 30, 2017, from https://www.pussyhatproject.com/.

Raven + Lily (2017). *Mission*. Retrieved on August 28, 2017, from https://www.ravenandlily.com/mission/.

Raven + Lily (2017). *Our Story*. Retrieved on August 28, 2017, from https://www.ravenandlily.com/our-story/.

(RED) (2017). *What Is (RED)?* Retrieved on August 30, 2017, from https://red.org/what-is-red/.

SiiZu (2017). *Our Philosophy*. Retrieved on August 30, 2017, from https://siizu.com/pages/philosophy/.

Social Enterprise Alliance (2017). *About Social Enterprise?* Retrieved on August 4, 2017, from https://socialenterprise.us/about/social-enterprise/.

Sseko Designs (2017). *Our Story*. Retrieved on August 8, 2017, from https://ssekodesigns.com/our-story.

Sudara (2017). *Our Story*. Retrieved on August 28, 2017, from https://www.sudara.org/pages/our-story.

Sustainable Communities (2017). *About Sustainable Communities*. Retrieved on August 4, 2017, from http://www.sustainable.org/about.

The Giving Keys (2017). *About Us*. Retrieved on August 10, 2017, from https://www.thegivingkeys.com/pages/about-us.

The Shoe That Grows (2017). *About Us*. Retrieved on August 8, 2017, from https://theshoethatgrows.org/about-us.html.

Toad&Co (2017). *More than a Warehouse*. Retrieved on August 26, 2017, from https://www.toadandco.com/doing-good.

TOMS (2017). *Improving Lives*. Retrieved on August 26, 2017, from http://www.toms.com/improving-lives.

Warby Parker (2017). *History*. Retrieved on August 30, 2017, from https://www.warbyparker.com/history.

Case Study: Conscious Step: Marketing Socks to Fight Poverty

Conscious Step was founded in 2013 by Prashant Mehta, Hassan Ahmad, and Adam Long, who were "concerned with the lack of awareness and the gravity of issues faced by their generation, they sought to create a way for the conscious individual to support global solutions in a way that was convenient, tangible, and recognizable" (Trahant, 2015). Headquartered in Brooklyn, New York, USA, and sourced in India, Conscious Step is a social enterprise that took "the most comfortable socks you'll every wear" and "matched them to key issues in the fight against poverty" in order "to fund organizations making the world a better place" (Conscious Step, 2017). For every pair of socks purchased, a donation is made to one of Conscious Step's nonprofit organization partners. These partners include Action Against Hunger, Global Citizen, and Water.org. Conscious Step is also a member of the 1% for the Planet industry initiative. In addition, Conscious Step socks are made using Global Organic Textile Standard certified organic cotton in fair trade working conditions.

Marketing strategies for social enterprises can be a challenge. Companies such as Conscious Step want to understand the lifestyles and values of their target customer and provide them with information about the important work the company is doing while at the same time promote products that meet the needs of their target customer. Currently, customers of Conscious Step can select and purchase online or at specialty stores throughout the United States, individual pairs of socks and/or collections of socks specifically around particular causes. For example, a "Collection Mens: Water, Books, Poverty" includes three pairs of socks, each with an embroidered emblem indicating donations were made to Room to Read, Water.org, and Global Citizen. The Conscious Step website and product packaging includes information about their manufacturing strategies, causes, and products themselves. An analysis of Conscious Step's current marketing efforts can provide important information to them about what is working and what they may do to improve their marketing strategies.

Questions

1. Who is the target customer for Conscious Step socks?

2. Go to the Conscious Step website (https://consciousstep.com/). Review Conscious Step's product offerings and effectiveness of their website as an informational and marketing tool. Provide Conscious Step with four suggestions (and rationale

for these suggestions) on how their website may be improved to share their story about their contributions to sustainable communities.

3. Create a fifty-word marketing communication message for Conscious Step target customer about the advantages of purchasing socks from Conscious Step.

4. What are four strategies Conscious Step could use to enhance their marketing efforts? Describe each strategy and the advantages and disadvantages of each.

5. Which of the four strategies would you recommend Conscious Step implement first? Why?

Note: The background for this case study is based on publicly available information. The business problem is speculative only and not based on publicly available and/or documented information from Conscious Step.

References

Conscious Step (2017). *Home*. Retrieved on October 15, 2017, from https://consciousstep.com/.

Trahant, Grant (2015). "Q&A with Conscious Step, On Fashion, Socks, and How to Sustainably Impact the World." *Causeartist*. Retrieved on October 15, 2017, from http://www.causeartist.com/conscious-step/.

Call to Action Activity: Becoming Part of the Solution

Fashion brand companies that are social enterprises address problems including poverty, hunger, modern slavery, homelessness, environmental issues, and/or social injustice through creating and selling fashion products. What local, regional, and/or global problem or cause would you be most interested in helping to address? This call to action activity is designed to inspire you to play a role in assisting a current organization or company in the fashion industry in addressing the problem or cause you have identified.

1. What is your passion? That is, what local, regional, or global problem or cause would you be most interested in helping to address?

2. Identify a fashion brand company whose social objective, activities, or foundation address this same problem or cause. Examples of companies are included in this and other chapters in this book and/or can be researched online. You may also be familiar with or research organizations that partner with fashion brand companies to address the problem or cause.

3. How does the fashion brand company address the problem or cause you have identified?

4. How can you become involved? Identify three activities in which you could participate in assisting with addressing the problem or cause. Select at least one of the activities and create an action plan for your participation.

5. Create a report that includes

    a. Background information on the problem or cause you have identified

    b. The fashion brand company and its role in addressing the problem or cause

    c. Three activities in which you could participate in assisting with addressing the problem or cause

    d. Your action plan for participating in at least one of the activities

Making a Difference in Communities: Conversation with Treana Peake

Treana Peake

Founder and Creative Director, Obakki https://obakki.com

Founder, Obakki Foundation https://obakkifoundation.org/

Treana Peake founded the luxury women's apparel brand, Obakki, in 2005. Based in Vancouver, B.C., Canada, the Obakki collection includes dresses and separates—tops, bottoms, and jackets. According to the Obakki website (Obakki, 2017), the "label is an extension of Peake, an avid traveler and leading humanitarian. From cross-country road trips to the cattle camps of South Sudan, her diverse inspirations lead Peake to create special and versatile pieces that connect customers to a real story."

Q: You are a fashion designer, philanthropist, and humanitarian. How did you come to combine these varied roles?

A: It all started with a white envelope. Every year around the same a white envelope of money would slide under the door to help my family get through the year. No return address. No letter enclosed. Just a plain white envelope—a beautiful act of kindness—one that would sculpt my views and actions. Why would someone do this so quietly? Never receiving any thanks, recognition, or praise for these actions. I thought of this person often and they became the benchmark of the person I would want to become and how I wanted to live my life.

At a very young age I started fundraising—concerts, events, school plays. I spent my early adult years doing development work around the world to help those in need, first in Romania and then in Africa—drilling water wells, building schools, and working with orphans and refugees. During this same time, I began my fashion career—launching collections around the world and truly living the creative dream. However, as my fashion brand grew, my interest in it began to fade. My two worlds—fashion and development—seemed very distant from one another. While I loved the creative exploration of fashion, it began to create a huge void in me because of its apparent superficiality. On the other hand, people loved what I was doing in fashion? At that point, I knew I needed to give meaning to my craft and to apply creativity to my development. And my worlds came together. I knew I could apply my passion to create change.

Q: How is your design work influenced by your philanthropic work? How do you balance authentic narrative and business?

A: When I first started as a designer, I searched for inspirations for my work—culling the world through art, books, internet, travel, and so forth. I was on a plane ride back from Africa and feeling inspired from my experiences. I realized that this is where I was drawing my inspirations—that my design work reflected what naturally moved me. For me now, the cause comes before the collection. Now when I travel the world—I look first at the need and then I look at how I can use the fashions to address the need. However, to a lot of people my worlds do not fit. How do you take what was going on in an African village and turn it into a $500 jacket? It took me years to figure it out. The stories I tell are authentic and real, considerate and respectful. And I tell the story of a hopeful, creative and happy Africa.

For example, my philanthropy work has taken me to Cameroon. I am inspired by the landscapes, shapes, contrasts, textures, forms, silhouettes, rituals, people, strength, hope, and future optimism. I create mood boards and silhouettes—translating these inspirations into fashions. Using foundational colors, textures, and shapes, I tell the story of history, hope, and future. I often include a film about my inspirations and the story the fashion tells. The fashions I create highlight elements that will connect and inspire people. And as more people who hear the stories through these fashions, the more water wells we'll be able to build.

Q: The Obakki Foundation does amazing work in Africa. Tell me about some of the projects that the Obakki Foundation has been involved with.
A: Let me talk briefly about five projects—Alel Chok, Malou, the Scarves for Water program, and the St. Valentine's orphanage.

Alel Chok. In December 2010, we drilled the first water well in Alel Chok. One year later, we hardly recognized the place. Around the well a village had sprung to life. There are houses and a small church, green crops thriving in the bright sun. Everyone's health has greatly improved. The children are in school. The elders can sit in the shade of a favorite tree and know that they are home at last. There is always immense gratitude in the eyes of the people as I return year after year—the growing sense of trust between us. As I sit with these people I am reminded that we're all connected and there is an over-whelming sense of belonging that I feel when I'm there.

Malou. Once rejected from society, Malou is a small community of leprosy-affected people. Leprosy is a curable disease, but not in this part of the world where medical care is a luxury. Untreated, those with leprosy suffer numbness, debilitating muscles stiffness, and, eventually, blindness. It's difficult to carry out essential daily tasks like fetching water and tending crops. When I visited Malou in December 2012, I dropped off some garden tools and seeds. Those seeds have since sprouted into a flourishing crop of fresh vegetables thanks to the care the villagers put into them. The people of Malou now have added a nutritional layer to their diet, and if they grow enough produce to satisfy their nutritional demands, they can also start making an income from their residual produce by selling it at the market. Malou

continues to impress us with their dedication to growth—they are the definition of a self-driven, successful community and have found a way to celebrate their inner beauty.

Scarves for Water Program. The Obakki Foundation is bringing clean water to villages in need, one scarf at a time. For every 500 of "limited edition" scarves sold, the Obakki Foundation drills a well, bringing clean water to 1,500 to 2,000 people in each community. To date we have drilled thirteen wells and impacted over 25,000 lives with our Scarves for Water program. For most people, a scarf is a stylish accessory. For villages in South Sudan, it's the gateway to a better life.

St. Valentine's Orphanage. When I first discovered the boys of St. Valentines Orphanage in Cameroon, they were living in a truly heartbreaking system, without access to schools or medical care, barely surviving on ten shared cups of rice every week in a shelter that lacked a roof, electricity, and water. We were able to provide them with basic necessities. And as I have returned every year to Cameroon, I have watched the original boys of St. Valentines grow into productive young men who are now working to become accountants, lawyers, and government administrators.

Q: What are the most important take-aways from your work with the Obakki Foundation? And your advice to those in the creative fields?
A: Those of us in the creative fields have so many opportunities to contribute. We spend years building networks and brands. I use the Obakki brand as a platform to do good in the world. I would encourage everyone in the creative fields, whether its fashion, music, or film, to use their platform for something good and to provide inspiration for others to be involved. By using the creative arts, others can be inspired and moved to take action.

I may never know who slipped that white envelope under my door year after year, but their kindness has had a ripple effect on many people. I can only hope that through my own actions and through the projects of the Obakki Foundation that I can inspire other people to do the same. I often get asked why I do what I do. That really isn't an easy question to answer. But, what I can tell you is that my heart is full and I wake up every morning with a passion to do more. We may not realize the impact we have when we give, but do it now—because someone somewhere is in need.

What I learn from the people in Africa has shaped and molded my life. I have spent so many years in Africa, I honestly feel that am leaving with more than I came with. And the very things that I learn from the villagers I now pass down to my family:

- To take risks and be courageous

- To love life and to embrace friendships

- To chase after your dreams

- To share one another's burden

- To be thankful for what you have and

- To dance to the beat of your own drum

- But, really above all, to be kind and compassionate

References and Resources

Creative Mornings (2013, February 18). "Obakki: Treana Peake Speaks at Creative Mornings Vancouver." Accessed from https://www.youtube.com/watch?v=kzZf5x6fKco on April 17, 2017.

Obakki (2017). *About Obakki.* Accessed from https://www.obakki.com/about/ on April 13, 2017.

Obakki Foundation (2017). *Projects.* Accessed from https://obakkifoundation.org/projects/all/ on April 13, 2017.

Saeedi, Mahyar (2016, July 2). "Designed To Speak—Fashion and Philanthropy—Treana Peake." Accessed from https://www.youtube.com/watch?v=7Bwnz7Tfc3c on April 17, 2017.

Company Highlight

Krochet Kids intl.: Together, We Empower People to Rise Above Poverty

Headquartered in Costa Mesa, California, USA, Krochet Kids intl. (KKi) has a mission to "empower people to rise above poverty." This mission is achieved through sustainable economic development programs in communities living in poverty. Programs focus on building capacity among women who live in poverty by providing them with training and work creating and manufacturing apparel and accessories. Merchandise is sold through the KKi website and through retailers including Whole Foods, Zumiez, and specialty retailers.

Currently, programs and local production facilities are located in Gulu, Uganda and Lima, Peru. In Gulu, Uganda over 150 women and their families have been assisted through the training and work program. With a minimum of three years of training and support, women are taught how to crochet a variety of apparel and accessory products. In 2008, 10 women in the program started a Village Savings and Loan Association to offer small low-interest loans to other women, family members, and neighbors; thus, empowering others in building a sustainable community.

In Lima, Peru the Cut & Sew Initiative is providing work to over 35 women creating apparel and accessories (e.g., t-shirts, travel bags). Work in the cut and sew facility is coupled with education and mentoring to assure long term economic sustainability. A Kickstarter campaign in 2011 allowed KKi to expand the Krochet Kids Peru programs.

Transparency is a key component to KKi's approach. The KKi website includes images and videos of the beneficiaries of these programs. An online "tour" of the facility shows images and provides explanations of each of the processes in creating the products. In addition, each product bears the signature of one of the women who made the product. Consumers can go on the Krochet Kids intl. website, find a photo of the woman who made your product, learn more about her, and even thank her (see Figure 7.12).

Reference

Krochet Kids intl. (2017). *What We Do*. Retrieved on August 8, 2017, from https://www.krochetkids.org/what-we-do/.

Figure 7.12 Consumers of KKi products know who made their products and can thank them through the KKi website.

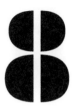

Goals, Plans, and Trends in Creating Sustainable Supply Chains

Objectives

- Explain the importance of a systems approach in developing and implementing sustainability plans.
- Explain interconnected strategies for creating a circular fashion system, including redefining fashion consumption.
- Summarize trends in social and cultural sustainability that result in capacity building and enduring and equitable business relationships throughout supply chains.
- Describe economic sustainability in terms of scalability of strategies around environmental, social, and cultural sustainability.
- Outline initiatives and strategies used to educate and empower consumers.
- Discuss the importance of leadership across and collaborations among fashion brand companies in achieving sustainable fashion supply chains.

> "My 30-year plan is for us to be a powerful force for change in the world."
> —Eileen Fisher

From its beginnings in 1984, Eileen Fisher, Inc. has been a design-driven company with the motto: "Good design is a result of paying attention to what women want and need." Through "simplicity, sustainability, and great design," Eileen Fisher creates "beautifully simple clothing designed to move with real life." A certified B Corporation, Eileen Fisher was an early advocate for sustainability in fashion. In 1997 the company created a social consciousness team to focus on

- Supporting women through social initiatives that address their well-being.
- Practicing business responsibly with absolute regard for human rights.
- Guiding our product and practice toward sustaining our environment.

Eileen Fisher fashion products embody environmental sustainability; made from organic cotton and linen, Tencel® lyocell, and other sustainable fibers dyed with bluesign® certified dyes. The designs of the fashions embody longevity of use; high-quality merchandise in seasonless styles. The company's sourcing decisions embody social sustainability through a human rights program that provides "people with dignified work that will enhance their livelihood, empowering them socially and economically." Sustainable communities are at the heart of their programs to support women's and girls' empowerment. The committed employees and culture of the company embody leadership at all levels with a focus on collaboration. Understanding that their organization encompasses "organic systems" that are continually evolving, Eileen Fisher embraces creativity in new directions. For example, the company recently launched Eileen Fisher Renew to give pre-owned Eileen Fisher merchandise a second life through resale and upcycling initiatives (see Figure 8.1). Eileen Fisher Renew products are now available through several Eileen Fisher retail outlets. In addition, the company's Vision 2020 sustainability plan focuses on all aspects of sustainability: environmental, social, cultural, and economic. With this holistic approach to sustainability in fashion, it's no wonder that Eileen Fisher, Inc. was used as an example throughout this book!

Figure 8.1 Eileen Fisher speaks about the Eileen Fisher, Inc. Vision 2020 sustainability plan at the Copenhagen Fashion Summit 2017.

As discussed throughout this book, multiple and interconnected strategies across the fashion supply chain are necessary to address the ever-changing dynamics of sustainability issues in the fashion industry including design and merchandising strategies around

- Diversity, equity, inclusion, and social change
- Product life cycle
- Longevity of use
- Supply chain assurance and transparency
- Sustainable business logistics and distribution
- Sustainable communities

It is now time to bring it all together. This chapter explores a holistic systems approach to sustainability and social change in fashion that companies such as Eileen Fisher, Inc. personify. When taking a holistic **systems approach** to sustainability and social change, companies focus "on the interactions and on the relationships between parts in order to understand an entity's organization, functioning and outcomes" (Mele, Pels, & Polese, 2010). In other words, they utilize **systems thinking** in their strategic planning and implementation. According to Ken Webster, Ellen MacArthur Foundation's Head of Innovation, systems thinking is the "understanding bigger contexts over longer periods and looking at the connections, not the parts, for insights" (Waldegrave, 2017). The global fashion industry is not only a holistic system in and of itself, it is also part of larger environmental and community systems. Therefore, when systems thinking is applied to sustainability and social change in fashion, the interconnected nature of and interactions among environmental, social, cultural, and economic sustainability in fashion inform companies' strategic planning and implementation of these plans.

The chapter begins with an overview of sustainability plans and goals of fashion brand companies including examples of exemplary efforts. Trends and future directions in the fashion industry around environmental, social, cultural, and economic sustainability are then discussed, focusing on their interconnections and relationships. The chapter

ends with a call to action around leadership throughout the fashion supply chain and throughout organizations. Industry leaders often voice that effective collaborations are imperative to address the issues facing the global fashion industry. Therefore, collaborations among companies and organizations are highlighted throughout the chapter.

Sustainability Goals and Plans

Industry and organizational systems are goal oriented and rely on continual feedback and assessments to adapt, improve, and foster innovation. This is certainly true of goals around systems that affect sustainability. In 2015, the United Nations adopted a plan of action called the *2030 Agenda for Sustainable Development* including seventeen goals and partnership strategies (United Nations, 2015). These high-level goals encompass all aspects of sustainability and reflect the interconnectedness among environmental, social, cultural, and economic sustainability. Although the goals are voluntary and dependent on each member country to take action, they give policy direction for countries. Using these goals as a foundation, in 2016 the Youth Fashion Summit (in conjunction with the Copenhagen Fashion Summit) outlined seven demands of the global fashion industry to be achieved by 2030 (Hendriksz, 2016).

1. As a group of CEOs, business and opinion leaders, academics and students, would you be here today without equal access to education? As inheritors of your roles, we demand empowerment and education of workers and consumers.

2. As inheritors of your roles, we demand that the fashion industry take drastic and immediate action toward closed-loop water systems to ensure that the industry is not dependent on fresh water as a resource.

3. As inheritors of your roles, we demand a long-term investment in the well-being of the community as a whole, through: fair wages; improving infrastructure; ensuring food security.

4. What do capital, profit and success mean to you? What if, by 2030, they meant something

completely different? As inheritors of your roles, we demand you all to collaborate as active investors in a fashion industry where capital, profit and success are redefined and measured in more than monetary value.

5. As inheritors of your roles, we demand that by 2030 fashion is no longer the second-largest polluting industry in the world.

6. As the next generation and inheritors of your roles, and our waste, we demand that designers, brands and governments collaboratively invest in the recycling technology and infrastructure that is needed to secure and enable a circular system.

7. As inheritors of your roles, we demand economic consequences in order to reverse standards.

Meeting these demands will take intentional, focused, and collaborative commitments of all companies in the global fashion industry, working together and using multiple and interconnected strategies. Utilizing a systems approach, coalitions of companies and organizations with the fashion industry are addressing the challenges being faced by the fashion industry within the larger environmental and community systems. For example, Fashion for Good is a "global coalition of brands, producers, retailers, suppliers, non-profit organizations, innovators and funders united in their genuine ambition to make all fashion good" (Fashion for Good, 2017). The goal of Fashion for Good is to reimagine "how fashion is designed, made, worn, and reused. Through innovation and practical action, we demonstrate a better way for the fashion industry to work that allows companies, communities, and our planet to flourish" (Fashion for Good, 2017). Partners include C&A, Cradle to Cradle Products Innovation Institute, Kering, Made-By, Sustainable Apparel Coalition, and Zero Discharge of Hazardous Chemicals.

Sustainability Plans

In addition, individual companies are moving forward with sustainability plans that encompass goals and multiple and interconnected strategies

around sustainability as well as their commitments towards industry-wide initiatives and collaborations. Development and continual assessments of sustainability plans over time with authentic feedback on impact of the plans are imperative for fashion brand companies to positively impact the larger environmental and community systems. The following steps are offered for creating, implementing, assessing, and adapting sustainability plans (Strähle & Müller, 2017; Wilson, 2015).

1. Develop and document a **sustainability plan** *with commitments, goals, implementation plans, and assessments.* For example, Marks & Spencer's Plan A (described in greater detail later in this chapter) focuses on three areas: zero carbon, zero waste, fair and healthy. The overall sustainability plan must be authentically adopted throughout the organization—leadership throughout the organization is imperative including leadership from the highest levels within the organization. In addition, appropriate and effective collaborations with other companies and/or organizations may be instrumental in meeting the goals of the company's sustainability plan.

2. Identify strategy and initiative priorities. Every fashion brand company comes to this process with different needs and priorities. In addition, fashion brand companies cannot implement all sustainability strategies and initiatives at once. Therefore, fashion brand companies must identify and prioritize initiatives. In some cases, the founder or CEO of the fashion brand company sets the priorities and overall philosophy of the company. Other fashion brand companies prioritize initiatives by conducting general risk assessments for their supply chain. Risk assessments were discussed in Chapter 5. Through these general risk assessments, the company realizes where the largest needs are in their supply chain and tackle these largest needs first.

3. Establish metrics, benchmarks, and processes for measuring performance around environmental, social, cultural, and economic sustainability. How does a fashion brand company determine their

progress on meeting their sustainability goals? When establishing the sustainability plan and goals, companies need to establish **metrics** (i.e., methods by which progress toward a goal will be measured), benchmarks (i.e., standard or point of reference used in comparing metrics), and processes (including continual audits) to measure progress and achievements as well as note areas for improvement.

4. Start small. When implementing strategies, start small with pilot programs and/or a limited number of operations. Learn from these pilot programs who to engage in the process, strategies that work, and strategies that need additional work.

5. Be transparent within and beyond the company. Be transparent by reporting metrics, benchmarks, and key performance indicators to internal stakeholders (e.g., employees, partner companies, and organizations) and external stakeholders (e.g., investors, customers).

    a. Engage employees through training, education, and incentives.

    b. Engage suppliers through product innovation using sustainable materials, design processes, reduction of waste, and transparency.

    c. Engage communities and customers through education and incentives. Marketing communications that connect with their stakeholders—informing them of initiatives, progress, learnings, and achievements—are imperative.

6. Remember that the sustainability plan is a journey not a destination. The plan must be updated on a periodic basis to reflect feedback, new technologies and processes, and changes in external environment.

Examples of Sustainability Plans

Both fashion brand companies and international organizations have developed sustainability

Figure 8.2 UK-based fashion retailer Marks and Spencer is a leader in sustainability, as evidenced by their Plan A\2025.

plans including all aspects of sustainability—environmental, social, cultural, and economic. One of the most comprehensive and progressive is the sustainability plan of UK-based fashion retailer Marks and Spencer (see Figure 8.2) called Plan A\2025 (Marks and Spencer, 2017). A general overview of this sustainability plan is provided as an exemplary example of fashion brand company's commitment to all aspects of sustainability, attainable metrics, strategies for implementation, and feedback for continual improvement (Marks and Spencer, 2017).

The Marks and Spencer Plan A\2025 focuses on three overarching pillars:

1. Nourishing our well-being

2. Transforming lives and communities

3. Caring for the planet we all share specific targets to achieve the goals

More specifically, Marks and Spencer set out a number of goals to be reached by the year 2025:

1. To be the world's leading retailer on engaging and supporting customers in sustainable living.

    a. Fully integrate sustainability into our brand and deliver a step change in the way we engage and support our customers. This will be achieved through new products and services, through even stronger community partnerships, and by providing advice and incentives on areas such as healthy living.

2. To help 10 million people live happier and healthier lives.

   a. We will extend the work we've done on our food products to our clothing, home and beauty offers too. We will have a particular focus on addressing issues of mental wellbeing, ensuring people are connected and happy as well as physically healthier. We will also work hard to ensure we support our customers and colleagues with cancer, heart disease, dementia and mental health issues.

3. To help transform 1000 communities.

   a. Starting in 10 communities (Birmingham, Bradford, Derry~ Londonderry, Glasgow, London Borough of Newham, Liverpool, Merthyr Tydfil, Middlesbrough, Norwich, Rochdale) we are going to undertake a range of activities to identify how our stores and people can make a positive and measureable difference to their neighbourhood. We'll rollout this approach to a further 100 communities by 2023 and then share any transformative learning with the other 1,000 communities we serve.

4. To champion Human Rights by taking a lead on addressing in-work poverty, modern-day slavery and inclusive society.

   a. Now we want to build on this position through an important new collaboration with Oxfam and by taking a lead on tackling issues such as in-work poverty and the living wage, modern day slavery and social inclusion.

5. To ensure 100% of our products address 100% of their material, social and environmental impacts.

   a. We have an existing commitment that every one of the 3 billion food, clothing, home and beauty products we sell every year has at least one Plan A attribute by 2020. An attribute being, for example, Fairtrade certified tea or coffee or FSC certified timber in furniture. We believe it's vital that Plan A should apply to everything we sell and not be a niche "ethical range" in the corner of a store. Today, 79% of our products have a Plan A attribute—putting us well on the way to our 2020 goal. However, we are now extending this commitment so that by 2025 every one of our products will have Plan A attributes that address every single one of its material social and environmental impacts. For example, covering the key raw materials, factory, use and disposal stages in a product's life cycle. This will put all our products well on the path to being truly sustainable.

6. To ensure 100% of factories are on a sustainability ladder with 50% of our products coming from the very highest Gold Standard.

   a. Currently, every factory that supplies M&S food is on a Bronze/Silver/Gold sustainability ladder to drive measurable improvements in its social and environmental performance. By 2025, every factory producing products for us will be systemically improving its environmental and ethical performance

7. To ensure our 50 key raw materials (80% by volume of what we use) come from a sustainable source.

   a. We are setting a goal that 100% of the key raw materials we sell will come from sources respecting people, communities, planet, and animal welfare. These key raw materials will represent at least 80% by volume of the raw materials used in our business

8. To set a science-based target to accelerate our shift to a low carbon business.

   a. The new plan includes a bold new (approved) science-based target to further improve the efficiency of our own operations as well as cutting 13.3m tonnes of CO_2 e from our wider value chain. We will also continue to invest in carbon offsets for our own operations to in order to remain carbon neutral.

9. To be a circular business generating zero waste.

   a. Plan A 2025 sets a bold new goal to be a zero waste business across all that we do—our operations, our supply chains and of course when our customers come to remove packaging and use our products. This includes designing our products and packaging to underpin the creation of a circular economy in the markets we serve.

10. To be a leader on transparency.

   a. Over the past 12 months we have published digital transparency maps identifying all the factories that produce food, clothing, home and beauty products for us. With Plan A 2025, we'll add information on the raw material sources we use and also translate this into 'on product' information to help guide our customers' decision making.

Many other fashion brand companies also have sustainability plans with targeted goals. Examples include:

- The Vision outlined in the sustainability plan of Swedish fashion brand, H&M, focuses on three ambitions: 100% Leading the Change, 100% Circular and Renewable, and 100% Fair and Equal. More specifically, under the 100% Circular and Renewable ambition, H&M has a goal to use 100% recycled or other sustainably sourced materials by 2030 (H&M Group, 2016).

- U.S. fashion brand, Eileen Fisher's, Vision 2020 sustainability plan focuses on six areas: Fibers, Color, Resources, People, Mapping, and Reuse. More specifically, under the Fibers area they have a goal that "all of our cotton and linen will be organic by 2020" (Eileen Fisher, 2017b).

- As part of the Hanes for Good initiative of U.S. corporation HanesBrands (brands include Hanes, Champion, Bali, and Gear for Sports), their 2020 Goals for Environmental Sustainability plan uses baseline data from 2007 as benchmarks for goals to reach by 2020. More specifically, Hanes is committed to reducing energy consumption by 40 % and water use by 50 % by 2020 (HanesBrands, 2017).

- The sustainability plan of Italian denim company Candiani, S.p.A., Europe's largest denim manufacturing companies, focuses on use of sustainable fibers as well as the development and use of innovative technologies associated with dying, weaving, and finishing denim (Szmydke-Cacciapalle, 2017). Their Denim 2.0 will be produced "with the least possible use of chemicals, it will reduce water consumption and waste in the dyeing and finishing process, as well as in the processing of samples. The goal is to be as close as possible to '0' By 2020" (Candiani, 2017).

- The sustainability plan of U.S.-based PVH (brands including Calvin Klein, Tommy Hilfiger, Van Heusen, Izod, and Speedo) consists of commitments that "represent a holistic, interconnected approach to creating positive impacts across three key areas: empowering people, preserving the environment, and supporting communities." More specifically, under the heading of Human Rights, PVH is committed to "promote adherence to our code of conduct for business partners, *A Shared Commitment*, and go beyond compliance to improve the lives of workers within our supply chain." Metrics include number of assessments, non-assessment engagement meetings, and trainings (PVH, 2017).

Trends in Environmental, Social, Cultural, and Economic Sustainability

Across the sustainability plans of fashion brand companies are trends and future directions in environmental, social, cultural, and economic sustainability. These trends reflect not only new technologies and processes, but also commitments by and collaborations among fashion brand companies as they address current and future challenges and issues associated with environmental, social, cultural, and economic sustainability.

Environmental Sustainability: Creating a Circular Economy

Environmental sustainability in the fashion industry requires fashion brand companies to 1) reduce their use of non-renewable resources in products and operations and 2) not use renewable resources in products and operations that exceeds the long-term rates of natural regeneration of these resources. Meeting these requirements takes intentional and incremental plans and strategies.

Fashion brand companies with progressive environmental sustainability plans incorporate both aspects of environmental sustainability through strategies associated with a circular economy. "A **circular economy** is an alternative to a traditional linear economy (make, use, dispose) in which we keep resources in use for as long as possible, extract the maximum value from them whilst in use, then recover and regenerate products and materials at the end of each service life" (WRAP, 2017). Moving towards a circular economy in fashion requires systems thinking; "by intention and design the feedback loops work to enrich, nourish, and add value. They therefore enable regeneration and restoration instead of lead to degeneration and consumption" (Webster, 2017). In 2017, Global Fashion Agenda called on fashion brand companies "to sign a commitment to accelerate the transition to a **circular fashion system**" (Global Fashion Agenda, 2017). Signatories committed to and set targets around one or more of four action points:

1. Implement design strategies for recyclability.
2. Increase the volume of used garments collected.
3. Increase the volume of used garments resold.
4. Increase the share of garments made from recycled textile fibers.

Fashion brand companies implement a number of strategies associated with the circular economy in creating a circular fashion system including:

- Sourcing environmentally sustainable fibers and materials.
- Creating fashions using zero-waste fashion design techniques.
- Designing and manufacturing high quality timeless designs that extend the life of the fashion.
- Creating opportunities for collecting previously worn fashions.

- Upcycling pre-consumer and post-consumer textile waste.
- Creating opportunities for repairing, sharing, renting, and/or reselling previously worn fashion merchandise.
- Engaging consumers as integral participants of the process.

All of these strategies have a goal of creating alternatives to the traditional linear economy of "make, use, and dispose." As discussed in Chapter 3, often a first (and important) step for fashion brand companies is the practice of sourcing environmentally responsible fibers and materials that do not rely on non-renewable resources or that are manufactured by reusing and/or recycling raw materials to create multiple lines of new fashions each year. Increased sourcing of sustainable materials by fashion brand companies is a result of research and development of these materials by textile companies and subsequent increased availability of these materials to fashion brands. For example, continuing their leadership in sustainable materials, Austrian textile producer, Lenzing Group recently launched filament fiber, Tencel™ Luxe branded lyocell, which creates fabric with a similar drape and texture as fabric made from silk. As with other Tencel™ fibers, Tencel™ Luxe is made from wood pulp sourced from sustainable wood using Lenzing's closed-loop lyocell production processes (Lenzing, 2017). Another textile company, Unifi, headquartered in Greensboro, North Carolina, USA, developed and sells REPREVE®, a fiber/yarn manufactured with 100 percent recycled materials (Repreve, 2017). According to Unifi, REPREVE® is used by fashion brands including prAna, United by Blue, Yukon Outfitters, Patagonia, Roxy, Adidas, Polartec, and Timberland (Unifi, 2017).

Going the next step of implementing multiple strategies together, non-renewable resources are reduced and precious resources are used for an extended period of time and reused in a regenerative circular process. Because most fashion brand companies are not vertically integrated; collaborations among companies are often necessary to implement a combination of strategies moving toward a circular economy. Fortunately, spurred by this environmental sustainability framework, companies throughout the fashion supply chain have contributed and partnered to achieve a more circular economy in fashion. The partnerships have often resulted in new fibers, materials, or products. For example,

- UK-based luxury brand designer, Stella McCartney, partnered with Bolt Threads, a biotech company based in the San Francisco Bay Area that specializes in advancing sustainable materials. Bolt Threads develops fibers from based on proteins found in nature, as well as clean, closed-loop manufacturing processes. An example of this partnership is a vegan-friendly silk created from yeast which McCartney will use in her collections (Stella McCartney, 2017).

- Singapore-based dye manufacturer, DyStar, partnered with fashion retailer C&A to create a T-shirt that received the Gold Level Cradle to Cradle Certified™ Material Health certificate by the Cradle to Cradle Product Innovation Institute. The shirt is made from 100 percent organic cotton and is dyed using DyStar Levafix® and Remazol® reactive dyes which received C2C Gold Level certification for Material Health in 2016 (DyStar).

Companies within the fashion supply chain have also created partnerships around upcycling pre- and postconsumer waste materials such as waste hosiery, plastic bottles, airline seats, even coffee grounds. For example,

- As part of Gildan Activewear's sustainability goal of finding alternative uses of textile waste (86 percent of which is already recycled or repurposed), they partnered with zero waste designer Katherine Soucie for her San Soucie collection. Gildan ships hosiery waste from its Gildan Apparel Canada Manufacturing facility located in Montreal, Quebec, to the San Soucie studio in Vancouver, B.C. (Gildan Activewear, 2017).

- Taiwan-based, Singtex Industrial Co. partners with local coffee shops in creating S.Café® yarns (see Figure 8.3). Used coffee grounds are collected

from the coffee shops and, through innovative processes, are embedded inside the yarn, changing the characteristics of the filament. S. Café® yarns naturally absorb odors and reflect UV rays (Singtex Industrial Co., 2017).

- In partnership with Thread, a certified B Corporation that transforms waste plastic bottles into fabric, Timberland created the Timberland X Thread line of shoes, T-shirts, and bags. The Thread™ Ground to Good™ fabric is made with postconsumer recycled PET from collected plastic bottles in Haiti. According to Colleen Vien, director of sustainability at Timberland, "This collection delivers good with every fiber, not just by recycling plastic bottles that would otherwise end up littering the streets, but also by creating job opportunities and cleaner neighborhoods in Haiti. Consumers

Figure 8.3 Because of their performance characteristics, S.Café® yarns, made with recycled coffee grounds, are often used in sports apparel.

can feel good about pulling on their Timberland®
X Thread™ boots or backpack, and know they are
making a positive impact in someone else's life"
(Timberland, 2017). "Each yard of fabric is traced
and tracked at every step of its journey, from bottle
collection and fabric creation to the delivery of the
fabric bolt to the manufacturer. This transparency
allows Timberland consumers to learn about the
vibrant people, stories and the impact metrics
behind each boot, shoe, bag and t-shirt they
purchase" (Timberland, 2017).

- Headquartered in Long Beach, CA, USA, Upcycle
  it Now has partnered with companies including
  Hurley, Patagonia, and Walt Disney in upcycling
  waste materials from these companies. Their
  goals are to "create a second life for promotional,
  pre-consumer, and post-consumer materials
  that no longer have any use" creating one of a
  kind products and custom-designed products.
  Examples include one of a kind dog coats made
  from well-worn Patagonia products and lunch
  bags made from street banners.

- Similarly, Looptworks (2017), headquartered
  in Portland, Oregon, has partnered with Alaska
  Airlines, Southwest Airlines, Langlitz Leathers,
  the Portland Trailblazers, and companies in the
  wetsuit industry to create limited edition apparel
  and accessories from excess and waste materials. For
  example, used leather from airplane seats is upcycled
  to create messenger bags; excess motorcycle
  jacket leather is upcycled to make tote bags excess
  neoprene, sourced from the wetsuit industry, is
  upcycled to create laptop and tablet sleeves.

City, company, and university collaborations on
upcycling initiatives are also an important trend. For
example,

- San Francisco State University, PeoplewearSF®,
  and the San Francisco Hotel/Non-Profit
  Collaborative collaborated on the Table Cloth
  Project (PeoplewearSF®, 2012; Ulasewicz, 2016) in
  which used table clothes from hotels were used to
  create innovative tote bags.

- Columbia College Chicago, United Airlines, and
  Re:new Project collaborated in transforming large

a

b

Figure 8.4 Columbia College Chicago design students
worked with surplus materials from United Airlines,
such as banners (a), in creating a variety of upcycled
products (b).

United Airlines banners into carry-on bags that
were then sold on the united.com website (see
Figure 8.4 and Zero Waste Design and University/
Industry Upcycling Collaboration: Conversation
with Elizabeth Shorrock at the end of this chapter).

Social and Cultural Sustainability:
Beyond Auditing

Social and cultural sustainability in the fashion
industry requires fashion brand companies to
contribute to the social well-being of individuals

and communities through shared structures and processes and through positive, equitable, and enduring relationships. Strategies associated with social and cultural sustainability implemented by fashion brand companies were described throughout the book including

- Designing, creating, manufacturing, and distributing inclusive and equitable products
- Implementing diversity and health and well-being programs for employees and for companies within their supply chain
- Advocating for policies that support their social objectives, equality, social justice, environmental sustainability, and sustainable communities
- Implementing, ensuring, and communicating responsible sourcing, production, and purchasing practices
- Contributing to initiatives that support the communities in which they operate and beyond
- Participating in industry-wide collaborations around responsible sourcing, production, and purchasing practices
- Creating positive, enduring, and equitable relationships among employees and with business partners that respect and value cultural representations and traditions
- Building capacity throughout their supply chain

As noted in Chapter 5, fashion brand companies' contributions to social and cultural sustainability often start 1) at the design stage with a commitment to inclusive and equitable fashions or 2) at the production stage with codes of conduct and factory auditing processes. From there, companies implement additional strategies that eventually result in more inclusive product offerings and imagery and capacity building and positive, enduring, and equitable business relationships throughout their supply chain.

Moving social and cultural sustainability in the fashion industry "beyond auditing" has been fostered by several industry-wide research projects and comprehensive reporting initiatives. The general goal of these research and reporting initiatives is to provide public disclosure of the status of the industry and/or fashion brand companies with the intent that the information will be used by companies to make changes and by consumers in informing their purchase decisions.

The Garment Workers Diaries is an ongoing research project documenting the lives of approximately 540 female garment workers in Bangladesh, Cambodia, and India (Garment Worker Diaries, 2017). A collaboration among Microfinance Opportunities, a U.S.-based nonprofit organization that conducts research on low-income households, Fashion Revolution, and C&A Foundation, the Garment Workers Diaries project researchers utilize Financial Diaries and cross-sectional surveys research methods to uncover economic realities that garment workers face. Data were drawn from weekly interviews and reports on workers' earnings and expenditures, and living and working conditions. Results indicated that on the average, participants worked 48 hours per week and worked overtime 45 percent of the weeks. Workers were reliant on overtime with 36 percent of gross wages coming from overtime hours. Expenditures were primarily for immediate consumption (e.g., 55 percent of expenditures for goods and services was on food) rather than for goods and services to improve standard of living (e.g., durable goods, education investment, medical care). Although many workers reported that they felt safe and healthy in their factories, 77 percent of participants reported not feeling safe all of the time in their factory; 40 percent had witnessed a fire and others were concerned with pollutants in the air. Workers also reported pressure from supervisors to work faster and discrimination in the workplace, against women (e.g., pregnant, too old) or belonging to a union (Garment Worker Diaries, 2017).

As discussed throughout this book, sustainable fashion brand companies are transparent and provide information about their materials, suppliers, workers, and practices around sustainability. In the past, if consumers wanted to know the policies and practices of their favorite brand, they would need to research each brand. To address this issue, several organizations have emerged to hold companies accountable by researching and publicly reporting companies' policies, practices, and strategies to around environmental, social, and cultural sustainability. Below are a few examples of these reports. Additional resources for consumers are discussed later in the chapter.

KnowTheChain, benchmarked the efforts of twenty publicly traded apparel and footwear fashion brand companies to eliminate forced labor within their supply chains (KnowTheChain, 2016). Companies included Adidas, Gap, H&M, Lululemon Athletica, Primark, Inditex (Zara), PVH, HanesBrands, Gildan Activewear, Nike, L Brands, Ralph Lauren, Hugo Boss, VF, Fast Retailing (Uniqlo), Under Armour, Kering, Prada, Shenzhou International, and Belle International. Business activities analyzed included: Commitment and Governance, Traceability and Risk Assessment, Purchasing Practices, Recruitment, Worker Voice, Monitoring, and Remedy. Fashion brand companies with the highest scores (e.g., Adidas, Gap Inc., H&M, Lululemon Athletica) demonstrated practices in all areas analyzed with notable activities in training, stakeholder engagement, traceability, risk assessment, and auditing processes.

Similarly, the Ethical Fashion Report (Nimbalker et al., 2017) focused on ethical practices of 106 multinational and New Zealand and Australian-owned companies covering 300 fashion brands. The report was researched and published through Baptist World Aid Australia's Behind the Barcode project and the Tearfund New Zealand. Scores given to each company were based on company policies, knowing their suppliers throughout the supply chain, auditing and supplier relationships, and worker empowerment. Top performing brands included Mighty Good Undies, Etiko, Kowtow, Liminal Apparel, and Patagonia.

In 2016, non-governmental human rights organization, Human Rights Watch, contacted seventy-two apparel and footwear companies to ask that they commit to and implement a Transparency Pledge including name and street address of factories, worker numbers, product type, and parent company of the factory, provided in a searchable and downloadable database. In 2017, they published the Follow the Thread (Human Rights Watch, 2017) report outlining their responses from the companies and their analysis of company commitment. Companies with full alignment with the pledge included Adidas, C&A, G-Star RAW, HanesBrands, H&M, Lindex, Levis, Nike, and Patagonia.

The Fashion Transparency Index, created by Fashion Revolution (see discussion in Chapter 5), annually rates fashion brands according to five key areas of supply chain transparency (Fashion Revolution, 2017, p. 15) using information that is publicly disclosed by the company around

- Policy and commitment—documentation and implementation of social and environmental policies, priorities, and future goals
- Governance—contact information for individual(s) who are responsible for the brand's social and environmental impacts and how the brand incorporates responsible sourcing and purchasing practices
- Traceability—public disclosure of suppliers, including tier one, two, and three suppliers
- Supplier assessment and remediation—policies and implementation strategies around supplier audits, worker empowerment, and remediation of any problems
- Spotlight issues (covering the business model, living wages, unions and collective bargaining)

Economic Sustainability: Scalability

Economic sustainability requires fashion brand companies to sustain a determined level of economic production over time. Fortunately, numerous fashion brand companies have debunked the myth that fashion brand companies cannot be economically sustainable and also practice strategies that contribute to environmental, social, and cultural sustainability. In fact, a fashion brand company's **competitive advantage**, the characteristics of the company that make it superior to its competitors, is often a result of their sustainability initiatives and efforts. In addition, examples of strategies associated with environmental, social, and cultural sustainability that enhanced the economic sustainability were provided throughout the book, including

- Inclusive fashion designs that expanded the fashion brand's target customers
- Life cycle analysis that provided the basis for reduced water and energy use by the company
- Health and well-being programs for employees that resulted in increased productivity and product quality
- Adopting environmentally sustainable packaging that reduced the costs of shipping

It is important to note that strategies associated with furthering environmental, social, and cultural sustainability in fashion often start small: a zero waste designer uses deadstock materials from a local mill, a social enterprise hires at-risk women in a community, a small group of artisans start a cooperative, a small specialty retailer sells only upcycled merchandise. In each case, the company's processes and systems start small with the idea that they will **scale** or expand in the future. **Scalability** is the capability of a company, system, and/or process to grow or expand while maintaining (or increasing) the performance, quality, efficiencies, and effectiveness of the company, system, or process. Scalability can be a challenge for social entrepreneurs and other small fashion brand companies wanting to grow and expand. Can the zero waste designer obtain enough deadstock materials to expand? Can the social enterprise effectively work with at-risk women in multiple communities? How will the cooperative be organized with additional artisan members? Will the specialty retailer need to focus on more than upcycled merchandise in order to grow? To answer questions such as these small fashion brand companies are advised to (LeBlanc, 2017):

1. If possible, think about scalability from the beginning by incorporating a solid foundation in systems, processes, and networks. For example,

at its beginning, the cooperative of artisans may create a document that outlines membership criteria and responsibilities.

2. When challenges arise, focus on scalable solutions. For example, when funding becomes an issue, the social entrepreneur could expand its facilities through grants that fund social enterprises.

3. Create and embrace strategic planning with goals, metrics, and benchmarks. Set priorities and adapt based on feedback. For example, the specialty retailer could develop a six-month merchandising plan with sales goals while at the same time expanding networks of companies creating upcycled merchandise.

4. Be flexible and take advantage of opportunities as they arise and/or are created. For example, the zero waste designer might take advantage of being approached by another mill who would like to sell their deadstock materials to the designer.

5. Be mission-driven with a focus on core strengths and values. For example, the social enterprise has articulated its mission around assisting at-risk women and addresses all strategies, challenges, and issues with this mission at the forefront.

6. Be patient as it takes time to build capacity in systems, processes, and people.

A great example of scalability is Patagonia's move into offering fair trade fashion merchandise. By their nature, fair trade facilities are typically small enterprises which have made it difficult for larger companies to utilize their services. However, Fair Trade Certification by Fair Trade USA has expanded the options for fashion brands. Patagonia now offers several collections, including swimwear and hemp workwear, in Fair Trade Certified facilities (Wright, 2017).

Consumer Engagement: Redefining Fashion Consumption

The economic sustainability of fashion brand companies is dependent on **fashion consumption**— acquisition, storage, usage, maintaining, and disposing of fashions. In the traditional linear economy, a consumer would purchase a new fashion item and then wear, maintain, and store it until the decision was made to dispose of it most likely by throwing it away, giving it to a charity, or reselling it. In moving to a circular economy, redefining fashion consumption is necessary. Consumers must consider fashion products as valued resources that are worn for as long as possible with materials that are then regenerated to create new products. Is this even possible in today's fast fashion consumption orientation? Do consumers really care? And, if so, how do companies engage fashion consumers to embrace a more circular economy in fashion?

Fashion consumption is a widely researched area. Scholars worldwide have investigated criteria consumers have used in making fashion purchase decisions and characteristics and purchasing behavior of specific groups of consumers, including the **sustainable apparel consumer**, consumers who use sustainability factors to inform their purchase decisions. According to the Global Environment Survey conducted by Cotton Council International and Cotton Incorporated (Cotton, Inc, 2017), overall 61 percent of their participants said sustainability had a moderate or great deal of influence on their apparel purchases. However, attitudes vary by country; 81 percent of participants in Italy, 69 percent of participants in the United Kingdom and Mexico, 64 percent of the participants in Germany, and 59 percent of the participants in the United States said sustainability had a moderate or great deal of influence on their apparel purchases. In general, participants perceived sustainability in terms of environmental sustainability and consumers were not always well-informed about environmentally sustainable fibers and materials. Only one-third of all consumers said that the fiber/fabric was "absolutely essential/extremely important" in determining sustainability. The survey found that participants considered cotton (83 percent), organic cotton (81 percent), and wool (79 percent) to be the most sustainable. That compared to recycled polyester (45 percent), rayon or viscose (41 percent), polyester (38 percent), and modal (37 percent). Another study

of consumer perceptions of sustainable fashion (sponsored by Oeko-Tex, 2017) was conducted with more than 11,000 consumers in ten countries. In general, participants held fashion brands accountable, counted on them for assurances of responsible production, and looked to them as role models in sustainability. As a short-cut to trust and transparency, participants often looked for particular fashion brands and certification labels that provided them with credible assurances of sustainable business practices. In addition, awareness and knowledge about sustainability issues in the global industry were important contributors to attitudes.

What does this mean for the fashion brand company that is committed to economic, environmental, social, and cultural sustainability? What are strategies to engage the sustainable apparel consumer as well as creating more consumers who take sustainability into account in their decisions? Initiatives and strategies by fashion brand companies and organizations can be used to educate and empower consumers. In addition, sustainable fashion influencers play important roles in heightening awareness among consumers.

Fashion Brand Company Initiatives to Educate and Empower Consumers

Moving to a circular economy requires that fashion brand companies engage, encourage, and lead fashion consumers through education, incentives, and evidence around environmental, social, and cultural sustainability in fashion. Below are examples of consumer engagement strategies. Depending on the size of the company, product offerings, current sustainability strategies, and future goals, fashion brand companies can be sustainability leaders in a number of ways.

Encourage consumers to only purchase what they need. The most famous example of a fashion brand encouraging consumers to think about their purchases before buying was Patagonia's Friday, November 25, 2011 (Black Friday) advertisement in the New York Times "Do Not Buy This Jacket." Of course, this advertisement drew criticism from some who believed that it was hypocritical of Patagonia to run such an advertisement because they are in business of creating and selling products. Patagonia countered these criticisms by noting "it would be hypocritical for us to work for environmental change without encouraging customers to think before they buy. To reduce environmental damage, we all have to reduce consumption as well as make products in more environmentally sensitive, less harmful ways. It's not hypocrisy for us to address the need to reduce consumption. On the other hand, it's folly to assume that a healthy economy can be based on buying and selling more and more things people don't need— and it's time for people who believe that's folly to say so" (Patagonia, 2011).

Focus on fashion as a valued resource. Heritage brands, slow fashion brands, and those that create and sell heirlooms often emphasize the value and longevity of their products, educating consumers about the value of purchasing fewer and higher quality pieces. For example, U.S. lifestyle fashion brand, Alabama Chanin's founder, Natalie Chanin, started with company with the vision of slow fashion and community. As noted on their website "We are a leader in elevated craft due to a strong belief in tradition and dedication to locally sewn garments and goods—both hand and machine-sewn. We maintain responsible, ethical, and sustainable practices holding ourselves to the highest standards for quality" (Alabama Chanin, 2017).

Educate and encourage consumers around sustainable practices. Fashion brand companies can engage consumers to take action around a number of sustainable practices. For example, REPREVE® fibers encourages consumers to recycle plastic bottles and to spread the word through social media. "Together, we can spread the word about what can be made with plastic bottles when recycled. Imagine all the potential uses for that recycled plastic bottle! Share on Twitter how you #TURNITGREEN!" (Repreve, 2017).

Report impact of strategies around environmental, social, and cultural sustainability. As discussed throughout this book, fashion brand companies

are making great progress in strategies around environmental, social, and cultural sustainability. Engaging and educating the consumer about these strategies is important. Fashion brand companies need to go beyond simply listing fiber content in their product information or posting their code of conduct. For example, in addition to indicating that fashions are made from 100 percent certified organic cotton, fashion brand companies can educate the consumer about the advantages of organic cotton. In addition to sharing codes of conduct, fashion brand companies can share the impact of implementing the codes along with images/videos of factories and stories about the workers.

Report impact of work in building community, inclusiveness, and social justice. Fashion brand companies are also contributing to communities, inclusiveness, and social justice. As such, they need to go beyond a statement of their work by sharing images and stories of the impact of their work on the individuals and community. Social enterprises and fashion brands that encourage the creation of shared communities are great examples of engaging and educating consumers about the broader context of their work. For example, size inclusive brand, Kade & Vos, notes on their website that they are "pushing the boundaries of size and fit" (Kade & Vos, 2018). US gender neutral brand, Wildfang, communicates their commitment to diversity and creates community around "the new neutral: 'cause your clothing doesn't get to define your gender" (Wildfang, 2017) (see Figure 8.5).

Encourage and report impact of consumers renting and purchasing pre-owned and/or upcycled fashions. As discussed in Chapter 6, opportunities for purchasing upcycled and pre-owned fashions continue to grow. Fashion brand companies such as Patagonia and Eileen Fisher now offer pre-owned merchandise through their own retail outlets. Fashion brands are also partnering with other companies to offer renewed and upcycled merchandise. Fashion brand companies can inspire consumers by information around advantages and role these efforts play in moving toward a circular economy.

Figure 8.5 Fashion brands, such as Wildfang, build shared communities that embrace diversity and inclusiveness.

Educate consumers around caring for and mending fashion products. As discussed in Chapter 3, less energy can be used in washing and drying fashions and as discussed in Chapter 4, life of fashion products can be extended through appropriate maintenance and care of the fashions. However, rarely do fashion brand companies provide guidance to consumers about the impact of caring and maintaining the fashions, beyond the mandatory care labels. However, fashion brand companies can play an important role in educating consumers. Patagonia's Worn Wear program includes product care guidelines that reduce energy use and easy fixes to common mending problems such as "how to repair a tear on the down jacket?" or "replacing cord in a hood" (Patagonia, 2017).

Provide education and opportunities around responsible disposing of fashions (donating, sharing, re-selling), upcycling and recycling. Educating and engaging consumers around a circular economy requires consumers to understand the importance of upcycling and recycling programs. In addition, in an effort to reduce postconsumer textile waste, opportunities are growing for consumers to recycle textiles, apparel, and footwear. Retail take-back programs, such as those discussed in Chapter 6, have become a trend. Charity organizations are promoting their recycling efforts; more communities are offering recycling options including drop-off recycling of used textiles and in some cases, curbside recycling for textiles, apparel, and footwear. Textile recycling bins operated by both for-profit and nonprofit organizations can be found throughout communities. For example, recycling bins operated by Recycle for Change, collect and recycle used clothing and shoes (see Figure 8.6) throughout California, USA. The clothing collected is sold to second-hand clothing dealers and graders and in the process "supports organizations in community-based sustainable development" (Recycle for Change, 2017). Companies can play an important role in providing information about what happens to donated fashions. For example, nonprofit organization, Planet Aid, headquartered in Maryland, USA, collects used clothing through its 19,000 bins in nineteen states. They provide an

Figure 8.6 Clothing collected through Recycle for Change recycling bins support community-based sustainable development.

excellent overview of "what happens to your used clothing" on their website (Planet Aid, 2017).

Organization and Industry-wide Initiatives to Educate and Empower Consumers

Associations and organizations have advanced industry-wide efforts to also engage, educate, and empower consumers around sustainability. Examples include

- GINETEX, the international association for textile care labeling, created the Clever Care website with practical tips on how to reduce the environmental impact of caring for clothing. Tips include don't wash your clothes too often, lower the temperature when machine washing, think of reducing the amount you tumble dry, think of ironing only when necessary, and use dry clean only when necessary.

- Fashion Revolution, a social enterprise headquartered in the UK, sponsors Fashion Revolution Week that includes the #whomademyclothes campaign (see Figure 8.7).

Figure 8.7 Who Made My Clothes campaign, sponsored by Fashion Revolution, is designed to empower consumers to ask fashion brands "who made my clothes?"

During this week, consumers are empowered to ask fashion brands "who made my clothes?" and fashion brands are encouraged to respond, resulting in greater supply chain transparency. Many brands post images of their workers with the sign "I made your clothes." In addition, Fashion Revolution's website includes images, diaries, and videos of garment workers throughout the world (Fashion Revolution, 2017).

- True Fashion Collective (2017) "provides fashion consumers with inspiring news and tangible tools to be part of the much needed positive change in the fashion industry." With a goal of taking sustainable "from 'niche' to 'norm,'" the True Fashion Collective offers resources including a listing of events and projects, consumer empowerment tools, and opportunities for sharing ideas and information.

- The groundbreaking 2015 documentary about the fast fashion industry, *The True Cost*, received worldwide acclaim and has been translated into 19 languages. As an important resource, in and of itself, that has influenced consumers around the world, The True Cost website (https://truecostmovie.com/) offers additional resources for consumers including "5 tips for shopping smarter," a listing of "brands we love," interviews, and links to educational and inspirational videos (The True Cost, 2017).

- Conscious Chatter (http://consciouschatter.com/) is a series of podcasts hosted by Kestrel Jenkins that focuses on topics related to sustainable fashions "that allows us to continue to learn more about the garment industry and how we can all be a bigger part of positive change in the industry" (Conscious Chatter, 2017). Podcasts include interviews with industry leaders, reports on issues, and calls to action for positive change.

Sustainable Fashion Influencers

In addition to fashion brand companies, organizations, and associations directly engaging consumers, **sustainable fashion influencers** are also important in building awareness and bringing attention to sustainable fashion brands, thus influencing consumer behavior. In marketing, **influencers** (also known as **opinion leaders** or **change agents**) are individuals who have the credibility and social visibility to influence the opinions, attitudes, and/or purchasing behaviors of consumers. Influencers are connected to consumers through media outlets, industry associations, brand communities, or **consumer tribes**, groups emotionally connected by similar consumption values and usage. Credibility or believability of influencers is based on their expertise or knowledge, trustworthiness, and/or attractiveness as an inspirational role model. A **social media influencer** has established credibility in a specific business and has access through social media, blogs, and social networks to a large number of consumers interested in the influencer, product category, or business. Brand marketing consultancy, Eco-Age, has created and advanced socially visible platforms for sustainable fashion influencers, thus heightening awareness of environmentally sustainable fashions (Eco-Age, 2017). These platforms include The Green Carpet Challenge® that pairs high profile celebrities with brands that create newsworthy designs worn on red carpets and the Green Carpet Fashion Awards, Italia 2017 that honored contributors to the sustainable supply chain, "Made in Italy." Designer Stella McCartney is an important sustainable fashion influencer through her partnerships with textile companies in developing and promoting innovations in sustainable materials, particularly for the luxury market. Actor Emma Watson has also emerged as an important sustainable fashion influencer through the publicity of her red carpet gowns made with sustainable materials (see Figure 8.8) and her Instagram account focused on sustainable fashion brands.

Leadership throughout the Sustainable Fashion Supply Chain

For fashion brand companies to effectively implement sustainability plans and for organizations and associations to effectively further initiatives around economic, environmental, social, and

Figure 8.8 Sustainable fashion influencer Emma Watson wore a Calvin Klein dress made from recycled plastic bottles to the 2016 Met Gala.

cultural sustainability, effective leadership is needed throughout fashion supply chains and throughout fashion brand companies. **Leadership** can be defined in many ways; however, the following definition of leadership by Kevin Kruse captures the type of leadership necessary to create sustainable fashion supply chains. According to Kruse (2013), "leadership is the process of social influence which maximizes the efforts of others, towards the achievement of a goal." This definition fits the role of leadership needed in fashion supply chains because it articulates that

- Leadership comes from social influence, not from title or position within a company. In fact, anyone within a company can influence others making a positive difference around socially responsible business practices, regardless of title or position.

- Leadership is goal oriented. Leadership is most effective when everyone has a clear vision and passion in achieving a common goal and have the opportunities and resources to achieve that goal.

- Leadership is about empowering others by creating environments in which their efforts are maximized. Effective leaders often indicate that their effectiveness is based on hiring great people and then "getting out of their way." Trust, encouragement, and inspiration are imperative.

- Leadership is not about having certain type of personality or communication style; there are as many effective leadership styles as there are people.

In their book, *The Necessary Revolution: How Individuals and Organizations Are Working Together to Create a Sustainable World* (2010), authors Peter M. Senge, Bryan Smith, Nina Kruschwitz, Joe Laur, and Sara Schley describe those who "'bring to life' a new way of thinking, seeing, or interacting that creates focus and energy." These leaders inspire others in companies and organizations to ask difficult questions and to respect multiple perspectives—all necessary to take the company or organization to new levels of creativity and impact. Similarly, María Almazán, fashion social entrepreneur "believes **intrapreneurs**—people who want to drive change from inside organizations—are key to the transformation process" in the fashion industry (Batist, 2017). As she noted in a *Forbes* magazine interview (Batist, 2017) "there are changemakers in every organization. They are not doing it to get rich but to change the industry. Because the ideas they introduce may sound alien at first, they need tools and evidence to show their peers how it can be done."

To create sustainable supply chains, Senge et al. (2010) challenge and provide strategies for individuals to engage in meaningful conversations around socially responsible business practices and ask difficult questions around "what would we do if . . .?" Applying these lessons to the fashion industry, questions might include: As a fashion brand company, what would we do if . . .?

- Zero waste design was the goal for every new fashion?
- Water scarcity meant that traditional dying methods would no longer be viable?
- The health and well-being of the factory workers who made our products were a priority to those purchasing the merchandise?
- Brand loyalty was dependent on complete supply chain transparency?
- We were required to take back all merchandise from consumers when the merchandise was no longer being worn/used?

For example, founders of French sportswear company Picture Organic Clothing asked the question "what would we do if our affordable performance sportswear advanced environmental sustainability?" (see Figure 8.9). The answer was the creation of sustainable fashion brand, Picture, made from 100 percent recycled, organic or responsibly sourced materials. As they note on their website: "Everything is connected. The Earth allows us to ride wonderful spots, to share incredible moments with our friends and we want future generations to be able to enjoy the same wealth" (Picture, 2017).

How do you get started having these conversations? If you are fortunate to be an employee of a fashion brand company that has a sustainability plan, then it makes sense to start with one of the areas already identified for your company as a priority. If your company does not have a sustainability plan, Senge et al. (2010) offers steps for moving conversations and initiatives forward. A summary is provided here.

1. What sustainability issues are the most important for you and your fashion brand company? What are the current practices of your company and why are you concerned? Ask "what would we do if . . .?" Communicate your thinking with your supervisor.
2. Talk with others in your company who may have similar concerns or passions around sustainability.

Figure 8.9 Co-founders of Perfect Organic Clothing, Jeremy Rochette (R) and Julien Durant (L), established their fashion brand to advance environmental and social sustainability.

Through these initial conversations, discuss who else need to be part of the conversations.

3. Convene a team of individuals from diverse perspectives who have common concerns. Include individuals who are directly involved with the processes under consideration for change as well as those who oversee and are involved with sustainability initiatives. Garner support to move forward with the conversations, assuring managers of the timeframe.
4. Develop a proposed plan for change including both practical (current situation) and strategic (future directions) perspectives.
5. From this proposed plan for change, develop a more detailed project plan to be presented to management and next steps for the team to engage the organization. Similar to a sustainability plan, the project plan should document commitments, goals, implementation plans, and assessments (metrics, benchmarks, and processes for measuring performance).

Whereas these steps appear simple and straightforward, organizational change is often difficult. For the "necessary revolution" and change to happen throughout fashion supply chain, leaders must question the status quo, create plans with metrics and benchmarks, implement necessary strategies, assess the outcomes, revise the plans, and continue to ask the question "As a fashion brand company, what would we do if . . .?"

Summary

As discussed throughout this book, multiple and interconnected strategies across the fashion supply chain are necessary to address the ever-changing dynamics of sustainability issues in the fashion industry. When taking a systems approach to sustainability and social change, companies focus "on the interactions and on the relationships between parts in order to understand an entity's organization, functioning and outcomes" (Mele, Pels, & Polese, 2010). Industry and organizational systems are goal oriented and rely on continual feedback and assessments to adapt, improve, and foster innovation. This is certainly true of goals around systems that affect sustainability. Utilizing a systems approach, coalitions of companies and organizations with the fashion industry are addressing the challenges being faced by the fashion industry within the larger environmental and community systems. In addition, individual companies, such as Marks and Spencer, Eileen Fisher, and HanesBrands, are moving forward with sustainability plans that encompass goals and multiple and interconnected strategies around sustainability as well as their commitments toward industry-wide initiatives and collaborations.

Fashion brand companies with progressive environmental sustainability plans incorporate multiple strategies associated with a circular economy. When these multiple strategies are implemented together, non-renewable resources are reduced and precious resources are used for an extended period of time and reused in a regenerative circular process. Because most fashion brand companies are not vertically integrated, collaborations among companies are often necessary to implement a combination of strategies moving toward a circular economy. In addition, in moving to a circular economy, redefining fashion consumption is also necessary. Consumers must consider fashion products as valued resources that are worn for as long as possible with materials that are then regenerated to create new products. Initiatives and strategies by fashion brand companies and organizations can be used to educate and empower consumers. Sustainable fashion influencers also play important roles in heightening awareness among consumers.

Fashion brand companies' contributions to social and cultural sustainability often start 1) at the design stage with a commitment to inclusive and equitable fashions or 2) at the production stage with codes of conduct and factory auditing processes. From there, companies implement additional strategies that eventually result in capacity building and positive, enduring, and equitable business relationships throughout their supply chain. It is important to note that strategies associated with furthering environmental, social, and cultural sustainability in fashion often start small and then are scaled as the company grows and expands. For fashion brand companies to effectively implement sustainability plans and for organizations and associations to effectively further initiatives around economic, environmental, social, and cultural sustainability, effective leadership is needed throughout fashion supply chains and throughout fashion brand companies.

Key Terms

circular economy
circular fashion system
change agents
competitive advantage
consumer tribes
fashion consumption influencers
intrapreneurs
leadership
metrics
opinion leaders

scalability
scale
social media influencer
sustainable apparel consumer
sustainable fashion influencers
sustainability plan
systems approach
systems thinking

References and Resources

Alabama Chanin (2017). About. Retrieved on October 24, 2017, from https://alabamachanin.com/about.

Batist, Danielle (2017, February 28). Incentivizing Sustainable Fashion: Lessons from Social Entrepreneurs. *Forbes*. Retrieved on October 25, 2017, from https://www.forbes.com/sites/ashoka /2017/02/28/incentivizing-sustainable-fashion-lessons-from -social-entrepreneurs/#252b7a277d3e.

Candiani (2017). Candiani Sustainability Report 2016. Retrieved on October 18, 2017, from http://www.candianidenim.it /download/Sustainability%20Report.pdf.

Conscious Chatter (2017). Home. Retrieved on October 25, 2017, from http://consciouschatter.com/.

Cotton Incorporated (2017, October 13). Sustainability Concerns: Americans Improving but Still Lag. *Lifestyle Monitor*. Retrieved on October 20, 2017, from http://lifestylemonitor.cottoninc. com/sustainability-concerns/.

Dystar (2017, June 8). DyStar Supports Circular Economy Initiative in Apparel Sector. Retrieved on October 18, 2017, from https:// www.dystar.com/dystar-supports-circular-economy/.

Eco-Age (2017). *Home*. Retrieved on October 25, 2017, from http://eco-age.com/.

Eileen Fisher (2017) *Meet Eileen*. Retrieved on October 18, 2017, from https://www.eileenfisher.com/meet-eileen/meet-eileen/.

Eileen Fisher (2017). *Vision 2020*. Retrieved on October 18, 2017 from https://www.eileenfisher.com/vision-2020/

Fashion for Good (2017). Home. Retrieved on October 25, 2017, from https://fashionforgood.com/.

Garment Worker Diaries (2017, August 31). http://www.articulate -story-demo.com.php7-32.phx1-2.websitetestlink.com/story _html5.html.

GINETEX (2017). *Clevercare.info*. Retrieved on October 22, 2017, from http://www.clevercare.info/en.

Gildan Activewear (2017, October 3). "Gildan Partners with Sans Soucie to Give New Life to Hosiery Waste." Retrieved on October 18, 2017, from http://3blmedia.com/News/Gildan -Partners-Sans-Soucie-Give-New-Life-Hosiery-Waste.

Global Fashion Agenda (2017). 2020 Circular Fashion System Commitment. Retrieved on October 25, 2017, from https:// www.copenhagenfashionsummit.com/commitment/.

H&M Group (2016). "The H&M Group Sustainability Reports." Retrieved on October 18, 2017, from https://sustainability. hm.com/en/sustainability/downloads-resources/reports /sustainability-reports.html.

HanesBrands (2017). Hanes for Good: Environmental Responsibility. Retrieved on October 18, 2017, from https://hanesforgood.com /environmental-responsibility/.

Hendriksz, Vivian (2016, May 20). Copenhagen Fashion Summit: "Sustainability Is the Norm." *Fashion United*. Retrieved on September 20, 2016, from https://fashionunited.uk/news /fashion/copenhagen-fashion-summit-sustainability-is-the -norm/2016052020477.

Kade & Vos (2018). *About Us*. Retrieved on February 23, 2018, from https://kadevos.com/pages/about-us.

Kruse, Kevin (2013, April 9). "What Is Leadership?" *Forbes*. Retrieved on October 24, 2017, from https://www.forbes.com /sites/kevinkruse/2013/04/09/what-is-leadership/#3a77105a5b90.

LeBlanc, Jeanette (2017, July 3). "What Is Scalability in Business? 5 Keys for Success + 3 Business Organization Tools." Retrieved on October 17, 2017, from https://learn.infusionsoft.com /growth/planning-strategy/what-is-scalability-in-business.

Lenzing (2017, October 9). "Lenzing Launches TENCEL™ Luxe." Press Information. Retrieved on October 20, 2017, from http://www.lenzing.com/en/press/press-releases/detail /article/2017/9/09/lenzing-praesentiert-tencelTM-luxe.html.

LooptWorks (2017). *About*. Retrieved on October 18, 2017, from https://www.looptworks.com/pages/about.

Marks and Spencer (2017). "Plan A/2025." Retrieved on October 15, 2017, from https://corporate.marksandspencer.com /documents/plan-a/plan-a-2025-commitments.pdf.

Mele, Cristina, Pels, Jacqueline, & Polese, Francesco (2010). "A Brief Review of Systems Theories and Their Managerial Applications," *Service Science*, 2(1–2): 126–35. https://doi .org/10.1287/serv.2.1_2.126.

Oeko-Tex (2017, October 23). "The Key to Confidence: Consumers and Textile Sustainability." Webinar retrieved on October 26, 2017, from https://www.oeko-tex.com/en /business/oeko_tex_webinars/webinar_2017_10_23_the _key_to_confidence.xhtml.

Patagonia (2011, November 25). "Don't Buy This Jacket, Black Friday and the New York Times." The Cleanest Line Blog. Retrieved on October 23, 2017, from https://www.patagonia .com/blog/2011/11/dont-buy-this-jacket-black-friday-and -the-new-york-times/.

Patagonia (2017). *Worn Wear*. Retrieved on October 23, 2017, from https://wornwear.patagonia.com/repair-and-care.

Planet Aid (2017). "What Happens to Your Used Clothing?" Retrieved on October 23, 2017, from http://www.planetaid .org/what-we-do/for-the-environment/what-happens-to-your -used-clothing.

PVH (2017). *Our Commitments*. Retrieved on October 18, 2017, from https://www.pvh.com/responsibility/our-commitments.

Recycle for Change (2017). *Home*. Retrieved on October 23, 2017, from http://www.recycleforchange.org/.

Repreve (2017). *Discover REPREVE*. Retrieved on October 22, 2017, from https://repreve.com/discover.

Senge, Peter M., Smith, Bryan, Kruschwitz, Nina, Laur, Joe, & Schley, Sara (2010). *The Necessary Revolution: How Individuals and Organizations are Working Together to Create a Sustainable World*. New York: Broadway Books/The Crown Publishing Group.

Singtex Industrial Co. (2017). "What Is S.Café®?" Retrieved on October 16, 2017, from http://www.scafefabrics.com/en-global /about/particular.

Speer, Jordan K. (2017, June 21) "Timberland Elevates Eco-Fashion Trash-Reducing Collection." *Apparel*. Retrieved on October 20, 2017, from http://apparel.edgl.com/news /Timberland-Elevates-Eco-Fashion-in-Trash-Reducing -Collection109951?rssid=Article109951&eid=363536749 &bid=1798405.

Stella McCartney (2017, July 20). "Stella McCartney and Bolt Threads Announce a New Partnership Focused on Sustainable Fashion and Luxury Materials Development." Retrieved on October 18, 2017, from https://www.stellamccartney.com /experience/us/press-room/stella-mccartney-and-bolt-threads -announce-a-new-partnership-focused-on-sustainable-fashion -and-luxury-materials-development/.

Strähle, Jochen and Müller, Viola (2017). "Key Aspects of Sustainability in Fashion Retail," in Jochen Strähle (ed.). *Green Fashion Retail* (7–26). Singapore: Springer Science+Business Media.

Szmydke-Cacciapalle, Paulina (2017, April 18). "Candiani Ups the Ante on Sustainability." *WWD*. Retrieved on October 18, 2017, from http://wwd.com/business-news/markets/candiani-ups -the-ante-on-sustainability-10866223/.

Timberland (2017, March 2). "New Timberland X Thread Collection Delivers Good with Every Fiber." Retrieved on October 20, 2017, from https://www.timberland.com /newsroom/press-releases/timberland-thread-collection.html.

True Fashion Collective (2017). *About*. Retrieved on October 22, 2017, from http://truefashioncollective.com/.

Ulasewicz, Connie (2016, April 22). Personal communication.

Unifi (2017). *Our brands*. Retrieved on October 26, 2017, from http://www.unifi.com/un_product_ourbrands.aspx.

United Nations (2015, September). "United Nations Sustainable Development Goals (SDG)." Retrieved on October 25, 2017, from http://www.un.org/sustainabledevelopment/sustainable -development-goals/.

Upcycle It Now (2017). http://www.upcycleitnow.com/partnerships/.

Waldegrave, Lou (2017, September 29). "What Is Systems Thinking?" *Circulate*. Retrieved on October 19, 2017, from http://circulatenews.org/2017/09/what-is-systems-thinking/.

Webster, Ken (2017, October 12). "4.5 Misconceptions About the Circular Economy." *Circulate*. Retrieved on October 20, 2017, from http://circulatenews.org/2017/10/4-5-misconceptions -circular-economy/.

Wilson, John P. (2015). "The Triple Bottom Line: Undertaking an Economic, Social, and Environmental Retail Sustainability Strategy." *International Journal of Retail Distribution Management*, 43(4/5): 432–47. https://doi.org/10.1108 /IJRDM-11-2013-0210.

WRAP (2017). "The Waste and Resources Action Programme. WRAP and the Circular Economy." Retrieved on October 15, 2017, from http://www.wrap.org.uk/about-us/about/wrap-and -circular-economy.

Wright, Beth (2017, August 4). "Patagonia Hemp Workwear to Be Made in Fair Trade Facility." *Just-style.com*. Retrieved on October 22, 2017, from https://www.just-style.com /news/patagonia-hemp-workwear-to-be-made-in-fair -trade-facility_id131369.aspx?utm_source=daily-html&utm _medium=email&utm_campaign=04-08-2017&utm_term =id98557&utm_content=109033.

Case Study: Scalability and LooptWorks: Use Only What Exists

The motto for Portland, Oregon-based LooptWorks is "use only what exists." In fact, all of the pre-consumer and postconsumer waste materials used to create LooptWorks products were at one time headed to the landfill; but instead the materials were rescued, upcycled, and repurposed into limited edition products. Starting with the materials as inspiration, LooptWorks designs apparel, bags, packs, laptop and tablet sleeves, and other accessories, which are then produced in factories that employ fair labor practices. Using zero waste pattern design techniques, LooptWorks uses as much of the waste materials as possible in the new upcycled products.

To be economically sustainable, LooptWorks must have continual sources of high quality materials for their upcycled products. In the past, LooptWorks has partnered with a variety of companies and organizations.

- The Portland Trail Blazers came to them with 4,000 obsolete game jerseys which were transformed into new limited edition backpacks, scarfs, and jackets.
- Southwest Airlines and Alaska Airlines/Horizon Air replaced heavy leather seat covers in their airplanes with lighter weight materials. Southwest Airlines'

80,000 seat covers were ready for a new life. The leather was repurposed by into bags and accessories.

- Langlitz Leathers needed a better way of using the leather trim leftover from the cutting patterns for their motorcycle jackets. The excess leather was transformed into a variety of bags and small leather goods.
- Excess neoprene materials from the wetsuit industry were used to create laptop and tablet sleeve covers.

As part of the team of designers and product developers at LooptWorks, you are always on the lookout for sources of materials for upcycling projects and for opportunities to get the word out regarding the mission and strategies of LooptWorks.

Questions:

1. What are three possible sources of materials that LooptWorks could use for upcycled merchandise? What types of merchandise might be made from each of these sources of materials? What are the advantages and disadvantages of using these sources of materials for their products?

2. The zero waste design process used by LooptWorks starts with the materials. What design challenges might be created by the sources of materials you identified in question 1?

3. What three strategies could LooptWorks use to get the word out regarding their mission and strategies for upcycling? What are the advantages and

disadvantages of each of these strategies? Which of these strategies would you recommend LooptWorks implements and why?

Note: The background for this case study is based on publicly available information. The business problem is speculative only and not based on publicly available and/or documented information from LooptWorks.

References:

LooptWorks (2017). LooptWorks and Langlitz Partner Up. Retrieved on October 18, 2017, from https://www.looptworks.com/blogs/looptworks-blog/69478915-looptworks-and-langlitz-partner-up.

LooptWorks Blog (2015). How to Make Bags and Travel Accessories with Airline Seat Covers. Retrieved on October 18, 2017, from https://www.looptworks.com/blogs/looptworks-blog/52319491-how-to-make-a-duffle-bag-and-tote-bag-with-airline-seat-covers.

Call to Action Activities: Fashion Transparency Index: Brand Analysis and Engagement

Do you know where and by whom your favorite brands were made? Are these companies committed to social, environmental, economic, and cultural sustainability? If so, how? These are questions we need to ask of all of the companies that create, produce, and distribute the fashion brands we love. To start this process, the Fashion Transparency Index provides basic information about many of our favorite fashion brands.

1. Go to the Fashion Transparency Index, http://fashionrevolution.org/about/why-transparency-matters/, and select a fashion brand included in the index that you wear or that you are interested in knowing more about.

2. Describe the fashion brand's scores on each of the five key areas assessed in the Fashion Transparency Index. What do each of the scores mean?

3. Select one of the key areas in which this fashion brand could improve their score? Describe three initiatives/activities that the fashion brand could implement that would improve their score. Why are each of these initiatives/activities important in improving transparency?

4. Write a professional email to the fashion brand (you can find contact information on the fashion brand's website) that describes your interest in the brand, your analysis of the scores on the Fashion Transparency Index, your recommendations for how the fashion brand could improve one of the scores, and the importance of this initiative/activity to you.

Call to Action Activities: **Upcycling Collaboration Project**

The goals of this call to action activity are for you to

- Identify postconsumer textile waste within your community that can be easily collected.
- Design and merchandise a product that utilizes the postconsumer textile waste.

1. Postconsumer textile waste is all around us—in homes, schools, businesses, hotels, restaurants, retailers, places of worship—anywhere where fabrics and textile products are used and thrown away. Look around! Where do you see postconsumer textile waste that ends up in landfill? Is it possible for this textile waste to be collected? If yes, brainstorm about upcycling this textile waste into a new product that could be merchandised and sold; thus extending the longevity of use of the material. For inspiration, check Etsy.com for a variety of upcycled textile products.

2. Identify the postconsumer textile waste to be used and connect with the users of the textiles to coordinate collection. Interview the users of the textiles to describe the amount of textile waste that could be removed from landfill if the textile waste was recycled, downcycled, or upcycled.

3. Design and create a new product that results in an upcycled textile product. Describe your inspiration, design process, and production method. Who is the target customer for your product? Create a brand name for your product.

4. Write a reflection paper (minimum of one page) on what you have learned from this project.

5. Turn in:
   - Paper (minimum of two pages) outlining the postconsumer textile waste identified, interview with the users, and description of inspiration, design process, and production method of the upcycled textile product. Describe the target customer for your product. Include the brand name of the product.
   - Photographs of the original postconsumer textile waste and the new product created from the textile waste.
   - Reflection paper (minimum of one page) on what you learned from this project.

Zero Waste Design and University/Industry Upcycling Collaboration: **A Conversation with Elizabeth Shorrock**

Elizabeth Shorrock, Assistant Professor
Fashion Studies
Columbia College Chicago
Chicago, IL USA

Q: How did you get interested in sustainability and social responsibility as a topic within fashion design?
A: My interest in second-hand and vintage clothing started when I was in college at the Rhode Island School of Design (RISD). This was before wearing second-hand and vintage clothing was associated with sustainability. However, the creative environment at RISD, the maker movement, my own desire for unconventional and quirky clothing, and my interest in textiles and fashion all came together. Upon graduation from RISD in 1981, I worked for a screen printer and then met my husband. We started our own business in 1984. At the time, the chemicals used in dry cleaning were an issue. Therefore, we decided to work with only natural fibers that were easy care and could be laundered. We designed and printed all of our own yardage. We wanted to work with the most environmentally responsible dyes and did a great deal of research on dyes; eventually using (biodegradable) pigments with a seaweed base. We sold our merchandise at juried arts and crafts shows—supporting the artist/

maker movement of the time. I continued to explore environmentally friendly materials (in this pre-Internet world) and discovered Sally Fox's Fox Fibre which we used for a couple of years. Because all of our fabrics were dyed, printed, cut, and sewn in-house, we accumulated and saved lots of textile scraps/waste. We challenged ourselves to create less waste in the cutting process—primarily with the motive to save money. This was the beginnings of designing using zero waste techniques. We produced a jacket made with scraps of fabric used in previous seasons and it became our best seller. Five or six women came to the studio every day—we paid well and our employees were very loyal. We marketed our line in NYC and as the business grew, it also became more stressful. I started to feel detached from design and wanted to make a difference in the world through teaching. I went back to school at the Rhode Island School of Design to earn my master's degree. I love the teaching process, engaging students in real-life initiatives, and empowering them—particularly around reducing industrial waste.

Q: How did you get involved with United Airlines upcycling project?
A: The American Association of Airport Executives sponsors an Airports Going Green Conference each year. The 2014 the conference, held in Chicago, included a Sustainable Fashion Show featuring Columbia College Chicago Designers who used fabrics donated by several airlines, including United Airlines. I asked representatives from United Airlines about the possibility of using a variety of materials that they had in their warehouses—seat belts, leather and upholstery from seats, and used banners. Students in my course, Design for Change, worked with surplus materials from United Airlines in creating a variety of upcycled products. United Airlines selected two of the students' designs to produce and sell on their website. All of the proceeds went to Re:New Project, a program that provides training and space for refugee women to learn viable skills for dignified work. The women create a number of handcrafted totes and bags using upcycled textiles. United documented every step of the way (Sustainable Brands, 2015).

Q: You are obviously passionate about creating social change through fashion. How do you currently integrate sustainability and social responsibility within the fashion curriculum? In your opinion what is needed to assure that sustainability and social responsibility are integrated into the curriculum of all fashion programs?
A: I'm fighting the fight through teaching—raising awareness and getting students to become actively involved in the human element of the industry. It is exciting and gratifying for me to watch a design student going from not caring to caring. Students need to come out of design schools with the mindset of reducing waste throughout the design and construction processes using the best sustainable practices. Sustainability issues and practices should be holistically integrated into every course we teach, from foundation level through senior level. Not doing so is a disservice. Therefore, I incorporate these concepts and practices into all of the courses I teach.

I also serve as a role model for students through my work as a designer and producer. And I am a founding member of a new organization in Chicago, Sustainable and Ethical Apparel Makers (SEAM), which will provide a platform for students and professionals to mentor, collaborate, produce and show their work as part of Chicago Fashion Week. We have garnered support from local business as well as bringing four area fashion design programs together to promote sustainable fashion within their design curriculum. We have opened an ethical production facility that teaches women from underserved populations the skills they need and then employ them within our SEAM Works Studio production company.

Reference

Sustainable Brands (2015, October 20). United Upcycles Banners into Bags to Benefit Re:new Project, Peruvian Forest Project. Sustainable Brands. Retrieved on October 25, 2017, from http://www.sustainablebrands.com/news_and_views/next_economy/sustainable_brands/united_upcycles_banners_bags_benefit_renew_project_pe?destination=node%2F113331.

Company Highlight

Loomstate: It's All Connected

In 2004 Rogan Gregory and Scott MacKinlay Hahn founded New York City based, Loomstate, LLC with a "vision, believing that whole clothing supply chains from cotton farm to fashion house can support sustainable clothing production" (Loomstate, 2017a). They use certified organic cotton and other sustainable fibers, design timeless and high quality styles, build long-term relationships with their customers and vendors, and value people and the environment as much as they do the products—apparel for men, women, and infants. For Loomstate, it's all connected: "when farmers, factories & brands work together transparently, best pricing, supply & quality happens. For us, a sustainable system is one where everyone wins environmentally, socially & economically" (Loomstate, 2017b).

Partnerships are one of Loomstate's strategies for creating these connections. In 2009, Loomstate partnered with Target to create a limited-edition collection of certified organic cotton apparel, Loomstate X Target. More recently, they partnered with Rockaway Herb + Dye on a limited edition collection of naturally indigo dyed shirts. In addition, Loomstate creates custom uniform and corporate apparel including promotional merchandise, corporate apparel, and employee/crew uniforms (Loomstate, 2017c). Since 2012, Loomstate has partnered with Chipotle Mexican Grill to outfit every Chipotle employee in 100 percent certified organic cotton clothing (Chipotle, 2017). Loomstate also creates Chipotle licensed products (T-shirts, hoodies, onesies, tote bags, and hats) that can be purchased on the Chipotle Store. Their "partnership is a joint commitment to environmental and social responsibility, with a focus on the highest standards in the ingredients we use, the materials we source, and our methods of production" (Chipotle, 2017). As Scott Mackinlay Hahn, Loomstate and Steve Ellis, Chipotle stated "It's all connected. Our meals, our clothing, our environment."

References

Chipotle (2017). The Connection: A Relationship that is a Natural Fit. Retrieved on October 19, 2017, from http://store.chipotle.com/connection.

Loomstate (2017a). About Us. Retrieved on October 22, 2017, from https://www.loomstate.org/about-loomstate.

Loomstate (2017b). Mission. Retrieved on October 22, 2017, from https://www.loomstate.org/mission.

Loomstate (2017c). Uniforms and Corporate Wear. Retrieved on October 22, 2017, from https://www.loomstate.org/direct-services/uniforms.

A

adapted clothing Clothing designed specifically for people with physical disabilities or have difficulty dressing themselves.

adaptive clothing See *adapted clothing*.

aesthetic obsolescence Obsolescence created because an aesthetic or style is no longer desired.

ageism Stereotyping and discrimination based on differences in age.

audit fatigue Situation whereby the workers and management of contract factories become overwhelmed by the number and frequency of audits by different fashion brand companies with different codes of conduct.

B

B Corporations™ Businesses certified by B Lab around "standards of verified, overall social and environmental performance, public transparency, and legal accountability" (B Lab, 2016, *see* Chapter 1 References and Resources).

barrier-free design See *universal design*.

big-and-tall clothing Men's clothing in sizes that are larger than the traditional sizing categories.

bonded labor Labor that is "demanded as a means of repayment of a debt or a loan and can apply to a whole family and be inherited through generations" (Skrivánková, 2017, *see* Chapter 5 References and Resources).

brand community "A group of ardent consumers organized around the lifestyle, activities, and ethos of the brand" (Fournier & Lee, 2009, *see* Chapter 4 References and Resources).

business logistics Coordination of forecasting need; purchasing materials, trims, and findings; and moving materials, semi-finished and finished products from the product's inception and distribution to the ultimate consumer.

business objectives Objectives of a company related to financial sustainability, profit, and business growth.

C

carbon footprint The amount of carbon dioxide and other carbon compounds emitted due to the consumption of fossil fuels and is typically expressed in equivalent tons of carbon dioxide (CO_2) for a particular time period (usually per year).

carbon intensity See *carbon footprint*.

change agents Individuals who have the credibility and social visibility to influence the opinions, attitudes, and/or purchasing behaviors of consumers.

child labor "Work that deprives children of their childhood, their potential and their dignity, and that is harmful to physical and mental development" (International Labour Organization, 2017, *see* Chapter 5 References and Resources).

circular economy "Alternative to a traditional linear economy (make, use, dispose) in which we keep resources in use for as long as possible, extract the maximum value from them whilst in use, then recover and regenerate products and materials at the end of each service life" (WRAP, 2017, *see* Chapter 8 References and Resources).

circular fashion system Fashion supply chain based on circular economy strategies.

classic fashion Fashion that continues to be in style over a long period of time.

closed-loop recycling systems Production processes in which postconsumer waste is collected, recycled, and used to make new products.

co-creator Engaging the consumer/user in the product creation process to enhance the connection the consumer/user has with the product.

codes of conduct Written principles, policies, and rules as the minimum standards a company requires of its suppliers in relation to human resources, employee health and safety, and labor and environmental laws.

collaborative consumption Activities in which goods and/or services are shared between private individuals, either for free or for a fee.

company-sponsored foundations Foundations supported by a company for the purpose of charitable activities.

competitive advantage Characteristics of a company that make it superior to its competitors.

conflict minerals Minerals (tin, tungsten, tantalum, and gold) that are mined under conditions that violate human rights or finance armed conflicts in Democratic Republic of the Congo or its adjoining countries (e.g., Angola, Republic of Congo, Uganda).

conscious capitalism From the book, *Conscious Capitalism: Liberating the Heroic Spirit of Business (2013)* by John Mackey and Raj Sisodia to describe four principles of business models: higher purpose, stakeholder integration, conscious leadership, and conscious culture and management.

consignment Process used by some resale fashion retailers in which the seller of the used fashion merchandise (consignor) contracts with a consignment retailer (consignee) to sell the fashion products for them.

consumer tribes Groups of consumers emotionally connected by similar consumption values and usage.

contractor "Company that specializes in the constructing, sewing, and finishing of goods or that specializes in a specific part of the production process (such as pleating piece goods)" (Burns, Mullet, & Bryant, 2016, p. 348; *see* Chapter 2 References and Resources).

cooperatives Companies and organizations owned and operated by their members for the benefit of their members.

co-producer See *co-creator*.

corporate foundations See *company-sponsored foundations*.

corporate responsibility (CR) Business initiatives that are part of a company's overall business plan and that contribute to sustainable development. Also, corporate social responsibility (CSR) and social responsibility (SR).

corporate social responsibility (CSR) See *corporate responsibility (CR)*.

cultural appropriation Unauthorized and inappropriate borrowing and/or using of symbolic elements representing a particular culture or ethnic group by individuals who are not part of that particular culture or ethnic group.

cultural identity Individuals' views of themselves as belonging to a particular cultural, racial, or ethnic group.

cultural sustainability Strategies for maintaining the aspects of culture that create positive, equitable, and enduring relationships among the current members and future members of the society, group, or organization and that retain the value of the physical artifacts that represent the culture.

culture Sum of knowledge, beliefs, attitudes, values, customs, and meanings that defines a group's particular way of life.

D

deadstock fabric Flawed fabrics/materials or fabrics left over by from textile mills.

design For the purposes of this book, the term *design* refers to the processes in creating a fashion product including design, product development, pattern making, and production systems.

designing for durability "Foster and amplify the skills, habits of mind, and abilities of users to create and engage with fashion from within a context of satisfaction and resourcefulness" (Fletcher, 2012, p. 235, *see* Chapter 4 References and Resources).

disability "Condition or function judged to be significantly impaired relative to the usual standard of an individual or group. The term is used to refer to individual functioning, including physical impairment, sensory impairment, cognitive impairment, intellectual impairment mental illness, and various types of chronic disease" (Disabled World, 2017, *see* Chapter 2 References and Resources).

distribution "Outbound flow of goods from the end of the production process to the consumer" (Encyclopedia of Business, 2017, *see* Chapter 6 References and Resources).

diversity Demographic mix of a people that includes both individual differences (e.g., personality, life experiences, perspectives) and group/social differences (e.g., race, ethnicity, socio-economic status, gender, sexual orientation, gender identity, country of origin, and ability as well as cultural, political, religious, or other affiliations).

domestic contractor Contract factory located in the same country as where the finished goods will be distributed.

due diligence "Pro-active assessment of risks and investigation of incidences of abuse anywhere in the supply chain, remedying those situations and publicly reporting on how they are addressed" (ETI, 2017, p. 14, *see* Chapter 5 References and Resources).

E

economic obsolescence Obsolescence created because it is less costly to purchase a new item than to repair and/or alter a worn item.

economic sustainability The ability for individuals, companies, communities, and countries to sustain indefinitely a defined level of economic production.

emotionally durable design Emotional and experiential relationship between a consumer and the products they purchase resulting in extending the life of the product.

environmental sustainability Reducing consumption of non-renewable resources and ensuring that consumption of renewable resources does not exceed their long-term rates of natural regeneration (US EPA, 2016a, *see* Chapter 1 References and Resources).

equity Goal of promoting justice, impartiality, and fairness within the processes and distribution of resources by systems and/or institutions within the society.

ethical production Production that reflects standards association with workers' rights, compensation, and workplace health and safety.

ethical purchasing Internal company decisions that mitigate negative effects on employees throughout the fashion brand company's supply chain.

ethical sourcing Sourcing decisions that result in socially, environmentally, economically, and culturally sustainable fashion products.

ethnic appropriation See *cultural appropriation*.

ethnic identity See *cultural identity*.

ethnicity Identification with a common cultural heritage including language, social, religious, and/or national experiences.

F

factory auditing Processes for verifying that standards associated with codes of conduct are being met by production facilities.

factory monitoring See *factory auditing*.

fair trade Global system that supports farmers and artisans in developing countries to make trade fair through paying a living wage, providing opportunities for advancement, employing environmentally sustainable practices, building long term-trade partnerships, ensuring healthy and safe working conditions, and providing financial and technical assistance.

fashion consumption Acquisition, storage, usage, maintaining, and disposing of fashions.

fashion cycle "Dynamic mechanism of change through which a potential new fashion is created and transmitted from its point of creation to public introduction, discernible public acceptance, and eventual obsolescence" (Sproles & Burns, 1994, p.13, *see* Chapter 4 References and Resources).

fashion process See *fashion cycle*.

fashion resale Selling fashion merchandise a second time with the goal of extending the life of the fashion products through multiple owners.

fashion retailing Process of selling fashion merchandise to ultimate consumers.

fast fashion On-trend fashions designed and manufactured using ultra-fast supply chain operations.

first-party audits Factory audits conducted by employees of the factory or company that owns the factory.

fit obsolescence Obsolescence created because a fashion product no longer fits.

floor-ready merchandise Merchandise with all hangtags, labels, and pricing information affixed so that the merchandise can be directly moved to retail selling floor or shipped directly to the ultimate consumer.

forced labor A type of modern slavery that "describes a situation in which a worker performs work or services involuntarily under threat of penalty" (Skrivánková, 2017, *see* Chapter 5 References and Resources).

for-profit organizations Commercial entities whose profits are shared among owners.

foundation "Entity that supports charitable activities by making grants to unrelated organizations or institutions or to individuals for scientific, educational, cultural, religious, or other charitable purposes" (Council of Foundations, 2017, *see* Chapter 7 References and Resources).

full-package contractor Contractor that offers design, pattern making, and manufacturing services.

G

gender Physical and/or culturally and socially constructed characteristics of women and men.

gender expression "An individual's presentation—including physical appearance, clothing choice and accessories—and behavior that communicates aspects of gender or gender role. Gender expression may or may not conform to a person's gender identity" (American Psychological Association, 2015, *see* Chapter 2 References and Resources).

gender identity How an individual conceptualizes and experiences their gender, regardless of whether or not it conforms with the gender culturally associated with their assigned sex at birth.

gender inclusive fashions Fashions that are worn by individuals of all genders.

gender neutral fashions See *gender inclusive fashions*.

grade rules Rules used by a fashion brand in creating patterns for the size range they produce resulting in variation in sizing among brands and styles produced.

H

healthwear Medically related apparel and accessories created to address challenges created by illness or disability using tools and techniques of fashion.

heirloom products (e.g., garments or accessories) that are saved and shared across generations (e.g., wedding dresses, handmade items).

heritage brand Older fashion brands characterized by quality materials, classic styling, and potential for longevity of use.

Higg Index A collection of self-assessment tools designed to empower "brands, retailers and facilities of all sizes, at every stage in their sustainability journey, to measure their own environmental and social and labor impacts and identify areas for improvement" (Sustainable Apparel Coalition, 2016, *see* Chapter 3 References and Resources).

High Wet Modulus (HWM) Process to create rayon that results in a rayon with increased wet strength over regular rayon.

home sewing Sewing apparel in one's home to create apparel that may be less expensive, higher quality, better fitting, and/or more creative.

human rights Rights afforded all individuals including civil and political rights; economic, social and cultural rights; and collective rights.

I

inclusion The degree to which diverse individuals are able to participate fully in the decision-making processes within an organization or group.

inclusive design See *universal design*.

Industrial Revolution Starting in the mid-1700s in England and continuing through the late 1880s in Europe and the United States, the societal change known as the Industrial Revolution brought us the introduction of machine-made products, use of steam power, and increased number of factories.

industrial textile waste Textile waste generated from industrial applications such conveyor belts, filters, geotextiles, wiping rags, etc. Some analysts use the term *industrial waste* to describe *pre-consumer waste*.

influencers See *change agents*.

intermodal transportation Using different modes of transportation for different needs within the supply chain.

internal audits See *first-party audits*.

intrapreneurs People who want to drive change from inside organizations.

investment dressing Purchasing high quality classically styled fashions with the intent to wear the fashions over time.

involuntary prison labor "Prison labour that violates international labour standards. It includes situations where prisoners are required to work for the benefit of a private company or an individual" (Skrivánková, 2017, *see* Chapter 5 References and Resources).

L

leadership "Process of social influence which maximizes the efforts of others, towards the achievement of a goal" (Kruse, 2013, *see* Chapter 8 References and Resources).

life cycle assessment (LCA) The scientific analysis and measurement of the environmental footprint associated with a product through the "compilation and evaluation of the inputs, outputs and the potential environmental impacts of a product system throughout its life cycle" (ISO 2016, *see* Chapter 3 References and Resources).

local sourcing Business strategy of purchasing materials and producing fashion merchandise within a close proximity to either the ultimate consumer or the company's distribution center.

longevity of use Extending the life of fashions through strategies incorporated throughout the life cycle of the product.

lyocell Generic name for a "cellulose fiber obtained by an organic solvent spinning process" and is considered a subclass of rayon.

M

manufactured fibers Fibers manufactured from cellulosic materials (e.g., rayon, acetate, lyocell), synthetic polymers (e.g., polyester, nylon, acrylic), protein (e.g., milk protein fiber), or inorganic materials (e.g., glass, metal).

merchandising For the purpose of this book, the term *merchandising* refers the various buying and selling processes across the supply chain including product and consumer research, marketing, and retailing of fashion products.

metrics Methods by which progress toward a goal will be measured.

modern slavery "An umbrella term that includes forced labor, debt bondage, servitude, and trafficking for the purposes of labor exploitation" (Skrivánková, 2017, *see* Chapter 5 References and Resources).

modular design "Strategy to build systems of complex products from small individual subsystems/modules that work as an integrated whole" (Ribeiro, et al., 2014, *see* Chapter 4 References and Resources).

mulesing Practice whereby flesh is stripped from the buttocks of Merino lambs to create scarred skin with no wrinkles or folds. This practice was intended to prevent blowflies from laying eggs in the folds of the animal's skin.

multimodal transportation See *intermodal transportation*.

N

national dress/clothing Clothing that reflects the history and identity associated with countries and/or world regions through symbolic elements (e.g., motifs, styles, accessories, etc.).

non-government organizations (NGOs) Non-profit voluntary citizens' groups that operate independent of governments.

nonprofit organization Organization whereby the revenues available after all expenses are paid are completely reinvested into the work of the organization.

non-renewable resources Resources of economic value that cannot be replaced by natural means on a level equal to its consumption.

not for profit organization See *nonprofit organization*.

O

obsolescence "The significant decline in the competitiveness, usefulness, or value of an article or property. Obsolescence occurs generally due to the availability of alternatives that perform better or are cheaper or both, or due to changes in user preference, requirements, or styles" (businessdictionary.com, 2017, *see* Chapter 4 References and Resources).

off-shore contractor Contract factory located outside the country in which the finished goods will be distributed.

one-for-one model Strategy used for social enterprises whereby every time a consumer buys one of its products the company donates a related product or service to someone in need.

operations Strategies, activities, and management systems required for a fashion brand company to operate on a day to day basis including human resource management, inventory management, facility and store design and maintenance, and merchandising strategies (e.g., buying, pricing, display).

opinion leaders See *change agents*.

organic cotton Organic cotton eliminates the use of synthetic fertilizers and pesticides and conserves water lessening irrigation and erosion (Global Organic Cotton, 2016a, *see* Chapter 1 References and Resources).

P

packaging "Wrapping material around a consumer item that serves to contain, identify, describe, protect, display, promote and otherwise make the product marketable and keep it clean" (Entrepreneur, 2017, *see* Chapter 6 References and Resources)

packaging filler Materials used to fill the "void" between the product package and shipping container to protect the merchandise during shipping.

personal protection equipment Clothing and accessories designed and worn to protect a worker from injury or illness.

petite clothing Clothing designed and sized for women who are 5 feet 4 inches tall or less.

physical distribution See *distribution*.

plus-size clothing Clothing in sizes that are larger than the historically traditional sizing categories.

policy advocacy Strategies used to make changes in local, federal, and/or global policies and legislation.

poly bags Polyethylene bags used to protect products from dirt, dust, and moisture during processing, shipping, and distribution.

postconsumer textile waste Textile waste created when apparel and household textiles are disposed of by the ultimate consumer.

pre-consumer textile waste Fabric selvages, left over fabric from the cutting process, and other fabric scraps created during the manufacturing process of textile products.

private label brands Brands that are owned and sold by a particular retailer.

product environmental footprint A multi-indicator summary of the product's environmental impact.

product life cycle The stages of a product from its inception, manufacturing, retail distribution, purchase or acquisition by a consumer, and its use and eventual disposition and disposal.

product life cycle assessment See *life cycle assessment.*

psychological obsolescence Obsolescence created because the fashion no longer represents the user's social role and/or self-image.

R

race A social construction created to interpret human differences and used to justify socioeconomic arrangements in ways that accrue to the benefit of the dominant social group.

racial identity See *cultural identity.*

ready-to-wear Mass-produced apparel sold in standardized sizes.

reclaimed fibers Fibers generated from collecting pre-consumer textile waste (e.g., fabric scraps and cuttings left from the cutting and sewing processes) and processing them to create a new fiber.

re-commerce Process of merchants buying used (pre-owned) merchandise from consumers and then reselling, recycling, or reusing the merchandise.

recruitment fees Fees paid by individuals to secure work; associated with bonded labor if the worker is forced to work to pay off the fees.

recycle Process by which waste materials are made suitable for reuse.

regenerated cellulosic fibers Manufactured fibers made from cellulosic materials.

renewable resources Resources of economic value that can be replaced or replenished naturally over time or are always available.

repurpose Process of using waste material/items again but with new purposes.

resale Selling merchandise a second time.

responsible production See *ethical production.*

responsible purchasing See *ethical purchasing.*

responsible sourcing See *ethical sourcing.*

restricted substance list Lists that reflect compliance with or exceeding legal limits of use of hazardous substances across their supply chains; include substances, test methods, prohibition or limitation values, and country or state specific requirements.

return on investment Calculated as (net profit/cost of investment) x 100.

return plan Processes a fashion brand company uses for merchandise returned to them by consumers.

risk management "The identification, analysis, assessment, control, and avoidance, minimization, or elimination of unacceptable risks" (Business Dictionary, 2017, *see* Chapter 5 References and Resources).

S

sales forecasting An ongoing process companies use for estimating future sales.

scalability The capability of a company, system, and/or process to grow or expand while maintaining (or increasing) the performance, quality, efficiencies, and effectiveness of the company, system, or process.

scale To expand operations in the future.

second-party audits Factory audits conducted by employees of the fashion brand company for contractors with whom they are vetting for possible contracts or with whom they already have a contract.

sharing economy See *collaborative consumption.*

size inclusive Fashion brands that offer a broader range of sizes and do not make distinctions among regular, plus, and/or petite.

slow fashion Movement within the fashion industry in which fashion designers create a more sustainable fashion industry through systems thinking, extending product life, enhancing consumer/user connections, and addressing all aspects of sustainability.

social change The discernible transformation of culture and social institutions (social processes, social interactions, organizations) over time; that is, apparent changes in how people within a society think and behave.

social compliance program "Continuing process in which the involved parties keep on looking for better ways to protect the health, safety, and fundamental rights of their employees, and to protect and enhance the community and environment in which they operate" (Business Dictionary, 2017, *see* Chapter 5 References and Resources).

social enterprise Business or organization that addresses "a basic unmet need or solve a social problem through a market-drive approach" (Social Enterprise Alliance, 2017, *see* Chapter 7 References and Resources).

social entrepreneurs Individuals who "work to solve critical social problems and address basic unmet needs through innovation" (Social Enterprise Alliance, 2017).

social firms Social objective driven companies and organizations that employ individuals who might otherwise find it difficult to find jobs or that create jobs in areas where the individuals may not have alternative employment.

social justice Process to ensure the distribution of resources is equitable so that all members of society are physically and psychologically safe and secure.

social media influencer Influencer who established credibility in a specific business and has access through social media, blogs, and social networks to a large number of consumers interested in the influencer, product category, or business.

social objectives Objectives of a company that are social in nature, e.g., reducing poverty, improving health.

social responsibility (SR) See *corporate responsibility (CR)*.

social sustainability Ability for a social system or social unit, such as a community, to function indefinitely at a defined level of social well-being through shared structures and processes (Business Dictionary, 2016, *see* Chapter 1 References and Resources).

socioeconomic status Social standing or class of an individual or group. It is often measured as a combination of education, income and occupation. Examinations of socioeconomic status often reveal inequities in access to resources, plus issues related to privilege, power and control" (American Psychological Association, 2017, *see* Chapter 2 References and Resources).

solution-based design Fashion design process approached from the perspective of creating fashions that are part of solutions to larger societal, economic, health, and political problems.

sourcing decisions Decisions around procuring materials, production systems, and distribution pipelines.

specialty store retailer of private label apparel (SPA) Specialty retailer that offers only their own private label merchandise.

style obsolescence See *aesthetic obsolescence*.

subcontractor Company or individual hired by contractors to complete orders or perform specific tasks (e.g., embellishments, embroidery).

sumptuary laws Laws used to regulate consumption. In the case of fashion, such laws restricted the wearing of particular materials (e.g., furs, metals, fabrics), colors, jewels, decorative techniques (e.g., embroidery), or clothing styles to those who were of particular rank or status.

supply chain Functions of a company's production and distribution of merchandise including supply of materials to a manufacturer, the manufacturing process, and the distribution of finished goods through a network of distributors and retailers to a final customer.

supply chain assurance Management systems designed to guarantee the integrity of suppliers that constitute the fashion brand company's supply chain and mitigate risks of modern slavery, faulty products, and worker and environmental resource exploitation.

supply chain management Planning and management of all activities involved in sourcing and procurement, conversion, and all logistics management activities.

supply chain traceability Ability for a fashion brand company to track and identify the entire supply chain for each product it distributes.

supply chain transparency Information about suppliers within the supply chain are readily available and publicly shared.

sustainability "The ability to maintain or improve standards of living without damaging or depleting natural resources for present and future generations" (US EPA, 2016b, *see* Chapter 1 References and Resources).

sustainability plan A company's written commitments, goals, implementation plans, and assessments around sustainability.

sustainable apparel consumer Consumer who uses sustainability factors to inform apparel purchase decisions.

sustainable community Community that "manages its human, natural, and financial resources to meet current needs while ensuring that adequate resources are equitably available for future generations" (Institute of Sustainable Communities, 2017, *see* Chapter 7 References and Resources).

sustainable development Broad term around business practices that take into consideration environmental impact, economic efficiency, and the quality of life.

sustainable fashion influencers Individuals who through their social visibility build awareness and bring attention to sustainable fashion brands, thus, influencing consumer behavior.

sustainable fashion retailing Business strategies of fashion retailers that promote environmental, social, economic, and cultural sustainability to improve the health and well-being of customers, employees, and communities.

sustainable operations Business strategies whereby economic, environmental, social, and cultural sustainability in all aspects of the company's operations.

sweatshops Factories characterized by low wages, long hours, and unsanitary and dangerous working conditions.

synthetic fibers Manufactured fibers made synthetic polymers.

systems approach Approach whereby companies focus "on the interactions and on the relationships between parts in order to understand an entity's organization, functioning and outcomes" (Mele, Pels, & Polese, 2010, *see* Chapter 8 References and Resources).

systems thinking "Understanding bigger contexts over longer periods and looking at the connections, not the parts, for insights" (Waldegrave, 2017, *see* Chapter 8 References and Resources).

T

technical obsolescence Obsolescence created because of new technologies or material/product failure or damage.

temporary inactive storage Storing but not wearing clothing with the intent of mending and/or altering the clothing and/or hope that the clothing may fit again in the future.

textile waste Waste textile materials created through the manufacturing, use, and discarding of textile products. Includes pre-consumer, postconsumer, and industrial textile waste.

third-party audits Factory audits conducted by individuals who work for a company or organization that is separate from either the fashion brand company or the contract factory.

thrift stores Resale fashion retailers that acquire merchandise through charitable donations.

tier one suppliers Direct suppliers to the fashion brand company; e.g., factory that manufacturers the apparel and accessory products.

tier three suppliers Suppliers to tier two suppliers; e.g., yarn suppliers, fabric print or dye producers, producers of plastics and metals for zippers and/or buttons.

tier two suppliers Suppliers to tier one suppliers; e.g., textile mills, zipper producers, button producers.

tomboy brands Fashion brands that focus on creating fashions with men's styling in traditionally female sizing.

traditional dress/clothing See *national dress/clothing*.

triple bottom line Term first used in 1994 by John Elkington to describe three bottom lines that companies need to address—economic prosperity (profit), social justice (people), and environmental quality (planet).

U

unisex fashions See *gender inclusive fashions*.

universal design Design and composition of an environment so that it can be accessed, understood, and used to the greatest extent possible by all people regardless of their age, size, ability, or disability.

upcycling Process by which discarded materials/items are transformed to create products with a higher value than what was being discarded without changing the composition of the original material.

V

value chain Supply chain with a process-orientation whereby the valued-added aspects of each step in creating a fashion product is emphasized.

vertical integration Business strategy whereby the same company is engaged in more than one segment within the supply chain.

vintage clothing and accessories Clothing and/or accessories that are at least twenty years old.

viscose Process to create rayon in which cellulose (wood pulp) is treated with caustic soda and carbon disulfide.

Z

zero waste design Design process that utilizes as much of the fabric as possible; thus reducing textile waste. Accomplished by using all scraps and remnants from the cutting or production process and/or creating patterns for a design that create a marker (pattern layout) that looks like a large jigsaw puzzle and results in 100 percent fabric utilization.

zero waste fashion design See *zero waste design*.

Chapter 1
1.1a & b Krochet Kids intnl.
1.2 B Lab
1.3 tonlé
1.4 Leslie Burns
1.5 Indigenous Designs Corp.
1.6 courtesy of Imperial Stock Ranch
1.7 Zakir Hossain Chowdhury / Barcroft via Getty Images
1.8 Mikael Valsanen/Corbis/Getty Images
1.9 © Paul Thacker

Chapter 2
2.1 Universal Standard
2.2 hadynyah/E+/Getty Images
2.3 Lise Gagne/E+/Getty Images
2.4 Care + Wear: Chat Razdan
2.5a & b Original photographs provided by the designers.
2.6 Stephanie Alves, ABL Denim™
2.7 Universal Standard
2.8 Wildfang
2.9 Photos @genderfreeworld
2.10 Angela Weiss/AFP/Getty Images
2.11 Bill McCay/Getty Images for Mizzen and Main
2.12 Stephanie Alves, ABL Denim™

Chapter 3
3.1 tonlé
3.2 Beowulf/Getty Images
3.3a & b Sustainable Apparel Coalition
3.4 Leslie Burns
3.5 Yulex
3.6 Shimon Karmel
3.7, 3.8, & 3.9 Leslie Burns

Chapter 4
4.1 Lyn Alweis/The Denver Post via Getty Images
4.2 Laura Chenoweth
4.3 Softstar Shoes
4.4 Sudara
4.5 Matthew Tobeck
4.6 THIERRY ORBAN/Sygma via Getty Images
4.7 Calzico
4.8 Because International
4.9 Fishman/ullstein bild via Getty Images
4.10 Shimon Karmel
4.11 The Renewal Workshop
4.12 Krochet Kids intnl.
4.13 Alabama Chanin
4.14 Shimon Karmel
4.15a & b Alabama Chanin

Chapter 5
5.1 George Frey/Getty Images
5.2 Softstar Shoes
5.3 Pascal Le Segretain/Getty Images
5.4 Leslie Burns
5.5 CPSC/Getty Images
5.6 Softstar Shoes
5.7 Thomas Trutschel/Photothek via Getty Images
5.8 & 5.9 Leslie Burns
5.10 2017 Better Buying
5.11 Fair Wear Foundation
5.12 Sustainable Apparel Coalition
5.13 Leslie Burns

Chapter 6
6.1, 6.2, 6.3, 6.4, & 6.5 Leslie Burns
6.6 The Renewal Workshop
6.7 Ferdaus Shamim/Wireimage/Getty Images
6.8 Sassafras
6.9 & 6.10 Leslie Burns
6.11 Sassafras

Chapter 7
7.1 Because International
7.2 Indigenous Designs Corp.
7.3 Because International
7.4 Paula Watts Photography
7.5 Raven + Lily
7.6a & b Clothroads.com
7.7a & b Warby Parker
7.8 Leslie Burns
7.9 Dominique Charriau/Getty Images
7.10 Mike Pont/Getty Images for OCRFA
7.11 Andrew Lichtenstein/Corbis via Getty Images
7.12 Krochet Kids intnl.

Chapter 8
8.1 Ole Jensen - Corbis/Corbis via Getty Images
8.2 Oli Scarff/Getty Images
8.3 Leslie Burns
8.4a & b United Airlines
8.5 Wildfang
8.6 Leslie Burns
8.7 Astrid Stawiarz/Getty Images for Zady
8.8 Dimitrios Kambouris/Getty Images
8.9 THIERRY ZOCCOLAN/AFP/Getty Images

A

ABL Denim 36–37, 52
Accord on Fire and Building Safety in
    Bangladesh 17, 128
acrylic 14, 213
adapted clothing 34, 210
adaptive clothing 34, 36–37, 52, 210
Adidas Group 12, 60, 128–129, 190, 194
advertising 31, 41–42, 45, 50–51, 66
aesthetic obsolescence 85, 93, 103, 210, 214
Africa 10, 162, 167–169, 172–173, 179–181
ageism 29, 46, 210
Airdye® 61, 74
air freight 144–145, 155
air quality 56, 66–68, 118, 163, 193
Alabama Chanin 102, 109–110, 197
Alliance for Bangladesh Worker Safety
    17, 128
All Myn 91
All Walks Beyond the Catwalk 41, 49–51
    (see also Franklin, Caryn)
Almazán, María 201
American Apparel and Footwear
    Association 18, 174
American Eagle Outfitters 12
American Foundation for AIDS
    Research 173
American National Standards Institute
    (ANSI) 70, 72
Argentina 26
Arkwright, Sir Richard 7
Armani, Giorgio 171
Arrow 92–93
Ashoka 164
Asics 129
ASTM International test methods 90
audit fatigue 126, 133, 210
Australia 13–14, 19, 26, 37, 154
    fashion brand headquarters 91, 105, 171

B

bamboo 14–15
Bangladesh 8, 17, 128, 130, 168
    Better Buying 138
    Garment Worker Diaries 193
barrier-free design 34, 46, 210
B Corporation 6, 21, 24, 210
    examples 4, 6, 24, 93, 167, 184
Because International 96, 162, 165–166 (see
    also The Shoe That Grows)

Belgium 63, 124, 172
Benneton 60, 128
Better Buying Project 128, 137, 138 (see also
    Dickson, Marsha)
Better Cotton Initiative 12, 67, 73, 79,
    172, 214
Better Work 129
big-and-tall clothing 37, 46, 210
bio-based materials 15, 59, 72
bio-rubber 63
Birkenstock 96
Blue Angel certification 67
bluesign® Standard and Certification 68, 73,
    80, 184
Bolt Threads 191
Bombas 170
bonded labor 117, 130, 133, 210, 214
Bono 171
Bourne, Debra 41, 50
brand community 100–101, 103, 197,
    200, 210
brand identity 34, 50, 146–147, 158, 215
Brazil 11, 138, 172
Brooks Brothers 83, 91, 92, 100
Buck & Buck 36
Burberry 60, 91, 92, 129
business frameworks 1, 4–6, 21, 89, 109,
    112–114
business logistics 141–144, 155, 185, 189,
    203, 210
business objectives 128, 161–166, 168–172,
    175–176, 210
business plan 4, 152, 155

C

C&A 60, 79, 128–129, 186, 194
    partnership with DyStar 191
    sustainability report 123
C&A Foundation 137, 138, 164, 172, 193
Calvin Klein 189, 201
Calzico 93–94
Cambodia 9, 54, 123, 167, 193
Cameroon 10, 172, 180
Canada 19, 37, 51–52, 72, 107–109, 191
    fashion brand headquarters 39, 75, 93,
    97, 99, 171–172, 179
    retailers 152, 154
Canada Goose 92, 105
Capilene®, Patagonia 59
carbon footprint 5, 62–63, 73, 75, 82, 210

Care + Wear 33
care of apparel 83, 101, 103, 198–199
    consumer education 20, 89–90, 96,
    198–199
    environmental impact 56, 60–63, 73
carpets and rugs 64, 70, 130
Carrefour 12, 128
Carter's Inc. 12, 128
Cartwright, Edmund 7
Carver, Jeanne 2, 13, 25 (see also Imperial
    Stock Ranch)
cashmere 92, 115
cellulosic fibers/materials 14–15, 21,
    212, 214
Chanel 114–115
change agent 179, 184, 201–202, 210
Chargeurs Wool 26
Chenoweth, Laura 59, 86
child labor 117–118, 127, 130, 132
    cotton production 11–12, 121
    definition 117, 210
China 9, 19, 129–130
    apparel production 16, 138
    cotton production 11, 55, 60, 117
Chouinard, Yvon 171
circular economy 79, 82, 164, 188–191, 203
    Cradle to Cradle Products 68, 77
    definition 190, 210
    fashion consumption 196–198
circular fashion system 68, 82, 107, 109,
    172, 186
    circular materials 78, 191
    definition 190, 210
    sustainability plans 188–189
classic fashion 91, 101, 103, 153, 159, 212
    definition 91, 210
    examples 56, 82, 91, 93, 105
climate change 4, 55–56, 61–62, 66
closed-loop recycling system 68, 73, 185,
    190–191
    definition 62, 210
    fiber recycling 15, 20, 62, 190
ClothRoads 169, 176
Coach 96, 174
co-creator 86, 100, 103, 210
codes of conduct 118–119, 123–126, 193,
    203, 210–211
    definition 124–125
    examples 75, 124–125, 129–130, 189

implementation 17–18, 115–116, 126, 131, 137–138
transparency 197
collaborative consumption 102–103, 210, 214
ColorZen™ 61
Columbia College Chicago 192, 207–208
Columbia Sportswear 5, 12, 19, 150
community development 5, 18, 21, 124, 131, 181
definition 163
economic development 10, 163
initiative examples 33, 87, 172
company-sponsored foundation 172, 176, 210
competitive advantage 194, 203, 210
conflict minerals 18–19, 21, 210
conscious capitalism 4–6, 21, 210
Conscious Capitalism: Liberating the Heroic Spirit of Business 5 (*see also* Mackey, John; Sisodia, Raj)
Conscious Chatter 77, 200
Conscious Step 171, 178
consignment 152–155, 159–160, 210
consumer education 88, 95, 101, 150, 195–197
fashion brand initiatives 61, 197, 200
consumer research 3, 90, 136, 213
consumer tribes 200, 210
contractor 7, 115, 117–119, 132
auditing 124, 126
definition 210–213
full-package contractor 114, 212
cooperative 166, 169, 176, 195, 210
examples 71, 109, 169
Copenhagen Fashion Summit 184–185
co-producer 86, 100, 103, 210
corporate foundation 166, 172, 176, 210
corporate social responsibility 113, 137–138, 214
framework 4–5, 21
cost-per-wearing 106–107
cotton, conventional 11, 55–56, 60
cotton, life cycle assessment 55–58, 60, 69
cotton, organic 12, 55–56, 72, 79, 197 (*see also* cotton certifications, organic)
assessment tools 57
definition 12, 213
Eileen Fisher 93, 184, 189
Indigenous Designs 12, 164
Patagonia 2
Preferred Fiber and Materials Market Report 12, 15, 59
use by other fashion brands 12, 47, 110, 152, 159, 167, 177, 191, 209

cotton, Uzbekistan 11–12, 117, 121, 130
cotton certifications 12, 57, 67, 128, 130, 191
fair trade 47, 79
organic 47, 69–71, 79, 177
Cotton Incorporated 196
cotton production 11–12, 18, 58, 60–61, 73, 121
Cradle to Cradle 68–69, 77–78, 82, 148, 186, 191
Creytex 114
Crystal Denim 63
cultural appreciation 40, 43, 108, 193
cultural appropriation 30–31, 33, 40, 211
cultural sustainability, definition 4, 25, 40, 193, 211
culture, definition 4, 30, 40, 211

D
deadstock fabric 97, 99, 103, 195, 211
de Castro, Orsola 64
Delivering Good 174
denim brands 20, 36, 52, 61, 63, 65, 96, 189
Denim North America 65
Denmark 92
design, definition 3, 184, 211
design, universal 27, 33–36, 45, 215
design, zero waste 63–64, 73, 86, 190–192, 195
definition 216
examples 2, 54, 64–65, 107–109, 191–192, 205–208
Design for Longevity resource 88–89
designing for durability 86, 88, 103, 211
Detox Catwalk 19
Detox My Fashion 19
Dickson, Marsha 128, 137 (*see also* Better Buying)
Dillinger, Paul 93, 100
Dior 171
direct to consumer 24, 28, 105, 109, 170
disability, definition 31, 211
Disney 174, 192
diversity, definition 29, 32, 211
diversity initiatives 32, 41–44, 51, 193, 197
domestic contractor 8, 115, 133, 211
Donna Karan 174–175
due diligence 116, 122, 130, 132–133, 211
DyeCoo 61
DyStar 191

E
ECO2cotton™ 65
Ecolabel Index 67

economic obsolescence 85, 94, 103, 211
economic sustainability, definition 3–5, 10, 163, 194–195, 211
operations 149
slow fashion 86–87
EcoSpun 62
Ecuador 59
Eileen Fisher 37, 78, 121, 152, 172, 184–185
B Corporation 4, 6, 24, 93
Renew take-back program 65, 150, 197
sustainability plan 189, 203
use of materials 15, 68, 78, 93, 121
emotionally durable design 99, 103, 211
energy consumption 18, 61–63, 69, 189, 195, 198
cotton industry 55–56
laundering and care of clothing 18, 73
LEED 150
environmental footprint 61, 72, 82, 144, 212
assessment tools 58, 71
definition 55, 213
environmental sustainability, definition 3, 5, 54–55, 118, 190, 211
equity, definition 31–32, 211
Esprit 60, 128
ethical marketing 42
ethical production 89, 124, 211 (*see also* responsible production)
ethical purchasing 120, 211 (*see also* responsible purchasing)
ethical sourcing 89, 112, 122, 124, 156 (*see also* responsible sourcing)
definition 119, 211
Ethical Trading Initiative 117, 129
ethnic appropriation 30–31, 40, 45, 211
ethnic identity 30, 32–33, 211
ethnicity 29–30, 45, 46, 211
Etsy.com 66, 100
European Union 14, 66–67, 70–72, 122, 144–145
Everlane 24, 124, 139–140 (*see also* Preysman, Michael)
Evrnu™ 21, 66

F
factory auditing 17, 119, 124–127, 131–132, 192–194, 203
auditing tools and services 129–130
definition 211
goals of 125
Fair Factories Clearinghouse 129, 137
Fair Labor Association 126, 129, 138

fair trade 79, 164, 169
   definition 12, 211
   fashion brands 11, 47, 152, 164, 167, 177, 195
Fair Trade USA 2, 130, 154
Fair Wear Foundation 130
Faller, Rachel 2, 64 (see also Tonlé)
fashion cycle 74, 84, 91, 93, 103, 211
Fashion for Good 186
fashion imagery 28–29, 31, 40–43, 45, 49–51, 193
Fashion Positive Initiative 68, 77–78
fashion resale 150, 152–155, 160, 184, 210–211, 214–215
Fashion Revolution 123, 172, 193–194, 199–200
Fashion Transparency Index 136, 194, 206
fast fashion 9, 91, 102, 196, 200, 211
   brands 114, 194
   definition 83–85, 211
Fast Retailing Co. Ltd 12, 128, 194
FedEx 145, 148
Fendi 92, 171
Ferragamo 92
Filson 82, 84, 91–92
first-party audit 126, 212
fit obsolescence 85, 94, 103, 211
floor-ready merchandise 146, 155, 212
Follow the Thread 194
Footprint Chronicles®, Patagonia 112, 124
forced labor 122, 125, 127, 130, 172, 194, 213–214
   definition 16, 117, 212
   Uzbekistan cotton industry 11–12, 117
forecasting, sales 138, 142–143, 154–155, 210, 214
Forest Stewardship Council 60, 63, 121, 150, 157
France 37, 42, 135, 171
Franklin, Caryn 41, 49 (see also All Walks Beyond the Catwalk)
Freeset 167
full-package contractor 114, 133, 212

G
Gallant International 154
Gandys Foundation 173
Garment Worker Diaries 193
gender equality initiatives 43–45
gender expression 29, 37, 212
Gender Free World (GFW) Clothing 2, 39
gender inclusive fashion 2, 37, 39, 197, 212, 215

geotextiles 64, 212
Germany 67, 92, 96, 171, 196
Gildan Activewear 191, 194
Giorgio Armani 171
Giving Keys 168
Global Goods Partners 168–169
Global Leadership Award in Sustainable Apparel (GLASA) 60
Global Organic Textile Standard (GOTS) 70, 72, 80, 121
   used by fashion brands 47, 59, 135
Global Recycled Standard 69, 121
Goodweave 130, 172
Goodwill Industries 65, 151, 154, 157
grade rules 37, 46, 212
Graham, Ashley 41
Granted Clothing 2, 99
greenhouse gas emissions 13, 19, 56, 61–62, 145
Greenpeace 19
Guatemala 63
Gucci 92

H
Haiti 65, 170, 191
HanesBrands 174, 189, 194, 203
hazardous chemicals 11–12, 19, 60, 118, 214
healthwear 33, 46, 212
heirloom products 97, 101, 105, 197
   definition 99, 212
   examples 2, 82, 99, 102, 105, 109–110
hemp 60, 195
heritage brands 92, 101, 197
   definition 91, 212
   examples 82, 84, 93, 100
Hermes 92
Hethorn, Janet 11
Higg Index 56–58, 73, 131, 138, 212
High Wet Modulus (HWM) rayon 14, 21, 212
home sewing 6, 7, 83, 102–103, 110, 117, 212
homework 7, 118
Howe, Elias 7
human resources 3, 9, 124–125, 149, 155, 163
   depletion of 2, 6, 11, 21
human rights 5, 19, 113, 116, 119–120
   campaigns and initiatives 45, 122–123, 130, 184, 188–189, 194
   child labor 117
   definition 212
human trafficking 87, 112, 121–123, 132, 166–167
   definition 116–117

I
Ibex 98
Icebreaker 14, 89, 156–157
ideals of attractiveness 28–29, 31, 41, 45
Ikea 129
Imperial Stock Ranch 2, 13, 25, 26 (see also Carver, Jeanne)
inclusion, definition 32–33, 43–45, 212
inclusive design 2, 33–34, 36–37, 193, 195, 203
India 20, 86–87, 130, 170, 193
   company headquarters 79, 98, 167
   cotton industry 11, 55, 60, 117, 142
Indigenous Designs Corp 12, 58, 98, 147–148, 164
   B Corporation 6, 24
Inditex 12, 15, 17, 60, 128–129, 194
Indonesia 130
Industrial Revolution 7, 21, 83, 212
industrial textile waste 64, 73, 208, 212, 215
influencer, media 41, 196, 200–201, 203, 212, 214–215
intermodal transportation 145, 148, 155, 212–213
internal audits 126, 133, 212
internal diversity initiatives 28, 43–45
International Labour Organization 117, 122, 129
International Organization for Standardization (ISO) 69
Intertek 126, 130
intrapreneurs 201, 203, 212
investment dressing 101, 103, 212
involuntary prison labor 117, 127, 133, 212
Ireland 97
Italy 16, 37, 41, 196, 200
   fashion brand headquarters 92, 171

J
Janska 34, 47
Japan 19, 34, 37, 40, 72
   company headquarters 61 (see also Uniqlo)
JCPenney 17, 128
Jeanologia 61

K
Kade & Vos 37, 197
Kenneth Cole 173–174
Kenya 162, 170
Kering 42, 78, 186, 194
Kirrin Finch 38
Knowthechain 194

Kowtow 47, 48, 194
Krochet Kids intl. 2, 100, 123, 181, 217

L
labeling programs 16, 67, 69, 70, 73
Lazlo 167
Lbrands 60
Leadership in Energy and Environmental
    Design (LEED) 150
leather 15–16, 87, 98–99, 121, 192, 205, 208
leather, finishing 16, 189, 210
leather tanning process 15, 16
Leather Working Group (LGW) 121
Lee, Kenton 162, 164
legislation 16, 41, 44–45, 213
Leonard, Scott 164
LeSouk 59
Le Tote 102
Levi Strauss & Co. 44, 60, 92–93, 100, 129
    Evrnu® partnership 66
    LCA of a pair of Levi's® 501® jeans 56, 61
    Responsible Sourcing Network 12
    restricted substance list 19
    take-back program 150–151
    Worker Well-being programs 127–128
life cycle assessment 54–58, 66, 72, 195
    definition 55, 212
    Levi's® 501® jeans 56, 61
    organic cotton 55
    standards and certifications 69, 71
Liminal 194
Lindex 15, 43, 44
local sourcing 100, 167, 170, 181, 212 (see
    also sourcing decisions)
    slow fashion 20, 86, 88, 103
longevity of use
    definition 82–85, 103, 212
    strategies 83, 88–91, 101, 103, 184, 197
Loomstate 209
Looptworks 99, 192, 205, 206
lululemon athletica 12, 75, 76, 101, 194
LVMH Moët Hennessy Louis Vuitton 42,
    92, 115

M
McDonough, William 68, 82
Mackay, John 5 (see also Conscious
    Capitalism)
Macy's 19, 114, 128
Made-By 130, 186
Malaysia 167
Mango 17, 128
manufactured fibers 14, 21, 59, 212, 215

Marimekko 45, 129
Marks & Spencer 60, 123, 128–129,
    152, 203
    Principles of Responsible Marketing 42
    sustainability plan 186–187
Martex Fiber Co. 65
Material Connexion 59
merchandising, definition 3, 142, 149,
    155, 213
merino wool 13, 89, 156, 213
Metawear® 68–69
metrics, sustainability 72, 186–187,
    189, 213
Mexico 172, 196
Microfinance Opportunities 193
Modal HWM rayon 14, 196
modern slavery 112, 118–119, 132, 166,
    188, 212–213
    definition 16, 116–117, 212–213
    supply chain assurance and
        transparency 121–123, 215
Modern Slavery Registry 78, 123
modular design 88, 93–94, 103, 213
Moschino 172
mulesing 13, 14, 21, 213
multimodal transportation 145, 155, 213
Muttonhead 39
mycelium packaging 148

N
national dress 30, 40, 45, 213, 215
Nau 20, 58, 171
Nest 164
Netherlands 130, 172
net income 164
net profit 164, 214
New Balance 60
New Zealand 13–14, 26, 47, 89, 156, 194
Nike 19, 60, 105, 114, 123, 129, 194
    code of conduct 125
    ColorDry 61
    Community Impact Fund 172
    energy use program 18
    use of materials 12, 15, 79
non-government organizations 163, 165,
    172, 176, 213
nonprofit organizations 155, 186, 192, 198
    definition 165, 213
    examples 6, 24, 68–69, 128–129,
        164–168, 174, 193
    partnerships with fashion brands 151,
        154, 159–160, 170–172, 177
    social enterprises 152, 165, 167, 175

non-renewable resources 55–56, 62–63, 203
    definition 213
    reducing consumption of 3, 15, 18, 190,
        203, 211
Nordstrom 43, 44, 128, 158
NotEqual 39
NSF International 69, 70, 112
Nudie Jeans 20, 96, 97
Nuu-Muu 171
nylon 14–15, 61–62, 107, 108, 213

O
Obakki 10, 172–173, 179, 180 (see also
    Peake, Treana)
Obakki Foundation 10, 172–173, 179–180
obsolescence, forms of 83–85, 93–94,
    103, 213 (see also economic
    obsolescence, fit obsolescence,
    style obsolescence, technical
    obsolescence)
ocean freight 144–146, 155
O'Connor, Erin 41, 50
Oeko-Tex® 70, 73, 135, 196
off-shore contract production 8, 115,
    133, 213
Oliberté 6, 130, 171
Oliver Cabell 124
Olukai 6
OneCert 72
one-for-one model 169–170, 176, 213
1% for the Planet 171
Open Arms Shop 165, 167
operations, definition 113, 132, 149–151,
    155, 213, 215
Organic Cotton Sustainability Assessment
    Tool (OC-SAT) 57
Outdoor Industry Association 174
Outerknown 12, 130, 154
Oxfam 138, 165, 188

P
packaging
    definition 146, 148, 155, 213
    environmental 70, 146–148, 150, 155,
        157, 189
    filler 148, 155, 213
Pakistan 11, 61, 117, 167
Patagonia 26, 129, 152, 160, 174, 192
    B Corporation 4, 6, 24
    "Do Not Buy This Jacket" advertisement
        196–197
    Drive-Less Program 150
    Fair Trade USA 2, 130, 154, 195

Patagonia, (*continued*)
  Footprint Chronicles® 112, 124
  1% for the Planet 171
  on-site child care 168
  packaging 147
  Responsible Sourcing Network 12
  Social and Environmental
      Responsibility Program 113,
      124, 194
  use of materials 2, 15, 58–59, 63, 79, 190
  Worn Wear program 20, 96, 198
Peake, Treana 173, 179 (*see also* Obakki)
Pendleton Woolen Mills 91–92, 105–106
personal protection equipment 120,
      133, 213
Peru 30, 100, 167, 181
pesticides 11–12, 18, 19, 55, 67
petite clothing sizing 37, 46, 213–214
Picture Organic Clothing 12, 135–136, 202
Pinterest 102
Planet Aid 198–199
plus-size clothing sizing 37, 46, 50, 159, 213
plus-size model 41, 50
policy advocacy 19, 28, 44, 66, 213
  by fashion brand companies 44,
      173–174, 194
  Outdoor Industry Association 174
  United Nations 122, 185
polybags 146, 155
polyester 14–15, 60–62
polyester, recycled 62, 65, 72–73, 80,
      196, 213
  Preferred Fiber and Materials Market
      Report 15, 59
  use by fashion brand companies 20,
      58, 135
postconsumer textile waste 19–20, 72–73,
      82, 84–85, 103
  definition 64, 213, 215
  materials made from 65, 191
  recovering and reusing 21, 62, 65–66,
      97, 191, 198, 205, 210
Prada 92, 194
prAna 98, 130, 147, 148, 190
Pratibha Syntex 60, 61, 79
pre-consumer textile waste 64, 143
  definition 63, 212–213, 215
  materials made from 64, 97–98,
      108–109
  recovering and reusing 64–66, 73,
      97–98, 190, 192
  zero waste design 64, 73

Preysman, Michael 24, 139, 140 (*see also*
      Everlane)
Primark 12, 128, 194
Pringle 91, 92
private label brands 114, 133, 152, 213–214
product integrity 90, 116, 118, 132
psychological obsolescence 85, 103, 213
Puma 60, 129
Pussy Hat Project 175
PVH Corp. 60, 128, 129, 174, 194
  Responsible Sourcing Network 12
  sustainability plan 189

R
race, definition 30, 213
racial identity 30, 46, 213
Rad Hourani 39
rail freight 144–145, 155
Ralph Lauren 25–26, 107, 174, 194
Ramblers Way 152–153
Rana Plaza 8, 17, 128
Raven + Lily 167
rayon 14–15, 60, 80, 196, 212, 216
ready-to-wear
  definition 36, 95, 103, 213
  history 7–8, 16, 29, 84, 102, 117
Reclaim to Wear 64
reclaimed fibers 64–66, 73, 213
re-commerce 152–155, 214
recruitment fees 117, 125, 133, 214
Recycled Claim Standard 71, 121
recycled packaging 146–148
recycled plastic bottles 2, 59, 62, 65,
      197, 201
(RED) 171, 172
regenerated cellulosic fibers 14–15, 21, 64,
      73, 214
REI 87, 129
renewable resources 68, 72–73, 150, 189, 190
  definition 3, 211, 214
  increasing consumption of 18, 58–59,
      61–63, 73
  textile fibers 14–15, 58–59, 62
Rent a Runway 102
REPREVE® fiber/yarn 190, 197
repurpose 65, 73, 82, 89, 157, 191, 205, 214
resale retailer 150, 152–155, 160, 184,
      210–211, 214–215
Responsible Down Standard 25, 71, 121
responsible production 73, 109, 128, 132,
      193, 196
  definition 119, 214
  Fair Labor Association 129, 138

responsible purchasing 119–120, 125, 128,
      132, 193, 214
  Better Buying 137–139
  Patagonia Responsible Purchasing
      Practices Program 124
responsible sourcing 119–120, 128,
      193–194, 211, 214
  Fair Labor Association 129, 138
  of production 112, 125, 156
  of textiles and materials 72, 88–89,
      160, 190
  Responsible Sourcing Network 12, 130
  Responsible Wool Standard 2, 13, 25–26,
      71, 121
restricted substance list 18–19, 21, 214
ReTuna Återbruksgalleria 154
return on investment 164–165, 176, 214
return plan 148–149, 155, 214
Reynolds, Matt 164
Ricci, Fillippo 64
risk management 70, 131–132, 186, 194
  definition 116, 214
Rissanen, Timo 64
Rivoli, Pietra 16

S
St. James, Tara 64
sales forecasting 138, 142–143, 154–155,
      214
Salvation Army 107, 157
Salvatore Ferragamo 92
Sans Soucie 64, 97, 107, 109 (*see also*
      Katherine Soucie)
Sassafras 152, 158–160
S. Café yarns 191
scalability 164, 194–195, 203, 205, 214
Scotland 92
sea freight 144–145, 155
search for the cheap needle 7, 8
Secondary Materials and Recycled Textiles
      (SMART) 21, 65
second-party audits 126, 131, 133, 214
self-assessment tools 54, 56–58, 72,
      130–131, 212
sharing economy 101–102, 160, 190,
      198, 214
Shorrock, Elizabeth 192, 207
Siizu 171
silk 3, 6, 36, 59, 68, 190–191
Singapore 191
Single Market for Green Products
      Initiative 71
Singtex Industrial Co. 191

Sisodia, Raj 5 (*see also* Conscious Capitalism)

size-adaptable 162

size inclusive 28, 36–38, 45, 197, 214

slow fashion 85–88, 99, 103, 158, 197
    brands 86–88, 91, 107–109
    definition 20, 214
    Kate Fletcher 20

social change, definition 4, 10–11, 21, 176, 185, 214
    business frameworks 6
    spurred by Rana Plaza building collapse 8, 17

social compliance programs 17, 117, 119, 124–126, 128, 132
    hierarchy of 131

social enterprise 163–166, 175–176, 195, 197
    definition 163–164, 214
    examples, 123, 152, 162, 164, 166–171, 199
    types 166–171

social entrepreneurs 163–164, 175, 195, 214
    examples 162, 164, 168, 201

social firms 166, 176, 214

social justice 5, 28, 43–45, 163, 193, 197
    definition 32–33, 214
    fashion brand advocacy 10, 43–45, 169

social media influencer 200, 214

social objectives 128, 162–166, 168–176, 193, 214

social sustainability, definition 3–5, 192–193, 214

socioeconomic status 29, 31–33, 45, 214

Softstar Shoes 86, 114–115

solution-based design 33, 46, 214

Soucie, Katherine 64–65, 97, 98, 107–108, 191

sourcing decisions 116, 119, 126, 132, 190
    (*see also* local sourcing)
    definition 113, 214
    environmental impact 18, 144
    fashion brand examples 128, 184
    resources 72

Sourcing Network's Pledge, Uzbek cotton 12

Spain 41

specialty store retailer 47, 66, 105, 151, 178, 181
    example 158

specialty store retailer of private label apparel (SPA) 114, 133, 152, 214

Stella McCartney 79, 129, 191, 200

Streetwires 169

Study NY 64, 88

style obsolescence 85, 93–94, 103, 214

subcontractor 7, 117–118, 122, 132, 138
    codes of conduct 124–125, 128
    definition 115, 214

Sudara 87, 166–167

Sugoi 93

sumptuary laws 31, 46, 215

Super Saturday fundraiser 174–175

supply chain, definition 8, 113–115, 132, 215
    sustainable development 18, 60, 70, 87, 185

supply chain assurance, definition 113, 119–120, 132, 215

supply chain traceability 120–122, 132, 194, 215

supply chain transparency, definition 120–121, 123–124, 132, 215

supply chain transparency, forms of 123–124, 132, 139, 202, 215

sustainability plan 184, 186–189, 195, 202, 215

sustainable apparel consumer 101–102, 154, 168–169, 195–197, 200, 215

sustainable community, definition 3, 163, 166, 215

sweatshop 7, 16, 117, 215

Sweden 20, 43, 96, 154, 189

Switzerland 129, 135, 150

Sword & Plough 97–98

synthetic fibers 14–15, 62–63, 73, 212, 215

systems approach, definition 185–186, 190, 195, 203, 215

systems thinking 20, 85, 87, 184–185, 190, 215

T

tagua nut buttons 58–59

Taiwan 61, 72, 191

Tanzania 55

technical obsolescence 84, 94, 96, 103, 215

temporary inactive storage 85, 215

Tencel® lyocell 15, 59–60, 66, 72, 93, 121, 190

Ten Thousand Villages 152

Textile Exchange 12, 15, 55, 57, 59, 172
    standards and certifications 13, 25, 69–72, 121

textile finishing 11, 14, 18, 60, 61, 78, 80, 189, 210

textile waste 10, 19, 63–66, 84–85, 103, 143
    (*see also* pre-consumer textile waste, postconsumer textile waste)
    definition 63, 215
    materials made from 109, 190–191, 208
    recovering and reusing 20–21, 65–66, 82, 152, 154, 198
    types of 63–66

Texture Clothing 158

The Curvy Fashionista 37

The Green Carpet Challenge 200

The Necessary Revolution 201–202

The Renewal Workshop 98, 148–149

The Shoe That Grows 95–96, 162, 164–165
    (*see also* Because International)

The True Cost 200

The Zip Yard 97

third-party audits 131, 215

third-party certification 25, 114, 129, 154

Thread International 65

Threads 4 Thought 6, 154

thredUP 154, 160

thrift stores 152, 154, 160, 215

tier one suppliers 114–115, 132, 194, 215
    examples 112, 123, 135, 139

tier three suppliers 114–115, 194, 215
    examples 112, 123

tier two suppliers 114–115, 194, 215
    examples 112, 123, 135, 139

Timberland 67, 91, 92, 105, 190–192

Tipton, Amy 152, 158

Toad&Co 98, 168

Tobeck, Matthew 88

tomboy brands 38, 39, 215

Tommy Hilfiger 114, 129, 189

TOMS 169–170

Tonlé 2, 9, 54, 64, 123, 146, 147

Topshop 64

traditional dress 30, 40, 45, 215

traditional production techniques 86, 89, 103, 109

trans-seasonal lines 28, 89, 91, 93

Triangle Shirtwaist Factory 7, 16

triple bottom line 5, 21, 215

TRMTAB 98

trucking 144–145, 155

True Fashion Collective 200

Turkey 55, 130

Turkmenistan 117

U

U.S. Environmental Protection Agency 3, 20, 62, 64, 66, 144

Uganda 2, 19, 100, 167, 181, 210
Ulasewicz, Connie 11, 192
Uniqlo 12, 65, 114, 150, 151, 194
unisex fashions 37, 39, 45, 215
United Kingdom (UK) 37, 50, 52, 82,
        95, 196
    fashion brand headquarters 39, 64, 92,
        97, 101–102, 171
    history 7, 83
    organization headquarters 123, 130, 199
United Nations 40, 116–117, 120, 122, 185
United States (US, USA) 11, 26, 60, 71,
        138, 146
    certifiers and certifications 70, 129
    consumer/user behavior 19, 65, 196
    fashion brand headquarters 91, 152,
        154, 170, 172, 178
    history 7–8, 83
    laws and regulations 66–67
    organization headquarters 172
universal design 27, 33–36, 215
Universal Standard 28, 37, 38 (see also
        Veksler, Polina; Waldman,
        Alexandra)
upcycle (upcycling) 21, 72–73, 82, 84,
        103, 155
    circular process 56, 68, 78, 190 198
    definition 65, 97, 154, 215
    do-it-yourself 66
    fashion brands 54, 64, 97–99, 167, 184,
        191–192, 197
    take-back programs 151
Upcycle It Now 192
Uruguay 26
USDA Certified Bio-based Product
        Label 72

USDA National Organic Program 12, 67,
        70–71
Uzbekistan 11–12, 117, 121, 130

V
value chain 4, 113, 132, 188, 193, 216
Value Village 154
Van Bergen, Rebecca 164
Veksler, Polina 28 (see also Universal
        Standard)
Verité 126
vertical integration 114–115, 125,
        132, 216
VF Corp 19, 63, 114, 128, 129, 194
Vietnam 112, 130, 138
vintage clothing 153, 216
viscose rayon 14–15, 72, 80, 196, 216

W
Waldman, Alexandra 28 (see also Universal
        Standard)
Walmart (Wal-Mart Stores) 17, 52, 128
Warby Parker 170
Waste Resources Action Plan 95
wastewater 11–16, 18, 60–61, 73
water consumption 15–16, 18, 58–61, 69,
        72–73, 189, 195
    cotton industry 11–12, 55–56, 60, 73,
        79–80
    laundering and care of clothing 63, 73
    wool industry 13
water risk tools 58
Watson, Emma 200, 201
Who Made My Clothes? campaign 123,
        199, 200
Wildfang 38, 197, 198

wool 3, 6, 12–15, 90, 196
    certifications 2, 13, 25–26, 71, 121
    production 2, 12, 25–26
    recycled and reclaimed 15, 21, 59, 66
    use by fashion brands 14, 26, 89, 93,
        105, 152, 156–157
Woolrich 91, 92
Worker Rights Consortium 59, 126, 131
World Fair Trade Organization 130
World Resources Institute 58
World Trade Organization 8
Worldwide Responsible Accredited
        Production (WRAP) 126–127, 131
World Wildlife Fund 165
Worn Wear Program, Patagonia 20,
        198, 202

Y
Yarn Ethically and Sustainably Sources
        (YESS) 130
Youngone 112
Yulex 63

Z
Zara 12, 15, 17, 114, 129, 194
Zero Discharge of Hazardous Chemicals
        Program 60, 186
zero waste design 63–64, 73, 86,
        190–192, 195
    definition 216
    examples 2, 54, 64–65, 107–109,
        191–192, 205–208
Zumiez 181